CONVERTING BOHEMIA

Prior to the Thirty Years War, almost all of Bohemia's population lay outside the Catholic fold yet by the beginning of the eighteenth century the kingdom was clearly under Rome's influence. Few regions in Europe's history have ever experienced such a complete religious transformation; because of this, Bohemia offers a unique window for examining the Counter-Reformation and the nature of early modern Catholicism. *Converting Bohemia* presents the first full assessment of the Catholic church's re-establishment in the Czech lands, arguing that this complex phenomenon was less a product of violence and force than of negotiation and persuasion. Ranging from art, architecture and literature to music, philosophy and hagiography, Howard Louthan's study reintegrates the region into the broader European world where it played such a prominent role in the early modern period. It will be of particular interest to scholars of early modern European history, religion, and Reformation studies.

HOWARD LOUTHAN is Associate Professor in the History Department, University of Florida. He is the author of *The Quest for Compromise: Peacemakers in Counter-Reformation Vienna* (Cambridge, 1997).

NEW STUDIES IN EUROPEAN HISTORY

Edited by

PETER BALDWIN, University of California, Los Angeles
CHRISTOPHER CLARK, University of Cambridge
JAMES B. COLLINS, Georgetown University
MIA RODRÍGUEZ-SALGADO, London School of Economics and Political Science
LYNDAL ROPER, University of Oxford

The aim of this series in early modern and modern European history is to publish outstanding works of research, addressed to important themes across a wide geographical range, from southern and central Europe to Scandinavia and Russia, from the time of the Renaissance to the Second World War. As it develops the series will comprise focused works of wide contextual range and intellectual ambition.

For a full list of titles published in the series, please see the end of the book.

CONVERTING BOHEMIA

FORCE AND PERSUASION IN THE CATHOLIC REFORMATION

HOWARD LOUTHAN

University of Florida

CAMBRIDGE
UNIVERSITY PRESS

CAMBRIDGE UNIVERSITY PRESS
Cambridge, New York, Melbourne, Madrid, Cape Town, Singapore, São Paulo, Delhi

Cambridge University Press
The Edinburgh Building, Cambridge CB2 8RU, UK

Published in the United States of America by Cambridge University Press, New York

www.cambridge.org
Information on this title: www.cambridge.org/9780521889292

First published 2009

Printed in the United Kingdom at the University Press, Cambridge

A catalogue record for this publication is available from the British Library

Library of Congress Cataloguing in Publication data
Louthan, Howard, 1963–
Converting Bohemia : force and persuasion in the Catholic Reformation / Howard Louthan.
p.   cm.
Includes bibliographical references.
ISBN 978-0-521-88929-2
1. Bohemia (Czech Republic) – Church history.   2. Catholic Church – Czech
Republic – Bohemia – History.   I. Title.
BR1050.C9L68   2008
282′.437109032–dc22
2008041686

ISBN 978-0-521-88929-2 hardback

To Bob and Sue

Contents

Illustrations

Acknowledgments

In the process of writing this book I have accrued a series of debts that I cannot possibly repay. But unlike the current international banking crisis where debt is divided and redistributed in increasingly arcane and mysterious ways, I know who my creditors are and can at least begin to acknowledge their contributions. This project took shape a decade ago while I was resident at the Center of Theological Inquiry in Princeton, New Jersey. Fittingly, the final editorial work was undertaken back at the same institute where I was warmly received by its new director, Will Storrar. In between I was supported by a series of grants and fellowships from the Alexander von Humboldt Foundation, the American Academy of Learned Societies, the Newberry Library, the International Research and Exchanges Board, and the National Council for Eurasian and East European Research. Special thanks and acknowledgment must be made to the School of Historical Studies at the Institute for Advanced Study in Princeton, New Jersey where I spent a congenial and profitable year in 2001–2. Jonathan Israel and Giles Constable were gracious hosts and the comments and critique of members of our early modern seminar (Allison Coudert, Robert von Friedeburg, Dale Kent, Karin MacHardy, Malcolm de Mowbray) helped shape the contours of the project.

I have also been assisted by a very generous and insightful group of colleagues and mentors who read portions of the book and helped me situate the Bohemian story in a broader European context. Here let me thank Phil Benedict, Robert Bireley, Mirjam Bohatcová, Tom Brady, Gary Cohen, Zdeněk David, Simon Ditchfield, R. J. W. Evans, Paula Fichtner, David Frick, Barry Graham, Rachel Greenblatt, Brad Gregory, David Holeton, Markéta Holubová, Bruce Janacek, Trevor Johnson, Hillel Kieval, Ivo Kořán, Diarmaid MacCulloch, John Marino, David Mengel, John O'Malley, Jim Palmitessa, James Parente, T. K. Rabb, Michal Šroněk, Henry Sullivan, Michal and Martin Svatoš, Jim Tracy, Thomas Winkelbauer and Daniel Woolf. During my research stays in Prague,

Vladimír Urbánek was of inestimable assistance, not only as a critical reader but also in such practical matters as ordering archival material and settling into a new living and working environment. Though I could not single out all who helped me working in the libraries and archives of Prague, Jan Pařez of the Strahov Monastic Library was particularly accommodating. Conversations with Petr Maťa, who took much time reading significant portions of the book, were extremely valuable. My stay in the city would have been much the poorer were it not for the hospitality of Klára and Marie Homerová. Through the kind offices of Eliška Fučíková I was able to live and work for two memorable trips in the Prague Castle, and travels with Jacek Soszynski across the Silesian landscape in an antique Mercedes sedan were memorable not just for our mishaps but were important for what we uncovered in the libraries.

In the latter stages of the project I was assisted by an able group of critics and associates. The three anonymous readers of Cambridge University Press offered advice that strengthened and clarified my major arguments. The editorial staff of Michael Watson, Helen Waterhouse and Chris Hills carefully shepherded the text to completion. On the technical level I am grateful for Maxim Tsypin who with characteristic aplomb solved a number of puzzling problems with my digital illustrations. My colleagues in the history department at the University of Florida were particularly solicitous as I approached the finish line. Nina Caputo arranged a venue with the Jewish Studies colloquium where I could air my ideas on Simon Abeles and Catholic sanctity. I profited much from the astute advice of Jon Sensbach who read my introduction with an ear for the broader early modern audience I have sought to reach. Finally and most importantly, my wife and departmental colleague, Andrea Sterk, has served as my best critic and friend over these past ten years. She has been willing to uproot the family and live as an academic nomad for what seems to be the majority of our married life. It is my hope that our three children, who still have not recovered from our many moves, may one day forgive me.

Material from chapter 1 has appeared in modified form in "New perspectives on the Bohemian crisis of the seventeenth century," in *Early Modern Europe: From Crisis to Stability* (University of Delaware Press, 2005). Portions of chapter 8 have appeared as "Breaking images and building bridges: the making of sacred space in early modern Bohemia," in *Sacred Space in Early Modern Europe* (Cambridge University Press, 2005) and "Religious art and the formation of a Catholic identity in baroque Prague," in *Embodiments of Power: Building Baroque Cities in Europe* (Berghahn Press, 2008). All material is used with permission.

Note on orthography

For any scholar working on central Europe, the spelling of proper names can be a delicate and complicated issue. The manner in which a specific place or family name is spelled (or misspelled depending on perspective) can stir nationalist passions very quickly. Is the busy Silesian metropolis along the banks of the Oder (or is it the Odra?) Breslau, Wrocław or Vratislavia? Should we refer to the family of the great generalissimo of the Thirty Years War as Wallenstein, Waldstein or Valdštejn? I have approached this issue pragmatically. For English readers the standard source on the Habsburg lands of central Europe during this period remains R. J. W. Evans, *The Making of the Habsburg Monarchy 1550–1700*. In nearly all cases I have followed the variants used by Professor Evans. No political or cultural judgments are intended by choice of names.

Abbreviations for periodicals and reference works

AnPr	*Analecta Praemonstratensia*
AÖG	Archiv für österreichische Geschichte
AUC,	Acta Universitatis Carolinae,
HUCP	Historia Universitatis Carolinae Pragensis
ČČH	Český časopis historický
ČKD	Časopis katolického duchovenstva
ČL	Český Lid
ČMKČ	Časopis Musea království českého
FHB	Folia Historica Bohemica
HJ	Historisches Jahrbuch
HZ	Historische Zeitschrift
Knihopis	Knihopis československých tisků od doby nejstarší až do konce XVIII. století
LF	Listy filologické
MVGDB	Mitteilungen des Vereins für Geschichte der Deutschen in Böhmen
OSN	Ottův Slovník Naučný
SbAPr	Sborník archivních prací
SbH	Sborník historický
SbH (Rezek)	Sborník historický (ed. A. Rezek), *1883–5*
SbHKr	Sborník historického kroužku
SbNMP	Sborník Národního muzea v Praze (Řada C–Literární historie)
VKČSN	Věstník královské české společnosti nauk (třída filosoficko-historicko-filologická)
WSJ	Wiener slavistisches Jahrbuch

Introduction
A tale of two windows: framing the history of early modern Bohemia

Surveying the religious landscape of seventeenth-century Europe, the perceptive observer would find few regions where events unfolded as dramatically as Bohemia. After the pivotal battle of White Mountain in 1620, a revitalized Catholic church led an aggressive program of reconversion that completely transformed the kingdom's confessional identity. This book examines that transformation. The religious strife of the seventeenth century, however, had a long history. Over 200 years of confessional conflict had a profound effect in shaping the Catholic response of the seventeenth century. White Mountain and its aftermath were in many respects the final act of a drama that had begun two centuries earlier.

On 30 July 1419 many of the Prague faithful rose early and gathered at the church of St. Mary of the Snows to hear the popular but increasingly radical Hussite priest, Jan Želivský. Though little is known of Želivský's past, this charismatic figure evidently arrived in Prague in the heady years following the 1415 execution of the great progenitor of Bohemia's first Reformation, Jan Hus.[1] Želivský initially served the parish of St. Stephen's in New Town, but a royal decree intended to suppress the new heretical movement deprived him of this post. Allying himself with Prague's urban poor, Želivský moved to the nearby church of St. Mary's and solidified his reputation with this constituency through his inflammatory rhetoric aimed at the city's secular and spiritual authorities. That Sunday, word had circulated among Želivský's followers that they should attend services well armed and ready for action. His incendiary oratory reached new heights that morning. Preaching from a series of bloodcurdling Old Testament texts, he drew from the prophet Ezekiel who had icily intoned:

---

[1] A. Molnár, "Želivský, prédicateur de la révolution," *Communio viatorum* 2 (1959), 324–34; A. Molnár, ed., *Jan Želivský. Dochovaná kázání z roku 1419* (Prague: NČAV, 1953).

Behold, I, even I, will bring a sword upon you, and I will destroy your high places. And your altars shall be desolate, and your images shall be broken: and I will cast down your slain men before your idols. And I will lay the dead carcasses of the children of Israel before their idols; and I will scatter your bones round about your altars.[2]

The words evidently achieved their intended effect, for after the sermon Želivský's passionate partisans left the church following the priest, monstrance in hand, to his old parish of St. Stephen's. The Hussites broke through the locked doors, drove out the priest who had been celebrating mass and held their own service. But Želivský and his frenzied worshipers were not finished. The swelling throng now turned its fury towards the city's secular authorities. The New Town Hall was a short, ten-minute walk from the church. There, four of the city's magistrates were consulting with a number of burghers when the mob arrived. Želivský's followers demanded the immediate release of Hussite prisoners who had been jailed for their missionary activity. The magistrates tried to stall as they waited for reinforcements from across the river, but playing for time did not work with this angry crowd. Želivský, still holding his monstrance with the Host exposed, exhorted the faithful to action. As the Catholic chronicler later related, they stormed the well-fortified but undermanned tower, assaulted those who sought to defend themselves and most significantly hurled thirteen of their Catholic opponents from the upper story of the town hall to the cobblestones below. Prague, the great city of spires, had witnessed its first defenestration.

Nearly 200 years later another angry mob reenacted this same ritual on the other side of the Moldau. This time it was the Habsburg emperor Matthias who had stirred up popular passion. Matthias had sided with Bohemia's Catholics in a dispute that challenged the interpretation of the 1609 Letter of Majesty, the kingdom's most recent religious ceasefire between feuding confessional factions. In May 1618 the escalating tensions resulted in a coup staged at the Bohemian Chancellery in the Prague Castle. Two royal officials along with a secretary were seized and then thrown from a high window of the building, an event that helped trigger the most devastating war central Europe experienced before the twentieth century. These two defenestrations, then, serve as convenient benchmarks framing an unprecedented period of religious violence in the Czech lands.

---

[2] Howard Kaminsky, *A History of the Hussite Revolution* (Berkeley: University of California Press, 1967), pp. 292–4.

Confessional conflict during the Reformation era has been perhaps most closely studied in the French or Dutch context. The wars of religion between Huguenot and Catholic, the excesses of the Duke of Alba and the uprising in the Low Countries are all part of the standard story of religion and violence in the Age of Reform. It is the Bohemian kingdom, however, that offers the most protracted setting of such activity in the late medieval and early modern periods. Here religious conflict lasted more than two centuries. A full-scale revolt began in Bohemia after Hus's execution at the Council of Constance. Pope and emperor launched five crusades to crush the rebellion, but under the leadership of the legendary blind general, Jan Žižka, Hussite armies were able to drive off the numerically superior forces of the crusaders. The period of fiercest conflict came to an end in the 1430s. The Council of Basel recognized the basic tenets of Hussitism in 1433, an agreement known as the *Compactata*. The following year the revolution imploded when the movement's radical wing was defeated by a coalition of Catholics and more moderate Hussites at the battle of Lipany. The cease-fire, however, lasted only a few decades. In 1458 Bohemia elected King George of Poděbrady as its first and only Hussite king. In 1462 Pope Pius II formally repudiated the *Compactata*, and shortly thereafter the armies returned when the Hungarian king Matthias Corvinus renewed the crusades against the heretic kingdom. Though formal hostilities drew to a close with the accession of the Catholic Jagiellonians, confessional tensions still ran high even during the relatively calm periods of the late fifteenth and early sixteenth centuries and on occasion led to open conflict such as the Prague uprising of 1483 and a series of urban disturbances in the early sixteenth century.[3]

An important juncture was reached, however, in 1526 when the Habsburgs came to the throne. Unlike the weaker Jagiellonians, they sought to centralize power and laid the foundation of future Catholic success. Ferdinand I invited the Jesuits to begin work in the Czech lands, and after a vacancy of 140 years, he appointed an archbishop to fill the Bohemian see. His actions helped trigger yet another revolt. In 1547 the Czech estates sided with the German Lutherans who had turned against Ferdinand's brother, Emperor Charles V. Though the rebellion was suppressed and a type of confessional détente was reached with Ferdinand's immediate successors, even during the kingdom's "golden age" under Rudolf II (1576–1612), Prague and other Bohemian towns

---

[3] F. Šmahel, "Epilog husitské revoluce. Pražské povstání 1483," in A. Molnár, ed., *Acta reformationem bohemicam illustrantia* (Prague: Kalich, 1978), pp. 45–127; Winfried Eberhard, *Konfessionsbildung und Stände in Böhmen (1478–1530)* (Munich: Oldenbourg, 1981), pp. 125–7.

continued to experience periodic outbreaks of religious violence. In 1605 a Corpus Christi Day procession in the imperial capital turned into a bloody brawl, and some six years later all civic order gave way when an army under the bishop of Passau invaded the city while mobs of townspeople murdered monks and looted churches.[4]

The resolution of this protracted crisis was equally dramatic. The cycle of violence reached its crescendo in the years 1618–20. The coup of the Bohemian estates, the defenestration at Prague Castle, the decision to depose the kingdom's legally elected sovereign, Ferdinand of Habsburg, and replace him with the Calvinist Elector Palatine, Frederick V, all inexorably led to the 1620 clash at White Mountain. On this small hill outside Prague, in a confrontation that hardly merits the word battle, an imperial army skirmished with troops loyal to the Bohemian estates, a force primarily composed of poorly paid mercenaries supported by a thin line of Hungarian cavalry. In a two-hour struggle the Habsburg coalition eventually broke the flanks of its opponents and then marched into the Bohemian capital virtually unopposed. Though White Mountain may not have been a military struggle of epic proportions, it was a critical turning point in the kingdom's long confessional struggle. For nearly two centuries Bohemia's Catholics had been an embattled minority struggling to stay afloat in a Hussite sea. Now they were at last masters of the situation and acted accordingly. They implemented an aggressive campaign of recatholicization. The religious pluralism that had characterized the Bohemian kingdom for generations was replaced by a more uniform set of beliefs, practices and rituals. The cults of older but neglected saints were revived while newer ones were established. Missionaries and musicians, poets and preachers, created a new Catholic literature. A veritable army of artists and architects fashioned a confessional landscape of baroque churches and chapels, pilgrimage complexes and renovated monasteries. Nearly every town had a Marian column in its central square while Loreto shrines quickly covered the countryside.

That confessional transformation is the focus of this study. Before the Thirty Years War nearly 90 percent of Bohemia's population lay outside the Catholic fold, yet by the beginning of the eighteenth century the kingdom was clearly under Rome's sway. The Czechs themselves developed a great reputation for their piety which was often criticized by outside observers for its credulity and devotional excess. In 1730 a German chronicler wryly

---

[4] Joseph Fischer, "Blutige Excesse bei einer Prager Frohnleichnamsprocession im Jahre 1605," *MVGDB* 38 (1900), 413–16; James Palmitessa, "The Prague uprising of 1611: property, politics and Catholic renewal in the early years of Habsburg rule," *Central European History* 31 (1998), 299–328.

observed, "The inhabitants of this country ... are very superstitious and great connoisseurs of religious fables and tales."[5] Later in the century an Englishman visiting Prague noted concerning the famous Charles Bridge and its celebrated statuary:

> In every part of the city people are seen kneeling before statues, but especially on the big bridge across the Moldau where there is the greatest crowd of passersby. This bridge is richly decorated by statues of saints, so that the walker must pass them on both sides like two rows of musketeers. Travelers, especially those coming straight from Berlin, will marvel at the piety of the people here, specifically at the burning passion they display before the saints of the bridge.[6]

This anecdotal evidence that suggests a solid Catholic identity had developed in the Bohemian lands by the end of the early modern period is supported statistically as well. In 1781 when Joseph II issued the Edict of Toleration, a mere 1–3 percent of the population joined either the Lutheran or Calvinist church. As late as 1913, 96.5 percent of the Czech population reported themselves as Roman Catholic.[7]

Any understanding of seventeenth- and early eighteenth-century Bohemia must begin with religion. The confessional transformation of the kingdom was nothing short of breathtaking. A *longue durée* of active dissent that stretched back to the fourteenth century was effectively mastered and replaced in a span of two generations with an outward allegiance to Rome. The kingdom's Counter-Reformation was not, however, a simple confrontation between Protestant and Catholic. Bohemian society at the eve of White Mountain was religiously complex. The Czech lands comprised an intriguing patchwork of religious communities. There were scattered groups of Protestants: a Calvinist faction centered around the new king from the Palatinate, a circle of influential Lutheran nobility and a small group of Moravian Anabaptists. There were also the Catholics and the tight-knit communities of the *Unitas Fratrum* or Bohemian Brethren, a fifteenth-century offshoot of the Hussite Reformation. The majority of the population, however, were descendants of the original Hussites and known as the Utraquists for their insistence on receiving the Eucharist in both the bread and the wine (*sub utraque specie*).

[5] J. B. Küchelbecker, *Allerneueste Nachricht vom Römisch-Käyserl. Hofe* (Hanover: Förster, 1730), p. 83.
[6] Cited in Zdeněk Hojda and Jiří Pokorný, *Pomníky i zapomníky* (Prague: Paseka, 1996), p. 24.
[7] M. E. Ducreux, "La reconquête catholique de l'espace bohémien," *Revue des Études Slaves* 60 (1988), 685; Cynthia Paces, "'The Czech nation must be Catholic!' An alternative version of Czech nationalism during the First Republic," *Nationalities Papers* 27 (1999), 425.

The story of the Utraquist church is critical for a proper understanding of Bohemia's Counter-Reformation. Its ultimate demise in the seventeenth century marks the only large-scale disappearance of an entire church in European history! Despite the revolutionary nature of Hussitism's early years, mature Utraquism was a relatively conservative movement theologically. The adoration of the Host, the veneration of images and relics, and the belief in the intercessory power of the saints were all retained. The church hierarchy continued to affirm apostolic succession. Even after the split with Rome, Utraquist leaders sought out sympathetic bishops to ordain their priests.[8] The impact of the Reformation on the Utraquist church is difficult to gauge. An earlier generation of historians maintained that the church had become moribund by the early sixteenth century and was slowly but inexorably drawn towards Lutheranism. More recent research has suggested that after 1517 Utraquism was far more vibrant than most scholars have assumed.[9] Though the dust has yet to settle from this debate, it is clear that sixteenth-century Utraquism was far from monolithic. Without an archbishop from the last third of the fifteenth century, the Utraquists became a decentralized community and represented a significant range of theological views in the sixteenth century. On the eve of White Mountain, Bohemia was not a thoroughgoing Protestant land. German Lutherans who traveled through the region were not infrequently astonished and scandalized by the "papist" rituals they found in the Utraquist churches. On the other hand, Catholics such as the devout Vilém Slavata, a victim of the 1618 defenestration, could cynically observe, "Each man thought and believed whatever suited him best, so that those who were known in the Bohemian kingdom as Utraquists could really have been called by any name you please."[10]

By recognizing Bohemia's religious pluralism, we can better appreciate the confessional changes that were implemented after 1620. It has often been assumed that White Mountain was a confrontation between two distinct cultures and religious systems. Even the most recent assessments of this period have essentially recycled old stereotypes that emphasize stark contrasts. The

---

[8] Enrico Molnar, "The Catholicity of the Utraquist church of Bohemia," *Anglican Theological Review* 41 (1959), 260–70; Barry F. H. Graham, "The evolution of the Utraquist mass 1420–1620," *Catholic Historical Review* 92 (2006), 553–73.

[9] An older view of Utraquism is best represented by Ferdinand Hrejsa, *Česká konfese: její vznik, podstata a dějiny* (Prague: Nákl. České akademie císaře Františka Josefa pro vědy, slovesnost a umění, 1912). For a revisionist position see Zdeněk David, *Finding the Middle Way* (Baltimore: Johns Hopkins University Press, 2003).

[10] Jaroslav Pánek, "Čechy, Morava a Lužice v německém cestopisu ze sklonku 16. století," *FHB* 13 (1990), 221; cited in R. J. W. Evans, *Rudolf II and His World* (Oxford: Oxford University Press, 1973), p. 33.

Canadian sociologist, Derek Sayer, in what is an otherwise insightful overview of Czech culture, describes this era as "something little short of cultural genocide." Michael Mullett in his survey of the Catholic Reformation avers, "Above all, in the Czech lands of Bohemia, Catholicisation was the religious accompaniment to political enslavement to Austria." Andrew Rossos is even stronger with his claim that after 1620 the Habsburgs and the Catholic church "set about obliterating the memory of its [the Czech] past."[11] On one level it is certainly true that the recatholicization of Bohemia was carried out by brute force. A new constitution revoked the kingdom's elective status and passed the throne as a hereditary right to the Habsburg family. A fifth to a quarter of the nobility and burgher class were sent into exile while the estates of non-Catholics were confiscated. The religious and cultural confrontation of this period, however, was significantly more complex, but all too frequently historians have reduced this complicated situation to a simplified set of binary oppositions: Czech against German, nation against empire, tradition against innovation and Protestant against Catholic. Before White Mountain, Bohemia's confessional identity was neither unified nor coherent. Afterwards, its new Catholic masters creatively drew much from the past in their quest to reconfigure the confessional contours of the kingdom. Indeed, traditional ecclesiastical beliefs and practices preserved by Utraquism help explain the relative ease many found in converting back to Catholicism.

With these observations in mind, we can better understand the two central goals of this study. Most importantly, Bohemia offers a unique window for examining the problem of Counter-Reformation. How Europeans were won over to Protestantism is a well-told story. For generations scholars have investigated the reasons why people became Protestant. Far less attention has been given to the question of turning Catholic. Bohemia offers an ideal setting for this subject, for there are few regions on the continent that can match the broad-scale confessional changes that occurred here during the course of the seventeenth century. As such, it is essential to remove the Bohemian kingdom from what at times seems like a hermetically sealed historiography and examine it in the wider world of early modern Catholicism. The study of the Catholic side of the Reformation is one of the most dynamic areas in the field of early modern religion. In recent years a number of surveys and important monographs have grappled with the

---

[11] Derek Sayer, *The Coasts of Bohemia* (Princeton: Princeton University Press, 1998), p. 50; Michael Mullett, *The Catholic Reformation* (New York: Routledge, 1999), p. 214; Andrew Rossos, "Czech historiography – Part I," *Canadian Slavonic Papers* 24 (1982), 253.

Converting Bohemia

nature of the Catholic experience during these tumultuous centuries.[12] New methodological approaches, new chronological schemes and a broader understanding of religion itself have expanded our view of the Catholic Reformation. Despite the assertions of nationalist historians, Bohemia's confessional transformation was actually quite complex and offers historians a marvelous opportunity to put the new tools to work.

Here a critical qualification must be added. Our focus will not be on interior patterns of belief but on public modes of representation. Whether or not the heretical Bohemians truly became good and faithful Catholics is frankly beyond the historian's grasp. Gerald Strauss, in what may be the most influential study of religious indoctrination in the Reformation era, concluded that the catechetical and pedagogical efforts of Lutheran reformers had limited impact on the actual lives of their parishioners.[13] There seems to be good reason to be skeptical regarding the Bohemian situation as well. In a region of mass conversions there was significant room for deception and dissimulation. There is the story of a priest who in 1628 was caught selling non-Catholics "confessional certificates," a document that authenticated an individual's conversion to the secular authorities.[14] Visitation records are likewise problematic. Bishops, in an effort to reform their diocese, often deputized commissioners to investigate the various parishes of their territory to determine whether confessional standards were being met and enforced in the countryside. In the case of the Upper Palatinate, a small German territory immediately to the west of Bohemia where Catholicism was also forcibly reimposed, these visitations were not always effective, and their reports were not consistently reliable.[15] Our focus, in contrast, will be on outward modes of confessional representation, the signs and markers of a new religious identity. For the great majority of the Bohemian populace, the Catholicism they were expected to observe demanded right actions and appearances. It was orthopraxy, rather than orthodoxy, that was paramount, and it is these forms of social behavior and cultural representation that will stand at the center of this study.

---

[12] John O'Malley, *Trent and All That: Renaming Catholicism in the Early Modern Era* (Cambridge, MA: Harvard University Press, 2000); R. Po-Chia Hsia, *The World of Catholic Renewal, 1540–1770* (Cambridge: Cambridge University Press, 2nd edn 2005); Robert Bireley, *The Refashioning of Catholicism* (Washington, D.C.: Catholic University Press, 1999).

[13] Gerald Strauss, *Luther's House of Learning* (Baltimore: Johns Hopkins University Press, 1978).

[14] R. J. W. Evans, *The Making of the Habsburg Monarchy 1550–1700* (Oxford: Clarendon Press, 1979), p. 118; Trevor Johnson, "The recatholicisation of the Upper Palatinate (1621–circa 1700)," unpublished Ph.D. thesis, Cambridge University (1991), p. 56.

[15] Johnson, "Recatholicisation," pp. 76–8, 92.

A second and more general objective of this text concerns the place of early modern Bohemia in the wider European context. Though the issues raised in the following chapters will certainly be of interest to Slavic specialists, this book was written with a broader audience in mind as it seeks to integrate the Czech lands into territory more familiar to Reformation and early modern scholars. The crisis of war and religion that gripped Bohemia in the first half of the seventeenth century loomed over the entire continent. From England to Poland, issues of authority and confessional identity were pressing matters of state. If the crisis had common roots, its resolution often followed recognizable patterns. The religious reconfiguration of Bohemia after 1620, though in certain ways extreme, unfolded in a manner similar to many areas of Catholic Europe. From baroque art and architecture to an emerging pantheon of Counter-Reformation saints, Bohemia was an integral part of a vibrant international Catholic society.

The book begins during the great crisis of 1618–20 when the Habsburgs nearly lost Bohemia and their dominant position in central Europe. The first third of the study examines the agents of reform who laid the foundation of a new Catholic state. It was the crown, church and nobility who were the prime architects of this society. In the sixteenth and early seventeenth centuries Europe's leading princes struggled to master the destabilizing effect of religious passion in their respective kingdoms. In France both Henry III († 1589) and Henry IV († 1610) were cut down by religious fanatics. William of Orange was assassinated by a zealous Catholic. Religion played a role in the execution of England's Charles I. In central Europe the moderate or at times vacillating religious policies of Maximilian II (1564–76) and his son Rudolf also contributed to political instability. Unlike his peers who were victims of religious violence, however, Emperor Ferdinand II (1619–37) was a tenacious survivor and able to initiate confessional changes that indelibly marked the Habsburg lands. The aristocracy, too, went through its own period of crisis. From the Parisian Fronde to the English Civil War, the seventeenth century was an age of noble rebellions. In Bohemia very few of the great families had not been swept up in the 1618 revolt. Nearly all had members who were tainted either by treason or heresy. In creative fashion these families exorcized their Protestant ghosts and then refashioned their image along more orthodox lines. The nobility was also instrumental in reviving lay piety. Their leadership in confraternities or promotion of other forms of corporate devotion was critical in the formation of a communal Catholic identity. Finally, there was the church, an institution that struggled mightily during the first decades of the seventeenth century only to reemerge as a vital force in Bohemian society after White Mountain. A young cardinal gave new life to the archbishopric and overhauled its administration. Religious orders such as the Franciscans and Piarists established cloisters and dispatched missionaries. It was the efforts of the Jesuits, however, that were most critical to the church's ultimate success. Over the past decade there has been a new surge of interest in the Society of Jesus. From studies of Jesuit theater in the Amazon basin to their pedagogical activities in the Philippines, scholars from a variety of disciplines and geographic fields are reevaluating the order's role and impact in the early modern world. The Jesuits devoted substantial resources to Bohemia, a frontline region in the struggle to recover central Europe for Rome. An assessment of their efforts to reshape the cultural and intellectual life of the kingdom, particularly in the area of education, sheds new light on the reconversion process.[16]

After considering the agents of reform, we shift our attention to focus more closely on the confessional culture these individuals and institutions were constructing. It has long been recognized that across the Catholic world a cultural revival was occurring in art and architecture, music and literature. In Bohemia, however, such developments have often been misinterpreted or passed over altogether. One of the enduring stereotypes of the post-White Mountain era is that of the dramatic decline of Czech letters or as an early pioneer of Slavic studies put it "the complete absence of anything that can be described as literature at all."[17] This generalization, however, hardly does justice to the tremendous body of confessional material that was busily being produced in Czech, German and Latin. Thick antiquarian treatises examining the Catholic roots of the kingdom, an engaging assortment of devotional and catechetical material, a Catholic vernacular Bible and piles of homiletic collections that have been neglected for generations are all part of a Catholic literature that was produced for a remarkably broad range of audiences. Music, too, experienced its own renaissance and was instrumental in the process of confessional formation. A new series of Catholic hymnals creatively incorporated elements of Bohemia's rich musical tradition as song became an effective tool of religious instruction. It was the kingdom's art and architecture, however, which were the most obvious signs of a new religious identity. Bohemia was one of the great showplaces of the European baroque. Few regions on the continent could match it. But

---

[16] John O'Malley, ed., *The Jesuits: Cultures, Sciences and the Arts, 1540–1773* (Toronto: University of Toronto Press, 1999). For Bohemia the standard source remains Alois Kroess, *Geschichte der böhmischen Provinz der Gesellschaft Jesu*, 3 vols. (Vienna: Opitz, 1910–38). More recent is the overview of I. Čornejová, *Tovaryšstvo Ježíšovo: Jezuité v Čechách* (Prague: Mladá fronta, 1995). For the Jesuits in the eighteenth century see Paul Shore, *The Eagle and the Cross* (Saint Louis: Institute of Jesuit Sources, 2002).

[17] R. W. Seton-Watson, *A History of the Czechs and Slovaks* (Hamden: Archon, 1965), p. 131.

though art historians have produced a specialized literature in this field, little work has been done to integrate aesthetic developments into a broader assessment of Bohemia's confessional transformation.

While the study of religion in seventeenth-century Bohemia has been generally marginalized, even less attention has been devoted to forms of popular piety. Scholars such as Louis Châtellier, Jean Delumeau and William Christian have for many years reminded us that confraternal activity, public rites and rituals, and the experience of the miraculous were all critical features of early modern Catholicism. More than any other type of religious expression, it was pilgrimage that tied these various strands together in the early modern period. Though in the popular imagination pilgrimage is most closely associated with the Middle Ages, this phenomenon actually reached its height in the seventeenth and eighteenth centuries. There was a massive revival of pilgrimage in the Bohemian lands during this period. A conservative estimate indicates that between 1620 and 1750 at least 150 pilgrimage shrines were either constructed or restored in the kingdom, and these often elaborate complexes began attracting significant numbers. By the end of the seventeenth century more than 300,000 visitors annually descended on three of the kingdom's most important pilgrimage sites. The seventeenth century was also a great age of saints. Along with Ignatius Loyola and Teresa of Avila, Bohemia celebrated the canonization of one of its native sons. Virtually unknown in the last decade of the seventeenth century, John Nepomuk, a fourteenth-century priest allegedly executed by a jealous king, became Bohemia's most recognizable saint if not its most famous celebrity in less than fifty years. His biography was translated into Mandarin and Tagalog while in Mexico City he was named patron of the university. Back in Europe his statue sat atop scores of bridges from Lisbon to Warsaw. Saints, however, were not always officially canonized and could come from unexpected corners. While Prague burghers may not have venerated a holy greyhound as did medieval villagers outside Lyon, the city did honor a bearded princess from Portugal and stranger still a Jewish boy who had died under mysterious circumstances. In 1700 Prague's ghetto was one of the largest Jewish communities in Europe. The intriguing story of the purported conversion and subsequent "murder" of one of its young inhabitants highlights the creativity and resourcefulness of Bohemian Catholicism. Here was a culture that could turn an obscure priest into a saint with a worldwide following and refashion a troubled Jewish adolescent into a heroic Christian martyr.

This study is not a narrative history of seventeenth- and eighteenth-century Bohemia though one is certainly long overdue. It is instead an interpretation of this formative period and as such a work that paints with broad strokes. A few comments, then, should be made regarding both its geographic and thematic scope. The words Bohemia, Czech lands and Bohemian kingdom are often used interchangeably throughout the text. In 1620 the crown lands of Bohemia included the kingdom of Bohemia proper, the margravate of Moravia, Upper and Lower Lusatia and the assorted duchies of Silesia. Saxony absorbed the Lusatias in 1635, and the Lutheran dukes also offered some protection to the Protestant communities of Silesia before the bulk of this territory was appropriated by the Prussians in the eighteenth century. Our primary focus will be the Bohemian kingdom itself with some consideration of Moravia, what is essentially the Czech Republic today. Even within this more limited geographic space, this study cannot do justice to a range of regional variations. In the early seventeenth century, Moravia could rightly boast of a more tolerant religious culture than even Bohemia.[18] Within Bohemia itself there were also important differences. In eastern Bohemia there were problems with secret Protestants up through the eighteenth century while in western Bohemia a city such as the beer-brewing Plzeň remained faithful to Rome during the Hussite and Reformation periods. Though regional studies would certainly enrich our understanding of these variations, it is still possible to chart the general contours of a new Catholic identity that emerged in Bohemia during the century after White Mountain. Likewise, a fuller investigation of rural missions, an analysis of institutional reforms or a more comprehensive assessment of popular religion would undoubtedly offer further insights. Nonetheless, the scope of this study is vast. From theology and philosophy to art and architecture, from literature and music to antiquarianism and hagiography, this wide-ranging assessment of Bohemia's history and culture reintegrates this region into the broader European world where it played such a prominent role in the early modern period.

Unfortunately, scholars in the English-speaking world have traditionally drawn attention to Bohemia only when events in the kingdom have had a decided impact on broader European developments – the Hussite wars of the fifteenth century, the late Renaissance court of Rudolf II, or the Czech revolt that touched off the Thirty Years War. In surveys such as the venerable *New Cambridge Modern History* Bohemia is rarely treated as an independent entity. The desultory comments on the kingdom normally

---

[18] Josef Válka, *Dějiny Moravy*, vol. II (Brno: Muzejní a vlastivědná společnost v Brně, 1995). On the role of Charles the Elder of Žerotín, Moravia's irenic Protestant leader who did not participate in the Bohemian rebellion, see Otakar Odložilík, *Karel Starší ze Žerotína* (Prague: Melantrich, 1936).

appear in chapters examining all of eastern Europe or those investigating the broader Habsburg lands. There are, of course, a number of reasons for this neglect. Politically, east central Europe stood apart from the process that historians have traditionally considered one of the landmark features of the period – the growth and emergence of the modern state. The decentralized polities of this region simply did not follow the political trajectories of France, Spain and England. More practically, there is a significant linguistic obstacle. Most historians of pre-modern Europe do not learn Czech, a language with a puzzling array of diacriticals and seemingly unpronounceable combinations of letters that the humorist Jerome K. Jerome once compared to Chinese.[19] There is also the issue of chronology. R. R. Betts described the Bohemian kingdom in the seventeenth century as "the land which has no history."[20] Though Betts was specifically referring to the region's misfortunes during this period, his words have a double meaning, for surprisingly in the English-speaking world there is no study that examines the Czech lands between 1620 and the middle of the eighteenth century.[21]

This lack of attention is frankly astonishing when one considers that, in the sixteenth century, the crown lands of Bohemia had a population exceeding 3 million, more inhabitants than contemporary England.[22] This was a region rich in natural resources. Agriculturally, the Elbe river basin and the flatlands of southern Moravia were among the most fertile areas of central Europe. Bohemian mines had from the Middle Ages provided the continent with a significant portion of its silver bullion. More recently, the great boom at the German settlement of Joachimsthal (Jáchymov) had been so important that the town gave its name to a new unit of currency, the dollar or "thaler." Politically, the kingdom was ruled by members of Europe's most prominent families including the Luxembourg, Jagiellonian and Habsburg dynasties. In the sixteenth and early seventeenth centuries Prague outshone Vienna. The city on the Moldau had a larger population, a stronger economic base and arguably a more vibrant cultural life than its rival on the Danube. Prague reached its zenith during the reign of Rudolf II with a population of possibly 60,000 and one of the continent's most brilliant courts. Though the Thirty Years War had a substantial impact

---

[19] Joseph Wechsberg, *Prague: The Mystical City* (New York: Macmillan, 1971), p. 15.
[20] R. R. Betts, "The Habsburg lands," in *The New Cambridge Modern History*, vol. V, F. L. Carsten, ed., *The Ascendancy of France (1648–88)* (Cambridge: Cambridge University Press, 1964), p. 494.
[21] Best at present are the chapters on Bohemia in Evans, *Making*.
[22] R. J. W. Evans, "The Habsburg monarchy and Bohemia, 1526–1848," in Mark Greengrass, ed., *Conquest and Coalescence* (London: Arnold, 1991), p. 134.

on this region, the kingdom did recover. By 1700 its population had surpassed pre-war levels.[23] Bohemia regained its economic strength. Without its tax receipts, the Habsburgs would have been hard pressed to maintain their dominant position in central Europe. After 1648 the kingdom also revived culturally and once more became an important center of artistic activity, this time as a showplace of the baroque.

Nonetheless, within Bohemia the post-1620 era has been a problematic field of study. Though a promising younger generation is examining this period with fresh eyes, until relatively recently both the scholarly community and the more educated public simply referred to these years as Bohemia's "dark ages" and devoted little study to what they perceived as a bleak chapter of the Czech past. Not unrepresentative is the recent survey, *Bohemia in History*, assembled by a distinguished group of Czech historians. After an insightful essay examining the significance of White Mountain, coverage jumps to the second half of the eighteenth century and the beginnings of the Enlightenment. The four generations after 1620 are simply ignored.[24] When it was not ignored, attention given to this era was primarily negative. In the late nineteenth century, the French historian Ernest Denis summed up what was then the general assessment of Czech scholars when he bluntly stated, "For close to two centuries there was nothing but lamentation in Bohemia. Many times on the Calvary which the nation began to climb it stumbled under the weight of its sorrows and fell prone and inanimate, lying as if dead."[25]

The older, negative assessment of this era is connected to a predominantly nationalist orientation of Czech historiography. Following the lead of Bohemia's most important nineteenth-century historian, František Palacký, many have seen the Habsburg domination of the Bohemian lands in the seventeenth and eighteenth centuries merely as part of the long and difficult road to political independence, best suited for analysis within a narrower nationalist framework. As a consequence, the multiethnic character of the Bohemian kingdom during this period was often obscured and the study of its international connections frequently neglected. One Czech scholar has recently observed, "The refusal to view the history of Bohemia or even 'the Czech destiny' in connection with the development of neighboring countries has run for decades like a red thread

---

[23] Thomas Winkelbauer, *Ständefreiheit und Fürstenmacht: Länder und Untertanen des Hauses Habsburg im konfessionellen Zeitalter* (Vienna: Ueberreuter, 2003), vol. I, p. 21.

[24] Mikuláš Teich, ed., *Bohemia in History* (Cambridge: Cambridge University Press, 1998).

[25] Ernest Denis, *Fin de l'indépendence bohème* (Paris: A. Colin, 1890), vol. II, p. 556.

through Czech historical research. This peculiar orientation has always rested primarily on a non-scholarly, political foundation."[26] The recatholicization of the Czech lands, however, was accomplished by a remarkable international coterie of scholars and religious leaders. Here native priests mingled and worked with Spanish philosophers, German architects, Flemish theologians, Polish missionaries, Italian mystics and Dutch artists. This complex mosaic of peoples and cultural traditions makes post-White Mountain Bohemia such a fascinating region of study while challenging us to rethink basic assumptions concerning the society and culture of early modern central Europe.

---

[26] Ivana Čornejová, "Das 'Temno' im mitteleuropäischen Kontext: Zur Kirchen- und Bildungspolitik im Böhmen der Barockzeit," *Bohemia* 34 (1993), 344.

CHAPTER I

Severed heads and holy bones: authority and culture in post-White Mountain Bohemia

"All eies are directed upon Bohemia," wrote an unusually excited Henry Wotton in August 1618.[1] Wotton, a seasoned English diplomat, was referring to the dramatic flurry of events that had happened in the wake of the famous defenestration in late spring. By hurling two Habsburg officials and the chancery secretary from a window high in Prague's royal castle, the Bohemian estates had initiated a revolt that plunged the kingdom into a great crisis of authority. In 1617, late in the reign of Emperor Matthias, Ferdinand of Austria had been elected to the Bohemian throne. In 1619 he was deposed and replaced by his Calvinist rival, Frederick of the Palatinate. As European princes watched anxiously, these two sovereigns engaged each other in a fierce contest for this critical central European kingdom. Their struggle for legitimacy and authority in Bohemia is one of the best documented chapters of the Thirty Years War. As publicists rushed to chronicle this confrontation through illustrated broadsheets, both claimants drew from a well-stocked arsenal of ideological weapons.[2] Frederick portrayed himself as the defender of traditional Czech liberties brazenly trampled underfoot by the Habsburgs. Ludwig Camerarius and Abraham Scultetus provided the constitutional and religious justification for his intervention.[3] Ferdinand, on the other hand,

---

[1] Cited in Theodore Rabb, "English readers and the revolt in Bohemia, 1619–1622," in *Aharon M. K. Rabinowicz Jubilee Volume* (Jerusalem: Bialik Institute, 1996), p. 153.

[2] Johannes Gebauer, *Die Publicistik über den böhmischen Aufstand von 1618* (Halle: Niemeyer, 1880); Rudolf Wolkan, *Deutsche Lieder auf den Winterkönig* (Prague: J. G. Calve, 1898); for a fascinating collection of broadsheets in Prague's National Museum (102A 1–199) that highlights the confrontation between Frederick and Ferdinand see Mirjam Bohatcová, "Vzácná sbírka publicistických a portrétních dokumentů k počátku třicetileté války," *SbNMP* 27 (1982).

[3] See for example *A Declaration of the Causes, for the which, Wee Frederick … King of Bohemia … have accepted of the Crowne of Bohemia, and countryes thereunto annexed* (Middleburg: Abraham Schilders, 1620); F. H. Schubert, *Ludwig Camerarius 1573–1651* (Kallmünz: Lassleben, 1955). For the identity of Abraham Scultetus and the provenance of a significant portion of this literature see Jaroslav Miller, "Tištěné prameny o českém stavovském povstání z let 1618–1621 v anglických knihovnách," *FHB* 20 (2002), 133–213.

decried the rebels' actions and insisted on his hereditary rights to the king-dom, which imperial jurists such as Melchior Goldast triumphed loudly.[4]

Though the Czech estates were routed and Frederick driven into exile, the Bohemian crisis was not magically resolved that fall morning of 1620 on the chalky uplands outside Prague. Ferdinand had considerable work ahead of him to bolster his claims of legitimacy and secure his authority. Nearly all historians who study this period emphasize that Habsburg hegemony and the subsequent campaign to recatholicize the kingdom was constructed on a series of harsh political, economic and social measures instituted shortly after White Mountain. It is difficult, indeed, to disagree with this initial assessment. Although Bohemia had been disciplined for its role in the Schmalkaldic War in the late 1540s, the severity of the punishment meted out by Ferdinand was unprecedented. The confiscations began in 1621. Imperial officials seized the estates of those who had been involved in the revolt while other Protestant nobles who were not directly implicated in the rebellion sold their lands at greatly reduced prices. By the time of Ferdinand's death in 1637, up to 50 percent of landed wealth had changed hands. Religious changes were also quickly instituted. In 1621 communion *sub utraque* was forbidden. Three years later Catholicism was proclaimed the only official religion of the kingdom. In May of that year all non-Catholic clergy were expelled from Bohemia proper. Five months later they were forced out of Moravia as well.

On the political front the Habsburgs pursued an aggressive program that greatly accelerated a longer process of centralization that had actually begun in 1526 with the accession of Ferdinand I to the Bohemian throne. The Bohemian Chancellery was moved from Prague to Vienna in 1624, and then three years later the Czech estates experienced what many historians have considered their death knell of independence. After defeating Denmark on the battlefield, Ferdinand issued the infamous Renewed Constitution (*Obnovené zřízení zemské/Verneuerte Landesordnung*) which finalized the redistribution of political power in the kingdom.[5] The elective monarchy was formally revoked. Habsburg succession was declared hereditary and

---

[4] Typical in this regard is the anonymous tract *Iustitia Caesarea, Imperialis, circa declarationem banni, contra Comitem Palatinum Electorem & circa nuperam Executionem* (n.p., 1621). For Goldast see *Melchioris Goldasti Heiminsfeldii De Bohemiae regni* (Frankfurt: Impensa I. I. Porsii, 1627).

[5] Jiří Mikulec, *31.7.1627* (Prague: Havran, 2005); Hans-Wolfgang Bergerhausen, "Die 'Verneuerte Landesordnung' in Böhmen 1627: ein Grunddokument des habsburgischen Absolutismus," *HZ* 272 (2001), 327–52; R. J. W. Evans, *The Making of the Habsburg Monarchy 1550–1700* (Oxford: Clarendon Press, 1979), pp. 198–200; Eila Hassenpflug-Elzholz presents a more benign interpretation of the decree and its implementation in her *Böhmen und die böhmischen Stände in der Zeit des beginnenden Zentralismus* (Munich: Oldenbourg, 1982).

guaranteed on both the male and female side of the family. The Bohemian Diet lost many of its traditional rights. With a few exceptions it could no longer initiate legislation. The estates themselves were transformed. A new clerical estate was added while the once powerful burgher class was reduced to virtual insignificance. Linguistically, German was given the same status as Czech, and a final pronouncement was made regarding religion through the Patent of Recatholicization. Non-Catholics had six months either to convert or to leave the kingdom. Not surprisingly, this new legislation precipitated a mass emigration. Between one fifth and one quarter of the nobility and nearly an equal percentage of townspeople packed their belongings and left their homeland.[6]

This standard historiographical treatment of White Mountain and its immediate aftermath constitutes an important chapter of a broader narrative tracing the development of Habsburg absolutism in which Ferdinand II figures prominently. From his early years in Inner Austria when he declared to the Styrian estates that he was a *princeps absolutus* to the heady days of the late 1620s that culminated with the Edict of Restitution, Ferdinand has been seen as a great centralizer in the history of the dynasty, a prince whom one historian has called the "founder of the Habsburg monarchy."[7] Geoffrey Parker has characterized Ferdinand's policies between 1621 and 1629 as "the practice of absolutism." When evaluating the emperor's reign, Dieter Albrecht has used the phrase "early absolutism," Hans Sturmberger has described a "practical absolutism," while Robert Bireley has developed the notion of "confessional absolutism."[8] As these varying terms suggest, there has been considerable debate concerning the nature and scope of Ferdinand's rule. The notion of absolutism needs to be qualified carefully in the Habsburg context. Recent work calls the model into question.[9] Despite his often strident rhetoric, Ferdinand was by nature a conservative prince who in his own mind sought to uphold the traditional structure of the Empire. As many have noted, even his boldest stroke, the 1629 Edict of Restitution, actually

---

[6] For an overview see Jaroslav Purš and Miroslav Kropilák, *Přehled dějin Československa I/2 (1526–1848)* (Prague: Academia, 1982), pp. 167–93.

[7] Robert Bireley, "Ferdinand II: founder of the Habsburg monarchy," in T. V. Thomas and R. J. W. Evans, eds., *Crown, Church and Estates* (London: Macmillan, 1991), pp. 226–44.

[8] Geoffrey Parker, *The Thirty Years War* (New York: Military Heritage Press, 1988), pp. 88–102; Dieter Albrecht, "Ferdinand II. 1619–1637," in A. Schindling and W. Ziegler, eds., *Die Kaiser der Neuzeit* (Munich: Beck, 1990), p. 127; Hans Sturmberger, *Ferdinand II und das Problem des Absolutismus* (Munich: Oldenbourg, 1957), p. 19; Robert Bireley, "Confessional absolutism in the Habsburg lands in the seventeenth century," in C. Ingrao, ed., *State and Society in Early Modern Austria* (West Lafayette: Purdue University Press, 1994), pp. 36–53.

[9] Petr Mat'a and Thomas Winkelbauer (eds.), *Die Habsburgermonarchie 1620 bis 1740: Leistungen und Grenzen des Absolutismusparadigmas* (Stuttgart: Steiner, 2006).

appealed back to existing law from the Peace of Augsburg. He merely sought to apply a Catholic interpretation of the settlement including the implementation of the "Ecclesiastical Reservation," which Protestant princes had simply ignored when they seized and secularized church lands after 1555. In Bohemia his aggressive actions were predicated on the belief that the kingdom's estates had forfeited their rights through rebellion.

More importantly, the overwhelming attention that has been devoted to the issue of absolutism and political authority has obscured a critical aspect of Ferdinand's reign. Though nearly all scholars recognize that the emperor's militant Catholic piety differed markedly from his predecessors' more ambiguous convictions, there has been no systematic study of the confessional shift that Ferdinand helped initiate that transformed the character of the dynasty. While substantial attention has been given to the late Renaissance world of his cousin, Rudolf II (1576–1612), the cultural and intellectual currents of Ferdinand's own court have not been studied in a thoroughgoing fashion. Ferdinand is stereotypically portrayed as a stern and ascetic figure unsympathetic to the whimsical proclivities and extravagant tastes of the Rudolfine era. Such a characterization, however, seriously underplays the emperor's activities in this area. In the long run Ferdinand's influence was even greater than that of his cousin, for his interests were focused squarely on the church.

During his years as archduke and emperor Ferdinand was instrumental in reshaping the ecclesiastical culture of the Habsburg lands. He instinctively realized that the church's authority was in large part based on a renewal of its culture, specifically a revival of its ceremonies and rituals in the public sphere. In this regard he differed markedly from his predecessors. His uncle, the moderate Maximilian II (1564–76), was reluctant to participate in popular ecclesiastical ceremonies such as the annual Corpus Christi day processions while the quizzical Rudolf refused the last rites on his deathbed. Ferdinand offered a new model of imperial leadership. With no equivocation he identified directly with the church, linked his reign to its fortunes and worked hard to portray himself as a great Catholic champion. The emperor's public persona and image were carefully cultivated. Ferdinand's court artist, Giovanni Pietro de Pomis, executed a series of commissions that celebrated the young Habsburg as the church's faithful ally. The most famous of these paintings shows a mature Ferdinand high in the heavens leading a cosmic struggle against Protestantism. An anonymous printmaker later depicted the emperor as a suffering Christ in Gethsemane who with a constant but sorrowful faith awaits the betrayal of his church and kingdom in Bohemia. In what is certainly one of the most dramatic depictions of any Habsburg

1. Portrait of Ferdinand II, Aegidius Sadeler

emperor, the Flemish engraver Aegidius Sadeler portrayed a militant Ferdinand on horseback at the height of his powers (Figure 1).[10] A banner at the top of the illustration refers directly to Ferdinand's divine calling, the restoration of Catholicism. Flanking the emperor are the figures of Piety with a flame rising from her head and Justice who is crushing the dragon of Heresy. As lightning flashes from the heavens, the emperor and his charger lunge forward to trample their confessional opponents. A critical detail lies partially obscured in the background. A priest bearing a crucifix solemnly accompanies a celebratory procession of soldiers dressed in full regalia, yet another reference to the importance of public rites and ceremonies in the restoration of the church's power and authority in central Europe.

How was ritual deployed in Bohemia after Ferdinand's triumph at White Mountain? Edward Muir has recently observed that in the early modern period Catholics effectively used it to express a sense of cohesion and conformity within divided communities. Ritual in itself does not create unity and consensus. Instead it fosters an experience of solidarity in its absence.[11] In this respect it was an ideal tool for Ferdinand as he sought to bring Bohemia back into the Catholic fold. For over two centuries Czech society was confessionally and culturally divided. Though the Habsburgs may have been able to impose new political and economic policies on the conquered kingdom, they could not immediately overcome the region's deep-seated religious differences. While the most obdurate of heretics could be expelled and their estates confiscated, much work lay ahead before a new Catholic identity could replace that which had been forcibly repressed. Ritual offered a means to begin this process. It papered over differences and divisions and helped create a sense of solidarity without necessarily compelling common belief. It bought time for the Habsburgs and the church to solidify confessional gains on the ground through the work of missionaries, educators and parish priests. Ritual also pointed towards the future setting forth an idealized view of community, an adumbration of a fully reformed Catholic society. It is thus appropriate to begin our study by examining two important civic ceremonies that took place in the years

---

[10] Kurt Woisetschläger, ed., *Giovanni Pietro de Pomis* (Graz: Styria, 1974), p. 149; Paul Monod, *The Power of Kings* (New Haven: Yale University Press, 1999), pp. 82, 86–93; Dorothy Limouze, "Aegidius Sadeler (c.1570–1629): drawings, prints and art theory," unpublished Ph.D. thesis, Princeton University (1990), pp. 277–9.

[11] Edward Muir, *Ritual in Early Modern Europe*, 2nd edn (Cambridge: Cambridge University Press, 2005), p. 225; David Kertzer, *Ritual, Politics and Power* (New Haven: Yale University Press, 1988), pp. 69, 96.

immediately following White Mountain. Considered together, they help elucidate the goals, methods and rationale that underpinned a program of religious reform that lasted more than a century and radically transformed the confessional character of the Bohemian kingdom.

Once the Czech estates had been overcome militarily, the emperor faced a serious dilemma. How should he treat the defeated? Clemency or harsh justice? Though a number of the rebels had fled with the Winter King, many of the key leaders had been apprehended and awaited imperial judgment. Others were soon tracked down. Ferdinand's decision had significant ramifications, for those confined included some of the most respected personalities of the kingdom. He spent considerable time deliberating this matter. The ultimate result was the most celebrated execution in Czech history. On 21 June 1621, twenty-seven prisoners were led on to a platform erected in Old Town Square and there before a stunned audience put to death. Executions were always ritualized pageants of punishment or, as Huizinga described, "spectacular plays with morals," but in the seventeenth century the staging of these events became even more elaborate and dramatic.[12] The scaffold was thus the ideal showplace for the emperor. Prague's citizens rose early that day bumping and jostling each other in the darkness as they moved en masse towards the square. Those unable to find room to stand headed for the roofs while the luckier ones were able to peer from windows of nearby buildings. Ferdinand surely knew that there would also be an explosion of broadsheets detailing through image and word the somber proceedings in Old Town Square. Therefore, the planning was meticulous and the emperor spent months consulting his deputy Karl von Liechtenstein.[13] Together they devised a carefully crafted statement that helped frame his subsequent program to restore Catholicism in Bohemia.

---

[12] Cited in Pieter Spierenberg, *The Spectacle of Suffering* (Cambridge: Cambridge University Press, 1984), p. 43; Richard van Dülmen, *Theatre of Horror: Crime and Punishment in Early Modern Germany* (Cambridge: Polity Press, 1990), p. 135.

[13] Čeněk Zíbrt, *Bibliografie české historie* (Prague: Nákl. České akademie císaře Františka Josefa pro vědy, slovesnost a umění, 1904), vol. IV, pp. 486–502; essential here is the correspondence between Ferdinand and Liechtenstein collected in Christian d'Elvert, ed., *Die Bestrafung der böhmischen Rebellion insbesondere die Correspondenz Ferdinand II. mit dem Fürsten Liechtenstein* (Brünn: A. Nitsch, 1868). The best overall narrative of the actual proceedings is Josef Petráň, *Staroměstská exekuce* (Prague: Rodiče, 2004).

From the various tracts produced after the execution, it is not difficult to reconstruct the events of those June days.[14] Activity began on Thursday, 17 June when a garrison of 700 Saxon soldiers rode into Prague to secure Old Town Square from any form of unrest. The following day, under the watchful gaze of the soldiers, a team of carpenters started work on the scaffold which they attached to the town hall. Thirty wagon-loads of sand, forty-four large pieces of black cloth, and over 2,000 nails were among the materials used in the construction of the platform.[15] On Saturday the prisoners were escorted under heavy guard to the castle. They assembled in a stately audience hall before Liechtenstein, who sat above them on a throne of violet samite. The imperial jurist, Otto Melander, stepped forward and formally pronounced their sentence. Not all were condemned to die, but those who received the ultimate penalty were detained that evening in the castle prison where they were visited by Jesuits who sought their last-minute conversion. The final preparations were made on Sunday. The scaffold was draped in a new black cloth, and the prisoners were brought down from the castle to more convenient cells in Old Town. As the clock struck five on Monday morning, a deafening fusillade of canons inaugurated the proceedings. The condemned men were escorted by an armed guard, and one by one led on stage. The order of execution was determined by social standing. Twenty-four were beheaded while three were hanged, two from a window post protruding from the town hall and one from a separate gallows erected at the side of the square (Figure 2). Though the grisly task was completed in approximately four hours, the full ceremonies did not conclude until the next day. On Tuesday morning Mikuláš Diviš, a minor official who had celebrated Frederick's entry into Prague dressed as the Hussite hero Jan Žižka, had his tongue nailed to the gallows in Old Town Square where he remained for two hours that morning. Three other city councilors were flogged for their participation in the revolt and then driven out of the city.

Such are the details of that traumatic summer week. Their interpretation, however, is far more problematic. Substantial debate has arisen concerning the meaning and significance of early modern executions. The discussion has normally oscillated between two interpretive poles. At one extreme, J. A. Sharpe has contended that the English state used the ceremonies to

---

[14] Concerning the main details of the execution, there is very little disagreement in the varying accounts. I am relying primarily on the *Prägerische Execution* (Prague: Albin, 1621), the source from which many other reports based their narrative. See Friedel Pick, ed., *Die Prager Execution i. J. 1621. Flugblätter und Abbildungen, Pragensia* 5 (1922), 89–90.

[15] Petráň, *Staroměstská exekuce*, p. 9.

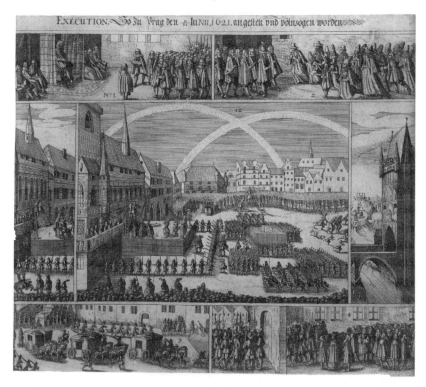

2. 1621 execution, Old Town Square, Prague

undergird its claims of authority and legitimacy. He contends that final speeches on the scaffold, where the condemned publicly confessed his guilt before the axe fell, were a Tudor innovation to strengthen the power of their regime. In the German context Richard Evans has put forward a similar argument.[16] At the other end of the spectrum are views expressed by scholars such as Thomas Laqueur. Drawing from Bakhtin, Laqueur maintains that these genuinely popular ceremonies were akin to carnival. The masses were able to subvert rituals of execution and subtly or in some cases

---

[16] J. A. Sharpe, "'Last dying speeches': religion, ideology and public execution in seventeenth-century England," *Past and Present* 107 (1985), 144–67; Charles Carlton, "The rhetoric of death: scaffold confessions in early modern England," *The Southern Speech Communication Journal* 49 (1983), 66–79; for Germany see Richard Evans, *Rituals of Retribution* (Oxford: Oxford University Press, 1996), pp. 102–4.

more directly challenge the existing social order.[17] Peter Burke long ago pointed out that "a crowd did not necessarily interpret proceedings in the same way as the authorities."[18] As we see in cases of religious executions, whether the victim died as a heretic or a martyr was very much in the eye of the beholder.

Czech historiography of the 1621 execution is relatively thin. Though the event itself figures prominently in any treatment of the period, traditional examinations have rarely moved beyond a superficial level. Most have treated the proceedings in a customarily nationalist fashion, decrying the inhumanity of the Habsburgs and lamenting the loss of Bohemia's stalwart patriots.[19] But as the broader literature suggests, there are deeper complexities here. The most salient fact that confronts the historian is the sheer number of pamphlets and broadsheets produced in the wake of the executions. According to one source, there were approximately sixty accounts, both in manuscript and printed form, in addition to nearly a dozen illustrations.[20] Some of the reports clearly favored the cause of the estates. These were often written by the exiles in the form of martyrologies or were composed abroad by Habsburg opponents.[21] Others definitively supported the imperial position.[22] Many texts and illustrations, however, were frequently more ambiguous in nature. The *Prägerische Execution*, one of the most important descriptions of the bloody exercise in Old Town Square, is a typical example. There has been some debate concerning the author of this anonymous pamphlet, which served as a basis for many other accounts. One scholar maintains that it was written by Georg Schwind, a Catholic official who worked under Vilém Slavata, the future chancellor of

---

[17] T. A. Laqueur, "Crowds, carnival and the state in English executions, 1604–1868," in A. Beier, D. Cannadine and J. Rosenheim, eds., *The First Modern Society* (Cambridge: Cambridge University Press, 1989), pp. 305–55; Peter Lake and Michael Questier, "Agency, appropriation and rhetoric under the gallows: Puritans, Romanists and the state in early modern England," *Past and Present* 153 (1996), 64–5; Pascal Bastien, "Fête populaire ou cérémonial d'Etat? Le rituel de l'exécution selon deux bourgeois de Paris (1718–1789)," *French Historical Studies* 24 (2001), 501–26.

[18] Peter Burke, *Popular Culture in Early Modern Europe* (London: T. Smith, 1978), p. 198. More recently see the comments of Catherine Bell in "The power of ritualization," in Catherine Bell, *Ritual Theory, Ritual Practice* (Oxford: Oxford University Press, 1992), pp. 197–223.

[19] J. J. Vrabec begins his account of the actual execution by dramatically declaring, "21 June – The Good Friday of the Czechs, Old Town Square – the Bohemian Golgotha!" J. J. Vrabec, *Popravy na Staroměstském náměstí, 21. VI. 1621* (Prague: Kočí, 1908), p. 135. Also see Petráň's comments comparing the Habsburgs to the Turks, *Staroměstská exekuce*, p. 23.

[20] Pick, ed., *Die Prager Execution*, pp. 89–90.

[21] See for example the account of Jan Rosacius, the Utraquist priest who attended the prisoners on the scaffold. See his *Koruna neuvadlá mučedlníkův božích českých* (n.p., 1621). For a fuller discussion of these texts see chapter 4.

[22] *Iustitia Caesarea*; Michael Caspar Lundorp, *Östreichischer Lorberkrantz Oder Kayserl: Victori* (Frankfurt: Schönwetter, 1627).

3. Illustration of 1621 execution from the workshop of Andreas Güntsch

Bohemia.[23] There is also evidence, however, that it may have been composed by a Protestant sympathizer.[24] The text as a whole is full of intentionally obscure passages. There were reports that at the time of the execution a rainbow appeared in the sky. While more partisan chroniclers saw this as a clear sign of divine support for the prisoners, the *Prägerische Execution* was more cryptic. The author cautiously commented, "What this sign meant God knows, but many different opinions were expressed."[25] Visual representations of the executions are even more difficult to interpret. What from one perspective could be seen as an advertisement of Habsburg cruelty could be viewed from another quarter as a just warning to those who harbored thoughts of revolt. Illustrative is a print from the workshop of Andreas Güntsch in Augsburg that inaccurately captured the goriest aspects of the execution. While at first glance the engraving may be read as an indictment of Habsburg bloodlust, it is actually an endorsement of imperial justice (Figure 3).[26]

---

[23] Vrabec, *Popravy*, p. 110.

[24] The anonymous author of the text commented positively on the fact that the condemned were steadfast in their beliefs. The tract also included an account of a sermon preached on the Thursday after the execution by a Lutheran pastor who praised those who were executed. *Prägerische Execution*, Biiv–Biiir, Bivr.

[25] Ibid., Biir.

[26] Pick, ed., *Die Prager Execution*, 210–11. This was a popular illustration slightly modified from a French account of the execution (*Discours veritable* [Lyon: Vincent de Coeursilly]).

Assessing the reception of the 1621 executions is thus quite difficult. Plausible arguments could be made interpreting the event both as a celebration of state power and an attempt to undermine the new imperial order by partisans of the Czech estates. What we can do more effectively is gauge the intent of the ceremony and consider imperial efforts to limit the subversion of its rituals. The first point to note in this regard is the setting of the execution. Some seventy years earlier, another Ferdinand had also faced a revolt in Prague. The city had risen against the Habsburgs as part of the Schmalkaldic War. After the revolt was quelled, Ferdinand staged a series of trials that ultimately culminated with the death of four of the conspirators. Imperial authorities led the unfortunate men to a scaffold on the other side of the Moldau, in front of the royal palace on Castle Square.[27] By putting the rebels to death in the shadow of the castle, Ferdinand spoke to the specific nature of their crime. They had committed treason against the king of Bohemia, who now administered royal justice from his own residence. The decision of Ferdinand and Liechtenstein to hold the execution in Old Town Square was equally significant. Old Town Square, dominated by the town hall and the historic Týn church, the central Hussite house of worship, was the city's civic and spiritual center. In Ferdinand's mind it was the locus of the religious and political dissent he sought to eradicate. Royal authority, as it were, was moving down from the castle, invading the space of the city and leaving an indelible mark at its very core. A platform overlooking the scaffold was erected for official witnesses of the ceremony: high ranking judges and officers, a deputation from the city councils, and Prince Liechtenstein himself. Old Town Square offered other advantages as well. Unlike the somewhat tighter confines of Castle Square, the public space of Old Town could accommodate a larger audience. Additionally, it is important to note that Ferdinand I had quietly struck a compromise with the Czech nobility who had been involved in the earlier rebellion. In the end only "second-stringers of the gentry or middle classes" were dispatched with the sword.[28] Though Ferdinand II also commuted a few of the sentences, unlike his predecessor he was not afraid of alienating the nobility through his decisive actions. Without hesitation he sent some of the most respected and dignified members of Czech society to the block. Many were in their sixties and seventies. The oldest was the knight Kašpar Kaplíř, who at eighty-six is reported to have said before the sword fell,

---

[27] Winfried Eberhard, *Monarchie und Widerstand: Zur ständischen Oppositionsbildung im Herrschaftssystem Ferdinands I. in Böhmen* (Munich: Oldenbourg, 1985), pp. 481–5.
[28] Peter Demetz, *Prague in Black and Gold* (New York: Hill and Wang, 1977), p. 177.

"In the name of God, I have already waited long enough!"[29] More ambitious in scope and intent, the 1621 execution was a far bolder statement of imperial prerogative than the earlier spectacle on Castle Square.

The actual staging of the event is also important to consider. In the early modern period executions were frequently unruly and upon occasion could degenerate into disorderly brawls. Rituals of justice were not always formalized. In the sixteenth century there are accounts of drunken executioners who were pelted with stones for their failure to cut off the heads of prisoners with a single blow. In 1591 such an incident occurred in Prague itself. A riot broke out after a headsman had botched the execution of five criminals. The following day he was put on trial for his incompetence.[30] In contrast, the 1621 execution was carefully planned, elaborately produced and rigorously controlled. Liechtenstein ordered the city gates closed and stationed soldiers that Monday morning at critical parts of Prague to prevent any unrest.[31] Presumably for security reasons, the prisoners had been transferred from the castle area to the Old Town on the previous day. They had spent the night in the holding cells of the town hall and were thus only a few paces away from the scaffold. The blowing of pipes and rolling of drums accompanied the condemned as they were escorted into the square the next morning. A line of musketeers surrounded the scaffold on three sides. Small squares of infantry and a contingent of cavalry were scattered around the plaza while the crowds pressed in from behind. The execution itself progressed smoothly. Prisoners were led on to the stage in an orderly manner, normally attended by one or two servants and a priest. After a moment of final reflection and prayer, the executioner stepped in and completed the ceremony with a swift stroke to the neck. Prague's headsman, Jan Mydlář, worked efficiently that morning. He finished his task by nine o'clock, going through four swords in the process. Liechtenstein rewarded him handsomely for his efforts. His wages, in fact, were large enough to purchase a small house.[32]

The most critical juncture of an execution was the moment before the final punishment was administered. Here the prisoner was often allowed a last speech. With cases of treason the criminal frequently confessed his guilt to the audience. Before he was put to death, the swashbuckling Wilhelm von Grumbach, the leader of a knights' revolt against the Habsburgs in the late sixteenth century, begged forgiveness for his sedition.[33] Not all

[29] Petráň, *Staroměstská exekuce*, p. 11.
[30] Evans, *Rituals of Retribution*, p. 50; van Dülmen, *Theatre of Horror*, p. 115.
[31] *Prägerische Execution*, Biir. [32] Petráň, *Staroměstská exekuce*, p. 15.
[33] Volker Press, "Wilhelm von Grumbach und die deutsche Adelskrise der 1560er Jahre," *Blätter für deutsche Landesgeschichte* 113 (1977), 396–431. On the execution itself see van Dülmen, *Theatre of Horror*, pp. 93–4.

offenders, however, were so accommodating. Those executed for religious reasons often used their final moment to rally fellow believers with a passionate call to stand firm in the faith. A ritual intended to cleanse heresy from the community could thus be subverted and transformed into a dramatic ceremony of martyrdom.[34] Liechtenstein was well aware of this possibility and took appropriate countermeasures. Though in later imperial sources there is mention of remorse among a few of the rebels, in general this was a steadfast group of individuals whose opposition to Ferdinand remained firm.[35] Václav Budovec of Budov was a senior leader of the Bohemian Brethren. Johannes Jessenius was a former rector of the university. The erudite Kryštof Harant of Polžice was an experienced man of politics and author of a well-known travel account to the Holy Land. These were eloquent and learned men unlikely to renounce their beliefs. Many expected quite the opposite. Not a few were drawn to Old Town Square to hear their dying remarks. Liechtenstein, however, disappointed the crowd. Under his direction, the drums and pipes grew even louder and continued for the entire time so that "no one could hear his own words, much less the final speeches which had been so eagerly anticipated."[36] The prince masterfully choreographed the entire affair using a variety of techniques to help control the psychological reception of the drama. After the first ten prisoners were executed, the eleventh, Jan Theodor Sixt of Ottersdorf, was led on to the stage. As he began to kneel before the block, it was suddenly announced that he had been pardoned. This strategic break deflected attention away from the prisoner as a potential martyr by reminding the audience that it was the emperor who was ultimately directing the proceedings. The last-minute pardon raised the dramatic tension on the scaffold considerably as the crowd now realized that others might unexpectedly be granted the same merciful fate.[37]

Liechtenstein was decidedly concerned with the ramifications of this entire affair. The trial and punishment of the rebels was an extremely delicate matter. Some argued that if handled improperly, it could provoke still further revolt in the region.[38] In his correspondence with Ferdinand, Liechtenstein pointed back to previous examples of *lèse-majesté* in Bohemia. He argued that in these earlier cases the Habsburgs had proceeded

[34] See for example David Nichols, "The theatre of martyrdom in the French Reformation," *Past and Present* 121 (1988), 49–73.

[35] Franz Christoph Khevenhiller, *Annales Ferdinandei* (Leipzig: Weidmann, 1724), vol. IX, pp. 1307–12.

[36] *Prägerische Execution*, Biir.   [37] Petráň, *Staroměstská exekuce*, p. 14.

[38] Anonymous memorandum to the emperor concerning the execution, March 1621. D'Elvert, ed., *Die Bestrafung*, pp. 46–9.

overzealously and had created an unfavorable impression of arbitrary despotism.[39] Though he did not believe that unusual clemency was in order, he urged Ferdinand to move forward carefully, avoiding the mistakes of the past. It was generally agreed that the emperor should not be present at the execution. The prosecution of the insurgents should be turned over to the properly designated authorities from the Czech estates.[40] Otto Melander was entrusted with the task of compiling a legal commentary and a "history of this crime from its beginning to end." The verdicts reached on the prisoners were to be posted prominently throughout Prague, both in Czech and German.[41]

Liechtenstein's ideas concerning judicial moderation were also in evidence on the scaffold. Executions for treason could be particularly gruesome.[42] Though some form of dismemberment normally took place, headsmen could be extreme in their actions. In 1567 Wilhelm von Grumbach was carried to the scaffold, undressed, and then bound hand and foot. In a manner more akin to an Aztec ritual of human sacrifice, the executioner proceeded to excise the knight's heart from his thoracic cavity, hold it momentarily aloft and then dramatically throw it back at Grumbach's mouth. Such appalling displays of gore and blood had the potential of merely horrifying a shocked audience, distracting it from any underlying moral lesson the authorities sought to communicate. Conscious of the spectacle they were designing, Ferdinand and Liechtenstein gave careful consideration to the specific mechanics of the execution, down to the actual details of dismemberment.[43] The ceremony they devised was an undeniably strong statement, but it avoided gratuitous mutilations and bloody excess. All but three of the prisoners were beheaded. Most were spared the torment of losing a limb while alive. Only one individual was singled out for special attention. Johannes Jessenius, one of the most prominent of the rebel leaders and its chief ideologue, received an especially harsh sentence. As many broadsheets illustrated, Jessenius was roughly

---

[39] Liechtenstein to Ferdinand, 5 March 1621. Ibid., pp. 37–8.
[40] Anonymous memorandum to the emperor concerning the execution, March 1621. Ibid., *Die Bestrafung*, pp. 46–9. Typically, the prince did not attend early modern executions. See Spierenberg, *Spectacle of Suffering*, p. 54. Liechtenstein was intending to stage a dramatic entry for Ferdinand into Prague three weeks after the execution, an event that would be cancelled for military reasons. Petráň, *Staroměstská exekuce*, p. 258.
[41] Liechtenstein to Ferdinand, 7 April 1621. D'Elvert, ed., *Die Bestrafung*, pp. 50, 53.
[42] W. R. J. Barron, "The penalties for treason in medieval life and literature," *Journal of Medieval History* 7 (1981), 187–201.
[43] See the addendum to Liechtenstein's report on the judgment of the rebels, 22 May 1621. D'Elvert, ed., *Die Bestrafung*, pp. 65–7. Also relevant is the report of the imperial judicial council sent to Liechtenstein, 2 June 1621. Ibid., pp. 72–3.

secured to a chair before his tongue was sliced off by the executioner. Thereafter he was decapitated. His body was later brought outside the city where it was quartered and then displayed. A final matter of staging discussed between Ferdinand and his governor concerned the heads of the prisoners. Twelve of them were impaled on spikes atop the Old Town Bridge Tower. Here, as Liechtenstein explained, they were easily seen from both sides of the river. Additionally those crossing the Charles Bridge were forced to pass under them.[44] For ten years the heads remained on the tower, a constant reminder to the city of the price of rebellion.

From the staging to the setting, the 1621 execution was a means to buttress Ferdinand's claims of political legitimacy in Bohemia. The twenty-seven prisoners were officially executed for treason against their lawful king. On the surface, then, these proceedings were not about religion. Confessional freedom had been guaranteed to the Czech estates in 1609 with the Letter of Majesty. But though the rebels were technically guilty of a political crime, an underlying religious dynamic was driving the entire affair. Three months before the execution, Liechtenstein had written Ferdinand, "I know that Your Imperial Majesty has had the intention of regarding this matter not as a religious but as a civic revolt."[45] Liechtenstein's words were actually less of a statement of fact than a cautiously phrased reminder for the emperor to proceed carefully on the religious front. In Ferdinand's mind there had always been a close link between confessional deviance and a political factionalism that would ultimately lead to rebellion. For what was heresy in the first place but rebellion against God and his church! Sooner or later, those who had revolted against divine authority also turned against his representatives on earth. As the correspondence between the two attests, Ferdinand saw the execution as the first stage of a broader campaign to rid Bohemia of heresy and the sedition it engendered. On 3 June he instructed his governor to publish an edict two or three days after the execution that banned all "preachers, professors and schoolmasters of the Calvinist or Picard persuasion" (usually a reference to the *Unitas Fratrum*) from the Bohemian kingdom.[46]

---

[44] Liechtenstein noted, "As some of the heads should be displayed as a public example, one could think of no better space than the Old Town Bridge Tower, not far from the toll house. When one goes from the bridge directly into Old Town or back from Old Town [across the bridge] to the Lesser Town and then back into Old Town, the passerby will always be able to see them." Liechtenstein's report on the judgment of the rebels, 22 May 1621. Ibid., p. 65.

[45] Liechtenstein to Ferdinand, 28 March 1621. Ibid., p. 44.

[46] Imperial resolution concerning the *negocium religionis*, 3 June 1621. Ibid., pp. 73–4. Liechtenstein was evidently reluctant to execute this order.

It is evident that had Ferdinand followed his own judgment the cere-monies in Old Town Square would have been very different in tone. Liechtenstein effectively moderated some of the emperor's more extreme inclinations. At times he was an actual advocate of the prisoners as in the case of Vilém Popel of Lobkovic. Liechtenstein argued for clemency, noting that Lobkovic was no true rebel but "merely a stupid idiot" whose capital sentence should be commuted in large part due to his family's long and distinguished record of service for the Habsburgs.[47] Without Liechtenstein, it seems likely that Ferdinand would have planned a ceremony closer in line to the *autos-da-fé* of his cousins in Spain. As it was, the most prominent feature of the scaffold was a crucifix nearly three meters high positioned before the block. The cross was decorated with a painting of Mary gazing in sorrow upon her crucified son. Clearly, the crucifix was intended to help create a suitably Catholic atmosphere on stage. Adding to the solemn mood was the new black drapery that covered the entire platform. Ferdinand had originally intended to forbid all Protestant clergy from attending the prison-ers in their last moments before death. In addition, he planned to deploy Catholic soldiers of Bavaria as the guard in Old Town Square. These two decisions troubled Liechtenstein. As he argued, the Bavarians had been at best a general nuisance in Prague ever since their victory at White Mountain in November.[48] Their presence in the square would undoubtedly heighten confessional tensions. A detachment of Lutheran soldiers from Saxony was far more palatable to the predominately non-Catholic audience. Likewise, the decision to allow only Catholic priests on stage was equally dangerous and unnecessarily provocative.[49]

On both these points Ferdinand relented. Nonetheless, the punishments that were administered to the rebels resembled in certain respects those traditionally meted out to those accused of religious crimes. Catholic authorities frequently cut out the tongues of Protestants who had been apprehended for blasphemy. Many of those at the execution surely drew the connection between human and divine treason with the treatment of Jessenius. From the Catholic perspective was not this former rector of Luther's old university in Wittenberg also guilty of *lèse-majesté* before God? The treatment of Protestant iconoclasts was also echoed in Prague.

---

[47] Liechtenstein's report on the sentencing of the prisoners, 17 May 1621. Ibid., pp. 60–1.

[48] Liechtenstein's report concerning the Bavarian garrison in Prague, 5 March 1621. Ibid., *Die Bestrafung*, pp. 36–7.

[49] Liechtenstein's report concerning the execution, 12 June 1621. Ibid., pp. 75–7. Even the Jesuits were concerned with such a measure and urged Ferdinand to allow non-Catholic clergy on the platform. A. Gindely, "Popravy v Praze po bitvě Bílohorské a jejich následky," *ČMKČ* 53 (1879), 372.

The hands of "image breakers" were often nailed to the church where they had committed their crime.[50] Severed hands of the prisoners had been placed above the heads on Old Town Bridge Tower. Though this was a reference to their broken oath of loyalty to Ferdinand, it could also have been seen as an allusion to the controversial "cleansing" of the St. Vitus Cathedral when Frederick's supporters cleared the church of many of its relics and destroyed much of its religious art.[51] As time passed, the imperial party more forcibly emphasized the confessional aspect of the revolt. In the *Annales Ferdinandei*, an eighteenth-century study of Ferdinand's reign, there is an interesting account concerning the only Catholic who was executed on 21 June. According to Franz Khevenhiller, the remorseful Diviš Černín requested a three-day reprieve in order not to die with the other heretics. He also informed his wife that he was not worthy to be interred in the family plot. Instead, he requested to be buried outside the church on his estate as a warning for future generations.[52]

Examined from a slightly different perspective, the 1621 execution can be viewed as the last and most formalized act of ritual violence in the protracted confessional struggle that had gripped the Bohemian kingdom since the death of Hus. For over two centuries competing religious communities had used such ritualistic weapons as iconoclasm and defenestration to defend their interests and attack their opponents. Ferdinand II clearly saw the revolt of 1618 as part of this long continuum of confessional strife. As the emperor argued in his 1627 Patent of Recatholicization, the troubles had begun during the reign of Wenceslas IV (1378–1419) when "all possible error and heresy crept into our hereditary kingdom, and then immediately disorder, quarrels, and mischief arose among our subjects ... and continued during the reigns of nearly all subsequent kings."[53] Seen from this vantage point, the execution in Old Town Square was for Ferdinand an appropriate ritual to close two centuries of turmoil and division.

Anthropologists of religion have argued that ritual acts of violence are often needed during times of crisis to restore equilibrium and stability in society. As René Girard has reminded us, sacrificial practices were developed to appease

---

[50] Nichols, "Theatre of martyrdom," 58–60.

[51] The correspondence between Ferdinand and Liechtenstein clearly shows that the emperor had been deeply troubled by the iconoclastic outburst on Castle Hill and made the restoration of the cathedral a high priority in the months immediately after White Mountain. See Liechtenstein's report on the castle chapel (17 February 1621, D'Elvert, ed., *Die Bestrafung*, p. 26) and the account of Archbishop Lohelius (18 February 1621, ibid., pp. 29–30).

[52] Khevenhiller, *Annales Ferdinandei*, vol. IX, p. 1309.

[53] Reproduced in Zdeněk Veselý, ed., *Dějiny českého státu v dokumentech* (Prague: Victoria Publishing, 1994), p. 194.

the divine and quell unrest within the community.[54] The imagery of sacrifice is particularly striking in the context of our discussion. Nearly all the broadsheet illustrations of the event depict the condemned kneeling humbly before the crucifix with the executioner poised with sword in hand.[55] While a Protestant audience might have viewed the scene in martyrological terms, from a Catholic perspective this was a moment of necessary violence when the collective sins of the kingdom were being symbolically cleansed through the death of the guilty. Mitchell Merback has recently noted, "Crime brought a taint of corruption and infamy upon the social body, and a proper execution held the potential to lift the miasma."[56] Ferdinand, himself, commemorated the events of 21 June in quiet retreat at the Austrian shrine of Mariazell. There, according to his chroniclers, he petitioned God to pardon the sins of the Bohemian heretics.[57] If the executions were on the one hand rites of expiation, they also celebrated the definitive expulsion of impurity from the community.[58] It is important to remember that the very last event of the 1621 ritual did not occur on the scaffold Monday morning but the following day in Old Town Square. Here a large audience watched as heresy was literally driven from their midst. Three of the minor conspirators were brought out before the crowds and then flogged in front of the town hall. They were then led down what is today Celetná Street, stopped opposite the city mint, and once more beaten. For the third and final flogging they were taken further along and whipped in front of the Inn of the Black Stags (Hybernská Street) before being sent beyond the walls into permanent exile. As people lined the route to witness the sad spectacle, the prisoners sang Psalms 70 and 112, calling for God's judgment on the wicked and deliverance of the righteous.[59]

IMPORTING PIETY: THE 1627 TRANSLATION
OF ST. NORBERT

The symbolic counterpart to the 1621 execution occurred six years later. While the drama in Old Town Square had been designed to rid dissent from society, it did little in a positive sense to strengthen the Catholic cause. Bohemia's Catholic community before 1620 constituted only 10–15 percent

[54] René Girard, *Violence and the Sacred* (Baltimore: Johns Hopkins University Press, 1977), esp. pp. 1–38.
[55] Pick, ed., *Die Prager Execution*, pp. 213–31.
[56] Mitchell Merback, *The Thief, the Cross and the Wheel* (Chicago: University of Chicago Press, 1999), p. 146.
[57] Pick, ed., *Die Prager Execution*, pp. 245–6.
[58] See for example Natalie Zemon Davis, "The rites of violence: religious riot in sixteenth century France," *Past and Present* 59 (1973), 51–91.
[59] Petráň, *Staroměstská exekuce*, p. 23.

of the populace. Though critical steps had been taken in the sixteenth century to renew the institutional grounding of the church, its leaders were shrewd enough to realize that though property and traditional ecclesiastical rights could be restored by imperial decree, cultural authority could be regained neither so quickly nor in such a peremptory fashion. Forced conversion combined with the expulsion of the most obdurate heretics could swell the church's ranks numerically, but such harsh tactics would obviously not create loyal Czech Catholics overnight. In response the church waged a lengthy cultural campaign to win the loyalty of its new members and restore its tarnished legacy, but religious deviance had deep roots in the kingdom. Thus, as the emperor and clerical leaders reasoned, if heresy had to be expelled, sanctity needed to be reintroduced in an equally dramatic fashion. Working closely with Ferdinand, Bohemia's leading churchmen seized the initiative with an important celebration of their own. The elaborately orchestrated translation of St. Norbert from Magdeburg to Prague in 1627 was a carefully constructed statement of renewed ecclesiastical authority and prestige.

Norbert of Xanten was the founder of the Premonstratensian order and archbishop of Magdeburg.[60] Born in lower Lorraine in the late eleventh century, Norbert had been designated for an ecclesiastical career at an early age. Through his family's connections, he was first appointed canon at the cathedral of Xanten. His hagiographers relate that, as a young man, Norbert was caught in a storm and knocked from his horse by a bolt of lightning. This traumatic experience prompted him to enter a life of religious seclusion from which he emerged three years later as an energetic reformer. He started his work in Xanten, but after a lukewarm reception he began to spread his message further afield preaching moral reform in the Low Countries and France. With the encouragement of Pope Callistus II he established a religious community that eventually evolved into the Premonstratensian order. He ended his career on Europe's eastern frontier as a missionary to the Sorbs, a reluctant archbishop of Magdeburg and close adviser of Emperor Lothair III (1133–7). He died in 1134 and was interred in the Premonstratensian church of Magdeburg. There his earthly remains resided until 1626.

The connection between Norbert and Bohemia may seem somewhat tenuous at first glance. The Premonstratensians, however, did have a long history in the Czech lands. Their first house in this region, the famous

---

[60] For a general overview on Norbert see Kaspar Elm, ed., *Norbert von Xanten* (Cologne: Wienand, 1984).

monastery of Strahov perched on a hill above Prague, was founded in 1140.[61] The order flourished here until the Hussite wars of the fifteenth century. Strahov was destroyed in 1420 while Catholicism itself was brought to the verge of extinction in the Bohemian kingdom. Recovery did not come until the late sixteenth century. The church's most important leader in this period was the new abbot of Strahov, Johann Lohelius.[62] A German from western Bohemia, Lohelius rebuilt Strahov and transformed it into a vibrant center of reform for the entire region. He was appointed archbishop of Prague in 1612, and though driven from the city in 1618, he returned triumphant after White Mountain to lead the church into a new period of expansion.

Not surprisingly, during his early years at Strahov, Lohelius's mind turned towards Magdeburg and Norbert as he sought to revitalize his weak and demoralized order. Norbert's cult, which had languished for several centuries, was now rapidly growing with papal support.[63] The forceful Lohelius first spearheaded an attempt in the late 1580s to bring the saint's relics to Prague. He faced, however, a number of serious obstacles. There were many in the predominantly Lutheran city of Magdeburg who strenuously objected to Norbert's proposed departure. The patriotic burghers were reluctant to give up their city's patron and protector. Lohelius also confronted stiff competition within his order. The vital Premonstratensian community of the Low Countries vied with Bohemia for the honor of housing their founder. The Habsburg court of Brussels began serious negotiations with Magdeburg in 1613 to acquire the relics.[64] In the end neither branch of the order was successful in prying the bones loose from the Germans, and with the onset of war in 1618 further attempts had to wait.

---

[61] Dominik Čermák, *Premonstráti v Čechách a na Moravě* (Prague: Nákl. Kanonie Strahovské, 1877); Hedvika Kuchařová and Jan Pařez, "Strahovští premonstráti a rekatolizace. Přístupy a problémy," in Ivana Čornejová, ed., *Úloha církevních řádů při pobělohorské rekatolizaci* (Prague: Univerzita Karolva, 2003), pp. 36–75.

[62] Gottfried Johann Dlabacz, *Leben des frommen Prager Erzbischofs Johann Lohelius* (Prague: Schönfeld, 1794); K. Pichert, "Johannes Lohelius," *AnPr* 3 (1927), 125–40, 264–83, 404–22.

[63] François Petit, "La Dévotion à St. Norbert au XVIIe et au XVIIIe siècles," *AnPr* 49 (1973), 198–213. Norbert was never officially canonized. In July 1582 Gregory XIII authorized the celebration of his feast day (6 June) for the Premonstratensian order. In 1621 Gregory XV included Norbert's office in the *Breviarum Romanum* and authorized the celebration of his feast day for the entire church. In 1625, however, the Premonstratensians made the request to move his feast day to 11 July. My thanks to Simon Ditchfield for this information.

[64] Elm, ed., *Norbert von Xanten*, p. 283; P. LeFevre, "Une tentative de transférer en Belgique le corps de Saint Norbert (1613–1626)," *AnPr* 26 (1950), 113–26.

The translation of Norbert's relics remained a high priority for the Bohemian church during the early years of the war. The job of securing them fell to Lohelius's successor at Strahov, Abbot Caspar Questenberg, and the young archbishop, Ernst Adalbert von Harrach. In 1625 Questenberg turned to Ferdinand II for assistance. According to the emperor's confessor, Ferdinand understood the importance of this enterprise and was eager to help. To facilitate the transfer of relics, he supplied Questenberg with a series of letters that were sent to the Magdeburg cathedral chapter, the city council, and the prior of the cloister where Norbert was buried.[65] This gentle form of persuasion did not succeed, and though the city was promised a number of privileges for their cooperation, when an attempt was made to remove the bones in March 1626, the Bohemian party was met by armed resistance and was forced to retreat.[66] A turning point came the following month. The imperial army under Wallenstein's direction won a decisive victory at Roßlau. Although negotiations still dragged on for a number of months, Questenberg with Wallenstein as an ally had the clear advantage. In late November 1626, Norbert's relics were taken from the city and carefully transferred to the Premonstratensian house of Doksany in preparation for their final journey into Prague.

At a time when Bohemia's Catholic community was confronted by so many serious challenges, it may seem strange that so much attention and so many resources were devoted to a project that at least on the surface seemed peripheral to the real needs of the church. The entry and procession of the relics into the city cost nearly 11,000 *Reichsthaler*.[67] Countless hours were spent planning the choreography of the celebrations down to the finest detail. The efforts to run and coordinate the crowded events of an eight-day festival that included the participation of nearly every religious order in Prague, not to mention municipal, regional and imperial representatives along with foreign dignitaries and visitors, must have been overwhelming. And all this was done for a saint whose direct contact with Bohemia had been limited. Why then was this project so important from the perspective of the kingdom's religious leaders? There was certainly an internal rivalry in the Premonstratensian order, and the honor to house the relics of its

[65] W. Lamormaini, *Ferdinandi II. Romanorum imperatoris virtutes* (Antwerp: Apud Ioannem Meursium, 1638), pp. 67–8; for a collection of these documents see *Narratio translati e Saxonia in Boemiam sacri corporis beatissimi viri, Norberti* (Prague: Paulus Sessius, 1627), q4r–y1v; E. Neubauer, "Die Fortführung der Gebeine des Erzbischofs Norbert aus Magdeburg im Jahre 1626," *Geschichts-Blätter für Stadt und Land Magdeburg* 25 (1890), 15–46.

[66] Neubauer, "Die Fortführung," 22–8.

[67] C. Straka, "Litteratura de translatione S. P. Norberti a. 1627 eiusque iubilaeis," *AnPr* 3 (1927), 336.

founder was a distinct mark of prestige. Rituals of translation in the Reformation era were also frequently a Catholic response to Protestant attacks on relics, and, undoubtedly, Norbert's translation was seen by many as a response to Frederick's iconoclastic regime.[68]

There is, however, a more general explanation that helps clarify the motives of Abbot Questenberg, Archbishop Harrach and Emperor Ferdinand, an explanation that points to an important feature of the quest to create a Catholic identity in the Bohemian kingdom. Robert Scribner and others have devoted substantial attention to the ways in which Protestants inverted or perverted Catholic rituals to attack traditional religious culture. Mock processions or parodies of liturgical rites were an effective means to critique and ridicule confessional opponents.[69] But while most Catholic regions had faced a Protestant challenge for a relatively short period, Bohemia's Catholic culture had been under serious assault for over two centuries. Hussites had burned monasteries and destroyed books. More moderate Utraquists had popularized a rival set of ecclesiastical symbols and celebrations while Lutherans and Calvinists launched direct attacks on Catholic practices and observances. Viewed in this context, translation ably addressed Catholicism's cultural decline. As opposed to rituals of pilgrimage where people are brought to the holy, with translation the holy is brought to the people. From Duke Wenceslas in the tenth century to Emperor Charles IV in the fourteenth, importing relics had always been an important tool in building a Czech ecclesiastical identity, but now it offered the church a way to reintroduce sanctity in a kingdom where the stain of heresy had become almost indelible.[70] Questenberg, Harrach and other leading churchmen instinctively realized that Bohemia's delicate ecclesiastical culture needed to be tended with much care and attention. Outside assistance, such as the bones of St. Norbert, was of inestimable value in this process. To counteract the centuries of heresy and impiety, the Czech lands needed a massive infusion of hallowed and sanctified relics. Norbert's translation, in fact, was the most famous of many such incidents

---

[68]   See the comments of Simon Ditchfield in "Martyrs on the move: relics as vindicators of local diversity in the Tridentine church," in Diana Wood, ed., *Martyrs and Martyrologies, Studies in Church History*, vol. XXX (Oxford: Blackwell, 1993), pp. 286–7. Jan Sixt of Lerchenfels devoted a substantial portion of his account of the translation to the defense of Catholic funerary practices. Jan Sixt of Lerchenfels, *Přenešení sv. Norberta* (Litoměřice, 1628), esp. Air–Aivr.

[69]   Robert Scribner, "Ritual and Reformation," in R. Po-Chia Hsia, ed., *The German People and the Reformation* (Ithaca: Cornell University Press, 1988), pp. 122–44.

[70]   One of the best accounts of this massive import of relics is provided by Tomáš Pešina in his history of St. Vitus Cathedral, *Phosphorus septicornis, stella aliàs matutina* (Prague: Joannis Arnolti de Dobroslavina, 1673), pp. 399–524.

during these early decades of Catholic recovery. Archbishop Harrach also acquired the remains of early church martyrs from Italy while the Capuchins initiated an even more aggressive program of importing relics.[71]

Norbert remained at the cloister in Doksany for the winter months. Back in Prague craftsmen labored feverishly to complete the necessary work for his entry. Special attention was devoted to the construction of a chapel for the relics in the Strahov monastery. All was ready by midspring, and the journey from Doksany to Prague was planned for 1 May. The procession did not begin on the most auspicious of notes. It had snowed the day before, and due to the distance to the city gates, final preparations began in the early hours of the morning.[72] The train moved out in darkness led by a drummer and eight trumpeters on horseback. With them was a small honor guard followed by eighty porters bearing torches and twenty-five priests singing psalms and hymns along the route. The carriage pulling Norbert's remains was drawn by three large white horses directed by coachmen wearing spotless white cloaks matching the color of the Norbertine habits. Abbot Questenberg and Prior Kryšpín Fuk flanked the car with a small group of other church officials marching solemnly after. At the very rear of the procession were fourteen carriages of the nobility while people out from the city or drawn from the surrounding countryside quickly filled in behind. By midafternoon they had reached the gates of Prague. Here Archbishop Harrach had come with his own large retinue of priests and musicians to greet the saint.[73]

The meeting of these two parties before the city walls marked an important transaction. Only a few weeks earlier in April, Prince Liechtenstein, and the high chamberlain, Jaroslav Martinic, had conferred with the archbishop regarding the upcoming festival. To heighten the impact of Norbert's arrival, they suggested that the saint be named an official patron of the kingdom. Harrach agreed and a public announcement to this effect was made at the end of April.[74] Now at the very doors of Prague, he led the assembled throng through an antiphonal reading of II Samuel 6, a passage that describes the reception of the Ark of the Covenant into Jerusalem after long years of absence. As David and the Israelites

[71] NA, ŘK, 52/I: 6, 8, 9, 11, 13, 24–6, 33–5, 37, 49; Johannes Miller, *Historia Beatissimae Virginis Glacensis* (Glatz: Pega, 1690), pp. 140–2. The Czech musician and cleric, Mauritius Vogt, would later boast that after Rome and Cologne, Prague boasted the largest collection of relics on the continent. See V. Schwarz, ed., *Město vidím veliké: cizinci o Praze* (Prague: Borový, 1940), p. 59.

[72] The best primary account of the procession is offered in *Octiduum S. Norberti triumphantis* (Prague: Paulus Sessius, 1627). Some contended that the snow was actually a sign of divine approval as the white ground covering matched the color of the Premonstratensian robes. C. Straka, *Přenešení ostatků Sv. Norberta z Magdeburku na Strahov (1626–1628)* (Prague: Kuncíř, 1927), p. 78.

[73] *Octiduum S. Norberti triumphantis*, f2r–f3v.   [74] Ibid., e4v–f1v.

jubilantly welcomed this treasured object that signified the very presence of God, so the archbishop and his congregation joyfully acknowledged and celebrated the arrival of this physical token of divine grace and mercy.

This transaction at the gate signified a type of spiritual contract between the patron and the people. A new lord was entering Prague, and its citizens had come to pledge their allegiance and loyalty. He was offering both his protection for the present and a general amnesty for the sins of the past. His entry was staged as a rallying point for the entire city. In the late antique period the *adventus* of a saint's relics could help broaden the bounds of a community by including the widest possible range of social orders in the celebrations. At times prisoners were even granted roles in such ecclesiastical festivities.[75] Though the jails may not have been emptied, church authorities clearly structured this event as a means to unite a city that had been divided by creed for over two centuries. The Catholic priest Jan Sixt of Lerchenfels described the eight-day proceedings as a homecoming, a curious but cleverly strategic phrase to be applied to an individual who had never visited Prague during his lifetime.[76] Questenberg, himself, was careful to avoid designing the ceremonies as an exclusive Premonstratensian celebration. Preaching and liturgical leadership rotated between the orders during the eight-day festival as homilies were delivered in Czech, German and Latin.[77]

Involvement in the proceedings, however, extended far beyond the clergy. Various representatives of the city government, confraternities, schools and the trades were at the gate with Harrach that first day to greet the carriage bearing the saint's remains. The university students in partic- ular were a lively presence during the week. On the fourth day they engineered a dramatic scene on the river. Elaborately rigging a fleet of boats, they mounted an allegorical representation of Norbert's translation on the Moldau.[78] The nobility, too, played a quiet but critical role. It was their financial support that stood behind so much of the costly staging. Considering their large donations for Norbert's new chapel in Strahov, it does not seem unlikely that at least some of the nobility were appropriating the saint as a special type of patron, what Friedrich Prinz has described as an *Adelsheilige*.[79] Apart from the open-air sermons and a spectacular fireworks

---

[75] Peter Brown, *The Cult of the Saints* (Chicago: University of Chicago Press, 1981), pp. 99–100.

[76] According to Lerchenfels, a "righteous son of God" had been delivered from the "fire of the heretics to be worthily greeted by Prague with drums, trumpets, songs and great rejoicing." Lerchenfels, *Přenešení sv. Norberta*, *ivr.

[77] *Octiduum S. Norberti triumphantis*, esp. n1v, n4v, p2r–s3v.   [78] Ibid., n2r–n4v.

[79] Straka, "Litteratura de translatione," 338–44; Friedrich Prinz, "Stadtrömisch-italische Märtyrerreliquien und fränkischer Reichsadel im Maas-Moselraum," *HJ* 87 (1967), 1–25.

display, a number of events were also specifically organized for the townspeople. The most important of these occurred on the second day of the
celebrations. In a ceremony mixing the secular with the sacred, a huge
crowd was urged to swear allegiance and devotion to Norbert before the
town hall while thousands of medals minted to commemorate the occasion
were distributed among them.

Like the execution, the focal point of this week's celebration was Old
Town Square. After the initial meeting at the gate on the first day, the
assembled crowds continued with Norbert's remains on to the Týn church
where the ceremonial coffin was temporarily laid to rest on the high altar.
Here in this important space in the heart of Prague, Harrach and
Questenberg endeavored to transform the archbishop of Magdeburg into
a distinctively Czech saint. The earlier decision to declare Norbert a patron
of the Bohemian kingdom was clearly calculated to help achieve this end,
but both civic and spiritual leaders certainly understood that this public
pronouncement was only the beginning of a longer campaign to secure
Norbert's status as patron and protector in the minds and hearts of the
broader populace. A significant portion of the celebrations was designed
with this goal in mind. Early in the morning of the festival's second day, a
group of clergy exited the Týn church with the saint's bones as they led
another lengthy procession through the city. Winding their way back
through Old Town Square, the column stopped in front of an elaborately
decorated arch for a short dramatic performance. Emerging from the
shadows was a figure arrayed in royal robes and followed by twelve attend-
ants. This was *Bohemia* accompanied by twelve representatives of the
provinces. Together they greeted the assembly and then stretched out
their hands to the reliquary symbolically pledging their loyalty to
Norbert. At the same time, through the help of a mechanical device,
Saints Wenceslas, Vitus, Ludmila, Procopius, Adalbert and Sigismund
descended from the upper story of the arch. Once on the ground, these
six patron saints of the kingdom gestured to an empty throne that was
reserved for their new colleague.[80] Similar displays of patriotic piety were
staged throughout the entire week. In a further effort both to advance and
protect Norbert's position as Bohemia's new patron, Questenberg sought
assistance from the pope. He was concerned that Premonstratensian houses
across the continent would deluge him with requests for bits and pieces of
the saint. His fears were quickly justified. Even before the May translation, a
French abbot had requested a part of the leg or shoulder for his monastery.

---

[80] *Octiduum S. Norberti triumphantis*, g4r–h3v.

The Premonstratensians of Antwerp were the most insistent as they directed a series of appeals not only to Questenberg but also to the archbishop and emperor. Though the abbot did give St. Michael's Monastery a portion of mummified skin and a segment of Norbert's small toe, a papal bull of Urban VIII, *Non licet dare*, extricated Questenberg from this difficult situation, helping him preserve what remained of Norbert's earthly remains in Prague.[81]

On the most general level the translation of Norbert and the promotion of his cult was an attempt by the church to recover lost prestige and reassert its cultural authority. But the saint's arrival also had a more specific meaning in the Bohemian context. In light of the kingdom's recent history, Norbert was a figure of exceptional relevance. Prague's religious and civic leaders cleverly highlighted those aspects of his career which expressly addressed the problems of heresy and sedition that had long plagued their region. On that first day of the festivities, when the saint arrived at the city's gates, he was greeted by a parade of twenty flags portraying various scenes from his life. Two images in particular predominated: Norbert as missionary proclaiming the true faith and Norbert as archbishop presiding over his flock in a peaceful and orderly fashion.[82] These two sides of Norbert's career were at the center of the entire eight-day celebration and the focus of its iconographic program.

The large triumphal arch that had been erected in Old Town Square and had served as the backdrop of the dramatic scene staged on the second day of the celebrations specifically emphasized Norbert's dual role as missionary and archbishop. The front part of this structure, which was over sixty feet tall and nearly thirty feet wide, was dedicated to Norbert's victories over heresy.[83] There were two episodes from Norbert's long wanderings across Europe that had special meaning in the Bohemian setting. His missionary activity had eventually led him to the edge of the Slavic world where he worked to expand Lothair's spiritual and secular authority. The archbishopric of Magdeburg had been a focal point of a long power struggle for control of the church's new territories in Poland. Otto I (962–73) had seen the archbishop as a virtual "warden of the Slav marches."[84] But with the creation of the archdiocese of Gniezno during the reign of Bolesław the Brave (992–1025), Magdeburg slowly lost its once preeminent position in

---

[81] *Octiduum S. Norberti triumphantis* concludes with the reproduction of this bull, s5r–v.
[82] Ibid., c4r–e2v.   [83] Ibid., n1v–n2r.
[84] A. P. Vlasto, *The Entry of the Slavs into Christendom* (Cambridge: Cambridge University Press, 1970), p. 119.

the affairs of the Polish church. With Norbert and Lothair we see the last serious attempt of the German *Reichskirche* to reassert its power in the lands to the east and dominate the dioceses of its Slavic neighbors. Ferdinand could have hardly found a more suitable model to match his own aspirations.[85]

Norbert was also known for his defense of the Eucharist against his opponent, Tanchelm. A native of Zealand, Tanchelm had also begun his career as a reformer attacking the corruption of the church. He attracted a large following in Antwerp but gradually moved away from orthodox Christianity. He supposedly distributed his bath-water to his followers as a substitute for the Eucharist. Norbert has been given credit for suppressing this heretical movement and bringing the city back to the true faith. The many images of the saint that were produced in the sixteenth and seventeenth centuries normally portray him with monstrance in hand as a champion of the Eucharist or as defender of orthodoxy with one foot resting on the splayed body of Tanchelm. Most commentators have noted that this iconography spoke well to the specific concerns of Catholics in the Low Countries where instances of Host desecration were not uncommon among the region's Calvinists.[86] But Norbert may have been an even more relevant symbol in the Czech lands. For over two centuries Hus's adherents had stubbornly contested the "proper celebration" of the Eucharist. The inscriptions on the front of the arch in Old Town Square, celebrating Norbert as a militant suppressor of heresy and tireless renewer of the faith, spoke to the major tasks facing the church in the difficult years ahead. Indeed, a climax of the festival was a public abjuration of heresy by more than 600 people on the last day of the celebrations.[87]

On the reverse of the arch was a very different portrayal of the saint. Norbert's missionary zeal was balanced by a pronounced pastoral instinct. The back of the vault was decorated by a series of statues personifying the chief virtues of the ideal bishop: love, justice, moderation, watchfulness and

---

[85] Julius Soliman, one of the Jesuit preachers active in the ceremonies, drew attention to this parallel. *Octiduum S. Norberti triumphantis*, p4v–q4r.

[86] See for example the early seventeenth-century engraving of Cornelius and Theodor Gallé. Reproduced in Elm, ed., *Norbert von Xanten*, p. 357. Also illustrative is a broadsheet that depicts Norbert literally sitting on Tanchelm. It seems likely that this illustration was produced in the Low Countries to celebrate the 1627 translation. Reproduced in Wolfgang Harms, ed., *Deutsche illustrierte Flugblätter des 16. und 17. Jahrhunderts* (Munich: Kraus International, 1980), vol. III, pp. 118–19.

[87] Julius Soliman specifically highlighted the connection between the heresy of Tanchelm and Hus. *Octiduum S. Norberti triumphantis*, r4v. For the mass conversion on the last day of the celebration see Cornelio Hanegravio, *Compendio della vita, miracoli, et instituto del glorioso Patriarcha S. Norberto* (Rome: Giacomo Mascardi, 1632), pp. 115–16.

generosity. An inscription extolled Norbert's gifts as a "leader, defender and educator of his flock."[88] The celebration of episcopal authority highlighted here iconographically again spoke directly to the needs confronting the Czech ecclesiastical establishment. The archiepiscopal see, which had been vacant since the defection of Konrad von Vechta to the Utraquists in 1421, had only been restored in 1561. Even then, during those late years of the sixteenth century, the authority of Bohemia's senior churchman had been substantially restricted. It was only with Harrach's predecessor, Johann Lohelius, that more serious attempts to restore the power and prestige of the archbishop had begun in earnest. Harrach was continuing Lohelius's work through a variety of means. The near fanatic fervor that he devoted to the import of relics with the arrival of Norbert's remains as the highpoint must be seen as an essential part of this broader campaign. By sponsoring such operations he was bolstering both the power and authority of his office. In this context one thinks of Peter Brown's remarks on Bishop Ambrose of Milan. Brown contends that Ambrose's well-orchestrated efforts to gather relics and then strategically deploy them through the churches of his diocese were in large measure an attempt to strengthen his position as bishop. "He [Ambrose] was like an electrician who rewires an antiquated wiring system: more power could pass through stronger, better-insulated wires toward the bishop as leader of the community."[89]

A more contemporary comparison can be found in Bavaria during the late sixteenth century. Benno, an eleventh-century bishop of Meissen, had been canonized in 1523. His shrine had originally been located in the Meissen cathedral, but after the death of the last Catholic duke of Saxony in 1539, his cult suffered a significant setback. The Wittelsbach family of Bavaria, however, seized the initiative and after a long series of negotiations secured his remains in 1576 and transferred them to Munich. Benno became an effective tool in their hands. His "rescue" from Protestant lands strengthened their position as defenders of Catholicism both in their duchy and in the broader German world. On a more specific level, they used Benno in their quest to move the diocesan capital from Freising to Munich. They clearly hoped that the prestige of housing the recently canonized bishop would help them wrest episcopal control from the independent-minded canons of Freising.[90] The translation of Norbert spoke to similar concerns of Harrach and other high church officials. Their logic was simple. The

---

[88] Straka, *Přenešení ostatků*, p. 87.　　[89] Brown, *Cult of the Saints*, p. 37.
[90] Philip Soergel, *Wondrous in His Saints* (Berkeley: University of California Press, 1993), pp. 181–91. The attempt to move the diocesan capital never succeeded.

honor bestowed on the twelfth-century bishop automatically reflected on the episcopal office of their troubled times. By possessing the relics of a saint and German archbishop, they were simultaneously elevating the status and enhancing the standing of Bohemia's highest church official.

What broader conclusions can we reach when we consider these two civic ceremonies together? At first glance, they may seem like an odd pairing of events. The execution of 1621 figures prominently in any survey of Czech history and has become a great symbol of national defeat. The 1627 translation of Norbert, in contrast, has been long forgotten and remains of interest only to a narrow group of ecclesiastical historians and antiquarians. 1627 is far better known for the Renewed Constitution and the infamous edict that presented the nobility and townspeople with the stark choice of either conversion or exile. Such a pairing, though, highlights the promise of a new methodological approach to the study of post-1620 Bohemia, for these two incidents illustrate that the kingdom's new Catholic masters realized the limitations of force and physical coercion. Power and legitimacy could not be based on political, economic and social innovations alone. Authority also had to be constructed culturally. In the English context Peter Lake has argued that in the fight against heresy the state depended quite as much on the staging of rituals such as public executions as it did on the efforts of those entrusted to ferret out Jesuit priests hiding in the country-side.[91] Ferdinand and Harrach also used weapons from a cultural arsenal in their campaign to restore Habsburg authority and the Catholic faith within Bohemia. Though after the Westphalian settlement of 1648 the dynasty faced no serious political challenge in Bohemia until the War of Austrian Succession (1740–8), there were ongoing efforts to secure the people's confessional allegiance through such symbolic ceremonies. The translation of Norbert was only the beginning of a more extensive program of reintroducing sanctity in Bohemia. The cults of other saints were revived such as that of the hermit Ivan, the peasant Isidore and the martyr Wenceslas. This great flurry of activity culminated in 1729 with the canonization of Bohemia's home-grown saint, John Nepomuk.

Viewed from this longer perspective, then, we see how foundational these two ceremonies were in efforts to articulate a new confessional identity for this divided region. In a more general context, David Kertzer has observed concerning the power and importance of such ritualistic play, "It is the

---

[91] Peter Lake and Michael Questier, "Puritans, papists, and the 'public sphere' in early modern England: the Edmond Campion affair in context," *Journal of Modern History* 72 (2000), 587–627.

struggle of the privileged to protect their positions by fostering a particular view of people's self-interest. It is a process of defining people's identity for them."[92] Ritual in the early modern period was constantly disputed and contested. These events in Bohemia illustrate that the church and state quickly wrested control of this critical form of communication to create a new vocabulary that would be used to define post-1620 Bohemia. Ferdinand marked a significant turning point in the history of the Austrian Habsburgs. He was the first emperor whose public persona was so purposefully molded according to the confessional standards of the Counter-Reformation. According to his confessor William Lamormaini, the emperor helped shape many forms of corporate piety. Ferdinand's enthusiastic participation in ecclesiastical processions, his generous patronage of church music and his keen interest in religious drama effectively set the tone and direction of a resurgent Catholic culture that would characterize Bohemian society for more than a century.[93] The church for its part was awaking from its long slumber to reassume a position of leadership in the Czech lands. Norbert's translation set the pace of reform by promoting episcopal authority while enlisting lay piety by refocusing attention on the centrality of the Eucharist. Finally and most importantly, church and state were creating together the standards by which confessional identity would be measured in Bohemia. Significantly, the yardstick they were fashioning was calibrated to gauge not so much orthodoxy as orthopraxy. Confessional identity in post-1620 Bohemia was in many respects more about action than belief. Such an emphasis would have long-term consequences in the direction and ultimate nature of Catholicism in the kingdom.

[92] Kertzer, *Ritual, Politics and Power*, p. 175.
[93] Lamormaini, *Ferdinandi II. Romanorum imperatoris virtutes*, pp. 99, 121–2; musicologists have observed that the more dramatic innovations of Ferdinand's composers such as the use of trumpet ensembles in sacred works consciously reflected the emperor's zealous crusading demeanor. Steven Saunders, *Cross, Sword and Lyre: Sacred Music at the Court of Ferdinand II of Habsburg* (Oxford: Clarendon Press, 1995), p. 118.

CHAPTER 2

Reshaping identity and reforming the kingdom: confessional change and the Bohemian nobility

In 1599 Michael Adolf von Althan was a young and ambitious Lutheran noble eager to secure the patronage of Emperor Rudolf II. He had journeyed to Prague with this end in mind when an event occurred that changed his life forever. One day as he was crossing the Charles Bridge, he passed the famous crucifix that had become an important center of devotion for the city's Catholics. At that moment feelings of anger and scorn rose within him for the "intolerable folly of the Papists." Stubbornly refusing to doff his hat, the Freiherr urged his horse on when according to a Catholic chronicler a great miracle occurred.

Hardly had he passed the image when he saw at the feet of his horse that the bridge had apparently split. He believed that he had already fallen into this horrific chasm and abyss that opened to the water. He was shocked, however, to find that he had not been destroyed. After he had recovered, he realized how this danger had arisen. He was immediately sorry for the great dishonor that he had paid to the image of his crucified Savior. He quickly turned around, dismounted from his horse, and knelt before the crucifix honoring the monument with a degree of humility that far outweighed the disrespect he had earlier shown. From there he made his way to the Jesuit college. Although the unexpected guest was first received with astonishment, after his story was told, he was welcomed with joy and thereafter fully instructed in the Catholic faith.[1]

Whether or not we believe the veracity of the Jesuit account, the story of Althan's sudden conversion is significant for a number of reasons. Most obviously, it reminds us that Protestantism had gained a significant foothold among the nobility of central Europe. In the Austrian archduchies the old faith was clearly in retreat. The situation was even worse in Bohemia. As a class, the nobility was deeply implicated by heresy. Before 1620 only a

---

[1] The account, written by the Jesuits of St. Anna Church in Vienna, is reprinted in Thomas Winkelbauer, *Fürst und Fürstendiener: Gundaker von Liechtenstein, ein österreichischer Aristokrat des konfessionellen Zeitalters* (Vienna: Oldenbourg, 1999), p. 135.

quarter of the kingdom's lords and a mere seventh of its knights remained
faithful to the Catholic church.[2] Nearly all the great families of Bohemia
had members who had defected to the Protestant cause, and as we know in
retrospect, the revolt against Rome coalesced with a more general rebellion
against Vienna. To understand the subsequent recatholicization of the
Bohemian lands, we must consider the experience of the nobility. Like
Althan, they refashioned their religious identity, oftentimes quite dramatically, along more orthodox lines.

The Althan story also speaks to the significance of the Catholic nobility
in the actual process of recatholicization. Once Althan had converted, a
whole range of new opportunities opened to him. In 1600 he became
commander of the emperor's bodyguard and later served as the chief officer
of the Esztergom fortress. The emperor rewarded him by raising his family
to the *Grafenstand* in 1608. Althan also became a critical advocate and
patron of the Catholic cause. A great champion of the Jesuits, he supported
their colleges in Krems, Jihlava, Znojmo and Komárno.[3] It is difficult to
underestimate the significance of the nobility for the success of the
Counter-Reformation in Bohemia. Despite the political changes after
White Mountain, they continued to wield significant power. With the
emperor now resident in Vienna, they, more than ever, were responsible
for the kingdom's day-to-day administrative duties. In contrast to other
European regions where the prince could exercise some authority on the
lands of his grandees, in Bohemia the nobility actually solidified their grasp
on their own lands as the seventeenth century progressed.[4] They were in
many respects the crown's most important and reliable agents of reform.
They supplied the church with some of its most effective leaders, and
among the laity they were instrumental in reshaping the religious character
of local communities. On their estates they spearheaded effective campaigns
of recatholicization. In Moravia the Liechtenstein and Dietrichstein families
led thorough reforms of their lands while in Bohemia proper the efforts of
the Lobkovic and Martinic clans had a substantial impact transforming the
confessional culture of their territories.

---

[2] James Van Horn Melton, "The nobility in the Bohemian and Austrian lands, 1620–1780," in
H. M. Scott, ed., *The European Nobilities* (New York: Longman, 1995), vol. II, pp. 105, 111.
[3] There is some debate concerning the actual date of Althan's conversion. See Winkelbauer, *Fürst und
Fürstendiener*, p. 134.
[4] R. J. W. Evans, *The Making of the Habsburg Monarchy 1550–1700* (Oxford: Clarendon Press, 1979),
pp. 200–16; Eila Hassenpflug, "Die böhmische Adelsnation als Repräsentantin des Königreichs
Böhmen von der Inkraftsetzung der Verneuerten Landesordnung bis zum Regierungsantritt Maria
Theresias," *Bohemia* 15 (1974), 80–1.

Though there is a significant body of scholarship on the Bohemian aristocracy, it has often been situated within a narrower nationalist framework.[5] There
was, however, a similarity of experience for early modern elites, and we can
better appreciate the changes within the Czech lands when viewed from this
wider perspective. Three points are most salient. First, nearly all scholars of this
period have rejected a simple absolutist model that characterizes the seventeenth century as an era of steady royal advance at the expense of the nobility. In
central Europe the work of Robert Evans, Jean Bérenger and Petr Maťa has
helped rehabilitate the aristocracy as they have reassessed their prerogatives,
privilege and power after White Mountain and the Renewed Constitution of
1627. Second, as the seventeenth century progressed, as crisis passed to resolution, there was a growing disinclination towards violence among the nobility.
Compromises were reached between erstwhile rebels and their titular overlords.
A figure such as Le Grand Condé, a prominent leader of the Fronde, became a
great fixture at the court of Louis XIV. In Bohemia many old feuds were also
settled. Finally, it must be remembered that the mid-seventeenth century was a
great period of conversion for the nobility across central Europe as a whole.
With the consolidation of the *Reichskirche* after 1648, Catholicism offered a new
and growing degree of attraction for the Protestant nobility. One of the great
ironies of the Thirty Years War is that at least four of the Winter King's
children, including one named Gustavus Adolphus, became Catholics![6]

During this period the nobility emerged as a more coherent social class.
Across the continent there was a progressive thinning of the ranks as elites
struggled to survive the political, social and economic challenges of the
sixteenth and seventeenth centuries. This was an era of intense competition
when the spoils were unevenly divided. Weaker members of the order were
jettisoned while those who rode out the various storms emerged with greater
power and prestige.[7] Many have observed this same phenomenon of
economic and social consolidation in the Bohemian context. The data of

---

[5] Representative is J. Muk, *Po stopách národního vědomí české šlechty pobělohorské* (Prague: Nákl.
Politického Klubu Československé, 1931). For a summary of this literature see Václav Bůžek and
Petr Maťa, "Wandlungen des Adels in Böhmen und Mähren im Zeitalter des 'Absolutismus'
(1620–1740)," in Ronald Asch, ed., *Der europäische Adel im Ancien Régime* (Cologne: Böhlau, 2001),
pp. 287–321. Best on the nobility is Petr Maťa, *Svět české aristokracie (1500–1700)* (Prague:
Nakladatelství Lidové noviny, 2004).

[6] Volker Press, "*Denn der Adel bildet die Grundlage und die Säulen des Staates. Adel im Reich 1650–
1750*," in E. Oberhammer, ed., *Der ganzen Welt ein Lob und Spiegel* (Munich: Oldenbourg, 1990),
p. 23; Andreas Räß, *Die Convertiten seit der Reformation nach ihrem Leben und aus ihren Schriften
dargestellt*, 13 vols. (Freiburg i.B.: Herder, 1866–88); Howard Hotson, "Irenicism in the confessional
age: the Holy Roman Empire, 1563–1648," in Howard Louthan and Randall Zachman (eds.),
Conciliation and Confession (Notre Dame: University of Notre Dame Press, 2004), p. 260.

[7] Jonathan Dewald, *The European Nobility 1400–1800* (Cambridge: Cambridge University Press, 1996), xvi.

Josef Pekař clearly illustrate the diverging land-holding patterns of the upper and lower nobility. Whereas the knights controlled 27 percent of landed wealth in 1615 compared to the 37 percent managed by the lords, in 1684 their share had dropped precipitously to 8 percent while the portion enjoyed by the magnates had risen to 63 percent.[8] The development of entail, what was known as the *Fideicommissum* in the Habsburg lands, became a critical tool by which families consolidated their often far-flung holdings. In the early seventeenth century the Liechtensteins were one of the first to establish a *Fideicommissum*, a model quickly followed by other leading families.[9]

Though few Czech scholars would dispute these general trends, the actual process by which a new Bohemian nobility emerged after 1620 has not been an easy phenomenon to analyze and understand. One historian has argued that the reconstruction of the kingdom's elites was "comparable in scope to the Norman expropriation of the Anglo-Saxon nobility after 1066."[10] Although this claim may seem extreme, nearly one quarter of the older elites were forced into exile while over 50 percent of landed wealth did change hands. Additional confusion was created by the reshuffling of noble titles and the expanded use of the *inkolát*, the procedure of naturalization now controlled by the king.[11] A variety of models have been employed to sort the social chaos that ensued in the decades after White Mountain. Scholars have drawn distinctions between new and old nobilities, between native and foreign elites. In the end, however, the bewildering heterogeneity of the post-1620 nobility defies any systematic scheme of classification.[12] Instead of classifying and creating new categories, then, it may be more useful to examine the processes by which the nobility defined themselves. By the end of the seventeenth century they had emerged with a more unified and recognizable identity. Very few of these clans, however, had a pedigree untainted by heresy or rebellion. The powerful Waldsteins had to cope not only with the legacy of

---

[8] Findings summarized in Otakar Odlozilik, "The nobility of Bohemia 1620–1740," *East European Quarterly* 7 (1973), 20. This growing disparity was at least in part caused by "title inflation" as more knights proportionately were raised to ranks of higher nobility. My thanks to Petr Maťa for this observation.

[9] Melton, "The nobility," p. 127; Herbert Hofmeister, "*Pro conservanda familiae et agnationis dignitate.* Liechtensteinische Familien-Fideikommiß als Rechtsgrundlage Familien- und Vermögenseinheit," in Oberhammer, ed., *Der ganzen Welt ein Lob und Spiegel*, pp. 46–63.

[10] Melton, "The nobility," p. 110.

[11] The simple dual distinction between lords and knights (*pán* and *rytíř*) was now changed into a more complicated four-fold division (*kníže, hrabě, pán* and *rytíř*). Petr Maťa, "Šlechtic v soukolí absolutismu. Politická činnost Adama mladšího z Valdštejna po Bílé hoře," in Bronislav Chocholáč, ed., *Nový Mars Moravicus* (Brno: Matice moravská, 1999), p. 486; R. J. W. Evans, "The Habsburg monarchy and Bohemia, 1526–1848," in Mark Greengrass, ed., *Conquest and Coalescence* (London: Arnold, 1991), p. 142.

[12] Maťa, *Svět české aristokracie*, pp. 67–76.

the notorious Albrecht but also with their Protestant past. Nonetheless, four generations of this family, including one archbishop, subsequently served in the highest ranks of the Bohemian administration and at the imperial court as well. The Kinskýs could boast of two members who participated in the Czech revolt as well as a third who was murdered alongside Wallenstein. Still, two generations later Franz Ulrich became one of Leopold I's most trusted advisers. Even the Schlicks, whose members included a ringleader of the Czech rebels, Joachim Andreas, survived and eventually produced a Bohemian high chancellor.[13] These examples are indicative of a more general pattern by which an entire social class refashioned its identity to meet the new confessional and political exigencies of the post-1620 period.

To examine these changes we will follow the life and career of one of the most influential nobles after White Mountain, Vilém Slavata of Chlum and Košumberk. Though the Slavatas traced their line back to the late eleventh century, the real foundations of the family's strength and importance were not laid until the fifteenth as they consolidated and expanded their holdings under the Jagiellonians.[14] Vilém himself was the beneficiary of a strategic match with his cousin in 1602 that helped centralize the power and wealth of the family. Slavata is best known as one of the victims of the 1618 defenestration. His miraculous survival endowed him with near martyr status, and his dogged loyalty to the Habsburg cause secured his political fortunes. He served as Bohemia's high chancellor from 1628 until 1652. Slavata is a fascinating figure to study for a number of reasons. His long life (1572–1652) neatly spans a critical transitional period of the Czech past, and fortunately for the historian, the chancellor left a substantial literary legacy that specifically highlights the impact of confessional change on the Bohemian nobility. Slavata was one of the early converts to Catholicism, and his journey to Rome is an instructive example of a more general phenomenon. Slavata also helps us understand the significance of noble patronage in the revival of the old faith. Their leadership in confraternities, their promotion of new forms of piety and their financial support of the church helped solidify Catholic gains after White Mountain. Finally and perhaps most importantly, Slavata introduces us to the issue of identity formation. With a concern that often bordered on obsession, Slavata and other leading nobles molded their family's image to conform to new confessional standards.

---

[13] Evans, *Making*, pp. 200–16.
[14] Despite the rich source material there is no modern biography of Slavata. See J. Jireček, *Leben des Obersten Hofkanzlers von Böhmen Wilhelm Grafen Slavata* (Prague: Tempsky, 1876); J. Dobiáš, "Vilém Slavata," *Časopis historický* 1 (1881), 267–309; 2 (1882), 34–56; Winkelbauer, *Fürst und Fürstendiener*, pp. 107–19.

CONVERSION: CONFESSIONAL FORMATION
AND CULTURAL ORIENTATION

Recent Catholic converts played a surprisingly critical role in the imperial administration. New Catholics comprised a quarter of the emperor's Privy Council between 1600 and 1674. Their overall influence, however, was disproportionate to these more modest numbers. Cardinal Khlesl, Prince Eggenberg and Count Trautmannsdorf, the principal advisers of Emperors Matthias, Ferdinand II and Ferdinand III respectively, were all converts.[15] The career of Vilém Slavata follows a similar trajectory as he rose from a Protestant branch of an eastern Bohemian family that had lost a substantial portion of its wealth in the aftermath of the 1547 rebellion. According to tradition the Slavata family had enthusiastically embraced the Hussite cause in 1415. They drifted from their Utraquist moorings and eventually joined the Bohemian Brethren. Though Vilém's father, Adam, was a committed member of this church, he entrusted his son's education to his richer Catholic cousin who had been raised at the court in Madrid with Archdukes Rudolf and Ernst. Vilém was encouraged to travel to Italy where he stayed for four years, a study tour that had a substantial impact on his confessional imagination. Despite this background Adam Slavata was caught off guard when in 1597 his son made a very public conversion to Catholicism. Later that summer a distressed father initiated a lively correspondence with his son on this matter.[16]

The resulting letters offer a fascinating window on the issue of conversion and the emergence of a new sense of Catholic identity among central European elites. Materialist concerns have often been put forward as the prime motivating factor behind many of these celebrated conversions. Undoubtedly, the promise of court appointment or other lucrative incentives were in some cases the critical determinant in such decisions.[17] Slavata's letters to his father are important reminders, however, that the old faith exerted a genuine spiritual and intellectual appeal to many of the

---

[15] Winkelbauer, *Fürst und Fürstendiener*, pp. 66–7. Trautmannsdorf was a child when his family converted; more generally see Karin MacHardy, *War, Religion and Court Patronage in Habsburg Austria* (New York: Palgrave, 2003).

[16] Letters are reproduced in F. Teplý, "Proč se stal Vilém Slavata z Chlumu a Košumberka z českého bratra katolíkem," *SbHKr* 13 (1912), 205–21; 14 (1913), 25–41, 171–81.

[17] See Winkelbauer's systematic attempt to classify many of these conversions in this period. Winkelbauer, *Fürst und Fürstendiener*, pp. 66–148. On Slavata in particular see Petr Maťa, "Von der Selbstapologie zur Apologie der Gegenreformation: Konversion und Glaubensvorstellungen des Oberstkanzlers Wilhelm Slawata (1572–1652)," in Ute Lotz-Heumann, ed., *Konversion und Konfession in der frühen Neuzeit*, forthcoming.

nobility. Vilém's defection to Catholicism prompted an outcry of betrayal from the region's non-Catholic nobility who claimed that his reconciliation with Rome had been effected merely as a means to secure his own fortunes, a charge that stubbornly followed him as he rapidly ascended to great power and privilege in the next two decades. These letters, which he may have intended to circulate, were his first attempt to justify his own conversion and more generally defend the Catholic cause.[18]

One of the immediate issues that Slavata raised in these documents, and undoubtedly one of the great weaknesses that bedeviled Protestantism in central and eastern Europe, was its divisiveness. Vilém described in some detail his own search for spiritual certainty and his consequent confusion prompted by the conflicting claims of competing evangelical groups. His father argued that although these churches differed on minor points of faith, they all recognized an invisible body of believers. Vilém, who was keenly aware of the often violent nature of intra-Protestant squabbling, insisted, and not without reason, that many Lutherans would rather return to Catholicism than convert to Calvinism.[19] Disillusioned and perplexed by the failure of evangelical churches to address doctrinal matters with a single voice, he began to examine the Catholic alternative. After a period of investigation he concluded that there were three critical signs of the true church: its unity, ubiquity and antiquity.[20] For Slavata, Bohemia's past two centuries followed an old recurring pattern of church history. It was inevitable that the Hussites would splinter into correspondingly smaller heretical sects leaving the kingdom politically divided and spiritually confused. As it had in the past, the Catholic church would emerge from this schismatic chaos unbowed and unbeaten, a unified witness to the truth.[21] Slavata was also moved by the consistency of Catholic doctrine over time and place. In a later undated letter that he wrote to his cousin, Kryštof, he pointed to the Eucharist as an example. While the interpretation of Christ's simple words, "This is my body," had left Calvinists and Lutherans hopelessly divided, Catholics everywhere had "from the time of the godly apostles" believed the simple and direct meaning of this injunction. The

---

[18] Vilém to Adam, 2 August 1597, Teplý, "Proč," p. 214. He also mentions his intention of writing a short apology for his new faith as well.

[19] Adam to Vilém, 16 August 1597, Teplý, "Proč," p. 220; Vilém to Adam, 2 August 1597, Teplý, "Proč," p. 211.

[20] Vilém to Adam, 10 August 1597, Teplý, "Proč," p. 216. Here Vilém was merely repeating the famous fifth-century Vincentian canon most probably brought to his attention by a Catholic preceptor.

[21] Vilém to Adam, 2 August 1597, Teplý, "Proč," pp. 207–8.

universal and immutable teachings of the church offered the young noble-man security in a world that was rapidly changing.[22]

Slavata's letters are significant as they reflect more general confessional trends across central Europe. The themes he raised were echoed by many others. Valerian Magni, a Capuchin monk and one of the region's most effective Catholic controversialists, contrasted the unified teaching of the Roman church with the doctrinal inconsistencies of a divided Protestant community. In Hungary Baron Mihály Károlyi claimed his decision to embrace Catholicism was prompted by "the certain visibility of the true holy mother church."[23] Slavata complained that Protestant leaders had introduced innovations that were radical departures from a long and consistent ecclesiastical tradition. Foolishly, these men sought "to critique the church from a doctrinal standpoint and not doctrine from the perspective of the church."[24] He reminded his father that Europe had been settled by Catholic missionaries and united by a common ecclesiastical culture. "How many Edwards from England, Louis's from France, Leovigilds from Spain, Henrys from Saxony, Wenceslas's from Bohemia, Leopolds from Austria and Stephens from Hungary are to be found who believed and clung to this Roman Catholic church as the true church of Christ and the apostles?" How could one not be impressed by the physical memories of this ancient faith that filled the Czech landscape? Bohemia's churches, chapels and cloisters all spoke to the antiquity, grandeur and truth of this great tradition.[25]

Slavata's arguments, though not especially novel, expressed a set of concerns shared by a certain group of the Czech nobility. When considered as a whole, his polemic illustrates a twofold appeal of Catholicism. The old faith did provide a desperately needed sense of spiritual certainty. The Bohemian kingdom had been religiously divided for over two centuries, and the psychological fallout of near constant controversy and contention was not insignificant. There were many who sought like Slavata a definitive resolution to theological doubt and religious confusion. Secondly, Slavata's letters clearly illustrate a longing or even nostalgia for a world that had been shattered by the Hussite revolution. Though his reading of church history was selective and naïve, it did reflect a desire to recover an older and more

---

[22] Letter published in F. Teplý, "Vilém Slavata vybízí svého bratrance Krištofa Slavatu k návratu do církve katolické a do Čech," *SbHKr* 18 (1917), 68–9.

[23] Peter Schimert, "Péter Pázmány and the reconstruction of the Catholic aristocracy in Habsburg Hungary, 1600–1650," unpublished Ph.D. thesis, University of North Carolina (1990), p. 457.

[24] Vilém to Adam, 10 August 1597, Teplý, "Proč," p. 215; Vilém to Adam, 10 September 1597, Teplý, "Proč," p. 39.

[25] Vilém to Adam, 10 September 1597, Teplý, "Proč," p. 38.

unified cultural tradition. A recurring theme throughout the correspondence was an appeal to antiquity, a call for his family to rediscover its spiritual
heritage and return to the faith of its forebears.[26] Looking around him,
Slavata saw the devastation of the Hussite period. Empty and neglected
churches, ruined convents and plundered monastic libraries were decaying
memories of what had been a vibrant Catholic culture. The restoration of
this dignified ecclesiastical tradition and the reconnection of Bohemia to a
broader Catholic world became a prime concern for Slavata and many of his
peers.

This second point introduces us to a broader phenomenon that was
slowly but inexorably transforming the social world and cultural orientation
of the Bohemian elites. It was a process that had begun in the late sixteenth
century and culminated two generations after White Mountain. As early as
the 1560s, families like the powerful Pernstein clan were beginning to forge
wider international links and foster a more cosmopolitan outlook that stood
in contrast to the more rustic and parochial mentality of many of their
neighbors.[27] Vratislav Pernstein, Bohemian high chancellor from 1566 to
1582, was one of the region's early converts and his household served as a
model for many Bohemian and Moravian Catholic families. The Pernsteins
had close contact with Catholic circles in Vienna, Madrid and Rome, and
when the male line of the family faltered, the women continued to exercise
significant influence. Maria Manrique de Lara and her daughter Polyxena,
the widow of Vilém Rožmberk and future wife of the fiercely Catholic
Zdeněk Vojtěch Lobkovic, kept the family's international contacts fully
engaged. Polyxena in particular helped create a type of "salon" that became
a prominent intellectual center for Bohemia's Catholics.[28] Patterns of
thought and belief imported from the Mediterranean were adapted to the
Bohemian setting. A lifestyle characterized by the cultural mores and
attitudes typical of a more cosmopolitan Catholic milieu flourished here
and offered an attractive alternative to many Czech nobles who felt hemmed
in and restricted by the conventions and customs of surrounding Utraquist,
Lutheran or Brethren communities.

---

[26] Vilém to Adam, 10 August 1597, Teplý, "Proč," p. 218; Vilém to Adam, 10 September 1597, Teplý,
"Proč," p. 40.

[27] Melton, "The nobility," pp. 119–21; Otto Brunner, *Adeliges Landleben und europäischer Geist. Leben
und Werk Wolf Helmhards von Hohberg, 1612–1688* (Salzburg: Müller, 1949).

[28] Winkelbauer, *Fürst und Fürstendiener*, p. 73; Josef Janáček, *Ženy české renesance* (Prague: Čs. spis.,
1987), 106ff.; R. J. W. Evans, *Rudolf II and His World* (Oxford: Oxford University Press, 1973),
pp. 286–8.

What was happening with the Pernstein circle was fully evident in the life of Vilém Slavata. In his letters we find the rush and excitement of a young man leaving what he considered a local and more narrow religious tradition for a broader cultural and confessional world. Slavata's first trip to Italy (1592–6) was of considerable importance in his spiritual development. As he related to his father, he initially avoided any discussion of religion and refused to read controversialist literature. But surrounded by such a rich and vibrant Catholic culture, he could not resist the church's siren song. The dazzling rituals and beautiful buildings ultimately led him to a more serious theological consideration of the Roman faith.[29] During a second trip to Italy a year after his conversion, Slavata attended an elaborate ceremony celebrating the jubilee year of 1600 in St. Peter's Basilica. From his descriptions of these proceedings it is evident that the theatrical display of ecclesiastical power and prestige left a deep impression.[30] The pattern we see with Slavata was played out many times over. Whereas in previous generations Czech Protestants may have sent their sons to Wittenberg, Heidelberg or Geneva, Italy was now becoming a standard destination for children of the Bohemian nobility. After the ceremony at the basilica, Slavata described how he was joined by seven of his countrymen for a private audience with the pope.[31] Travel accounts and correspondence of Bohemian elites attest to the growing significance of these journeys as in the case of three other families who saw the expediency of reshaping their image after White Mountain.

The Kounices were one of the most prominent of Moravia's Protestant families. Oldřich, its patriarch, had been educated at Calvinist universities and maintained an active correspondence with Basel's important reformer Johann Jakob Grynaeus. A leading member of the *Unitas Fratrum*, he had sent his four older sons to visit Reformed communities of France, Germany and the Swiss lands. Two of them were consigned to the gloomy dungeon of Brno's Špilberk fortress for their participation in the Czech uprising while a third died in exile in Geneva. The youngest of his sons, Lev Vilém, had a very different experience, for he was only five at the outbreak of the rebellion and was left orphaned after the death of his mother in 1627.[32] Cardinal Franz Dietrichstein helped turn the family's fortunes as he became

[29] Vilém to Adam, 10 September 1597, Teplý, "Proč," pp. 172–3.
[30] "Popis oslav začátku jubilejního léta v Římě 31. prosince 1599," reproduced in Petr Maťa, "Oslavy jubilejního léta v Římě a česká šlechta," *Jihočeský sborník historický* 66–7 (1997–8), 115–17.
[31] Ibid., 117.
[32] František Hrubý, "Český poutník v Assisi roku 1636," *ČČH* 32 (1926), 284–5; František Hrubý, *Lev Vilém z Kounic, barokní kavalír* (Brno: Státní oblastní archiv, 1987).

Lev Vilém's guardian. He sent the boy to the Jesuit school in Olomouc and there carefully monitored his progress. As a capstone to his education, Lev Vilém traveled to Italy in 1635 where he followed a carefully designed route. Less of a grand tour and more of an extended pilgrimage, he charted an itinerary that included some of the peninsula's most important religious sites. From the cell of St. Francis to the furnishings of the Loreto, he carefully recorded the physical details of this journey and interspersed them with edifying anecdotes from saints' lives or accounts of miraculous legends connected to the sacred landscape. He noted in his diary that he "was visiting these holy places in order to better imagine them." Returning home with a decidedly Catholic imagination, he was well positioned to restore his family's fortunes.[33]

While the pilgrimage of Lev Vilém helped anchor the new confessional moorings of a former Protestant family, in many instances trips to Italy reinforced older family traditions and accelerated new social patterns as was the case with Heřman Jakub Černín who journeyed south in 1678. The son of a former ambassador to Venice, Heřman Jakub was part of a larger contingent of young nobles who went to Italy on a type of grand tour. As he noted in his diary, participation in ecclesiastical rituals was a central part of their experience. His entourage frequently broke their journey to visit a local church or monastery and hear mass. In Italy Heřman Jakub actually joined a confraternity and when visiting the local nobility regularly participated in their church celebrations. His reflections were also filled with a sense of wonder and awe characteristic of Slavata's earlier account. In Venice he toured St. Mark's and viewed with amazement a series of relics ranging from the stone on which John the Baptist had been beheaded to eight columns taken from Solomon's temple in Jerusalem. Rome was the climax of his trip, for, as he remarked, here he was able to see both the monuments of the classical world and the ancient remains of his own Catholic tradition.[34] Heřman Jakub also helps us evaluate the changing social patterns of the Bohemian nobility. He and his other Czech colleagues had embraced the sophisticated culture of international Catholicism. He discussed his Italian and French lessons as well as his attempts to master rudimentary skills of drawing. The diary itself points to the cosmopolitan character of Bohemian elites in the late seventeenth century. Apart from Czech and

---

[33] Hrubý, "Český poutník," 293. His son, Dominik Andreas, was named imperial vice chancellor while his great grandson, better known by his German name, Prince Wenzel Anton von Kaunitz, became Maria Theresa's most trusted minister.

[34] "Deník z cest po Itálii a Portugalsku, 1678–1682," in Josef Polišenský, ed., *Česká touha cestovatelská* (Prague: Odeon, 1989), pp. 385–6, 390, 392, 396, 399, 400.

German it includes passages in Italian, French and Spanish. An older culture, connected more closely to the vernacular and rooted in the late-humanist values characteristic of the Rudolfine era, was giving way to a very different world.

A final case to consider is that of the Liechtenstein family. They offer an instructive contrast to the overtly pious examples of Vilém Slavata and Lev Vilém Kounice. As opposed to Slavata's deep religious concerns, it seems that the conversion of Karl von Liechtenstein during the reign of Rudolf II was prompted more by the prospect of material advancement, and unlike the Slavata clan, the Liechtenstein family consistently had a more worldly orientation.[35] But despite these differences there was general agreement on the essential qualities of a proper Bohemian cavalier. For the Liechtensteins we can turn to a document from the middle of the seventeenth century, a text outlining the educational ideals of Prince Karl Eusebius.[36] He begins with a few commonplace observations regarding the place of religion. The fear of God must be cultivated in the hearts of young children as it creates discipline and respect. The Jesuits are effective at instilling these virtues though a careful father should make sure that his son does not become overzealous and actually enter a religious order.[37] In terms of travel he also favors the Mediterranean lands. The north has little to offer. A quick journey through the Low Countries to see its fortified cities or a brief stay in England for the hunt is sufficient.[38] Italy, France and Spain are far more important for the cultivated gentleman. In these lands due attention must be paid to the forms and structure of religious observance. In this respect a specific excursion to Rome is of particular value. Participation in the public rituals of the church, including pilgrimage, is an essential part of a young man's training and an older man's official responsibilities. A nobleman's life is played out on an open stage and mastering the etiquette of both the court and the church is a central component of his station.[39] Karl Eusebius's instructions are significant, for though they lack the fervor of a new convert like Slavata, they illustrate to what extent the religious ideals the high

---

[35] See Winkelbauer's assessment here, *Fürst und Fürstendiener*, pp. 89–93.

[36] Gernot Heiss summarizes much of the text in "*'Ihro keiserlichen Mayestät zu Diensten ... unserer ganzen fürstlichen Familie aber zur Glori'*: Erziehung und Unterricht der Fürsten von Liechtenstein im Zeitalter des Absolutismus," in Oberhammer, ed., *Der ganzen Welt ein Lob und Spiegel*, pp. 155–81. For an abbreviated version of this text see "Auszüge aus des Fürsten Karl Eusebius Instruction für seinen Sohn Hans Adam," in Jacob von Falke, *Geschichte des fürstlichen Hauses Liechtenstein* (Vienna: Braumüller, 1877), vol. II, pp. 395–408.

[37] Heiss, "*'Ihro keiserlichen Mayestät'*," p. 156.   [38] "Auszüge," pp. 406–7.

[39] Heiss, "*'Ihro keiserlichen Mayestät'*," pp. 163, 171.

chancellor had promoted had become a standard feature of noble identity scarcely a generation after White Mountain.

As these examples illustrate, the conversion of Bohemian elites was an interconnected phenomenon of confessional formation and cultural reorientation. It has often been assumed that the process of recatholicization was abrupt and dramatic. Though we should not underestimate the great disruptions that came after 1620, a cultural shift in certain Catholic circles was evident by the latter half of the sixteenth century. It is also apparent that for many nobles the transition from a Protestant to a Catholic world was accomplished with relative ease. Older forms of spirituality were simply replaced with new patterns, and it was not long before many of these noble converts saw themselves as the kingdom's principal guardians of religious orthodoxy.[40] Social scientists have spoken more generally of processes that they loosely label "reference group" formation. As individuals develop a sense of identity, they do so by finding a social reference point which serves as "an anchor for their sense of self and other."[41] Catholicism in many respects offered these nobles a more useful point of mooring for self and community than the Protestant alternatives.

MODELS OF DEVOTION AND PATRONS OF PIETY

It is evident both from his writings and activities that Vilém Slavata considered himself a trustee of this new Catholic culture. As a part of his official responsibilities, he devoted significant time to public religious observances. In 1644 he composed a checklist of regular activities intended for his own spiritual edification and ethical improvement. Though some of these pledges dealt with matters of personal morality (avoiding private conversations with women, refraining from cards and excusing oneself from overly lavish banquets), the most important of these exercises were public and communal in nature. The adoration of the Host in one or more of the city's many churches was the normal focus of his Sunday afternoons while he was resident in Vienna. On Mondays he attended the *Augustinerkirche* to pray for the dead while on Fridays he crossed town to the Jesuit house to participate in the activities of the local religious brotherhood. On special feast days he regularly marched with the emperor in

---

[40] See for example the case of Zuzana Černínová z Harasova whose father had been a key leader in the Bohemian rebellion. Foundational here is Zdeněk Kalista, ed., *Korespondence Zuzany Černínové z Harasova s jejím synem Humprechtem Janem Černínem z Chudenic* (Prague: Melantrich, 1941).

[41] Robert Hefner, "World building and the rationality of conversion," in Robert Hefner, ed., *Conversion to Christianity* (Berkeley: University of California Press, 1993), p. 25.

religious processions.[42] Slavata's busy ceremonial life mirrored broader changes occurring in various Habsburg courts of the period. The indifference to or even neglect of public religious ritual, typical of the reigns of Maximilian and Rudolf, had been replaced by more rigorous and regular forms of Catholic observance upon the accession of Ferdinand II. Prominent nobles were expected to adopt forms of piety central to the regime's confessional identity. By the 1640s in Habsburg Naples, the court had nearly complete control of the Congregation of the Holy Sacrament, one of the most important lay fraternities in the city. At the northern end of their domains Archduke Albrecht of the Low Countries (1598–1621) restricted membership of the St. Ildefonso Confraternity to his courtiers and actually fined those who were slow to join.[43]

Though the situation in the Bohemian lands was slightly different, the nobility was fundamental to the dissemination of public forms of devotion. Models set at court spilled over into the public sphere. Slavata was specifically instrumental promoting one of the Habsburgs' favorite forms of piety: devotion to the Immaculate Conception. In 1648 he was prefect of the Viennese confraternity established to support and foster this cult. Slavata has left us with the only eyewitness account describing the raising of Vienna's Marian column which celebrated the Virgin's elevation as patron of Austria.[44] In Bohemia as well, the nobility helped advance the Marian cult. After White Mountain Archbishop Harrach, Jiří Martinic and Adam Waldstein reestablished a confraternity dedicated to the Virgin. Though this sodality was open to all ranks of society, its leadership remained firmly in the hands of the kingdom's elites. From the end of the Thirty Years War to the middle of the eighteenth century, it was directed by members of the Lobkovic, Kolovrat, Lažanský, Sternberg and Vrbna families.[45]

Though the Bohemian nobility certainly helped propagate devotional ideals of the Habsburg family, they also promoted public forms of piety particular to the Czech lands. One of these indigenous cults was that of the

[42] Cited in Jiří Mikulec, *Pobělohorská rekatolizace v českých zemích* (Prague: SPN, 1992), pp. 39–40. See in particular Slavata's correspondence with Jaroslav Martinic from the early 1630s, *SbH* (Rezek) 1 (1883), 305–22; *SbH* (Rezek) 2 (1884), 32–7, 92–7; *SbH* (Rezek) 3 (1885), 193–202, 283–92, 361–4; *SbH* (Rezek) 4 (1886), 352–63.

[43] John Adamson, "The making of the ancien-régime court, 1500–1700," in J. Adamson, ed., *The Princely Courts of Europe* (London: Weidenfeld and Nicolson, 1999), p. 25; Luc Duerloo, "Archducal piety and Habsburg power," in W. Thomas and L. Duerloo, eds., *Albert and Isabella* (Louvain: Brepols, 1998), p. 268.

[44] Gulielmus Slavata, *Maria Virgo immaculate concepta publico voto Ferdinandi III. Rom. Imp. in Austriae patronam electa* (Vienna: Cosmerovius, 1648).

[45] Josef Svoboda, *Katolická reformace a marianská družina v království českém* (Brno, 1888), vol. II, pp. 45, 47, 59–60.

Jezulátko or the Infant Jesus of Prague. Though veneration of the Infant Jesus had a long ecclesiastical tradition, Teresa of Avila reinvigorated this practice during the Catholic Reformation. A series of statues of the infant Christ were produced in Spain in the late sixteenth century, and as legend has it, one of them came into the possession of the noblewoman Isabella Manrique de Lara y Mendoza. She gave it as a wedding present to her daughter, Maria Manrique de Lara, who brought it north to Bohemia when she married Vratislav Pernstein. She in turn handed it on to her own daughter Polyxena where it passed through the Rožmberk and Lobkovic households. After the death of her second husband in 1628, Polyxena retired to her residence at Roudnice nad Labem and bequeathed the figure to the discalced Carmelites in Prague, whose convent was adjacent to the church of Our Lady Victorious in the Lesser Town (*Malá Strana*).[46]

Within three decades this statue was transformed from an object of private devotion to the center of a public cult, a transition that was effected almost exclusively through the patronage of the nobility. The early legends that developed around this wood and wax carving focused on the connection between the general welfare of the Carmelite house in the Lesser Town and the physical condition of the statue. In 1637 the figure, which had been lost when Lutheran Saxons occupied Prague, was rediscovered damaged but still intact. As the priests began to examine it, the statue of the infant Christ miraculously spoke, declaring to his rescuers that the fortunes of the ransacked convent and church would be restored if he were accorded proper worship and honor.[47] The nobility answered his call and transfigured a Spanish cult into a devotional form with a more distinctly Bohemian character. In 1639 Alžběta Kolovratová attributed her sudden recovery from a serious illness to the Infant Jesus. As a token of her gratitude, she donated a small golden crown for the figure. Her husband provided the cloister with an annual subsidy and left funds in his estate for the purchase of a silver lamp and reliquary. The generosity of the Kolovrats was quickly matched by donations from other magnates. In 1641 Václav Eusebius Lobkovic contributed 100 ducats for the decoration of the carving's tabernacle while in 1642 Anna Polyxena Slavatová gave 6,000 florins for an altar adjacent to the shrine. In the same year Benigna Kateřina Lobkovic made a major financial contribution for the renovation of the church, and in 1654 the Talmberk family donated 2,500 florins for a side chapel that housed the

---

[46] Jan Forbelský, *Pražské Jezulátko* (Prague: Aventinum, 1992), pp. 48, 50.
[47] Emericus a Sancto Stephano, *Pragerisches Gross und Klein* (Prague: Höger, 1737), pp. 26–7.

Infant Jesus for over a century.[48] A number of these noble benefactors were memorialized in a series of paintings executed for the Carmelite cloister in the first half of the eighteenth century. Perhaps as a warning to those who were ready to honor the *Jezulátko* with their lips but not with their purse, this cycle, which highlighted the generosity and piety of the Bohemian elites, also included a scene of an unnamed noble who had suddenly died for failing to fulfill a vow he had made at the shrine.

The growth and spread of this cult was dependent not only on the financial support of the elites. More important in many respects was their aggressive promotion of this new form of devotion. Here Bernard Ignác Martinic, Bohemia's powerful grand burgrave (1651–85), played the most significant role. The Martinic household attributed at least two miraculous healings to the Infant Jesus, and in the year of his accession to office, he organized its first public celebration. On 14 January 1651 Martinic, Harrach, Liechtenstein and others of the high nobility were present at a ceremony honoring the *Jezulátko* in conjunction with the feast of Epiphany, a celebration that was observed yearly during the lifetime of the grand burgrave and the archbishop.[49] Even more dramatic were the events Martinic helped orchestrate four years later. Without the official approval of Rome, the grand burgrave with Harrach's complicit approval had pushed ahead and instituted what became an annual coronation of the Infant Jesus. For the occasion Martinic had commissioned a new crown for the figure along with a miniature replica of the Golden Fleece. Nearly all of Prague's leading families were present at the festivities officiated by the archdiocese's suffragan bishop. After the mass, the great spectacle drew to a close as the nobles solemnly approached the shrine and one after another reverently kissed the foot of the infant.[50]

The nobles also initiated the custom of dressing the statue. Over time the Infant Jesus acquired an extensive wardrobe. The type of gown with which he was clothed was dependent on the liturgical season or specific church feast. An elaborate ritual developed around the changing of the *Jezulátko*'s garments. Though this practice was eventually taken over by Carmelite nuns, it was initially restricted to women of the Bohemian nobility.[51] Finally, we should note that the elites were influential in promoting this cult to a broader audience. In 1644 Febronie Pernstein donated a portion of

---

[48] Alena Vodičková, "Soupis textilií určených pro Pražské Jezulátko," unpublished thesis, Týnská škola, Prague (1997), p. 19.

[49] Emericus a Sancto Stephano, *Pragerisches Gross und Klein*, pp. 193–6.

[50] Ibid., pp. 221–5.   [51] Vodičková, "Soupis textilií," pp. 19ff.

her estates in eastern Bohemia to the Carmelites where they began missionary work among the non-Catholic inhabitants. According to the missionaries nothing could sway the stubborn peasants until a devotional painting of the Infant Jesus was set before them. As the chronicler notes, such an irresistible expression of God's grace quickly melted even the hardest of hearts. The Pernstein lands were won back for the church, and this new expression of Catholic piety began to develop roots in the Bohemian countryside.[52]

During the course of the seventeenth century the nobility also introduced a form of piety that literally transformed the countryside. Many of them had traveled to Italy and had returned home with ideas to replicate patterns of Mediterranean devotional life. One of the mandatory stops on such a tour was the Loreto, a pilgrimage center constructed around a small building that was supposedly the home of the holy family once they had returned to Nazareth from Egypt. The *Santa Casa* had long been an important Christian shrine in Palestine, but after the expulsion of the Crusaders in the late thirteenth century, devotion to this site took on a new shape in the west. In 1291 angels purportedly transported the house to a village on the Istrian peninsula. Three years later they returned to move the structure to its final resting place outside the village of Loreto, not far from the Italian port of Ancona. The Loreto first became popular with pilgrims in the late fourteenth century. Later renovations of Bramante and Sansovino transformed the originally modest sanctuary into a lavish Renaissance complex that became in the post-Tridentine period one of the most important pilgrimage shrines in the entire Catholic world. Journeys to the Loreto frequently played a significant role in the religious formation of young Czech nobles who returned home eager to reproduce what they had found in Italy.[53]

The first Loreto chapel in the Czech lands and quite possibly the first north of the Alps altogether was constructed in 1584 by Kryštof Lobkovic. Inspired by his own trip to Italy, Lobkovic built a modest replica of the original on his estate in southwest Bohemia.[54] The success and spread of these chapels was in large part dependent on the enthusiasm of these early pilgrims. In some instances these Loretos became outposts of Catholic renewal in a hostile confessional environment. Such was the case in the

---

[52] Emericus a Sancto Stephano, *Pragerisches Gross und Klein*, pp. 176–80.
[53] Numerous references can be found in Kalista, ed., *Korespondence Zuzany Černínové z Harasova*. See in particular letters xv (63), xl (132), and lxxiv (223).
[54] Jan Bukovský, *Loretánské kaple v Čechách a na Moravě* (Prague: Libri, 2000), p. 24; Jan Diviš, *Pražská Loreta* (Prague: Odeon, 1972), p. 17.

village of Jílové outside Prague when in 1616 the brothers Štěpán and Jiří Beník established a cloister dedicated to the Virgin of Loreto with the assistance of Archbishop Lohelius.[55] In 1621 the recent convert Florián Jetřich Žďárský of Žďár along with his wife Eliška, the daughter of Jaroslav Martinic, traveled to the Italian Loreto where the young couple petitioned Mary to bless their marriage with a male heir. The son came two years later, and as an expression of their gratitude to the Virgin, they erected their own chapel just to the west of Prague. Their story attracted others to the shrine, and there were soon reports of miracles. Before long the Loreto of Hájek had become a popular pilgrimage destination.[56] In Moravia Cardinal Franz Dietrichstein began the construction of a series of Loretos that appeared like mushrooms across the region. After his visit to Italy where at the insistence of the Jesuits he visited the *Santa Casa*, he returned to the north and built his replica in Mikulov in 1623. In the confessionally plural-istic setting of southern Moravia, this chapel helped rally beleaguered Catholics and became an important focal point in Dietrichstein's subse-quent campaign to restore the old faith on the family lands.[57]

Forty-five of these chapels were built between 1584 and 1729. As opposed to religious orders, city councils or local dioceses, it was the nobility who were responsible for the creation and maintenance of nearly 80 percent of these shrines.[58] Equally significant is the range of these patrons. The construction of Loretos was not a phenomenon restricted to a mere handful of Bohemian magnates. Nearly all of the kingdom's great families partici-pated. Within Bohemia proper the old guard as represented by the Lobkovic, Waldstein, Martinic, Černín, Kinský, Sternberg and Kolovrat clans sponsored almost a quarter of all shrines raised. Even the Schlicks, despite the ignominy of Joachim Andreas, built their own Loreto near Jičín. In Moravia the Liechtensteins and Dietrichsteins led the way. The Habsburgs contributed as well when at the insistence of Archduke Leopold Wilhelm, bishop of Olomouc, a chapel was dedicated to the Virgin of the Loreto in the city's Wenceslas Church. Newer nobles were also involved including the Scottish Leslies, the Italian Clary-Aldringens and the Westphalian Sporcks. Together these families created a series of shrines that served not only as centers of devotion but also as physical markers of Bohemia's new Catholic identity. These Loreto chapels,

---

[55] Bukovský, *Loretánské kaple*, p. 24.

[56] A. Podlaha, *Posvátná místa Království českého* (Prague: Nákl. Dědictví sv. Jana Nepomuckého, 1913), vol. VII, pp. 230–54; *OSN*, vol. 27, p. 764.

[57] NA, ŘK, 52/I: 18.   [58] Numbers based on Bukovský, *Loretánské kaple*, pp. 143–51.

designed by the likes of Fischer von Erlach, Johann Lukas von Hildebrandt and Christof Dientzenhofer, are among the kingdom's most important baroque monuments.

A proprietorial sense often developed around these chapels. The kingdom's most famous Loreto on Prague's Castle Hill was in many respects a house shrine of the Lobkovic family.[59] The story begins in 1600 with Markéta Lobkovic. She was an early patron of the kingdom's Capuchins, who were great promoters of the cult. Markéta provided the property for their first cloister which was adjacent to the new shrine begun two decades later by another grande dame of the family, Benigna Kateřina. During the war years progress on the complex was slow and often interrupted though the original chapel was dedicated in 1631, but in the next generation Alžběta Apolonie continued construction with the completion of the cloister surrounding the *Santa Casa* in the 1660s. In the early eighteenth century Eleonora Karolina financed important renovations. The Prague Loreto was also well known for its treasure. Benigna Kateřina had begun what became an extensive collection of ecclesiastical objects that were a constant temptation to the cash-strapped Habsburgs. Its great masterpiece, the Diamond Monstrance, was commissioned by Václav Ferdinand in the late 1690s. Crafted by two goldsmiths from the Viennese court, the famous monstrance, which depicts the Virgin in triumph, comprises more than 6,000 diamonds.

The Loretos are but one example of how Bohemian elites helped create an infrastructure of devotional piety that contributed to the overall success of recatholicization. They also played an increasingly greater role in the church's administrative structures. Even before the disturbances of the Hussite period, the Bohemian church was hard-pressed to supervise and manage what was a very large archdiocese. The absence of an archbishop from 1421 to 1561 was catastrophic for its ecclesiastical administration. Though the Habsburgs appointed Antonín Brus of Mohelnice as the new archbishop in 1561, broader structural reforms were not implemented for nearly a century. Under the leadership of Archbishop Harrach (1623–67) two new dioceses were created in the Bohemian lands: Litoměřice in 1655 and Hradec Králové in 1664. There was also a corresponding change in the upper echelons of church leadership. After Harrach's accession high church office increasingly became a province of the nobility. Antonín Brus and his

---

[59] There is a rich assortment of archival documents in the Capuchin fond (ŘK) of the Národní archiv charting the Lobkovic involvement in the Loreto complex. See for example ŘK, 4:51; ŘK, 98:16; ŘK, 101:119.

successor Martin Medek (1581–90) were sons of simple burghers from the Moravian village of Mohelnice. Even more humble was the background of Prague's tenacious reformer Johann Lohelius (1612–22) whose father was an impoverished carter's assistant in the Eger (Cheb) region. The great transition occurred when young Count Harrach became archbishop in 1623. With only two notable exceptions a nobleman occupied this position until the early twentieth century. The pattern emerging in Bohemia was replicated in Moravia. Members of the Dietrichstein, Liechtenstein-Castelcorno and Habsburg families occupied the bishopric of Olomouc in the seventeenth century. Bohemia's elites controlled the church's administrative machinery at the lower levels as well. The Waldsteins, Sternbergs, Talmberks and Vratislavs of Mitrovice most frequently held the new sees of Litoměřice and Hradec Králové.

CREATING CATHOLIC IDENTITIES

Even more dramatic than these changes within the church was the transformation of the nobility itself. A tremendous amount of energy and financial resources were spent refashioning the image of the kingdom's leading families. As noted earlier, nearly all of these households had some connection to the rebellion or were more broadly implicated by religious inconstancy. But now after White Mountain *Kaisertreu* and *Katholisch* were the new virtues of the day, and the elites scrambled to remake their identity to conform to these standards. Vilém Slavata serves as an instructive example. Though undoubtedly devout, Slavata was also very ambitious. A marriage to his cousin Lucia Otýlia combined with the untimely death of her brother in 1604 had made Slavata head of his house, but this former member of the Bohemian Brethren had even greater aspirations. The lines of the Hradec and Rožmberk families, two of the most important landowners in southern Bohemia, came to an end in 1604 and 1611 respectively. Slavata subsequently laid claim to their lands. In so doing, he reshaped his family's past in a creative fashion.

Slavata's actual connection with the Rožmberks was somewhat tenuous, and to make his case he resorted to an intriguing genealogical argument that referred back to the legendary Vítkovci (Witigonen).[60] The Vítkovci were the supposed descendants of the princely Ursinus family who had fled Italy when Rome was overrun by barbarian tribes. The family eventually entered

---

[60] T. Wagner and F. Mareš, "O původu Vítkovců," *ČČH* 25 (1919), 213–35; Petr Maťa, "Zrození tradice," *Opera Historica* 6 (1998), 513–50; Maťa, *Svět české aristokracie*, pp. 95–8.

the service of the new emperors who had established themselves north of the Alps. In the tenth century one of their number, Vítek Ursinus, joined Emperor Otto I to finish the task of Christianizing Bohemia, a process that had been suddenly interrupted when Boleslav had treacherously murdered his brother Wenceslas, the future saint. Vítek joined the emperor in the campaign, successfully beat back Boleslav's pagan allies, reintroduced Christianity and then settled in the region. His descendants, the Vítkovci, eventually became the great families of southern Bohemia. Slavata boldly claimed that his wife was the last living member of this ancient tribe, and as her husband, he was heir of a renewed Vítkovci legacy. Slavata's claim to the Hradec title was on firmer ground. Lucia Otýlia was the rightful heir to this fortune when the line failed in 1604. Slavata, though, was careful to preserve continuity between the two families. One of the old traditions of the Hradec family, a practice that dated back to the Middle Ages, was the distribution of sweet porridge to the poor once a year on Maundy Thursday. In the sixteenth century Adam I of Hradec had considered this annual activity so important that he included a stipulation in his will mandating the continuation of this custom with stiff penalties for those who refused. Slavata immediately embraced this charitable ritual strengthening his connection to the old lords of Hradec. Over time the Slavatas even expanded this practice. By the 1670s there are reports of up to 3,000 people participating. As if to counteract his family's recent dalliance with Protestantism, Slavata insinuated himself into the myths and traditions of pre-Hussite Bohemia. As guardian of the Hradec legacy, he continued a practice of piety which Adam I had described as a "most ancient custom."[61] Identification with the Vítkovci was more audacious. Here he connected his house to an individual who had finished a task that even the holy Wenceslas had left incomplete.[62]

There were other families such as the Sternbergs who were also keen to eulogize their past. Assisting them was the Jesuit Jan Tanner who published a history of this old Bohemian house. Tanner had dug through the records and had compiled a detailed account of the early Sternbergs. Though the enterprising Jesuit claimed that the family's Bohemian origins could be traced back to Burghardus of Sternberg in the tenth century, he actually began his story a millennium earlier by linking the family to the Three Wise

[61] F. Teplý, *Dějiny města Jindřichova Hradce* (Jindřichův Hradec: Nákl. obce Hradecké, 1927), vol. I, pp. 128–9.
[62] This aspect of "family history" was celebrated in paintings and plays produced to honor the Slavatas. See for example the Jesuit play, *Rosa Novodomensis*, and the baroque oration of Jindřich Václav Zyvalda, *Věnec slávy* (Prague: Jezuitská tiskárna, 1655); Maťa, "Zrození tradice," 548–50.

Men!⁶³ On somewhat firmer ground he highlighted the great deeds of the Sternbergs during the Middle Ages. Listing the accomplishments of the family's most illustrious members, Tanner specifically praised them as great champions and defenders of the Catholic cause. In the thirteenth century Albrecht of Sternberg became the first grand master of the Crusaders with a Red Star. The following century another Albrecht was appointed archbishop of Magdeburg. During the Hussite revolt the family resisted the heretics while shortly thereafter the brave Zdeněk led a Catholic faction against Bohemia's Hussite king, George of Poděbrady.⁶⁴ These themes were also represented visually in a sumptuously illustrated thesis sheet executed for the family in 1661 (Figure 4). Produced for the university defense of the two brothers, Wenzel Adalbert and Johann Norbert, the nearly five-foot engraving depicts the long relationship of the Sternbergs with the rulers of Bohemia.⁶⁵ At the bottom of the sheet stand the two brothers who gaze heavenwards as the history of their family unfolds before them. The central figure of the scene is Leopold I, portrayed as the sun. Surrounding the emperor are six other "planets," former kings of Bohemia. Members of the Sternberg clan are represented alongside these princes. The series begins with Saturn, the Přemysl Otakar II (1253–78), who is accompanied by Grand Master Albrecht and the valiant Jaroslav, who fought off the Tatars. Pious Archbishop Albrecht joins Charles IV (1346–78) while a series of Sternberg martyrs attends Emperor Sigismund (1419–37), the fierce opponent of the Hussites. This pattern of pairing a ruler with a Sternberg patriarch carries through the early seventeenth century where appropriately enough _Luna_, the erratic Rudolf II, is steadied by the sage advice of Adam Sternberg. The Sternberg past was also celebrated on stage when in 1695 the Jesuits produced the drama, _The Golden Fleece_, which once more focused on the family's link with the three magi.⁶⁶

As these examples demonstrate, after White Mountain there was a growing demand for antiquarians to work through local archives or wade through the disorganized holdings of family libraries to find clues linking a specific house with some glorious moment of the Czech past. Far and away

---

⁶³ J. Tanner, _Geschichte derer Helden von Sternen, oder deß uhralten und Ruhmwürdigsten Geschlechtes von Sternberg_ (Prague: Hraba, 1732), pp. 19–26. This legend can be traced back to the early seventeenth century though it may well have been older. Maťa, _Svět české aristokracie_, p. 725.

⁶⁴ Tanner, _Geschichte derer Helden von Sternen_, pp. 93, 125, 141, 318ff.

⁶⁵ NK, inventory number 428; reproduced in Sibylle Appuhn-Radtke, _Das Thesenblatt im Hochbarock_ (Weißenhorn: A. H. Konrad Verlag, 1988), pp. 91–5.

⁶⁶ KNM, 49 A 20; also see the 1655 play celebrating a Slavata–Sternberg marriage that further developed the motif of the planets (NK, 52 B 44, no. 76); P. Zelenková, "Šternberské alegorie na grafických listech podle Karla Škréty," _Umění_ 54 (2006), 327–42.

4. Sternberg family thesis sheet (1661)

the most important of these amateur genealogists was the industrious Jesuit priest Bohuslav Balbín (1621–88). Balbín, himself of minor nobility, developed close relationships with many of Bohemia's great houses. He taught their children and integrated the histories of their respective households into many of his writings.[67] His crowning project in this regard was an undertaking he worked on for nearly three decades, a massive history of Bohemia, the *Miscellanea historica regni Bohemiae*. The second part of this study was to have been an exhaustive treatment of the kingdom's nobility. Although the project was never completed, enough of it survives to recreate its general contours. Balbín began with a general defense of the Slavic nobility. The word Slav, he maintained, was not etymologically derivative of *sclavi* (slave) but of *slovo* (word) and even more appropriately *sláva* (glory).[68]

Of greater importance for Balbín was the role of the nobility initially creating and then preserving the kingdom's ecclesiastical heritage. It was they who had built Bohemia's churches and cloisters and then filled them with relics they had gathered from abroad. Through their own examples of piety, and by their willingness to accept even martyrdom, they passed on these traditions, customs and beliefs from one generation to the next. When difficult times came, ostensibly Balbín's allusion to the Hussite period, the nobility was like the olive branch that the dove had brought to Noah as a sign that earth's ancient life cycle had not been destroyed by the flood.[69] Balbín was not content, however, with simply enumerating these virtues. He sought to connect the nobility in a more concrete and physical manner to Bohemia's sacred past. Through his genealogical research he brought many families into direct contact with the kingdom's holy men and women. Ludmila, Bohemia's first Christian martyr and the saint whom Balbín called "the great mother of dukes and kings," made frequent appearances in his genealogies.[70] The blessed Hroznata, a twelfth-century noble and pioneer of Bohemian monasticism, was claimed as an ancestor of the Černíns, Lobkovics and Vrbnas. The counts of Gutenstein had an even more impressive pedigree. In what may have been the most ambitious of these projects, Balbín, through a type of genealogical prestidigitation, connected this family to fourteen saints, ten individuals beatified by the church and thirty-eight founders or major patrons of churches and cloisters.[71]

Despite his commitment to his own heritage and culture, Balbín's view of the Bohemian nobility was in no sense parochial. This was not a

---

[67] Olga Květoňová-Klímová, "Styky Bohuslava Balbína s českou šlechtou pobělohorskou," *ČČH* 32 (1926), 522.

[68] Bohuslav Balbín, *Miscellanea historica regni Bohemiae, Decas II, Liber 1* (Prague: Georgii Laboun, 1687), p. 5.

[69] Ibid., pp. 3, 71, 90–6.   [70] Ibid., p. 6.

[71] Bohuslav Balbín, *Syntagma historicum quo illustrissimae et pervetustae stirpis, comitum de Guttenstein, origines et memoriae continentur* (Prague: Typis Universitatis Carolo-Ferdinandeae, 1665), pp. 42–3.

provincial aristocracy that merely reveled in local traditions and celebrated ties with regional saints. Balbín, in fact, endeavored to prove quite the opposite as he diligently sought connections that linked his elites with a broader Catholic world. An entire section of the *Miscellanea* was devoted to the relationship of Czech and Polish nobilities. Balbín also found closer bonds between his land and the Austrian archduchies, going so far as to argue that Austria's influential Harrach family was originally from Bohemia and only later emigrated to the south.[72] Most enterprising, however, were his efforts tracing the line of Bohemia's first Christian princes, Duke Bořivoj and his martyr wife Ludmila. Balbín developed an entire series of genealogical tables illustrating the blood ties between this holy couple and royal families ranging from England in the west to Poland in the east.[73] Jan Tanner was more concise in his *Via sancta*. According to his calculations this family had produced twelve emperors as well as five Spanish, thirteen French, fifteen Polish, three English, four Scottish, four Danish and four Swedish kings.[74] Balbín, Tanner and their other antiquarian colleagues thus defended the Bohemian nobility both vertically and horizontally. They connected the elites back through time to a holy past as well as integrating them through a web of interlocking relationships into a community of Catholic notables that extended beyond the borders of the Czech lands.

It was not only a family's past but also its present that could be shaped to conform to the new standards of the post-White Mountain period. Though Slavata celebrated his connection with the Vítkovci, his own personal history was an even more compelling testimony of his fidelity to both Rome and Vienna. The central event of his life was of course the famous defenestration of May 1618. In their first act of open defiance, the leaders of the Czech revolt stormed the royal castle, broke into the chancellery and there confronted Slavata, his colleague Jaroslav Martinic and the chancery secretary Philip Fabricius. They seized all three men and with angry words hurled them out of a high window. To the surprise of all, the Habsburg deputies survived the fall. News of the defenestration spread quickly as printers busily produced broadsheets depicting the events on Castle Hill.

---

[72] Balbín, *Miscellanea, Decas II, Liber 1*, pp. 25–33; on Harrach see part III, of book two of *Decas II, Tabula compendiosa Comitum ab Harrach ex quo e Bohemia olim in Austriam immigrarunt.*

[73] Balbín, *Miscellanea, Decas II, Liber 2, Tabulae genealogicae tredecim demonstrantes omnes prope reges Europae & principes & illustriores familias ex sanguine S. Ludmillae seu virili seu foeminea linea descendere.*

[74] Jan Tanner, *Swatá Cesta z Prahy do Staré Boleslawě* (Prague: Typis Universitatis Carolo-Ferdinandeae, 1679), unpaginated illustration.

Not unexpectedly, there were conflicting accounts of this confrontation. As a central participant in the drama, Slavata aggressively promoted his version of the story. It was a major theme of his memoirs. His interpretation was also reflected by a monument erected in the castle moat where the three men had landed. Here authorities raised two obelisks with a long Latin inscription describing how the men were saved through the miraculous intervention of the Virgin. The iconographical scheme of these columns also corresponds to what may be the most fascinating memorial of the defenestration, a votive picture commissioned by Slavata or one of his immediate descendants to commemorate the events of May 1618 (Figure 5).

This painting, an intriguing mixture of arcane symbols and popular religious imagery, captures in allegorical fashion the story of the defenestration. The actual events of 23 May are represented in the background where one sees a broad panorama of Castle Hill. To the right Slavata and Martinic are tumbling through the air while to the left two small figures are climbing a ladder into the safety of the Lobkovic-Pernstein palace. In the foreground the events are portrayed allegorically. Slavata, Martinic and Fabricius are gracefully coming to earth assisted by three figures of Fortune who catch them in the folds of a garment. In the top left corner is the hand of God extending martyrs' palms to the three men while to the right is the charitable Polyxena Lobkovic into whose residence Martinic escaped. The focal point of the painting is the Virgin who sits enthroned at the bottom of the picture. Her outstretched hands are holding two glass spheres on which the Fortunes stand. On her lap sits the Christ child whose eyes are turned heavenward towards the falling men.

The votive image had a clear didactic purpose. At the base of the canvas is a simple German poem that highlights the various lessons of the defenestration. Two themes in particular stand out. The first is martyrdom, alluded to most directly by the palms. Slavata elaborated on this interpretation in the *Memoirs*. A few days before the actual event both he and Martinic were in the cathedral and saw a vision that foretold their deaths. According to Slavata, Martinic had another vision at the moment of his execution. In an obvious allusion to the New Testament martyr Stephen, Martinic, as he was being pushed through the window, saw heaven in all its splendor opening before him.[75] For Slavata and the artist whom he commissioned, the

---

[75] Josef Jireček, ed., *Paměti nejvyššího kancléře království českého Viléma hraběte Slavaty* (Prague: I. L. Kober, 1866), vol. I, p. 83.

5. Slavata votive image of the Prague defenestration

defenestration was far more than a local skirmish between two opposing political factions. In the middle ground of the painting is a cross with the instruments of Christ's suffering and death, a device that links the story of Slavata and Martinic to a broader struggle between good and evil. The Habsburg officials embodied Bohemia's persecuted Catholic community which in the coup of 1618 was nearly destroyed. Nearly but not quite, for the second theme of this allegory is triumph. This is a votive image, an expression of thanksgiving, and it is Mary who is at the center of the celebration. The painting is filled with references to the Virgin's great victory. Wearing wreaths of red and white roses, all three men are dressed as members of a Marian confraternity.[76] In the *Memoirs* Slavata recounted how as Martinic was being bustled to the window, one of the rebels sarcastically barked, "Let Mary help you now." When he saw his victim emerge from the moat unharmed, he purportedly said in a markedly different tone, "I swear before God that his Mary truly did help him."[77] Both in the votive picture and in his writings Slavata emphasized the miraculous nature of the defenestration. From the castle fall to the remarkable escape to Bavaria, Slavata described the events of May 1618 as a cascading series of miracles. In the *Memoirs* he confronted skeptics who like the Protestant historian Pavel Skála of Zhoř had claimed that all three men had landed on a pile of rubbish. All such trash according to Slavata was burned and not deposited in the moat. When in 1620 a prominent member of the *Unitas Fratrum* argued that the Habsburg loyalists had been saved through some type of magic, Slavata responded that God had ordained this miracle to illustrate that Roman Catholicism was the one and only true faith.[78]

Slavata was certainly an exceptional figure. There were few who could shape their actions so dramatically and create a place for themselves at the center of Bohemia's *historia sacra*. Albeit more modestly, many other nobles followed Slavata's example and consciously fashioned identities according to the new confessional and cultural standards. Kašpar Kaplíř, the grandson of the famous rebel executed in 1621, is a case in point.[79] The young Kaplíř had actually fought against the Habsburgs in both the Dutch and Swedish armies before switching sides with the obvious intention of recovering his

---

[76] Jiří Dvorský and Rudolf Chadraba, "Votivní obraz Viléma Slavaty v Telči," *Umění* 38 (1990), 139.

[77] Jireček, ed., *Paměti*, vol. I, p. 83.   [78] Ibid., pp. 142, 144–5.

[79] Jaroslav Macek, "Kaspar Zdenko Kaplíř von Sullowitz (1611–1686)," *Jahrbuch für Geschichte der Stadt Wien* 39 (1983), 7–68; F. Mareš, "Hrabě Kašpar Zdeněk Kaplíř," *ČMKČ* 57 (1883), 3–45; F. Houdek, "Obránce Vídně proti Turkům Kašpar Kaplíř ze Sulevic v lidovém podání," *ČL* 23 (1913), 209–20; Zdeněk Kalista, *Čechové, kteří tvořili dějiny světa* (Prague: Garamond, 1999), pp. 127–36.

family's lost fortune. Slavata effected a reconciliation arranging an audience for Kaplíř with Emperor Ferdinand III who promised to reconsider the confiscation of family property if the new officer proved his loyalty in the army. During this era of Turkish conflict Czech antiquarians reinvigorated the ideals of the crusader, and Kaplíř shaped his image according to this model. He played a significant part in the 1683 defense of Vienna and was later praised as a stalwart Christian champion who helped turn back the Muslim hoards. Kaplíř himself wrote an impassioned apology defending his family's honor. What Kaplíř expressed verbally was for others represented visually, for the seventeenth century was the great age of the illustrated thesis sheet. A fascinating but neglected genre of baroque art, the thesis sheet was originally a simple printed announcement of an academic defense at the university.[80] In the Catholic lands, especially those of central Europe, these printed announcements evolved into intricate large-scale engravings that normally had very little to do with the actual thesis. A few weeks before the event these early modern posters appeared in prominent places around the city or town of the respective university. The collection of thesis sheets produced for Prague is particularly rich and worthy of study.[81]

As with most of these illustrations, the theses produced for Prague were dominated by themes central to the Catholic Reformation. From the veneration of John Nepomuk to the spread of Marian devotion, the Jesuits in particular fostered this form of visual expression. The thesis sheets were also an ideal means by which the nobility could carefully shape a public image of their family. From the Bubnas to the Vrtbas, nearly all of the kingdom's leading families participated to some degree in the production of these engravings.[82] In certain instances an actual member of a noble household instructed an artist to produce a thesis sheet for his own defense. Alternatively, a magnate family might support a member of the lower nobility or even burgher class who as a token of his appreciation commissioned a sheet in honor of his patron. Such was the case with the Nostitz family. Otto II (1608–64), a former Protestant, converted during the reign of Ferdinand II.

---

[80] Wolfgang Seitz, "Die graphischen Thesenblätter des 17. und 18. Jahrhunderts: Ein Forschungsvorhaben über ein Spezialgebiet barocker Graphik," *Wolfenbütteler Barock-Nachrichten* 11 (1984), 105–13; Appuhn-Radtke, *Das Thesenblatt im Hochbarock*.

[81] For this collection of 526 thesis sheets see Anna Fechtnerová, *Katalog grafických listů univerzitních tezí uložených ve Státní knihovně ČSR v Praze*, 4 vols. (Prague: Státní knihovna ČSR, 1984). A selection of these are reproduced in Oldřich Blažíček, *Theses in Universitate Carolina Pragensi Disputatae* (Prague: Pragopress, 1967).

[82] Fechtnerová, *Katalog*, vol. IV, pp. 734–8.

6. Nostitz family thesis sheet (1661)

The emperor consequently made him a member of the Privy Council and appointed him *Landeshauptmann* of the Silesian territories of Breslau and Schweidnitz-Jauer. In this capacity he was honored in a thesis sheet executed in 1661 (Figure 6).[83] In a region with a strong Protestant presence, the recent convert is portrayed as a great Catholic champion. Personifications of Schweidnitz and Jauer lay gifts of their cities before the central feature of the illustration, an altar-like structure that bears the Nostitz coat of arms. The prolific Karel Škréta, who designed the sheet, takes the sickle moon of the Nostitz arms and connects it directly to the iconography of the Catholic Reformation. The crescent moon, a reference to Mary's Immaculate Conception, is used by Škréta to frame the miraculous votive image of Schweidnitz which he places above the altar. Four of Bohemia's patron saints, Norbert, Ludmila, Wenceslas and Adalbert, flank the image while below and to the right the degree candidate holds a dedicatory scroll that explains the entire illustration. According to the inscription the lamp which hangs in front of the Virgin symbolizes both Nostitz's vigilance in public office and more specifically his patronage and protection of the precious votive image.

Though less dramatic than the votive image commissioned by Slavata, the Nostitz thesis sheet with Škréta's deft manipulation of heraldic devices is an instructive example of how families could use this new genre to burnish their image both confessionally and politically. Benno Martinic, the son of Jaroslav, ordered an engraving for his own defense in 1637. In straightforward fashion, the provost of Vyšehrad employed this illustration to highlight not only the virtues of Ferdinand III but more importantly the long faithfulness of his family to the Habsburg house and the Catholic religion.[84] An elaborate thesis sheet of 1676 praised the regime of new archbishop Johann Friedrich Waldstein (Figure 7). In honor of his accession representatives of the arch-diocese present gifts from their home regions while in the background homage is paid to Waldstein's illustrious family.[85] Lesser houses such as the Lažanskýs could exploit this medium to demonstrate both their local patrio-tism and their political loyalties. A 1679 engraving shows an image of Count Karel Maximilian transported in a chariot to the gates of the kingdom. There the Lažanský procession is greeted by a personification of Bohemia as angels carry a portrait of Leopold I overhead.[86] With images of Habsburg emperors in nearly all of these illustrations, the thesis sheets of the Bohemian nobility

[83] Reproduced in Appuhn-Radtke, *Das Thesenblatt im Hochbarock*, p. 157.
[84] NK, inventory number 425. Hana Seifertová, "Univerzitní teze Ferdinanda Leopolda z Martinic a její ikonografický program," *Umění* 20 (1972), 276–83.
[85] NK, inventory number 473. [86] NK, inventory number 50.

7. Waldstein family thesis sheet (1676)

express visually to what extent this class, as opposed to the fractious Hungarian aristocracy, had identified with the imperial cause by the end of the seventeenth century. There were engravings that specifically celebrated the accomplishments of Czech nobles in service of the dynasty. Sheets were produced honoring the diplomatic activities of both Franz Ulrich Kinský who helped negotiate the 1679 treaty of Nijmegen and Jan Václav Vratislav of Mitrovice who led a critical diplomatic mission to the court of St. James.[87]

---

[87] NK, inventory numbers 138, 472. For the mission of Vratislav of Mitrovice see Elke Jarnut-Derbolav, *Die österreichische Gesandtschaft in London* (Bonn: Röhrscheid, 1972). An overview of Kinský's activities is offered by Kalista in *Čechové*, pp. 157–63. More recent is Aleš Valenta, *Dějiny rodu Kinských* (České Budějovice: Veduta, 2004), pp. 62–72.

The Kinský engraving is particularly noteworthy, for only a few decades earlier three of the diplomat's great uncles had openly defied Ferdinand II. Now in baroque exaggeration Kinský is displayed as a loyal servant of the Habsburgs and a great defender of his country.

Though the nobility certainly manipulated the thesis sheet to reflect the claims and pretensions of their respective households, the reach and impact of this genre was ultimately limited, for these were ephemeral representations. More lasting were the funeral ceremonies and monuments that became increasingly elaborate over the course of the seventeenth and early eighteenth centuries. While Czech funeral rituals may not have matched the theatricality of those in Poland where nobles actually rode their horses into church and then threw themselves prostrate before the catafalque, they were a powerful form of cultural expression that mirrored the changing confessional sensibilities of the period. The seventeenth and early eighteenth centuries was a great age for the construction of funerary monuments in Bohemia.[88] Arguably, the most spectacular memorial built for a member of the Czech nobility was the tomb of Count Vratislav of Mitrovice. The man who had helped engineer the alliance of Eugene of Savoy and the Duke of Marlborough was interred in St. James Church of Prague. His brother-in-law, the Bohemian high chancellor Leopold Schlick, commissioned the Empire's leading architect Fischer von Erlach to design the tomb.[89] Begun in 1714, the resulting monument has no real equivalent in either Prague or Vienna (Figure 8). A reclining figure of the deceased count lies on top of the sarcophagus where the arms of the family are prominently displayed. He is supported by a female who is crowning him with a ringlet of stars. To the right stands *Chronos* with his hourglass while on the opposite side sits a mourner at the base of the tomb. The key to the entire structure is a long inscription that an angel is engraving on a pyramid above the sarcophagus. The actual author of this epigraph was the imperial inspector of antiquities, Carl Gustav Heraeus, who used this space to record the various accomplishments of the experienced diplomat. Linking the count directly to the revival of the Bohemian kingdom, Heraeus detailed the diplomat's efforts to repair the damage of the Thirty Years War.[90] While Fischer's tomb spoke to political and patriotic concerns, most of these monuments, as one would

[88] Jitka Helfertová, "Castra doloris doby barokní v Čechách," *Umění* 22 (1974), 290–308; Pavel Král, *Smrt a pohřby české šlechty na počátku novověku* (České Budějovice: Historický ústav Jihočeské university, 2004).

[89] Alistair Laing, "Fischer von Erlach's monument to Wenzel, Count Wratislaw von Mitrowicz," *Umění* 33 (1985), 204–18.

[90] Carl Gustav Heraeus, *Gedichte und lateinische Inschriften* (Nürnberg: Monath, 1721), pp. 295–7.

8. Tomb of Count Vratislav of Mitrovice (St. James Church, Prague)

expect, highlighted matters of piety. A number of families constructed memorials that connected their household more closely to forms of devotion that were popularized in the post-White Mountain period. The Clary-Aldringens and Thuns built Loreto shrines that also served as family burial chapels. Bernard Ignác Martinic commemorated his passing in even grander fashion. He stipulated that at his death his heart should be divided into three portions. One was to be buried beneath his Loreto at Slaný, another was to be given to the Theatines of Prague while the third was to be left with the Piarists on his home estate. His body was then to be interred in the family crypt in St. Vitus Cathedral.[91]

When viewed collectively, the Bohemian nobility had by the early eighteenth century emerged as a more coherent and homogeneous social class. The diversity that marked this group during the Rudolfine era had given way to a greater degree of outward uniformity. This new public image was constructed from a rich representational culture as Czech elites turned to a well-stocked iconographic arsenal of the baroque arts to enhance the character and standing of their families. The great palaces of the seventeenth century were part of this same phenomenon. The expansive city residence of Albrecht von Wallenstein with its elaborate sculpture garden, the monumental Černín palace with its imposing façade and the Sternberg's elegant chateau of Troja with its splendid murals employed this same pictorial language to reflect the claims and pretensions of their patrons. Appearance was all important and not just in architecture. This was the underlying theme of Karl Eusebius's short treatise on education. From a basic knowledge of the fine arts to proper riding habits, from the graceful pronunciation of Italian to the mastery of complicated court etiquette, a young nobleman's success was dependent on his comportment and bearing in public situations. The life of the nobility was carried out on a grand stage. Every gesture and action demanded careful calculation.

From this perspective, it is clear that the courtly world of the nobility was naturally inclined towards Catholic culture. The cosmopolitan and sophisticated milieu of international Catholicism had a far greater appeal to these elites than the more parochial and traditional environment of smaller Lutheran courts. More importantly, the church's liturgical practices, its emphasis on display and appearance, were adapted and then incorporated into the ritual life of the early modern court. Even the most stalwart of Protestant princes followed certain ceremonial practices that ultimately derived from the celebration of the mass or other Catholic rites.[92] The processions of feast days, the religious drama of the Jesuits and the public observances of confraternities spoke more directly to the noble lifestyle than the restrained architecture and decoration of Protestant churches or the custom of private Bible reading. Put simply, the Catholic world offered the Bohemian nobility a number of cultural resources that Protestantism did not have at its disposal. A representational culture needed a representational

---

[91] Bukovský, *Loretánské kaple*, p. 25.
[92] Press, "*Denn der Adel bildet*," p. 23; Adamson, "Making," pp. 27–33.

religion. One is reminded of Clifford Geertz's observations of Balinese society. Like the elaborate rituals of this Indonesian island, the complex ceremonial life of the Bohemian nobility was "an illustration of the power of grandeur to organize the world." From the complicated iconography of the thesis sheet to the careful design of the funeral monument, this world, to use Geertz's phrase, was a "metaphysical theatre designed to express a view of the ultimate nature of reality."[93]

---

[93] Clifford Geertz, *Negara: The Theatre State in Nineteenth-Century Bali* (Princeton: Princeton University Press, 1980), pp. 102, 104.

CHAPTER 3

"Monarchs of knowledge": mastering dissent in post-White Mountain Bohemia

In 1653 an anonymous writer, either a Jesuit or one of their supporters, wrote a short memorandum sharply critical of Archbishop Ernst Adalbert von Harrach. Harrach, one of the most influential figures in Counter-Reformation Bohemia, had become archbishop at the tender age of 24 in 1623. During his tenure of more than four decades he would implement a series of significant changes to revive the church's power and influence.[1] According to this critic, however, Harrach's efforts to renew Catholicism in Bohemia were failing. The archbishop was a naïve reformer who frequently sought compromise when discipline and order were the only means to restore orthodoxy with a people who had stubbornly clung to heresy for over two centuries. The greatest problem in this churchman's eye was Harrach's bungled attempt to reform institutions of higher learning. Here the stakes could not be higher. Success or failure of the entire Catholic program was dependent on education. Bohemia's problems could ultimately be traced back to its schools. They had started long ago at the Charles University when its original mission had been betrayed. In all of Europe there had been no school more subversive than the one in Prague, for it had long functioned as "a Trojan Horse from which various sects, dangerous innovations and rebellions had been produced."[2] Unless it was thoroughly reformed and rigorously controlled, all sorts of theological errors would inevitably creep back into the kingdom and plunge the region once more into crisis.

The image of the Trojan Horse was an apt metaphor and was repeated by others.[3] It was the deceptive Hus who had led the nation astray, and he had

---

[1] On Harrach see Alessandro Catalano, *La Boemia e la riconquista delle coscienze: Ernst Adalbert von Harrach e la Controriforma in Europa centrale (1620–1667)* (Rome: Edizioni di storia e letteratura, 2005).
[2] A. Rezek, "Tak-zvaná 'Idea gubernationis ecclesiasticae' z času kardinála Harracha," *VKČSN* (1893), 5.
[3] See for example M. X. Volckmann and Georg Weis, *Gloria Universitatis Carolo-Ferdinandeae Pragensis* (Prague: Typis Universitatis Carolo-Ferdinandeae, 1672), p. 45.

accomplished this end through the university. As dean and then rector, he had radically transformed the school by embracing the heretical notions of Wyclif. Young and impressionable students were seduced by these sweet-sounding lies. Priests were swayed and influenced by the demagoguery of heterodox masters, and once they returned to their parishes, they spread the contamination further. It was not long before the entire kingdom was corrupted. From the church's perspective, then, the key to Catholic renewal could be found in the schools. The Jesuits, in particular, were keenly attuned to the promise and potential of pedagogical reform. They had originally come to Bohemia in the sixteenth century to work with the schools, and they realized that the kingdom's *reconquista* must begin with a vigorous overhaul of its educational infrastructure. In an impassioned memorandum to Ferdinand II, William Lamormaini, the emperor's Jesuit confessor, argued that the broader Catholic project in Bohemia was in large part dependent on efforts to regulate the schools and universities.[4] Once the dust from White Mountain had settled, the church was ready to act. The kingdom's new Catholic masters proceeded to control, reorganize and ultimately transform Bohemia's intellectual life through their work at the university.

THE CHARLES UNIVERSITY AND THE DISSEMINATION OF DISSENT

Established in 1348, the Charles University was the oldest university in central Europe. The school was part of Charles IV's ambitious plans to transform Prague into a worthy imperial capital, but intellectually it had a brief era of prosperity and began to decline with the death of its founder.[5] Theological and ethnic tensions divided and weakened the school. Hus began teaching at the university in the 1390s, and soon many of the Czech masters espoused a form of Wyclifism. Their German colleagues resisted, and before long accusations of heresy were exchanged between the two groups. The crisis culminated in 1409 when the Czechs outflanked their German rivals by engineering an administrative coup that gave them control of the school. German masters and students promptly packed their bags and left, many heading to the new university in Leipzig. The outbreak of the

---

[4] Archivum Romanum Societatis Iesu, Rome, Aust. 23, fol. 7. My thanks to Robert Bireley for a copy of this text. Similar themes are stressed in Alois Kroess, "Gutachten der Jesuiten am Beginne der katholischen Generalreformation in Böhmen," *HJ* 34 (1913), esp. 35–9, 277–94.

[5] František Kavka and Josef Petráň (eds.), *Dějiny Univerzity Karlovy 1348–1990*, 4 vols. (Prague: Karolinum, 1995–8).

Hussite wars in 1420 was equally devastating as only the arts faculty survived this tumultuous period. By the 1450s the university was a shell of its former self and very clearly a Hussite institution. In 1458 school authorities passed a decree that stipulated mandatory adherence to Utraquism. This confessional orientation had a decided impact on its growth and development. Throughout the fifteenth century it remained isolated and outside the traditional orbit of late medieval universities. During this period the Bohemian nobility often sent their children abroad. At home Catholics viewed the institution as a dangerous threat to their church, for one of its traditional functions was the supervision of the kingdom's Latin schools. The university helped create an Utraquist infrastructure that ran the region. From parish priests and teachers to lawyers and government officials, Prague's university trained those who filled these positions.

As the Habsburgs quickly discovered, the university could also serve as a locus of political dissent if not outright rebellion. In the 1530s the Utraquist estates turned to the university for ideological support in their struggle against the Habsburgs. When resistance turned into open revolt in 1547, 300 representatives of the estates converged on Prague in March to protest Ferdinand's policies and swear an oath of mutual support and defense.[6] After the uprising had been suppressed, Ferdinand attempted to reform the university by loosening its moorings to the Utraquist establishment. The school had never been on a strong financial footing even in the mid-fifteenth century when it had enjoyed the favor of Bohemia's only Utraquist king, George of Poděbrady. For greater influence Ferdinand was willing to provide a much needed influx of capital. The masters, however, resisted his entreaties, and Ferdinand in turn developed an alternative strategy to recapture the minds of the Czech heretics. Sidestepping the university altogether, he invited the Jesuits into the country who established their own school in Prague in 1556. Ferdinand granted this new rival institution, the Clementinum, the right to award academic degrees in 1562. In 1616 it was raised to full university status.

With the founding of the Clementinum, intellectual exchanges between Utraquists and Catholics entered a new phase. Though varying degrees of tension had always existed between the two confessional groups, there had also been instances of collaboration especially among the learned. Examples of cooperation became increasingly rare as the century progressed. Rhetoric coming from the Clementinum helped raise confessional temperatures.

---

[6] Winfried Eberhard, *Monarchie und Widerstand: Zur ständischen Oppositionsbildung in Herrschafts system Ferdinands I. in Böhmen* (Munich: Oldenbourg, 1985), pp. 146–52.

One of the school's most famous instructors in the early years was the English Jesuit and future martyr Edmund Campion. In fall 1576 the fiery priest delivered the Clementinum's opening address by savagely attacking the Hussite legacy of the Carolinum. It was through the university and the work of "reckless preachers" and "a base apostate [Jan Hus]" that "so many sects, so many schisms, so much mischief, and so many vices" had been brought into the kingdom.[7] As the Jesuits continued their attacks in the latter half of the sixteenth century, it was clear to all that the Clementinum was quickly gaining ground on the Utraquist university. The Carolinum struggled on with its shrinking budget, decaying buildings and an increasingly smaller professoriate while the Jesuit college enjoyed ample resources. But there were currents of reform at work in the Charles University, and in 1609 yet another shift occurred that made open conflict with the Catholic church and the Habsburg regime all the more probable.

Though the Utraquists had been officially protected through the Basel Compacts, the 1609 Letter of Majesty removed all ambiguity from their legal standing. Guaranteeing religious freedom to all adherents of the Bohemian Confession (1575), a broad Protestant statement of faith, it helped solidify the institutional standing of the university in Czech society while transforming its confessional character. Encouraged by these developments, a former rector of the university put forward an ambitious plan to renew the academy along the lines of Protestant schools elsewhere in Europe. Theologically, it would adopt the Bohemian Confession, and any lingering Catholic influence would be eliminated. Older restrictions on celibacy would be lifted. There was also an effort to redress the institution's serious financial problems. With greater confidence the masters now began to speak of their intention to restore the higher faculties and expand the teaching staff with the addition of luminaries such as Johannes Kepler.[8] In many respects a new school was emerging in Prague. The older and more traditional Utraquist character of the Charles University was being replaced by a more aggressive Protestant spirit best represented by Johannes Jessenius, the rector who led the school in the heady days that culminated at White Mountain.

Jessenius, a native of Silesia, dramatically broadened the intellectual and theological scope of the university. He brought to Prague an important set

---

[7] Cited in Zdeněk David, "Confessional accommodation in early modern Bohemia," in Howard Louthan and Randall Zachman, eds., _Conciliation and Confession_ (Notre Dame: University of Notre Dame Press, 2004), p. 181.

[8] V. V. Tomek, _Geschichte der Prager Universität_ (Prague: Haase, 1849), p. 221.

of international Protestant contacts. He had spent his early years in the late-humanist center of Breslau before turning to the south and studying medicine in Padua, one of the few havens for Protestants in Italy. He then returned to the north, this time to Wittenberg where he taught at the university and lived with Caspar Peucer, Melancthon's son-in-law. Recommended to Rudolf II by Tycho Brahe, Jessenius came to Prague in 1600 where among other activities he performed the first public anatomy at the university. As strains between Catholics and Protestants worsened during the reign of Matthias, Jessenius's own views became more radical as he gradually assumed a higher profile and became a leading ideologue in the anti-Habsburg coalition. In 1614 he published in Padua a slim monarchomach tract entitled *Pro vindiciis contra tryannos.*[9] A second edition of the text appeared in 1620 as justification of the Bohemian uprising. Jessenius also served the Bohemian estates in a more practical fashion. After the defenestration he led a diplomatic mission to Hungary in an effort to secure an alliance with Bethlen Gábor. On his return trip he was intercepted by Habsburg forces and carted off to prison in Vienna. After a brief period of incarceration he returned to Prague where he continued his activities on behalf of the estates.

It was this orientation that the Silesian doctor brought to the university when he was elected rector in 1617. As rector, Jessenius pushed the school to take an active role in the rebellion. Though most of his colleagues were more ambivalent, Jessenius saw the university as a critical ally of new King Frederick. In 1619 he published an important manifesto that outlined his new program. In a manner more pronounced than any of his predecessors, he argued that the Carolinum was a means to complete the Reformation in Czech society. He recounted its history beginning with Charles IV who established the academy "to restore for the first time the original and authentic apostolic faith."[10] Though the school had been deflected from this mission, deprived of resources and attacked by its Catholic rival, disaster had been averted through the prompt actions of the estates culminating with the expulsion of the Jesuits and the timely arrival of God's anointed, Frederick of the Palatinate. Jessenius now called upon the king to finish the task at hand. As recompense for its sufferings, the university should immediately appropriate the abandoned assets of the Jesuits, both its

[9] Stanislav Sousedík, "Jan Jesenský as the ideologist of the Bohemian estates' revolt," *Acta Comeniana* 11 (1995), 13–24; Josef Polišenský, *Jan Jesenský-Jessenius* (Prague: Svobodné slovo, 1965).
[10] Friedel Pick, ed., *Denkschrift des Rektors Johannes Jessenius von Gross-Jessen an den Generallandtag von 1619 über Erneuerung der Prager Universität, Pragensia* 2 (1920), Diiv.

books and buildings. With this "Egyptian booty" it could return to its original purpose refreshed and replenished. Instead of studying abroad in foreign Protestant schools, sons of the Czech nation would now be able to drink their "mother's milk" as they grew in knowledge and devotion.[11] Jessenius was clear about the nature of this piety as he included a lengthy statement of faith that summarized the main elements of the Augsburg Confession in the text.[12]

Most histories of the Charles University do not sufficiently emphasize the radical nature of the changes proposed by the school's Protestant leadership in the years immediately prior to 1620. Jessenius was attempting to transform a sleepy and parochial Utraquist institution into a more militant Protestant outpost. He recruited faculty that matched this new profile including Wittenberg's leading theologian, Polycarp Leyser.[13] In hindsight, these efforts were counterproductive, for Jessenius's Protestant coup galvanized Catholic resolve to eradicate the intellectual center of the broader rebellion root and branch. Ferdinand was reportedly so upset about the university that no one could speak of it in his presence, fearing that its mere mention would throw him into paroxysms of rage. Jessenius, in fact, was singled out on the scaffold in 1621 as the greatest villain of the Bohemian rebellion. When a more mild Utraquist delegation traveled to Vienna after White Mountain to consult the Habsburgs on the fate of the university, they were greeted with a long harangue by the high chancellor, Zdeněk Vojtěch Lobkovic, who in animated fashion recounted the many sins committed by the school's leadership since 1609.[14] Worse, however, was still to come.

AFTER WHITE MOUNTAIN: NEW PLANS FOR THE UNIVERSITY

After White Mountain, the Habsburg regime represented by Prince Liechtenstein moved quickly against the university. The few professors who were still in Prague were not allowed to lecture and the school's property was immediately seized by troops entering the city. Shortly thereafter, a number of officers were actually quartered in the Carolinum. At the same time the Jesuits streamed back to Prague and were reinstated in the

---

[11] Ibid., Biiir. [12] Ibid., Biv–Biiv.

[13] C. A. Pescheck, *The Reformation and Anti-Reformation in Bohemia* (London: Houlston and Stoneman, 1845), vol. I, p. 191.

[14] Käthe Spiegel, "Die Prager Universitätsunion (1618–54)," *MVGDB* 62 (1924), 10; Tomek, *Geschichte der Prager Universität*, pp. 245–6.

Clementinum where they found their library significantly thinner. In early 1621 Liechtenstein issued an order sealing the university archives with the texts and charters that documented its historic rights and privileges. With slim hopes of finding redress from the emperor, the masters planned what was their demoralizing embassy to Vienna. School authorities also looked to Saxony for support, but a mission there in April proved equally unfruitful. Jessenius was executed in June along with the father of another master, Jiří Šultys, who shortly stepped down himself leaving only four professors at the Carolinum. As the end seemed imminent, Liechtenstein packed up the university archives and sent them off to Vienna in March 1622. The last rector of the school, Nicolaus Troilus, handed over the school's seal in April while in November the official decree was finally pronounced entrusting the Charles University to the Society of Jesus for reorganization.

The Jesuit plan for the university was remarkably broad in scope and reflected their dogged determination to eliminate heresy at its very source. Their controversial reforms were a blueprint for a virtual overhaul of higher education and intellectual life in Bohemia. Indeed, the changes they proposed and strove to implement helped set the intellectual trajectory of the Czech lands for the next 150 years if not beyond. Once authority had been transferred, they quickly outlined their program. In 1622 they issued a succinct statement of their pedagogical objectives while in 1623 upon the emperor's request they submitted a detailed letter that summarized their scheme to create a new Charles–Ferdinand University.[15] According to their plan the theological and philosophical faculties of the Clementinum would be expanded and united with the newly constituted law and medical divisions of the Carolinum. Teaching in the philosophical and theological faculties was to be restricted to the Jesuits alone. The position of chancellor was not to revert to the archbishop as in the pre-Hussite period but would remain within the order. The university's new rector, also a Jesuit, would enjoy expanded power and privileges and need not stand for election on a regular basis. He would approve all degree candidates and any curricular reforms. Though the law and medical faculties could elect their own deans, their decisions would be contingent on his final approval. Before any professor outside the order could take up a post at the university, he would be obliged to submit a confessional statement and swear an oath of

---

[15] "Ratio et modus, quo Carolina academia cum Patrum Societatis Jesu academia utiliter uniri et incorporari possit, servata augusta Caroli IV. memoriae," reproduced in H. Kollmann, ed., *Acta Sacrae Congregationis de Propaganda Fide res gestas Bohemicas illustrantia* (Prague: Typis Gregerianis, 1923), vol. I, pt. 1, pp. 67–75.

obedience to the rector. Finally, the rector was to oversee one critical aspect of intellectual life that extended far beyond the university, censorship.

Response to the Jesuit proposals was mixed. Though the emperor with encouragement from Lamormaini fully backed their plan, others on the Catholic side had reservations. Lohelius, who initially favored the Jesuit takeover, had second thoughts when the details emerged. The Dominicans and Franciscans, however, were less restrained in their opposition. Excluded now from the university's two major faculties, they went directly to the emperor and then to Rome to voice their protest. They found an ally with the papal nuncio in Vienna, Carlo Caraffa, who warned the pope of the tremendous power that had been entrusted to a single religious order. Urban VIII was a willing listener, and by 1625 the battle lines were clearly drawn. Ranged on one side were the Jesuits and the emperor, on the other the archbishop and the pope. The struggle over the university and its future was far more than mere factional squabbling. The dispute reflected deeper philosophical differences, and its resolution was critical in shaping the character of Catholic reform in Bohemia as a whole.

The Jesuits may have been caught off-guard by the stiff resistance they encountered in Prague. Archbishop Lohelius died in November 1622 and was replaced by the young and inexperienced Count Harrach who had the daunting task of overseeing an archdiocese that comprised all of Bohemia. The Jesuits, who assumed they could manage the new archbishop, were no doubt surprised by his energy and independent spirit. Harrach during this period was ably assisted by the Capuchin priest, Valerian Magni, who had been sent to Prague in 1623 as both the provincial superior of his order and perhaps more importantly as the informal mentor of the archbishop. Together, Harrach and his adviser waged a vigorous campaign to regain control of the Charles University.[16] In 1626 Magni traveled to Rome where he met with Urban concerning the Bohemian situation. He came back from his trip with a cardinal's hat for Harrach and a stern word from the pope warning the Jesuits that they "should in no way rebel against the archbishop."[17] The following year the pope suspended the Jesuits' rights to grant degrees at the university. After this small victory Magni remained on the offensive. In 1629 he was back in Rome advocating his cause before the newly established Congregation for the Propagation of the Faith. He argued

---

[16] For an overview of these complicated developments see I. Raková, "Cesta k vzniku Karlo-Ferdinandovy univerzity (Spory o pražské vysoké učení v l. 1622–54)," *AUC, HUCP* 24 (1984), 7–40; Catalano, *La Boemia*, pp. 111–61.

[17] Milada Blekastad, *Comenius* (Oslo: Universitetsforlaget, 1969), p. 116.

that the power of university appointment should be returned to the arch-bishop and exclusive Jesuit control of theological training terminated. The Jesuits, for their part, refused to back down. Confident of imperial support, they continued their work. The dispute, however, did not quietly go away. By the early 1630s it had escalated in intensity with both parties now noisily denouncing the other in print.

A turning point in the struggle came in 1637 with the death of Ferdinand II and the accession of his son, Ferdinand III (1637–57). Magni had continued his campaign against the Jesuits by targeting the imperial suc-cessor. In a bold petition to the new emperor he raised a series of issues that he hoped would sway the young ruler. Why, he queried, had the theological orientation of the institution been entrusted not to the pope and the broader body of the church but to a specific religious order? Why had the archbishop been impeded in his rightful responsibilities? Why had he been excluded for fourteen years from the administration of the university?[18] Magni's words may have carried some weight, for in 1638 the emperor re-separated the two institutions. Ferdinand, though, was concerned with the archbishop's aggressive tactics. Harrach had earlier decided that if the Jesuits were not willing to give up their monopoly on theological education, he would circumvent them by establishing his own seminary. Plans for such a school dated back to the mid-1620s, but due to the war they were not implemented immediately. Rome enthusiastically backed Harrach's endeavor, and in 1638 Urban issued a bull that granted the seminary the right to award degrees in theology. A livid Ferdinand wrote a stinging letter to the archbishop in which he reproved him for adding greater confusion to an already disordered situation by creating what was in effect a third university. Although Harrach's response was conciliatory in tone, Ferdinand saw the archbishop's appeal to Rome as an underhanded attack on his own authority.[19] Unlike his father, Ferdinand III was ready to act in a more unilateral fashion and was willing to oppose both the archbishop and the Jesuits in order to resolve the dispute once and for all.

In 1652 the emperor deputized a commission that included members of both parties to reach a definitive settlement. Though feelings still ran high, there was growing momentum pushing the committee towards compro-mise. The students, themselves, played an instrumental role in this story.

---

[18] NA, JS IId. 422, Clem. 20/4, *Libellus supplex apologeticus F. Valeriani Magni Capuccini ad Caesarem*, 17v, 19r.

[19] Spiegel, "Die Prager Universitätsunion," 45; Catalano, *La Boemia*, pp. 191–6; on the seminary see F. Tadra, "Počátkové semináře arcibiskupského v Praze," *SbH* (Rezek) 2 (1884), 193–279.

The drama at the university was unfolding against a backdrop of war. The school, in fact, had been briefly returned to the Protestants when the Saxons occupied the city in 1631. In 1648 when Prague was under direct attack again, the students of all three schools joined together and led a heroic defense against the Swedes. In the wake of these events they expressed a desire to unite once more into a single institution. By the early 1650s the main features of a compromise settlement seemed to be in place. The archiepiscopal seminary was to remain open but would be reduced in status and restricted solely to the training of clergy. The other two schools would be rejoined into the Charles–Ferdinand University. Although the position of chancellor would return to the archbishop, the Jesuits would continue to control the theological and philosophical faculties. Finally, the position of rector was to rotate among the four faculties. It was decided that the Jesuit Johannes Molitor would be appointed the school's first rector. On 4 March 1654, ecclesiastical and civic officials staged an elaborate ceremony in the Týn Church celebrating the reunion of the two schools.

JESUIT PEDAGOGICAL ACTIVITY IN CONTEXT

Though the settlement of 1654 reunited the university, significant tensions remained between the Jesuits and their rivals. This feud in Prague, however, was not an isolated incident. It was part of a broader pattern that played itself out across the Catholic world in the late sixteenth and early seventeenth centuries. From the universities of Paris and Louvain to those of Cracow and Padua, Jesuits and non-Jesuits vied with each other for dominance. Though these pedagogical disputes were often complex affairs, they are easier to comprehend by reviewing in more general terms the character and nature of the Jesuit educational enterprise. The Society of Jesus began a new period in the history of Catholic education. It was the first religious order to see the operation of schools as "a primary and self-standing ministry."[20] Despite Ignatius's initial reluctance, the Jesuits quickly found themselves as educators when their early leaders complained that the universities did not meet the needs and goals of the order. But what started as a movement to address internal concerns quickly grew and expanded. Jesuit colleges were originally intended to serve only as residences for potential members who were trained at a nearby university, but they soon began to offer instruction both for their own and for outsiders who were attracted to their schools. By 1600 they had established 245 colleges in

[20] John O'Malley, *The First Jesuits* (Cambridge, MA: Harvard University Press, 1993), p. 239.

Europe and the New World.[21] Jesuit professors had begun teaching in the universities on a temporary basis. Claude Jay, for example, filled the empty chair of Johannes Eck at Ingolstadt in 1543. By the end of the century, however, they had a substantial presence in the theological and philosophical faculties of Catholic universities, especially in central Europe.

A second feature to note concerns their intellectual orientation. As opposed to the more traditional Dominicans who approached "secular" culture cautiously, the Society of Jesus was far bolder in this respect both as scholars and educators. The Jesuits were fully engaged in the society around them. They were musicians and architects, astronomers and botanists, linguists and historians. In the classrooms they eagerly incorporated such worldly fashions as drama and transformed it into one of their most effective pedagogical tools. The Jesuits saw themselves as "guardians on the frontier," intermediaries between the church and the wider society.[22] As Christ's servants, they were called to be active in a sinful world, and through their involvement they sought to shape it, change it and ultimately save it. Viewed from this perspective, the Jesuit campaign to reform the Charles University must be seen as far more than a mere attempt to restore proper Catholic teaching in the school's theological and philosophical faculties. Their mandate was part of a larger mission to refashion the intellectual life of the Bohemian kingdom.

A final point to consider speaks to the specific nature of the Jesuit educational program in central Europe. In spring 1548, as Ignatius was completing his plans for the first Jesuit college, he had a formal audience with Pope Paul III. With great enthusiasm the pope encouraged him to expand his efforts as a means to combat Protestant error. Even before Ignatius's interview with Paul III, Claude Jay had recommended that the order commission half of its members in Germany to work in the schools so that "God, by means of learned, exemplary men, [may] bring the country back to the church."[23] When Ignatius asked Peter Canisius how the wavering Catholic cause in central Europe could best be served, he had a one-word answer – the colleges. In such a setting, where the teaching of theology became an important weapon in the arsenal of the Counter-Reformation, the schools quickly developed a more polemical and militant edge. At the Clementinum Edmund Campion railed against the Protestants, angrily declaiming that "Lutherans and Calvinists ought to be killed with the

[21] Rivka Feldhay, *Galileo and the Church* (Cambridge: Cambridge University Press, 1995), pp. 111, 116.
[22] O'Malley, *The First Jesuits*, pp. 241–2; Feldhay, *Galileo*, pp. 93–128.
[23] Cited in Feldhay, *Galileo*, p. 116.

sword; they ought to be banished and oppressed; they ought to be burnt with fire, sulfur and pitch; drowned in water; impoverished, exhausted, hunted down, deprived of their estates, and annihilated."[24] Though Campion's rhetoric was undoubtedly extreme, there was in general a shift in Jesuit pedagogy from the middle to the end of the century that in some respects matched the more hostile religious climate of central Europe. The early years of the schools were a creative period of experimentation when various innovations were introduced in an effort to combine learning with moral and spiritual formation. When reports from the colleges indicated that these goals were not being met, that piety was not always accompanying scholarship, the Jesuits adjusted their pedagogical strategy accordingly. The 1599 publication of their pedagogical manifesto, the *Ratio Studiorum*, reflected a conservative shift that had occurred, both in practice and theory. Greater emphasis was placed on governance and control. Jesuit educators became more concerned with matters of regulation and oversight while the schools became more hierarchical in nature.[25] At the same time there were forces both inside and outside the Society that were pushing the order to take a more active role in reshaping central Europe's Catholic universities in the fight against the Protestant threat, a development that did not go undisputed in many of these institutions.

The Jesuits slowly infiltrated Germany's Catholic schools in the course of the sixteenth and early seventeenth centuries.[26] They were invited to Ingolstadt by Duke Wilhelm in the 1540s, and after an extended struggle they took over the philosophy faculty in 1576. They began a *Gymnasium* in Cologne in 1556, and by the 1560s they were teaching theology at the university. The order also did well at the schools of the Empire's two other spiritual electors. They assumed responsibility for the theological and philosophical faculties of Trier and Mainz in 1561 and 1562 respectively. Apart from Bavaria, their success with secular princes in Germany was somewhat slower in coming. In 1620 they began their work at the university in Freiburg im Breisgau while nine years later they descended on Heidelberg and refashioned the curriculum of the former citadel of Reformed learning. It is Vienna and its university, however, that merits closest attention, for its

[24] Cited in Pescheck, *The Reformation and Anti-Reformation*, vol. I, pp. 327–8.
[25] G. Anselmi, "Per un'archeologia della *Ratio*: dalla 'pedagogia' al 'governo,'" in Gian Paolo Brizzi, ed., *La "Ratio Studiorum": Modelli culturali e pratiche educative dei Gesuiti in Italia tra Cinque e Seicento* (Rome: Bulzoni, 1981), pp. 11–42.
[26] Karl Hengst, *Jesuiten und Universitäten und Jesuitenuniversitäten* (Munich: Schöningh, 1981); Ernst Schubert, "Zur Typologie gegenreformatorischer Universitätsgründungen: Jesuiten in Fulda, Würzburg, Ingolstadt und Dillingen," in H. Rössler and G. Franz, eds., *Universität und Gelehrtenstand 1400–1800* (Limburg: Starke, 1970), pp. 85–105.

fate serves as an important reference point to Prague. The Jesuits came to Vienna in 1551 and quickly established a college. Like Prague, a great many of the city's residents had defected from Rome. The Jesuits saw themselves as key figures in the struggle against Protestantism and specifically worked towards the incorporation of their college into the larger university. Though their attempts to unite the schools initially met some resistance, a compromise settlement was ultimately brokered in 1623.

The details of this agreement constitute a significant contrast to that of Prague, for though the Jesuits won key concessions, they did not achieve a full monopoly of power in Austria. The so-called "Pragmatic sanction" which had been negotiated by imperial, Jesuit and university officials in 1623 was full of compromises.[27] The Society withdrew its demand stipulating that the university rector must be a Jesuit. The position of dean in the philosophy faculty rotated on a semester basis between a Jesuit and a non-Jesuit. For the examination of degree candidates in the arts faculty two non-Jesuits always had to be present. Classes between the university and the Jesuit college were coordinated to minimize competition between the two. It was this type of model that Ferdinand III envisioned for Prague, and the emperor's ideas were reflected in certain elements of the Bohemian settlement. The office of chancellor did revert back to the archbishop. But when one looks closer at the specifics of the 1654 union, it is obvious that it fell well short of the Austrian ideal. Emerging with full control of both the arts and theological faculties, the Jesuits retained their most important prize. Beneath a show of unity, they treated professors outside their order as at best junior partners. Johannes Molitor, the first rector of the renewed Charles–Ferdinand University, consistently fought to expand his own authority. The Jesuits continued to agitate for special status and often simply ignored the terms of the 1654 settlement. They carried on with the promotion of their students without consulting the archbishop as official requirements now stipulated. They refused to recognize university jurisdiction over their own members and students. This strategy ultimately succeeded as Emperor Leopold I later conferred many of the privileges they demanded.[28] In sum, by the middle of the seventeenth century there were few places in central Europe, if not the entire continent, where the Jesuits had a more dominant influence on higher education than in the Bohemian kingdom.

The militant stance the Jesuits adopted in Prague was at least in part a product of their experience in the Czech lands. If central Europe was a confessional battlefield for the Society, the Bohemian kingdom was the

---

[27] Spiegel, "Die Prager Universitätsunion," 83–5.   [28] Ibid., 74–81.

locus of one of its fiercest conflicts. Though the rhetoric of Campion may have been extreme, it was not atypical. From their vantage point no university in Europe could rival the heretical legacy of the Carolinum. Though founded by a pious emperor, the school had slipped its confessional moorings almost immediately, and for more than two centuries sailed through the choppy waters of theological error and doctrinal deviation. No one, it seemed, could pilot the school into safe harbor. During the reigns of Rudolf and Matthias the situation had deteriorated even further. Under their watch the university was becoming a new Heidelberg, a center of heresy and dangerous political dissent. The order alone had stood up to this challenge, and for their efforts they were rewarded with persecution and ultimately expulsion. What may have been most surprising for the Jesuits, however, was that their fight did not end with White Mountain. For their efforts they were greeted with resistance from fellow believers. A former student, the young and misguided archbishop, had unexpectedly turned on them. The Jesuits must have asked themselves how such an important mission as university reform could be entrusted to one so inexperienced. At the death of their patron Ferdinand II, they also faced imperial opposition. Ferdinand III could at times be openly antagonistic to their work. In the end antagonism and strife only strengthened their resolve to hold firm at the university, retain their grasp on the philosophical and theological education and complete the task to which they had first been called.

The Jesuit position was also buttressed by strong theological convictions. Nearly all apologists of Bohemia's Counter-Reformation diagnosed the confessional crisis in a similar manner. The doctrinal disputes that had begun with Hus had multiplied, spread quickly across the kingdom, and left nothing but chaos and disorder. The Jesuits, more than any other Catholic faction in Bohemia, believed that theological unity must be recovered and maintained at all costs. Division and innovation eventually led to heterodoxy and heresy. Critics of the Society frequently complained that the Jesuits overstepped their bounds as spiritual watchdogs. In late sixteenth-century Padua, Cesare Cremonini, a popular professor of philosophy at the university, led an attack on the Jesuit college complaining that the fathers were "making themselves *the monarchs of knowledge*" and in the end would destroy the school.[29] Though Cremonini's critical remarks were partially motivated by professional jealousies, his comments bear special relevance in

---

[29] Cited in John Patrick Donnelly, "The Jesuit college at Padua: growth, suppression, attempts at restoration: 1552–1606," *Archivum Historicum Societatis Iesu* 51 (1982), 62. Italics are my own.

Bohemia, for there the Jesuits certainly did see themselves as cultural arbiters with a broad intellectual mandate.

Back in Prague the Jesuits defended their educational monopoly with great vigor. In February 1623 a group of Franciscans and Dominicans put a request before the emperor asking for a restoration of their teaching privileges at the university. More specifically, they sought the creation of two chairs in theology, one dedicated to the Scotist tradition, the other to the Thomist. Ferdinand passed this request back to the Jesuits who responded with a lengthy memorandum justifying their refusal. They cited a number of practical difficulties and legal precedents supporting their position, but even more important from their perspective was the potential damage that could result from such an arrangement. These different theological traditions, specifically the "subtleties of Duns Scotus," could easily create dangerous confusion and division among the students. Unity must be maintained.[30] In 1649 a similar event occurred when, at the instigation of the Jesuits, Ferdinand III issued a decree mandating that all masters and degree candidates at the university in Vienna swear an oath supporting the doctrine of the Immaculate Conception. As the decree read, theological unanimity was critical to avoid "great varieties of opinion, conflicting and discordant views, confusion among the less learned and the division of minds."[31] A similar edict was passed for Prague the following year. Though Marian veneration was certainly an important end in itself, the Jesuits had an ulterior motive. They were using the decree as a means to exclude the Dominicans from the universities both in Vienna and Prague. They did not succeed in Austria. The Dominicans, who disputed this doctrine, had enough influence to ensure that a statute was passed exempting them from the oath.[32] There was no such allowance in Prague as the Society was able to construct yet another firewall blocking their rivals from the school.

Such background helps us understand the document that opened this chapter, the 1653 attack on Archbishop Harrach. Almost certainly written by a Jesuit, this stern critique of the archbishop's leadership was dedicated almost exclusively to educational issues. It was composed while final negotiations were being conducted concerning the fate of the university. Accurately articulating the concerns of the Jesuits, the writer had

[30] The Jesuit response is reproduced in Kollmann, ed., *Acta Sacrae Congregationis de Propaganda Fide*, vol. I, pp. 240–6.
[31] Cited in R. Perkmann, *Die Jesuiten und die Wiener Universität* (Leipzig: Wigand, 1866), pp. 235–9.
[32] Reprinted in Rudolf Kink, *Geschichte der kaiserlichen Universität zu Wien*, vol. II, *Statutenbuch der Universität* (Vienna: Gerold, 1854), no. 92, pp. 473–5.

particularly hard words for Harrach's seminary. He argued that the school had been established "not in the form and manner prescribed by Trent but according to its own inclination and the decisions and judgments of its supporters."[33] This lack of discipline, regulation and control in the theological community was the most significant weakness of Harrach's regime and the Jesuits' greatest fear. Our critic was even more specific with his assessment as he continued by naming those who were responsible for introducing dangerous doctrinal novelties. The Cistercian Juan Caramuel Lobkovic, the Franciscan Malachias Fallon and the Capuchin Valerian Magni were among those he singled out for censure. These individuals and their respective confrontations with the Jesuits are significant as they illustrate the changing nature of intellectual life in post-1620 Bohemia and how dissent was ultimately mastered.

MUFFLING DISSENT AND MANAGING OPPOSITION

Juan Caramuel Lobkovic (1606–82) is a difficult individual to categorize. Born in Madrid, Caramuel was an immensely precocious child who by the age of ten was composing astronomical tables. He wrote scores of works ranging from canon law to metaphysics and reputedly spoke more than twenty languages.[34] He became a Cistercian in 1623 and received a degree in theology from Louvain in 1638 where he taught for a number of years. Caramuel was a young, rising star within the church, but his ascent was unexpectedly interrupted and ultimately reversed by Pope Alexander VII whom the Cistercian had earlier offended. He ended his career in semi-exile as a bishop of two minor Italian dioceses. Caramuel's notoriety and reputation, however, were at their zenith when he was called to Prague at the end of the Thirty Years War to serve as abbot of the Emmaus monastery and vicar-general of the archdiocese. Caramuel's thought stubbornly defies systematization. R. J. W. Evans once described his *Trismegistus Theologicus* as a "*Finnegan's Wake* of Baroque philosophy."[35] The eclectic Cistercian certainly dabbled with a broad array of ideas that were circulating in the Catholic world of the mid-seventeenth century. While at Louvain he

---

[33] Rezek, "Tak-zvaná 'Idea gubernationis ecclesiasticae'," 6.

[34] The literature on Caramuel is substantial. For an introduction see Alessandro Catalano, "Juan Caramuel Lobkovicz (1606–1682) e la riconquista delle coscienze in Boemia," *Römische Historische Mitteilungen* 44 (2002), 339–92. In English see Henry Sullivan, "Fray Juan Caramuel y Lobkowitz O. Cist.: the Prague years, 1647–59," in Michael McGrath, ed., *Studies in Honor of John Jay Allen* (Newark: Juan de la Cuesta, 2005), pp. 339–74.

[35] R. J. W. Evans, *The Making of the Habsburg Monarchy 1550–1700* (Oxford: Clarendon Press, 1979), p. 325.

eagerly participated in the early Jansenist disputes. Of all the theologians and philosophers active in post-White Mountain Bohemia, his interaction with Cartesian ideas was the most substantive. Applying his interest in mathematics to moral theology, he boldly claimed that certain intractable doctrinal issues could be resolved with compass and ruler. His fascination with probabilism shaped his understanding of casuistry, earning him the unenviable nickname, the "Prince of Laxists."[36] Not surprisingly, a number of his texts ended up on the Index.

For the Jesuits, Caramuel was the proverbial bull in the china shop, a dangerous presence in a highly sensitive theological environment. He was an undisciplined and unpredictable thinker whose speculative ideas could provoke serious controversy. His use of Descartes was particularly disturbing as the Jesuits instinctively recoiled from Cartesianism. But though the high-flying Caramuel may have attracted greater attention, the obscure Malachias Fallon and his colleagues perhaps posed a more serious threat to the Jesuit establishment, for they offered a form of dissent that was institutionalized. While Caramuel had minimal pedagogical influence in Prague, the Irish Franciscans were active in the schools. Originally expelled from England, these Franciscans had settled in Louvain. In 1629 they accepted an invitation to begin a work in Bohemia. In Prague they taught at two small institutions: the new *Collegium Ferdinandeum* attached to the Franciscan cloister of St. James in the Old City and a school of the Observant Franciscans at St. Mary of the Snows. They assumed a higher profile, however, as instructors at Harrach's seminary where they gave their lessons from a Scotist orientation.[37] Though the Jesuits were not pleased that a Scotist alternative was being offered in the schools, they were in all likelihood more concerned with other ideas the Franciscans could be bringing with them from the Low Countries. In 1653 Innocent X issued the bull, *Cum occasione*, one of the early broadsides fired against Jansenism. The Jesuits were quick to respond and were the only religious order to support the pope's edict.[38] The Society feared that the Jansenist maelstrom of Louvain might also engulf Bohemia if the Franciscans were not closely controlled.

---

[36] For the challenge of probabilism to Catholic orthodoxy see Ian Hacking, *The Emergence of Probability* (Cambridge: Cambridge University Press, 1975). Note especially its connection to Jansenism, pp. 24–5, 57–9. On Caramuel and Descartes see Stanislav Sousedík, *René Descartes a české baroko* (Prague: Filosofický ústav, 1996).

[37] Stanislav Sousedík, "Der Scotismus in den böhmischen Ländern," *Collectanea Franciscana* 60 (1990), 477–503, esp. 494–503.

[38] William Bangert, *A History of the Society of Jesus* (St. Louis: Institute of Jesuit Sources, 1972), p. 230.

In the final analysis, however, it was neither the irascible Caramuel nor the Franciscans who posed the greatest challenge to Jesuit intellectual hegemony in the Bohemian kingdom. Their most significant foe was the Capuchin Valerian Magni (1586–1661).[39] The war of polemics between these two parties reached near epic proportions. The invective they heaped upon each other ranks among the very best of the seventeenth century. While Magni blasted the Jesuits for their duplicity and deception, they in turn described the Capuchin as a "toad bloated with poison" and a "wolf in the sheepfold of the church."[40] Born in Milan, Magni had come north with his family in 1589 and grew up in the cosmopolitan setting of imperial Prague. Shaped in this world of late humanism, Magni was well connected with the literati of his day, winning accolades from figures such as Pascal.[41] Though as Harrach's adviser he had first crossed swords with the Jesuits during the university dispute, his opposition to the order extended well beyond that affair, for Magni advocated an alternative approach to the restoration of Catholicism in Bohemia. In opposition to the harsher methods advocated by Lamormaini and others, Magni proposed a milder program that favored discussion and dialogue over expulsion and coercion. He sought engagement with prominent leaders of the Czech estates, and when the Saxons occupied Prague in 1631 bringing with them many of the former exiles, he remained in the city to debate his confessional opponents. A missionary with distinct irenic convictions, Magni subsequently served as adviser to the Polish king Władysław IV. In the Polish–Lithuanian Commonwealth he spearheaded attempts to reunite the region's Protestant and Orthodox communities with the Catholic church. Magni always lamented the stern tactics that were ultimately adopted in Bohemia. He went to his grave believing that had his methods been followed, many wayward Christians would have willingly returned to Rome.

Magni's critique of the Jesuits also had deeper intellectual roots. He was an outspoken opponent of the neoscholastic curriculum and philosophy imported by the Society into the Czech lands. The tradition of Vitoria and Suárez was best represented in Bohemia by Rodrigo Arriaga. Arriaga, one of the most influential theologians in Prague in the post-1620 generation, had come to Bohemia in the 1620s and played a significant role in the

---

[39] For an introduction to Magni see Howard Louthan, "Mediating confessions in central Europe: the ecumenical activity of Valerian Magni," *Journal of Ecclesiastical History* 55 (2004), 681–99.

[40] Hugo Bloth, "Der Kapuziner Valerian Magni und sein Kampf gegen den Jesuitenorden," *Materialdienst des Konfessionskundlichen Instituts* 7 (1956), 85.

[41] Blaise Pascal, *The Provincial Letters*, trans. A. J. Krailsheimer (Baltimore: Penguin Books, 1967), Letter 15 (25 November 1656), pp. 233–6.

reorganization of the university.[42] His massive *Cursus philosophicus* (1632) was one of the most important neoscholastic works of the seventeenth century. It went through numerous editions, becoming a model for theological text-books in Jesuit colleges across the continent. Magni, in contrast, was a fierce opponent of what he bluntly described as the "atheism of Aristotle."[43] Deeply influenced by both Cusanus and Bonaventure, Magni drew heavily from the Platonic and Augustinian traditions. As opposed to a neoscholastic model that lent itself to the sharpening of theological difference, Magni turned to Platonism and developed a system that offered a way for Catholics and Protestants to overcome their division. One of the most distinctive features of Magni's theology was its lack of attention to doctrinal detail. Magni's most famous treatise, his 1628 *De acatholicorum credendi regula iudicium*, was typical in this respect. In this spirited defense of Catholicism, Magni's argu-ments were decidedly more philosophical than dogmatic in nature. He engaged his Protestant opponents on their own terms, considering what he understood as the implications of a theology constructed around the premise of *sola Scriptura*. Magni argued that Protestants had put themselves in a difficult position logically by elevating the authority of the individual over the general councils of the church, for those who insisted on interpreting Scripture individually were in the end compelled to join "a confused com-pany of fanatics in which there is no order."[44]

Magni's pronounced rationalist impulse was a red flag to many in both the Protestant and Catholic worlds. The Dutch Calvinist Gisbertus Voetius was highly critical of the Capuchin's position, for "natural human reason is set up as the judge and norm of faith."[45] The Jesuits, too, were concerned with the implications of Magni's theology. It was difficult to pin him down on specific doctrinal issues. In debates he avoided technical theological discussions. Where the Jesuits insisted on clarity and precision, Magni consistently blurred distinctions and categories. When he admitted that papal authority was based on tradition, a number of prominent Jesuits condemned him immediately.[46] Many were also disturbed that his ideas had won significant

---

[42] Tereza Saxlová and Stanislav Sousedík, eds., *Rodrigo de Arriaga: Philosoph und Theologe* (Prague: Karolinum, 1998).

[43] See in particular Magni's tract *De atheismo Aristotelis* in his broader compendium *Principia et specimen philosophiae* (Cologne: Apud Jodocum Kalcovium, 1652), pp. 121–9; Franciszek Gabryl, "O Waleryan Magni Kapucyn (1586–1661). Anti-Arystotelik w XVII wieku," *Archiwum Komisji do Badania Historii Filozofii w Polsce* 1 (1915), 133–68.

[44] Valerian Magni, *De acatholicorum credendi regula iudicium* (Prague: Paulus Sessius, 1628), p. 44.

[45] Cited in Klaus Scholder, *The Birth of Modern Critical Theology* (Philadelphia: Trinity Press International, 1990), p. 22.

[46] Eduard Winter, *Ketzerschicksale* (Berlin: Union, 1979), p. 135.

support from certain quarters, especially with the Piarists who offered the only real alternative to Jesuit education on the primary level in Bohemia. The order established its second school in the Czech lands on the Moravian estate owned by Valerian's brother Francesco. These schools also posed a distinct ideological challenge to the Jesuits. Galileo and Campanella had close connections with the order, and the ideas of both the problematic astronomer and the wayward Dominican found a favorable reception with the Piarists. Magni realized the Piarists could serve as an important counterweight to the Jesuits and did all in his power to promote their cause. The Piarists, in turn, popularized the Capuchin's theology and philosophy by incorporating it into their own educational program.[47] In the end, however, Magni and his ideas were effectively marginalized. By the 1630s Magni was primarily occupied with Polish affairs and only on occasion focused more closely on the Bohemian situation. His opponents eventually gained the upper hand, and in 1661 he was arrested on charges of heresy. He died six months later before his case could be heard in Rome.

With Caramuel, Fallon and especially Magni the Jesuits addressed problems of doctrinal pluralism in an aggressive fashion. There were other ways, though, to master intellectual dissent in the post-White Mountain period. In certain situations the opposition could be co-opted. Though Jessenius led a radical Protestant faction that sought to transform the university, there was a more conservative wing of the school that was more ambivalent to the regime of the Winter King. Of the final four professors of the Carolinum, two converted to Catholicism. When Jan Campanus, the most famous of these men, died in 1622, the Jesuits were quick to seize the moment and commemorated his passing with a lavish public ceremony that drew huge crowds. Though the poetry and history of the humanist Campanus hardly constituted a significant threat to the Society's doctrinal program, his conversion conferred on the new university a certain continuity with the past and hence a greater sense of legitimacy.

There were yet other means to handle ideological opposition. As Mary Douglas has reminded us, institutions can create "shadowed places."[48] Though the Charles–Ferdinand University was technically a united institution between 1621 and 1638 and again after 1654, its faculties were in reality divided into two unequal camps. While the philosophical and theological

---

[47] Jerzy Cygan, "Der Anteil Valerian Magnis an der Verteidigung des Piaristenordens," *Collectanea Franciscana* 38 (1968), 364–72; Paul Grendler, "The Piarists of the pious schools," in Richard DeMolen, ed., *Religious Orders of the Catholic Reformation* (New York: Fordham University Press, 1994), p. 266.

[48] Mary Douglas, *How Institutions Think* (Syracuse: Syracuse University Press, 1986), pp. 69–70.

wing of the university enjoyed the bright sunshine of ample resources and attention, the medical and law faculties were languishing in the shadows. One can see the contrast by merely comparing the histories of the two sets of buildings that housed the university faculties. The teaching of theology and philosophy, which remained until the second half of the eighteenth century a Jesuit monopoly, took place in the Clementinum. This complex, which had originally belonged to the Dominicans, had been turned over to the Jesuits when they arrived in Prague in 1556. The Jesuits gave the former Dominican church and monastery an architectural makeover as they began an extensive building program in the 1570s.[49] They constructed school buildings, libraries, a printing house, an astronomical observatory and an apothecary. Among the new structures were some of Bohemia's most important baroque monuments including the magnificent Mirror Hall of Kilian Ignaz Dientzenhofer. By the time major construction had ended in 1726, the complex stretched over five acres and next to the rambling castle across the river was the second largest installation of buildings in Prague.

Quite the opposite was happening across Old Town at the Carolinum. The Carolinum was still officially the center of the university. Though the Jesuits fought for the right to promote their own students at the Clementinum, all degree candidates regardless of faculty were graduated here until the order finally prevailed in 1703.[50] The Carolinum was also home to the medical and law faculties which had been reconstituted after White Mountain. But while the Jesuits were enjoying the ever expanding resources of their college, the two secular faculties struggled along in cramped confines as their once resplendent building literally decayed around them. It was only in 1714 when the Carolinum was threatened with imminent collapse that repairs were authorized, and even then it was a struggle to find the necessary funds to finance the project.[51] Numbers also tell an important story. Between 1642 and 1648 only eight students were matriculated at the faculty of medicine. The situation at the Clementinum was strikingly different. During this period the Jesuit complex often serviced 500–600 students annually, earning it the title "bastion of orthodoxy."[52] Some caution needs to be exercised with these figures, for

---

[49] Petr Voit, *Pražské Klementinum* (Prague: National Library, 1990).

[50] Kavka and Petráň, eds., *Dějiny Univerzity Karlovy*, vol. II, p. 62.

[51] J. Klabouch, "K dějinám hospodářství pražské univerzity v 17. a 18. století," *AUC, HUCP* 4 (1963), 87–114; Kavka and Petráň, eds., *Dějiny Univerzity Karlovy*, vol. II, p. 63.

[52] M. Truc, "Příspěvek k dějinám lékařské fakulty v letech 1638–1954," *AUC, HUCP* 7 (1966), 9; J. Hemmerle, "Die Prager Universität in der neueren Zeit," in Ferdinand Seibt, ed., *Bohemia sacra* (Düsseldorf: Schwann, 1974), p. 417.

medical education in central Europe was still at an early stage. But while older universities (Tübingen, Leipzig and Vienna) and newer schools (Halle and Strassburg) were making substantial progress in this field, Prague was slipping behind.

The specific case of Marcus Marci is important to consider at this juncture as it illustrates how intellectual activity that was potentially subversive to neoscholasticism could be marginalized and relegated to the shadows. Marcus Marci (1595–1667) was Bohemia's most original thinker and acclaimed scholar in the century after White Mountain.[53] The leading professor of the medical faculty, Marci also served as the personal physician of Emperors Ferdinand III and Leopold I. Despite the difficulties of the war years, Marci maintained a significant network of international contacts. He had met William Harvey. He corresponded with Galileo and came to know Athanasius Kircher and the mathematician Paul Guldin.[54] Marci, who attended Jesuit schools in Bohemia and Moravia, completed his academic training in Prague with a 1625 dissertation on epilepsy. But even the field of medicine could be problematic in the theologically sensitive atmosphere of seventeenth-century Prague. In 1635 he wrote the *Idearum operatricum idea*, a controversial work on embryology that troubled his more orthodox colleagues.[55] Here he first articulated his ideas regarding the *world soul*, a Platonic force that stood behind the biological activity he was describing. Marci owed his greatest scholarly debt to Jan Baptist van Helmont whose work in the Low Countries had elicited significant opposition from both the Spanish Inquisition and the University of Louvain. In 1635 van Helmont, in fact, was under house arrest and his works condemned by the Louvain theological faculty. Marci's own ideas rested on equally questionable ground. His interest in the hermetic arts and Paracelsianism was a significant cause for concern. His work was linked to such heterodox figures as Campanella, Fludd and Bruno. Not unexpectedly, then, the *Idearum operatricum idea* landed the physician in some difficulties. He was reprimanded for not submitting it to the censors. Its publication also initiated a thirty-year quarrel with Rodrigo Arriaga who attacked Marci's ideas in later

[53] Zdeněk Servít, *Jan Marek Marci z Kronlandu* (Prague: Academia, 1989); Petr Svobodný, ed., *Joannes Marcus Marci: A Seventeenth-Century Bohemian Polymath* (Prague: Charles University, 1998).

[54] Walter Pagel and Pyarali Rattansi, "Harvey meets the 'Hippocrates of Prague' (Johannes Marcus Marci of Kronland)," *Medical History* 8 (1964), 78–9; Zdeněk Pokorný, "Dopis Jana Marka Marci Galileimu," *Sborník pro dějiny přírodních věd a techniky* 9 (1964), 7–19; John Fletcher, "Johannes Marcus Marci writes to Athanasius Kircher," *Janus* 109 (1972), 95–117.

[55] Walter Pagel, "Religious motives in the medical biology of the seventeenth century," *Bulletin of the Institute of the History of Medicine* 3 (1935), 225–31; Joseph Needham, *A History of Embryology* (New York: Abelard-Schuman, 1959), pp. 80–1.

editions of his *Cursus philosophicus*. As far away as England, Marci was cited as a staunch opponent of neoscholasticism.[56]

The response of Arriaga and his Jesuit colleagues to Marci offers an intriguing counterpoint to the Magni case. With Magni the struggle with the order was direct and unrestrained. Marci's situation, on the other hand, demonstrates that within certain parameters ideological differences could be tolerated as long as they did not pose a direct threat to the Jesuit pedagogical monopoly. Marci in many respects represented a loyal opposition. He was a product of Jesuit schools and devoted his entire career to the university. In 1648 he was among the professors and students of Prague who mounted the civilian defense against the Swedes. Though critical of Arriaga, he did not conduct his feud in the *ad hominem* manner characteristic of Magni. Perhaps more importantly from the Jesuit perspective, he was a good loser. Marci had been a disciple of Magni and had carried on the struggle to separate the Carolinum from the Clementinum. He had been part of an imperial commission to resolve this contentious matter and had journeyed to Rome as an advocate of an independent Carolinum. Marci's cause lost in the end, but gracious in defeat, he formally announced the union of the two schools at the Týn Church celebration. What is even more significant is the locus of Marci's dissent. He was a professor of medicine, and in this capacity his interaction with pupils was more restricted and limited. The number of students in his faculty was a tiny fraction of the volume that passed through the Clementinum, and though philosophical notions supported his under-standing of the natural world, he was not teaching from a platform that directly challenged the Jesuits' theological orientation. Although Marci did have a modest international reputation, he labored in relative isolation within Bohemia. His students and early biographers lamented the fact that his work received little notice in the Czech lands.[57]

Though Marci's challenge was politely but effectively sidelined, any frontal assault on the Society's educational ideals continued to be met with stiff resistance. The last significant critique of their pedagogical pro-gram in the seventeenth century came from Hieronymus Hirnhaim, the Premonstratensian abbot of the Strahov Monastery. Hirnhaim (1637–79) was from the upper Silesian town of Troppau (Opava) where he attended

[56] J. Smolka, "The scientific revolution in Bohemia," in R. Porter and M. Teich (eds.), *The Scientific Revolution in National Context* (Cambridge: Cambridge University Press, 1992), p. 226; Pagel, "Harvey meets the 'Hippocrates of Prague'," 79–80.

[57] F. M. Pelcl, *Abbildungen böhmischer und mährischer Gelehrten und Künstler* (Prague: Gerle, 1773), vol. I, p. 80.

the local Jesuit *Gymnasium*.[58] In 1658 he journeyed to Prague where he
entered the Strahov Monastery and there continued his studies at the
Norbertinum, the Premonstratensian college that had maintained its independence from the university. He later lectured at both the Norbertinum
and the archiepiscopal seminary until his election as the new abbot of
Strahov in 1670. In this position he oversaw an extensive building campaign
that culminated with the renovation and reorganization of Bohemia's most
important monastic library. Hirnhaim launched a direct attack on Jesuit
pedagogy in 1676 with the publication of *De typho generis humani*. Like
Marci, he had initially dodged the Jesuit censors by publishing his work at
the rival archiepiscopal press.

Hirnhaim minced no words in *De typho*. The colleges and universities of
his day, he claimed, were full of scholars who spent their hours in useless
argumentation. These individuals "endeavored to please greedy ears with
sophistry and paradox merely to prove the keenness of their wits." Why was
it necessary to debate "whether and what kind of fish live in the waters
beyond the heavens, or when the serpent was created, or whether the
caterpillar was made before the butterfly"?[59] Such were the heights of
philosophical activity in Prague from Hirnhaim's perspective. The abbot
was not slow in assigning blame. "I have great respect," he claimed, "for
St. Thomas, Duns Scotus and the other patriarchs of the schools. For their
interpreters, however, I do not have the same esteem."[60] Neoscholasticism
with its slavish attachment to theological texts of the High Middle Ages
helped create an intellectual atmosphere that was stultifying in the extreme.
Hirnhaim's critique was of course not unique. During the deliberations
surrounding the eventual union of the Clementinum and Carolinum,
Emperor Ferdinand III put forward his own reform plan for theological
education. He also believed that the Jesuits devoted too much attention to
speculative theology.[61] While the emperor addressed these educational
concerns in a composed and measured tone, Hirnhaim adopted a rhetoric
that was far less restrained. Hell, he claimed, is full of many erudite
theologians who had failed to recognize the true spiritual nature of their
calling and ministry.[62]

Though *De typho* missed the Jesuit censors in Prague, a copy was sent to
the University of Louvain for review. The Jesuits controlled the theological

[58] Ulrich Leinsle, "Hirnhaim, Hieronymus," in W. Kaspar, ed., *Lexikon für Theologie und Kirche* (Freiburg i.B.: Herder, 1996), vol. V, p. 150; Julius Klitzner, *Hieronymus Hirnhaim* (Prague, 1943).
[59] Hieronymus Hirnhaim, *De typho generis humani* (Prague: Typis Georgii Czernoch, 1676), pp. 9–10, 267, 275.
[60] Ibid., p. 263.   [61] Klitzner, *Hirnhaim*, p. 57.   [62] Hirnhaim, *De typho*, p. 377.

faculty there, and they had a stern reproof for Hirnhaim. The abbot, they claimed, was passing on the dangerous ideas of Paracelsus and van Helmont, rashly probing issues that were best left unexplored.[63] Once more, the *world soul*, that perennial philosophical bugbear of the Jesuit establishment, came to the fore. The censors, in fact, pointed to this issue as the most problematic feature of the book arguing that the *world soul* is "the worst plague of this age ... It has spread from England to the entire north, and it is feared that if its course is not stopped by God, many will be lost to Epicureanism or even atheism."[64] In the end, *De typho* was placed on the Index. Indebted both to Magni and Marci, Hirnhaim was the last major exponent of a philosophical tradition in Bohemia that could be traced back to the fascinating circle of late Renaissance thinkers at the Rudolfine court. With Hirnhaim the residue of late humanism mixed with elements of Christian mysticism to produce a theology that resisted the Aristotelian imperatives of neoscholasticism.

Unlike Marci, who was safely isolated in the medical faculty, Hirnhaim occupied a prominent position in the theological community and played a major role in both the Norbertinum and the archiepiscopal seminary. As such, he was a greater threat to the Jesuit teaching program. Though he died three years after the publication of *De typho*, his late years at Strahov were full of trouble. His opponents may well have detected elements of Jansenism in his work, for a devotional text he had authored also ended up on the Index for reasons of excessive piety.[65] The greatest difficulty he faced during his tenure as abbot was with his former student and future successor, Hyacinth Hohmann. In 1674 Hirnhaim established a chair for canon law at the Norbertinum, a position that was shared with the seminary. Hirnhaim's appointment of Hohmann surprisingly provoked considerable controversy. It was actually rare for Jesuits to interfere in academic matters outside the arts and theology faculties. Here was their prime if not exclusive area of ministry in the schools.[66] In this case, however, they were deeply troubled. The creation of a new chair in canon law obviously bestowed greater prestige on their institutional rival. They also saw this violating the spirit of 1654 union. According to the settlement the seminary

[63] The report of the censor is reprinted in Klitzner, *Hirnhaim*, pp. 103–8.   [64] Ibid., p. 106.

[65] H. Hirnhaim, *S. Norberti Archiepiscopi Magdeburgensis* (Prague: Typis Georgii Czernoch, 1676); in the eighteenth century Premonstratensian houses did serve as conduits of Jansenism to Bohemia especially in Moravia. Eduard Winter, *Tausend Jahre Gesisteskampf im Sudentenraum* (Salzburg: Müller, 1938), pp. 279–80.

[66] Hilde de Ridder-Symoens, ed., *Universities in Early Modern Europe, 1500–1800* (Cambridge: Cambridge University Press, 1996), vol. II, p. 141.

was to restrict itself to the training of clergy. A full position in canon law might lead to a change in the school's status. In the end, Hohmann was permitted to teach, but his appointment was officially retitled to avoid any infringement on university prerogatives.[67]

Valerian Magni, Marcus Marci and Hieronymus Hirnhaim were Bohemia's most important Catholic dissenters in the first two generations after White Mountain. The challenges they posed, though, were eventually mastered through a variety of stratagems. But Magni, Marci and Hirnhaim are also significant as they reflect critical changes that were occurring in the broader Czech landscape. By comparing the three, we can begin to delineate the collapsing horizons of Bohemia's intellectual world. Magni, who came of age in the cosmopolitan context of Rudolfine Prague, maintained a wide network of contacts across Europe as his career led him from France to the Ukraine, from Danzig to Rome. His literary legacy remains scattered across the continent.[68] Marci was also known outside the Czech lands though his interaction with literati abroad was more limited. His encounter with Harvey was fortuitous, and he would have never met Guldin or Kircher had he not been on a mission to Rome. News of his work was difficult to obtain. When the secretary of England's Royal Society attempted to contact him to initiate a correspondence, he discovered after considerable effort that Marci had been dead for two years.[69] Hirnhaim closes the circle, for the abbot was virtually unknown beyond Bohemia. Although *De typho* was a work of considerable learning, even in the eighteenth century it was difficult to find a copy of it outside the Czech lands.[70] Enrollment statistics tell a similar story. The number of foreign students attending the university consistently dropped in the course of the seventeenth and early eighteenth centuries. Between 1654 and 1660, 12 percent of students who received a bachelor's certificate in philosophy came from lands outside the Bohemian kingdom. By 1720 this number was under 5 percent. In the medical faculty, where traditionally there was a greater percentage of foreign students, the trend was equally pronounced. In the middle of the seventeenth century, they comprised close to 40 percent of the class. A century later, that percentage would be cut in half. While the enrollment of foreigners decreased, more Czechs were attending the university at home instead of

---

[67] Carl Barach, *Hieronymous Hirnhaim* (Vienna: Braumüller, 1864), p. 2.

[68] Jerzy Cygan, *Valerianus Magni (1586–1661): "Vita prima," operum recensio et bibliographia* (Rome: Institutum Historicum Capuccinum, 1989).

[69] Jiří Marek, "Jan Marcus a Londýnská Royal Society," *Sborník pro dějiny přírodních věd a techniky* 9 (1964), 81–2.

[70] See Pelcl's comments in *Abbildungen*, vol. I, p. 48.

studying abroad. These shifting patterns contributed in their own way to Bohemia's growing intellectual isolation.[71]

There were other factors that contributed to ideological climate change in the Czech lands. The brilliant culture of Rudolfine Prague was a product of imperial patronage. Rudolf's successors had different tastes and interests and moved their residence back to Vienna. Then there was the war. It is difficult to calculate the destruction, disruption and dislocation caused by the protracted conflict. The kingdom lost a substantial portion of its population while its capital city was invaded twice. Both of these forces helped initiate a process that eventually transformed Prague from an international center of culture to a more peripheral and provincial outpost. When Lady Mary Wortley Montagu passed through the city in 1716, she was disappointed with what she found, discovering only "remains of its former splendor."[72] At the same time there was an important shift occurring in the actual work of Bohemia's Catholic dissenters. The passion of Magni's energetic resistance to the Jesuits was never matched by an accommodating Marci or a more resigned Hirnhaim. Though *De typho* was an incisive critique of Bohemia's prevailing philosophical and theological culture, Hirnhaim did not propose a robust alternative. The pages of *De typho* are at times marked by a striking intellectual passivity. He pointed to the apostle Thomas as a spiritual ideal. Here was an individual who could believe without seeing. It is surely significant that while the Jesuit intellectual enterprise had lost some of its earlier vigor, Bohemia's most important dissenter in the last quarter of the seventeenth century argued that in matters of faith Christian believers should "swallow with simplicity" instead of "chewing with curiosity."[73]

CHALLENGES OF A NEW CENTURY

Hirnhaim's death in 1679 closes a distinct phase of intellectual life in the Czech lands, for after his passing the nature of dissent underwent an important change. From Magni to Marci, from Caramuel to Fallon, the Jesuits faced serious challenges within Bohemia to their philosophical and pedagogical program. Hirnhaim was their last major internal critic. The

---

[71] Kavka and Petráň, *Dějiny Univerzity Karlovy*, vol. II, pp. 244–5. The numbers of Bohemians receiving degrees in philosophy nearly tripled between 1654 and 1730. The process of intellectual marginalization that occurred in Bohemia during this period was accentuated by the general isolation of central Europe's universities in the seventeenth century. See R. J. W. Evans, "German universities after the Thirty Years War," *History of the Universities* 1 (1981), 169–90.

[72] Cited in René Wellek, "Bohemia in English literature," in his *Essays on Czech Literature* (The Hague: Mouton, 1963), p. 120.

[73] Hirnhaim, *De typho*, pp. 312, 314.

basic system that the Jesuits had established had prevailed and continued well into the eighteenth century without significant domestic resistance. Though ideological opposition did not cease in this period, it came from a different direction, from the outside. This shift began with the accession of Ferdinand III, who was not as accommodating to the Society as his father. At his insistence a new position of superintendent was created at the university. Answerable directly to the emperor, the superintendent could potentially undercut Jesuit authority. Nothing happened immediately. The Jesuits, in fact, were able to win even greater concessions from Ferdinand's successor, the pious Leopold I (1658–1705). It was during the reign of his iconoclastic son, Joseph I (1705–11), that they first encountered difficulties.

Like his future namesake, Joseph bore a measure of antipathy to the order. When a Jesuit once entered the Habsburg's bedroom disguised as a ghost in order to "advise" the young prince to dismiss his current religious instructor, a former Protestant, Joseph had the overzealous actor thrown out the window.[74] Towards the end of his short reign the emperor turned his attention to Prague and the university. In 1710 he commissioned Peter Theodor Birelli, the university's superintendent, to draw up a report assessing the strength of the institution. Birelli composed a stern and blunt memorandum that highlighted significant problems both with individual faculties and across the school as a whole. One of the greatest of these was holidays. With two months in the autumn, seventeen days at Christmas, eleven days during carnival, two weeks at Easter, a further sixteen days at Pentecost, forty during the summer, and the many saints' days scattered throughout the year, the school lacked a rigorous academic calendar that serious university work demanded.[75] More significantly, professors employed pedagogical techniques that were outmoded and ineffective. Following the traditional dictation method, instructors spent the hour reading verbatim to their students instead of commenting and discussing texts in a more critical fashion as law and medical professors did during their private lessons. Finally on a more general level, Birelli recommended a restructuring of university governance that allowed for greater participation. Here he specifically criticized the Jesuits who limited the number of candidates who could stand for university rector as well as restricting voter eligibility in the annual decanal elections.[76]

---

[74] Charles Ingrao, *The Habsburg Monarchy 1618–1815* (Cambridge: Cambridge University Press, 1994), pp. 112–13.
[75] Karel Kučera, "Raně osvícenský pokus o reformu pražské university," *AUC, HUCP* 4 (1963), 65–6.
[76] Ibid., 68.

The university superintendent also had strong words for the individual faculties. Despite Marci's leadership a generation earlier, the struggling medical faculty had never been able to secure itself on firm ground. Birelli criticized the lack of practical training and more cynically noted that students were so weak in botany, they prescribed medicines that could actually poison their patients.[77] Though the law faculty was ostensibly in better shape with healthier enrollments and a larger professorial staff, Birelli detected an intellectual torpor that was eroding its standing. Instructors showed little interest in the new approaches of legal reformers such as Arnold Vinnius, Johannes Voet and Hermann Conring.[78] The superintendent, however, reserved his most serious critique for the Jesuits. Their separatist agenda was undermining the institution as a whole. In the classroom they resorted to pedagogical methods that may have worked in the middle of the sixteenth century but were now decidedly stale and old-fashioned. The philosophy faculty wasted considerable time on useless material. A thorough training in medieval scholasticism had limited utility in a rapidly changing society. Why should students be forced to debate arcane philosophical questions when there were decidedly more pressing problems facing the kingdom? Instead, they should follow the model of the archiepiscopal seminary and devise a shortened two-year curriculum.[79] Theology, as well, needed substantial reform. To centralize the training of clergy, some type of union should be effected with the seminary. In both faculties less time should be spent on the speculative subjects while greater attention should be devoted to more practical courses such as geography, geometry and mathematics.

Though the emperor fully endorsed Birelli's report, not unexpectedly, it elicited a strong reaction from the Jesuits. In 1714 they submitted a formal response that defended their rights, traditions and practices with resolute defiance.[80] The text began with the proud observation that, for 158 years in Bohemia, the Society had followed a well-defined teaching program that had never been altered. The dictation method had proved its value over time and should not be discarded. The order unilaterally rejected the

---

[77] Ibid., 65.
[78] Ibid., 70–1. For a survey of legal pedagogy in this period see H. Coing, "Die juristische Fakultät und ihr Lehrprogramm," in H. Coing, ed., *Handbuch der Quellen und Literatur der neueren europäischen Privatrechtsgeschichte*, vol. I (Munich: Beck, 1973), pp. 3–102, and vol. II (Munich: Beck, 1977), pp. 39–128. Specifically on Prague see J. Klabouch, *Osvícenské právní nauky v českých zemích* (Prague: NČAV, 1958).
[79] Kučera, "Raně osvícenský pokus," 67.
[80] AUK, "Responsum academicum ad puncta ab inclyta Commissione Studiorum proposita, 2 December 1714," in *Acta et Conclusa Facultatis Philosophicae*, Tomus II, pp. 169–233.

proposals concerning university governance and the consolidation of theological faculties. They considered Birelli's curricular recommendations completely unacceptable. It was impossible to reduce the arts program to two years. The university was Bohemia's most important center of higher education, and to maintain its integrity the traditional curriculum must be preserved. The Jesuits were most concerned, however, with Birelli's apparent lack of understanding and appreciation of scholastic philosophy and theology. This was a discipline that had value for every educated Christian. Philosophy was the bulwark of the church, and if its study were weakened, religion itself was in jeopardy. Was this not evident in the medical faculty where the professors had foolishly accepted the work of Descartes with great enthusiasm?[81] Had they been firmly grounded philosophically, they would surely have realized that such tenets were incompatible with Catholic doctrine. Proper theological education was also essential, for the threat of heresy had not disappeared. Only a year earlier Clement XI had issued the bull *Unigenitus* that once more condemned the errors of Jansenism. The Jesuits contended that many in the schools harbored sympathies for this dangerous heresy. Those wavering souls could be brought back to the truth through careful training and instruction.[82]

The power struggle between the imperial party and the Jesuits ended anticlimactically. Birelli died the same year the Society issued its response, and a committee the emperor deputized to implement his proposals was slow to act. The committee's lack of initiative combined with staunch Jesuit resistance doomed all hopes of reform. On a broader level, the confrontation of Birelli and the Jesuits was a clash between a more modern cameralist mentality and a pedagogical philosophy that had not substantially changed since the sixteenth century and was still shaped by theological concerns of an earlier period. The long track record of dissent in Bohemia reinforced the Jesuit instinct to act as the kingdom's doctrinal watchdog, and the new Jansenist bogeyman was uncomfortably familiar to the Protestant heretic who had only been expelled a century earlier. Jansenist theologians contended that it was not Luther and Calvin but Catholic leaders at Trent who had erred on the contentious issue of justification by emphasizing human responsibility at the expense of divine initiative and grace. If ever there were a Trojan horse that held within its belly a terrible cargo of heresy, Jansenism was surely it. The Jesuits had first identified Jansenism as a threat in the middle of the seventeenth century. Though it may have been a latent influence on Hirnhaim, it emerged once more in the early eighteenth

---

[81] Ibid., p. 197.   [82] Ibid., pp. 188–203.

century, this time in a more mature form. By this period, Jansenism in central Europe was more than a mere doctrinal challenge to orthodox Catholicism. Across the region it had become an important tool for general reform against ultramontanism and baroque piety.[83] In Bohemia the Jansenist challenge came from one of the most remarkable personalities of this era, Count Franz Anton Sporck (1662–1738).

The son of a Westphalian noble, Sporck lived on a large estate in eastern Bohemia that his father had received for his service during the Thirty Years War.[84] Immensely wealthy, Sporck was a great patron of the arts. In Prague he constructed what became Bohemia's first opera house. On his country estate he built an elaborate spa complex around his chateau. As a young man, he had spent considerable time in France and returned to Bohemia a convinced Jansenist. In 1705 he established his own Port-Royal in northeast Bohemia. He founded a Celestine cloister where he installed his eldest daughter Marie Eleonore as abbess. There she translated important Jansenist texts that were published by her father. The printing press was at the center of Sporck's reform program. In an effort to dodge the censors he had played a clever shell game using presses in Prague, Nuremberg and other German cities on a rotating basis. But to avoid restrictions altogether, he set up a printing house on one of his smaller estates in 1709. An advocate of religious toleration and critic of Marian veneration, Sporck used the press aggressively to promote his agenda.[85]

It was only a matter of time before Sporck's activities provoked a response from the authorities. In 1711 functionaries from the archbishopric stepped in and forcibly shut his press. Two years later imperial officials swept down and leveled Sporck with a hefty fine for illicit publications that he continued to produce. While a more prudent individual may have modified his conduct after these relatively mild warnings, the spirited count continued on with his program undeterred. Sporck had friends in high places both in Prague and Vienna and may have thought he was immune from more serious reprisals, but the count had many enemies as well. The storm finally broke in summer 1729 when the Jesuits claimed that forbidden tracts and pamphlets were at the root of local peasant unrest. With orders from the

[83] Peter Hersche, *Der Spätjansenismus in Österreich* (Vienna: Verlag der österreichischen Akademie der Wissenschaften, 1977); T. C. W. Blanning, "The Enlightenment in Catholic Germany," in R. Porter and M. Teich, eds., *The Enlightenment in National Context* (Cambridge: Cambridge University Press, 1981), pp. 120–1.
[84] Pavel Preiss, *František Antonín Špork a barokní kultura v Čechách* (Prague: Paseka, 2003); Heinrich Benedikt, *Franz Anton Graf von Sporck (1662–1738): Zur Kultur der Barockzeit in Böhmen* (Vienna: Manz, 1923).
[85] Hersche, *Der Spätjansenismus*, pp. 45–6.

Bohemian Chancellery, fifty soldiers arrived on the night of 26 June and began removing books from his estate. In the end thousands of volumes were confiscated and turned over to the Jesuit vicar-general of the Hradec Králové diocese. The vicar-general had long been concerned by Sporck's activities. Now as the dragnet was finally closing, he prepared a detailed report enumerating the specific theological errors of the count's books. At the same time in Prague, church officials moved in on Sporck's palace, ransacked his library and confiscated all volumes that lacked the proper ecclesiastical imprimatur. Heresy proceedings were also begun against him. Threatened with loss of title and lands, not to mention life imprisonment and a monumental fine of 100,000 florins, the chastened Sporck proved himself as great a penitent as he had been rebel. Yielding to the mercy of the court, he was spared the worst of these punishments as his crime was commuted from heresy to the publication of heretical books. Now passive and pliant, he made peace with the Jesuits who continued to keep a watchful eye on him. In 1735 they led a summer mission on his estates where the count was reportedly foremost among the faithful. Three years later he died with a Jesuit hearing his final confession.

The story of the Birelli proposals and the fate of Count Sporck are important measures of intellectual climate change in early eighteenth-century Bohemia. In both cases the impetus for reform came from the outside, Birelli as the independent superintendent of the university and Sporck as the avid importer of French Jansenism. Both of these challenges were ultimately overcome as the Jesuits continued to dominate the intellectual life of the kingdom. Admittedly, there were divisions within the order. The Society was not monolithic. The prolific Bohuslav Balbín was regarded with suspicion from some quarters. The mathematician Caspar Knittel favored a Platonic system of thought, and Josef Stepling (1716–78), though slightly beyond our period, was a leader in the scientific community. As an institution, however, the Jesuits were wary of innovation, for they remained faithful to their original mission, the restoration of Catholic orthodoxy. In this task they were largely successful. A century after White Mountain, the legacy of Hus had at long last been mastered. Though there may have been small pockets of crypto-Protestants in the countryside, theological dissent, so characteristic of this region since the fifteenth century, had been replaced by a new spirit of confessional uniformity.

CHAPTER 4

Finding a holy past: antiquarianism and Catholic revival

Those who have studied Bohemia's Counter-Reformation have traditionally drawn attention to those vivid moments of crisis and conflict. They
have pointed to the protracted political crisis that culminated with the 1618
uprising literally launched by the defenestration of Slavata and Martinic.
They have examined the military confrontation that reached its fateful
denouement a cool November day at White Mountain. They have considered the draconian policies of expulsion and confiscation that followed the
Catholic victory. The great drama of these events, however, has overshadowed another struggle that was occurring at the same time, a battle for an
imagined Bohemia. Based not on force but persuasion, this conflict was
fought with ink instead of gunpowder, with metaphor instead of musket.
This was a contest for Bohemia's identity and in some respects was even
more significant than the 1620 confrontation outside Prague. Though force
could rid the kingdom of its heretics, tactics of violence and coercion had
their limitations and were not likely to create lasting bonds of confessional
loyalty. In contrast, this campaign for an imagined Bohemia was aimed at
hearts and minds and was more constructive in nature. The contest for the
kingdom's past helped chart its future course, for at its most basic level this
was a struggle about memory. How would the region be remembered – an
early outpost of Protestantism cruelly repressed or home of a persecuted but
ultimately triumphant Catholic community?[1]

After White Mountain and the decrees of expulsion, Bohemia's exiles
found safe haven in Poland, Saxony, the Low Countries and England.
During the war their thoughts remained focused on their homeland, for it
seemed quite possible that Protestant victories could secure their return.

---

[1] For an overview of historical literature of this period see František Kutnar and Jaroslav Marek,
Přehledné dějiny českého a slovenského dějepisectví (Prague: Nakladatelství Lidové noviny, 1997),
pp. 91–133; a fuller but more literary evaluation of this period is offered in Jaroslav Vlček, *Dějiny
české literatury*, 2 vols. (Prague: Československý Spisovatel, 1951).

Lutheran Saxons occupied Prague in 1631, and the early victories of the Swedes renewed hope that their displacement was only temporary. This optimism slowly faded as the war drew to a close, and it became evident that despite Habsburg setbacks, Czech Protestants would not be represented at the peace conferences. Exile would be prolonged indefinitely. In part as a political response, in part as an attempt to recapture the memories of a lost world, leading members of this community recreated the contours of their homeland through histories, martyrologies and memoirs. The historian Pavel Stránský recalled the freedoms granted the Bohemian kingdom during the reign of Emperor Charles IV. John Amos Comenius, the last bishop of the Czech branch of the *Unitas Fratrum*, helped compile a church history that related the sufferings of Bohemia's faithful Christians from the time of Cyril and Methodius to the new era of persecution under the Habsburgs. The doctor Ondřej Habervešl, an eyewitness to White Mountain, recorded the political narrative during the last days of an "independent kingdom" while the Utraquist priest, Jan Rosacius, memorialized the infamous 1621 execution.[2]

Back within Bohemia a very different vision of the region's past was emerging. Celebrating the kingdom's rich ecclesiastical heritage, a dedicated cohort of antiquarian scholars was producing a formidable corpus of research. This work had actually begun in the late sixteenth century. Through his writings Jiří Barthold Pontanus of Breitenberg (†1616), a dean at the cathedral, helped revitalize the cults of early Czech saints who had long been neglected. After White Mountain a larger and more organized group of learned clerics followed Pontanus's lead busily exploring local archives, private manuscript collections and monastic libraries in an effort to celebrate the glories of a *Bohemia sacra*. Bohuslav Balbín, the most assiduous of these antiquarians, produced over thirty texts ranging from a biography of Prague's first archbishop to a spirited defense of the Czech language.[3] His colleague and collaborator, Tomáš Pešina, focused his efforts primarily on Moravia's sacred and secular past while the Tanner brothers, Jan and Matthias, sought to recover the memory of Bohemia's many martyrs and

---

[2] Pavel Stránský, *Respublica Bohemiae* (Leiden: Elzevir, 1634), 190ff.; John Amos Comenius and Adam Hartmann, *Synopsis historica persecutionum ecclesiae Bohemicae* (Leiden: Apud Davidem Lopes de Haro, 1647); Ondřej Habervešl of Habernfeld, *Bellum Bohemicum* (Leiden, 1645); Jan Rosacius, *Koruna neuvadlá mučedlníkův božích českých* (n.p., 1621).

[3] Carlos Sommervogel, ed., *Bibliothèque de la Compagnie de Jésus* (Brussels: Oscar Schepens, 1890), vol. I, pp. 792–808. The contemporary term in English was "antiquary." I will be using the modern equivalent, antiquarian, in my description of these scholars.

missionaries.[4] In this golden age of ecclesiastical antiquarianism, forgotten pilgrimage shrines, neglected monasteries and ruined churches all found their eager chronicler.

These competing visions of imagined Bohemias were essential to the broader formation of group identities in the troubled years of the seventeenth century. Exiles and Catholics frequently formulated their respective histories with apocalyptic urgency and recourse to divine assistance. An anonymous Moravian historian chronicling the sufferings of his home region included an account of a vision from the winter of 1627. The townspeople of Olomouc awoke early on Christmas morning to see a dramatic struggle playing out above them in the heavens. A soldier armed with a sword menacingly approached a second man who was holding a chalice. Intent on destroying this most important symbol of Utraquist identity, the swordsman despite his every effort could not harm or even touch the cup, a clear sign that despite their present sufferings the godly would ultimately prevail. In like manner, John Amos Comenius included in his writings dire predictions concerning the ultimate collapse of the Habsburg regime. On the Catholic side there were similar stories of divine intervention. The Virgin provided help at White Mountain. St. John Nepomuk drove off those who sought to desecrate his tomb. Lightning struck scoffing Protestants, and miraculous images thwarted looting soldiers.[5]

What was occurring in the Bohemian kingdom was part of a broader phenomenon. The sixteenth-century Reformations had a dramatic impact on the writing of history.[6] Reformers such as Philip Melanchthon saw history as a powerful weapon in their campaign to restore the church to its original vigor and purity. Melanchthon helped Johannes Carion publish his world history from a Lutheran perspective in 1532 while a number of

[4] Tomáš Pešina, *Prodromus Moravographiae* (Litomyšl: J. Arnolt, 1663); Tomáš Pešina, *Phosphorus septicornis, stella aliàs matutina* (Prague: Joannis Arnolti de Dobroslavina, 1673); Matthias Tanner, *Societas Jesu usque ad sanguinis et vitæ profusionem militans* (Prague: Typis Universitatis Carolo-Ferdinandeae, 1675); Jan Tanner, *Muž apoštolský aneb život a ctnosti ctihodného pátera Albrechta Chanovského* (Prague: Typis Universitatis Carolo-Ferdinandeae, 1680).

[5] Josef Polišenský, ed., *Kniha o bolesti a smutku: výbor z moravských kronik XVII. století* (Prague: Nakladatelství Elk, 1948), p. 106; John Amos Comenius et al., *Lux e tenebris* (Amsterdam, 1665); Vincenc Kramář, *Zpustošení Chrámu svatého Víta* (Prague: Artefactum, 1998); Olivier Chaline, *La Bataille de la Montagne Blanche* (Paris: Éditions Noesis, 1999).

[6] P. Polman, *L'élément historique dans la controverse religieuse du XVIe siècle* (Gembloux: J. Duculot, 1932); Peter Meinhold, *Geschichte der kirchlichen Historiographie*, 2 vols. (Freiburg i.B.: Alber, 1967); Bruce Gordon, ed., *Protestant Identity and History in Sixteenth-Century Europe* (Brookfield: Ashgate, 1996); Irena Backus, *Historical Method and Confessional Identity in the Era of the Reformation (1378–1615)* (Leiden: Brill, 2003).

years later Flacius Illyricus headed a team of scholars who investigated the doctrinal corruption of the church through the *Magdeburg Centuries*. On the local level, wherever evangelical teaching was accepted, history had the power to mold and shape communal memories and create a past that could legitimize new confessional identities. Protestant historians were remarkably imaginative scholars. In Scotland George Buchanan reworked old humanist histories to convince his countrymen that they had always been Presbyterians. In his struggle against the papacy Luther was quick to appropriate late medieval heretics such as Hus and Savonarola while Protestant martyrologists ranged far and wide in their hunt for early witnesses of the evangelical message.[7] Less attention has been given to Catholics and their search for a usable past, but their use of sources was no less creative. In Italy a figure such as Pietro Maria Campi (1569–1649) churned out material vindicating local ecclesiastical traditions. In southern Germany Matthäus Rader's *Bavaria sancta et pia* replaced the *Bavarian Chronicle* of Johannes Aventinus, a much praised humanist history of the duchy which eventually ended up on the Index.[8] In the religiously divided lands of central Europe the writing of history was thus critical in the formation and maintenance of confessional identities. Calvinists and Catholics, Anabaptists and Utraquists, understood the power of the past and used it to help shape the character of their respective religious communities.

In Bohemia the writing of history had long been subjected to confessional standards. The Hussite drama had its partisan chroniclers from the very beginning, none more important than Petr of Mladoňovice, a former student of Hus who had witnessed his mentor's trial and subsequent execution in Constance. His account of these events, written in the form of a passion narrative, was even informally incorporated into the liturgy of the Utraquist church. At the annual 6 July feast to commemorate Hus's martyrdom, the Czech faithful heard a reading of the final chapter of this history after the Gospel lesson. In the sixteenth century Bohuslav Bílejovský continued this tradition through his *Bohemian Chronicle* (1537). He carefully sifted the past to find precedents supporting both the liturgical use of

---

[7] Roger Mason, "Usable pasts: history and identity in Reformation Scotland," *Scottish Historical Review* 76 (1997), 54–68.

[8] Though anticlerical in the traditional humanist spirit, Aventinus never left the Catholic church. For a fuller description of his confessional sympathies see Gerald Strauss, *Historian in an Age of Crisis* (Cambridge, MA: Harvard University Press, 1963), pp. 196–204. Alois Schmid presents an overview of history writing at the Wittelsbach court in his "Geschichtsschreibung am Hofe Kurfürst Maximilians I. von Bayern," in Hubert Glaser, ed., *Um Glauben und Reich Kurfürst Maximilian I* (Munich: Hirmer Verlag, 1980), pp. 330–40.

Czech and the distribution of the Eucharist *sub utraque*, a practice he claimed the church had consistently followed until the thirteenth century.[9] On the Catholic side there was the phenomenally successful *Czech Chronicle* (1541) of Václav Hájek. Completed with Habsburg support, the popular text reflected Hájek's conservative Catholic sensibilities. Even smaller groups such as the *Unitas Fratrum* had their own historians. Up to White Mountain, then, the writing of history in the Czech lands was with a few exceptions part of a broader confessional struggle.

The 1620 confrontation between the emperor and the Czech estates dramatically changed this intellectual landscape. On the political and military level the long confessional conflict was over. Culturally, the situation was less clear. Though Bohemia's Catholic elites now had a clear playing field, they stared out over two centuries of contentious debates and unresolved disputes concerning their kingdom's religious past. A daunting and challenging task lay before them. In the years ahead they confronted their history and from this troubled heritage constructed a coherent Catholic identity for the divided region. Their version of the past, though, did not go unchallenged. The exiles were busy writing their own histories of the region, and it is to them that we will turn first.

MEMORIES OF THE EXILES

The most important text that came out of this community was Pavel Stránský's *Respublica Bohemiae* (1634). It quickly ran through three editions and was republished multiple times in the eighteenth century as well.[10] Stránský was educated in the Prague of Rudolf II. When he finished his studies, he moved to the hills of northern Bohemia where he became a school teacher in the picturesque town of Litoměřice on the banks of the Elbe. Though he was involved in local politics as a town councilman, he was not an active participant in the estates' revolt. Nonetheless, he was a supporter of King Frederick, and due to his religious beliefs he was forced into exile in 1627.[11] Stránský's *Respublica Bohemiae* was published with the

---

[9] Matthew Spinka, ed. and trans., *John Hus at the Council of Constance* (New York: Columbia University Press, 1965), p. 80; Zdeněk David, *Finding the Middle Way* (Baltimore: Johns Hopkins University Press, 2003), esp. pp. 80–110.

[10] Stránský, *Respublica Bohemiae* (Leiden: Elzevir, 1634, 1643, 1648); (Amsterdam: Rüdiger, 1713); (Prague: Calve, 1790); (Prague: Calve, 1792–1803).

[11] For a biographical sketch see Bohumil Ryba's epilogue in Pavel Stránský ze Zápské Stránky, *Český stát/ Okřik* (Prague: Státní nakladatelství krásné literatury, hudby a umění, 1953), pp. 426–40.

Elzevir house in Leiden. It was part of a broader series the Elzevirs were producing on European "republics" which included studies of France, Poland, Hungary, the Hanseatic cities and Venice. Written in part as a response to the contentions of Melchior Goldast and other German publicists who defended the Habsburgs' hereditary claims to the Czech lands, the *Respublica* was a spirited defense of the laws and traditions of the "Bohemian republic." Though the history ranged from a description of the region's customs to an examination of its coinage, at the heart of the text were its legal arguments. The Bohemian state, according to Stránský, rested on a firm foundation of law. Municipal assemblies, independent courts and local magistrates had from time immemorial stood at the center of civic life. They guaranteed the kingdom's traditional rights and privileges. The capstone of all Czech freedoms was the elective monarchy. Tracing this institution back to the mythical Czech past, Stránský claimed that it was the legendary Krok who began this practice which in time became the central feature of the Bohemian constitution. All of Bohemia's kings, the Přemyslids, the Luxembourgs, the Jagiellonians, honored and safeguarded this ancient Bohemian tradition. It was only the reckless Habsburgs who dared overturn this fundamental right of Czech society.[12]

Stránský's argument was repeated by others in the exile community. Most similar in sentiment was the work of Ondřej Habervešl of Habernfeld, whose *Bellum Bohemicum* appeared in 1645. Habervešl came from a distinguished Prague family and was a member of the Bohemian Brethren. He trained as a doctor but later served as an officer in the army of the Winter King. He was present at White Mountain and reflected on this experience in his account of the war. Although Habervešl's text was essentially a narrative of the Czech uprising, its underlying theme was the immoral and unlawful suppression of Czech liberties. Habervešl published the *Bellum Bohemicum* in Leiden with the hope that it would influence the peace negotiations that were then underway. It may have been for that reason that his criticism of the Habsburgs was somewhat muted. Instead he singled out the Jesuits as the primary villain of the drama. Working behind the scenes, they had been able to manipulate the Habsburgs to crush Bohemia's freedoms and subjugate its people. Significantly, he concluded

---

[12] Stránský, *Respublica Bohemiae*, p. 203; Vladimír Urbánek, "The idea of state and nation in the writings of Bohemian exiles after 1620," in Linas Eriksonas and Leos Müller, eds., *Statehood Before and Beyond Ethnicity* (Brussels: Peter Lang, 2005), pp. 67–83; Eduard Maur, "Pojetí národa v díle českých pobělohorských exulantů," in M. Hrubá, ed., *Víra nebo vlast?* (Ústí nad Labem: Albis, 2001), pp. 174–83.

his treatise with a series of charters and letters that documented the imperial privileges the kingdom had enjoyed since the thirteenth century.[13]

The exiles also wrote texts that focused more closely on the religious dimension of the struggle and its tragic aftermath. The first of these tracts was Jan Rosacius's *The Unfading Crown of the Godly Czech Martyrs*. Rosacius was an Utraquist priest of St. Nicholas Church in the Lesser Town and author of several popular devotional texts for the sick and dying. His reputation prompted a visit from imperial officials in June 1621. He was asked to minister to the twenty-seven rebels who had been condemned for their involvement in the uprising. He consoled them in prison and was even allowed to accompany them onto the scaffold itself. From this experience he composed his martyrology. *The Unfading Crown* recalled the prisoners' final hours as the priest highlighted the simple piety of these brave Christians who died for their faith and fatherland. Rosacius's account of the execution became one of the standard sources of this event for the exiles and was regularly reprinted up through the early twentieth century.[14] Outside the Czech community it was the *Unitas Fratrum* who took the lead in publicizing Bohemia's confessional catastrophe. John Amos Comenius and Adam Hartmann collected material for the *Historia persecutionum ecclesiae Bohemicae* (1648). Though the text begins with the conversion of the Bohemian kingdom in 894, its primary focus is the sufferings of Czech evangelicals at the hands of the Habsburgs and Jesuits. Aimed at a broad Protestant audience, this volume was originally intended to be part of a new edition of Foxe's *Acts and Monuments*.[15]

A final and arguably the most remarkable text produced by the exile community was the mammoth *Church History* of Pavel Skála of Zhoř. After a brief period of study at the Charles University, Skála left his native Prague for Wittenberg where he studied with a circle of humanists who endeavored to preserve Melanchthon's irenic legacy in an increasingly confessionalized atmosphere. Skála's history reflected this spirit. The title of the manuscript

---

[13] Ondřej Habervešl of Habernfeld, *O vojně české od roku 1617*, trans. E. Tonner (Prague: E. Grégr, 1867), pp. 49–89; Josef Polišenský, ed., *Historie o válce české 1618–1620. Výbor z historického spisování Ondřeje z Habernfeldu a Pavla Skály ze Zhoře* (Prague: Státní nakladatelství krásné literatury a umění, 1964).

[14] Jan Rosacius, *Koruna neuvadlá mučedlníkův božích českých* (Prague: Šolc, 1913).

[15] There were two related Latin editions of this text. *Historia persecutionum* is actually an expanded edition of the 1647 *Synopsis historica persecutionum ecclesiae Bohemicae*. A Czech version, *Historia o těžkých protivenstvích*, was published in Leszno in 1655. For a modern edition of both the Latin and Czech text see vol. IX, part 1 of the series *Johannis Amos Comenii Opera Omnia* (Prague: Academia, 1989). On Comenius as historian see Josef Polišenský, "Komenský a české dějepisectví bělohorského období," *Acta Comeniana* 22 (1963), 61–83.

is in some respects a misnomer, for though Skála certainly traced the
development of Bohemia's various confessional communities, the final
four volumes of this project were in essence a political history of the
Bohemian revolt. They are without doubt the most valuable source of the
uprising, unmatched in detail and style. Though it remained in manuscript
form until the nineteenth century, most scholars consider the *Church
History* one of the great masterpieces of early modern Czech literature.[16]
Before White Mountain, Skála worked in Frederick's chancellery and drew
from that experience in his narration of the revolt. What he described was
objective in tone, at points even sympathetic to the Habsburgs. In a detailed
narrative of White Mountain he used over a dozen sources and cited seven
lengthy accounts of the battle.[17] In similar fashion he recounted the 1621
executions from the perspective of the estates and the Habsburgs.
Charitable to individuals on both sides of the conflict, Skála avoided strong
religious rhetoric in his search for the broad and underlining causes of the
disaster that had overtaken Bohemia in the seventeenth century.

These texts of Stránský and Skála, of Habervešl, Rosacius and Hartmann,
are the most important histories produced by the exile community. But
what do they tell us collectively concerning the broader process of identity
formation in the Czech lands after White Mountain? Most obviously, the
texts are linked by the experience of exile. The trauma of displacement
frequently radicalized religious communities. The growing militancy of the
Calvinist movement, for example, has been at least in part attributed to this
phenomenon.[18] For Bohemia's emigrés, their bitter experience is reflected
in the histories by a tangible sense of loss. There are almost wistful passages
in Skála and Stránský, a longing for a world that has passed and will most
likely never be regained. Stránský reflected back on the age of Rudolf II
when the customary freedoms of the kingdom were still preserved while
Skála quietly lamented the changes instituted after 1620 that transformed
Czech society and culture. But there was also a more militant aspect to this
sense of loss. Ondřej Habervešl began his text with the clarion call, "Wake
up! Wake up! Wake up, you apathetic Bohemians! Do you not see the
sword that is taking your freedoms away?"[19] Frederick's former officer
shared the Winter King's exile in the Low Countries and wrote the

---

[16] Pavel Skála ze Zhoře, *Historie česká*, ed. Karel Tieftrunk, 5 vols. (Prague: I. L. Kober, 1865–70); for a
modern abridgement with an assessment of Skála's career see Pavel Skála ze Zhoře, *Historie česká: od
defenestrace k Bílé hoře*, ed. Josef Janáček (Prague: Svoboda, 1984).
[17] Skála, *Historie česká*, vol. III, pp. 90–2; vol. IV, pp. 337–88.
[18] Ole Peter Grell, ed., *Calvinist Exiles in Tudor and Stuart England* (Brookfield: Ashgate, 1996).
[19] Habervešl, *O vojně české*, p. 7.

Bellum Bohemicum to refute the claims of the imperial legation negotiating at Westphalia.[20] John Amos Comenius, too, was active diplomatically as he energetically lobbied Oxenstierna and the Swedes on behalf of his church. This was polemical literature written to achieve a specific end. Skála's history was in some sense the exception, and it is not coincidental that it remained in manuscript form until the nineteenth century.

The exile experience shaped these histories in other ways as well. The stunning collapse of the Winter King's regime, the swift retaliatory Catholic reaction, the forced emigration, and the long-term distress of displacement had a profound psychological effect on these writers. In an effort to understand the great tragedy that had overtaken them so suddenly, they focused on contemporary events most relevant to understanding their present situation. After a brief nod to the past, Habervešl centered his text on the crisis that led up to White Mountain. Rosacius's *Unfading Crown* was a memorial to the fallen heroes of the Bohemian uprising. Comenius and Hartmann quickly ran through the pre-Hussite period to investigate more modern developments. Of the text's 107 chapters, 78 are concerned with the religious situation under the Habsburgs. Skála in telescopic fashion progressively narrowed the focus of his *Church History*. While the first two volumes of the ten-volume work chronicled nearly a millennium of the Czech past, the final four covered only the first decades of the seventeenth century. This close attention to the present, so characteristic of these writers, offers an important point of contrast to the kingdom's Catholic antiquarians who frequently dismissed the recent past for what would appear to the exiles as the distant mists of antiquity.

The exile texts also follow a broader pattern of Protestant polemics characteristic of the period. The *Magdeburg Centuries* are generally considered the watershed text of Protestant ecclesiastical historiography. With this work Flacius and his colleagues initiated an important shift in methodology. Breaking with a tradition that could be traced back to Eusebius, Flacius focused on doctrine rather than events or personalities as the main theme of his narrative.[21] This was a historical tradition that critically dissected the

---

[20] Ibid., pp. 121–37. Habervešl is a particularly intriguing figure as he was involved in the broader European struggle between Catholic and Protestant towards the end of the Thirty Years War. See for example the short tract, *Rome's master-peece. Or, the grand conspiracy of the Pope and his Iesuited instruments, to extirpate the Protestant religion, re-establish popery, subvert lawes, liberties, peace, parliaments, by kindling a civill war in Scotland, and all his Majesties realmes, and to poyson the King himselfe in case he comply not with them in these their execrable designes* (London: Michael Sparke, 1643).

[21] John Headley, *Luther's View of Church History* (New Haven: Yale University Press, 1963), 270; Ronald Diener, "The Magdeburg Centuries: a bibliothecal and historiographical study," unpublished Ph.D. thesis, Harvard Divinity School (1979); Gregory Lyon, "Baudouin, Flacius, and the plan for the Magdeburg Centuries," *Journal of the History of Ideas* 64 (2003), 253–72.

past. In the case of the *Magdeburg Centuries*, Flacius directed his gaze on the doctrinal deviations of the Roman church. It was also a tradition that placed less emphasis on social and cultural developments. Johannes Sleidanus devoted little attention to these themes in his *Commentaries*, the most famous contemporary narrative of the Lutheran Reformation.[22] Both of these characteristics are typical of the exile histories. Comenius, Hartmann and Rosacius used their texts to critique Catholic theology. The fifth chapter of the *Historia persecutionum* presents a sampling of the doctrinal errors of the Roman church in the years before Hus. The reformer, of course, helps restore true worship and pure teaching but is condemned and ultimately destroyed for his efforts. Rosacius's martyrological account, though more narrow in scope, also features the confrontation between truth and error. In significant detail he described how one of the condemned, a senior lay leader of the Bohemian Brethren, spent his last hours refuting a Jesuit interlocutor in an impromptu theological debate.[23]

Though Stránský and Habervešl did not focus on doctrinal history, their approach was similar. Their critical eye was focused not on theology but law. They developed constitutional and legal arguments to support the now abrogated freedoms of the Czech estates. Habervešl pointed to a variety of documents that guaranteed Bohemia's sovereign rights beginning with the Golden Bull of Frederick II (1212). Stránský's work was significantly more sophisticated. As mentioned earlier, his text was part of a multi-volume series sponsored by the Elzevir press on various early modern states ranging from England to China. There was an underlying political agenda to the project as a whole. In the main, these were texts written by historians intent on probing the ancient and medieval past to uncover the origins of modern political liberties, a search for "ancient constitutions" to legitimize more republican forms of government.[24] Ubbo Emmius, the author of *Graecorum respublicae* (1632), was a friend of Althusius and a significant figure in the Dutch revolt. Johannes Angelius Werdenhagen was a German Lutheran whose analysis of the Hansa cities was intended as a political model for the Dutch provinces. Piet van der Cun was a colleague of Hugo Grotius. His

[22] A. G. Dickens, "Johannes Sleidan and Reformation history," in R. B. Knox, ed., *Reformation, Conformity and Dissent* (London: Epworth Press, 1977), p. 41.

[23] Comenius, *Historia persecutionum*, pp. 208–10; Rosacius, *Koruna neuvadlá*, pp. 33–5.

[24] J. G. A. Pocock, *The Ancient Constitution and Feudal Law* (New York: Cambridge University Press, 1987); Peter Miller, *Peiresc's Europe* (New Haven: Yale University Press, 2000), pp. 76–101; Vittorio Conti, "*Consociatio civitatum*. L'idea di repubblica nelle *respublicae* Elzeviriane," in Chiara Continisio and Cesare Mozzarelli, eds., *Repubblica e virtù* (Rome: Bulzoni, 1995), pp. 207–26; Georg Frick, "Die Elzevir'schen Republiken," *Hallesche Abhandlungen zur neueren Geschichte* 30 (1892), 1–35.

examination of the ancient "Republic of the Hebrews" has been described by Richard Tuck as "one of the most remarkable pieces of political theory to come out of the early seventeenth-century United Provinces."[25] Stránský's volume fell very much in line with these other works. Though the text was intended as a general overview of the kingdom's past, Stránský laid particular emphasis on Bohemia's constitutional history as he emphasized the elective nature of the crown and the critical function of the estates within the kingdom. His republican arguments in fact bore distinct parallels to those of François Hotman.[26]

This polemical cast the exiles gave their histories speaks directly to the issue of identity formation. In most general terms, the exiles were not trying so much to reconstruct the past as they were attempting to deconstruct the present. Stránský and Habervešl challenged the constitutionality of Habsburg innovations while Comenius and Rosacius highlighted the doctrinal failings of the new regime. The emphasis of their texts was on the recent past. Events before the Habsburgs, much less before Hus, were generally not of great concern for them. Questions concerning the origins of the Czech people were of value to them only inasmuch as they provided support for their more general political or theological agenda. Comenius and Hartmann skimmed over the early history of the Czech church, paying scant attention to those many saints and martyrs who figured heavily in the Catholic revival of the seventeenth and eighteenth centuries. Stránský gave the briefest of descriptions to Wenceslas, the kingdom's patron saint. Concerning his place in contemporary Bohemian society, he curtly remarked, "He is considered by our people today in the number of the sacred martyrs." Somewhat surprisingly, even Hus received relatively little attention.[27]

What these authors did present contrasted sharply with that of their Catholic counterparts. With Skála we see the end of a vibrant culture, a society that is entering the gloom and darkness of a long winter. What optimism there may have been in the early volumes of his history is absent in the final section of the text that chronicles the changes instituted by the Habsburgs and their proxies after White Mountain. Apart from the stern laws imposed by the imperial victors, the Bohemians must also deal with

[25] Cited in Conti, "*Consociatio civitatum*," p. 224.
[26] Urbánek, "The idea of state," pp. 71–3; see the parallels of Stránský's project with those of the English antiquarians in Colin Kidd, "Whose ancient constitution? Ethnicity and the English past, 1600–1800," in Kidd, *British Identities before Nationalism* (Cambridge: Cambridge University Press, 1999), pp. 75–98.
[27] Stránský, *Respublica Bohemiae*, pp. 169–71, 259–63, 321.

rampant inflation, conditions of famine, an unsupervised army systematically looting the countryside and the direct impact of war itself.[28] The normally stoic Skála now more frequently injects his own voice into the narrative. He concluded his account of the expulsion of Moravian Protestants with the lament, "It would fill the Christian heart with sorrow and pity to look at this grief-stricken people, especially the women and small children, who left their homeland with bitter tears and mourning."[29] Nothing, he seems to be saying, is sacred in this society. Perhaps for metaphorical flourish, one of the last events he described in the entire history is a series of church robberies emptying Prague of its ecclesiastical treasures.[30]

If with Skála the dominant image is of a society in twilight, the emphasis is slightly different with Stránský and Comenius. *Respublica Bohemiae* emphasizes the distinctive nature of Czech society, most specifically its constitutional and legal traditions. Here the issue of plurality comes to the fore. What separates Bohemia from the German lands in Stránský's mind are the broad privileges that have been granted to the Czech estates over generations. This is a society, he claims, that is composed of many communities. He makes the same argument when examining religion. Dissent for Stránský was a traditional feature of Czech culture and distinguished it from individual German states. In an effort to defend the religious freedoms that had been recently revoked by the Habsburgs, he contended that the Christian community in Bohemia had always been divided. Initially, there had been competition between the Greek and Roman rites. Later, as the Orthodox community dwindled in numbers, Waldensian missionaries found eager converts. Then came Hus and the many splinter groups of his movement, and finally the Reformation of the sixteenth century added further diversity to the already complex religious mosaic of the Bohemian lands.[31] In similar fashion, the *Historia persecutionum* is a story of dissent. From traditional Utraquists to radical Taborites, Hartmann and Comenius carefully considered the full range of religious expression in their homeland. What is significant for these authors, then, is that Czech identity could not be reduced to a single and uniform set of cultural characteristics. Their society, instead, was marked by division and diversity. This was a region of multiple identities constantly shifting and sliding in the vast kaleidoscope of central Europe.

---

[28] Skála, *Historie česká*, vol. 5, esp. pp. 267–315. [29] Skála, *Historie česká*, vol. 5, p. 269.
[30] Skála, *Historie česká*, vol. 5, p. 315. [31] Stránský, *Respublica Bohemiae*, pp. 249–96.

CREATING A CATHOLIC PAST

While Stránský and Comenius highlighted the pluralistic nature of Bohemian society in their arguments for political and religious freedoms, the kingdom's Catholic antiquarians viewed this situation from a decidedly different vantage point. The variations in creed and custom the exiles pointed to as a broader pattern of the Czech past were for them serious aberrations that had plunged the region into crisis. Unlike the exiles, however, who viewed 1620 as the great break in the continuum of Czech history, the antiquarians saw the troubles beginning two centuries earlier. They frequently cited a famous passage from Aeneas Silvius Piccolomini's *Historia Bohemica* (1458) where the future Pope Pius II praised the kingdom's flourishing ecclesiastical culture that had existed before Hus:

I believe that there was no kingdom at this time in all of Europe that had as many magnificent and beautiful churches as Bohemia. There were churches soaring into the heavens of remarkable length and breadth capped by massive stone vaulting. There were altars covered with gold and silver that housed the relics of saints. There were ecclesiastical vestments interwoven with pearls and richly adorned with jewelry. There were valuable liturgical vessels. High above light flowed into these buildings through windows of exquisitely cut glass. One could find these types of churches not only in the larger and smaller cities but also in the villages.[32]

For these seventeenth-century antiquarians, it was not only the region's churches, monasteries and cloisters that were being ravaged by the Hussites. Bohemia's identity as a Christian kingdom was itself in serious jeopardy. By the beginning of the sixteenth century, the Czech lands had developed a well-known reputation as a homeland of heresy. At Leipzig Eck had used the epithet "Hussite" to attack Luther while in more popular circles similar stereotypes were very much in force. A proverb that widely circulated at the time proudly proclaimed that Germany was admirably self-sufficient as Swabia provided her prostitutes, Franconia her thieves, Frisia her perjurers, Saxony her drunkards, and *Bohemia her heretics.*[33]

Heresy, however, was not the only concern of the Czech antiquarians. The events of 1620 had brought other problems to the fore as well. Issues of identity had never been clearly delineated in the Bohemian kingdom. This was a region after all where ethnicities, religions and languages frequently

---

[32] Aeneas Silvius Piccolomini, *Historia Bohemica*, ed. Joseph Hejnic and Hans Rothe (Cologne: Böhlau, 2005), vol. I, p. 255.
[33] Cited in Gerald Strauss, *Sixteenth-Century Germany: Its Topography and Topographers* (Madison: University of Wisconsin Press, 1959), p. 11. Italics are my own.

mixed. But in the minds of many of these individuals what traditions and sense of identity this area did share were threatened in the aftermath of White Mountain. Ironically, some of these dangers were posed by the nominal allies of Czech Catholics – the Habsburg dynasty and the Roman church. There were fears that an over-dominant Habsburg presence could reshape Bohemian culture and society in a peculiarly Austrian fashion. In like manner, there was an apprehension that the new direction of the church taken at Trent to make the rites and practices of the faith more uniform could possibly destroy the distinctive character of Czech Catholicism. In many respects, then, White Mountain was the culmination of a great identity crisis that confronted the region. As the Catholic antiquarians faced the challenges of a heretical past, a Habsburg present and a possible Tridentine future, the task of defining the kingdom's identity was of primary concern for these individuals. The solutions they found were remarkably inventive and indicative of a more general strategy Czech Catholics adopted to reclaim their lands from more than two centuries of religious division and cultural confusion.

Memory was the key issue for the antiquarians, and in this context the observations of John Pocock are particularly relevant. Pocock once noted, "If a traditional relationship with the past has been ruptured, the first instinct of society's intellectuals may be to restore it … by reshaping myth, by historisation or by the construction of a new image of the past in terms of some new continuity of which society has become aware in the present."[34] In Bohemia there was a concerted effort on the part of Catholic elites to bridge the discontinuity of the fifteenth and sixteenth centuries and remember a world that had existed before Hus. What the antiquarians were doing in the Czech lands was mirrored across the Catholic world, for memory played a key role in the church's revival. Seventeenth-century Catholicism was in many respects a memorial culture. Cardinal Borromeo, the reforming archbishop of Milan, had enjoined his bishops to collect and record the deeds of their predecessors. Many heeded his injunction. In Italy, Ferdinando Ughelli and a team of ecclesiastical scholars compiled the *Italia sacra* (1644–62), an important historical account of the country's bishoprics. *Gallia Christiana*, the French equivalent of Ughelli's undertaking, appeared twelve years later.[35] The most famous product of this period was Cesare Baronio's massive *Ecclesiastical Annals* (1588–1607). In his

---

[34] John Pocock, "The origins of study of the past: a comparative approach," *Comparative Studies in Society and History* 4 (1962), 217.

[35] On Borromeo see the well-used *Acta ecclesiae Mediolanensis*. For Ughelli, Denys Hay, "Scholars and ecclesiastical history in the early modern period: the influence of Ferdinando Ughelli," in P. Mack and M. Jacob, eds., *Politics and Culture in Early Modern Europe* (Cambridge: Cambridge University Press,

wide-ranging survey of the church's past, Baronio assembled a broad range of evidence to defend the Roman church from its critics and detractors. At the very heart of his program was the conviction that the Tridentine church had not deviated from the truth but was one and the same with the Apostolic institution. From Borromeo to Baronio, memory, then, was at the center of this broad enterprise of Catholic scholarship in the early modern period.[36]

Who were Bohemia's antiquarians, and how did their actual work contrast with that of the exiles? The literature produced by the emigré community was in some respects more disparate in nature with their martyrologies, memoirs and histories. The literature of the kingdom's Catholic antiquarians, in contrast, was more unified, for though their research varied widely, these scholars in the most general sense were concerned with origins. Here a sharper distinction needs to be drawn between antiquarian and historical research. To this point I have used these terms somewhat interchangeably. Though there was certainly an overlap between the two genres in the first half of the seventeenth century, there were also distinctions. In their quest to uncover the past, antiquarians placed significant emphasis on the examination of artefacts and material objects. As opposed to historians who studied their subject chronologically, antiquarians examined the past in systematic fashion frequently ignoring strict chronology. While the historian selected facts for a defined purpose or argument, the antiquarian was more concerned with collecting as much material as possible connected to a specific subject. In the early modern period antiquarianism was most fully developed in England. William Camden's *Britannia* (1586) inspired an entire generation of antiquaries intent on recovering England's past through an investigation of the kingdom's archaeological and literary remains.[37]

1987), pp. 215–29; Eric Cochrane, *Historians and Historiography in the Italian Renaissance* (Chicago: University of Chicago Press, 1981), pp. 458–63. Important with Ughelli is the role of Nicolò Coleti who produced a revised edition of *Italia sacra* in Venice (1717–22).

[36] The seventeenth-century French scholar Claude Fleury commented on Borromeo's efforts to bring antiquity to bear on every aspect of church life as he noted, "On sait combien saint Charles a travaillé pour ramener l'esprit de l'Antiquité jusque dans les moindres parties de la religion." Cited in Bruno Neveu, "L'érudition ecclésiastique du dix-septième siècle et la nostalgie de l'antiquité chrétienne," in Keith Robbins, ed., *Religion and Humanism, Studies in Church History*, vol. XVII (Oxford: Basil Blackwell, 1981), p. 213.

[37] Foundational is the seminal essay of Arnaldo Momigliano, "Ancient history and the antiquarian," in Momigliano, *Studies in Historiography* (London: Weidenfeld & Nicolson, 1969), pp. 1–39; F. J. Levy, "Antiquarianism," in Daniel Woolf, ed., *A Global Encyclopedia of Historical Writing* (New York: Garland, 1998), vol. I, pp. 36–9; Daniel Woolf, "Varieties of antiquarianism," in his *The Social Circulation of the Past* (Oxford: Oxford University Press, 2003), pp. 141–82.

There were parallels to English antiquarianism on the continent, most directly in France and Italy. There were resonances in Bohemia as well. Where Stránský was part of a late humanist historical tradition, these scholars moved in a somewhat different direction, adapting antiquarian methodologies for their particular purposes. Antiquarianism in Bohemia had distinct religious overtones. Nearly all of these scholars were clerics intent on recovering the memories and remains of a pre-Hussite ecclesiastical culture. In Prague learned priests systematically marched through the city's archives. Others moved out into the countryside and scoured the libraries and manuscript collections of noble houses, monasteries and cloisters. Apart from literary remains, they also collected those physical vestiges of the past such as relics. Though antiquarians pursued interests that might appear today as wildly divergent, their projects were not an eclectic assortment of unrelated activities. Methodologically there was a rationale to their scholarship, and in their quest to uncover origins, they left few areas of the past untouched. As John Donne observed, antiquarians would "digg and thresh out the words of unlegible hands."[38] Bohemia's erudite clerics, however, did more than simply decipher the cramped scrawl of ancient scribes. They were amateur archaeologists, numismatists and genealogists. They were epigraphers and geographers, folklorists and natural scientists. They crisscrossed the countryside returning from their rambles with songs of peasants, legends of mountain giants and inscriptions from remote churches and monasteries.

The most industrious of these individuals was the Jesuit Bohuslav Balbín.[39] Born in eastern Bohemia the year after White Mountain, Balbín was a precocious child who had a particular love for the past. He later claimed that by the age of seven he had read through Hájek's *Czech Chronicle* several times. He was sent to the Jesuits for his formal education and eventually joined the order himself. The Jesuits were constantly shifting their personnel in Bohemia, and Balbín soon grew accustomed to packing his bags. In one span of thirteen years he taught at six different schools across the Czech lands. He also participated in itinerant mission work, an activity that took him to some of the more distant corners of the kingdom.

---

[38] Cited in Graham Parry, *The Trophies of Time: English Antiquarians of the Seventeenth Century* (Oxford: Oxford University Press, 1995), p. 15.

[39] The fullest treatment of Balbín is the confessional biography of A. Rejzek, *Bohuslav Balbín T. J., jeho život a práce* (Prague: Nakladem dědictví Sv. Prokopa, 1908). More recent is Jan Kučera and Jiří Rak, *Bohuslav Balbín a jeho místo v české kultuře* (Prague: Vyšehrad, 1983). Of more limited utility is the conference volume, Z. Pokorná and M. Svatoš, eds., *Bohuslav Balbín und die Kultur seiner Zeit in Böhmen* (Cologne: Böhlau, 1993). In general for the Empire see Stefan Benz, *Zwischen Tradition und Kritik. Katholische Geschichtsschreibung im barocken Heiligen Römischen Reich* (Husum: Matthiesen, 2003).

From these travels he collected piles of notes and documents that served as the basis of his monographs. In Moravia he was nearly matched by the energy of his colleague Tomáš Pešina, who worked his way through the region's archives, monastic libraries and private manuscript collections. In the introduction to his *Prodromus Moravographiae* (1663) Pešina outlined an exhaustingly long list of local archival collections he had visited in the production of the volume.[40] The labors of Pešina and Balbín were not carried out in isolation. Antiquarian activities were by nature a collaborative effort. These scholars regularly corresponded with each other, busily trading information and sharing rare books and manuscripts. In the *Prodromus Moravographiae* Pešina effusively thanked fellow Jesuits Jiří Kruger and Jan Tanner for providing important source material for the text.[41] The results of this cooperative work were impressive. With the prolific Balbín leading the way and Pešina, the Tanner brothers, Jiří Kruger and others close behind, post-White Mountain Bohemia was awash in antiquarian literature.

The most distinctive feature of this literature is its confessional character. Many of these scholars were Jesuits, and this institutional infrastructure gave the movement a significant boost, facilitating the exchange of information and providing a means to publish. Jiří Ferus, who managed the press for many years at the Clementinum, was particularly active as a publisher and editor of important Catholic sources including the letters of Vilém Slavata.[42] With such a wealth of documentary evidence, it is somewhat surprising that this material has received relatively little scholarly attention, but these antiquarians occupy an ambiguous position in the dominant nationalist narrative of the Czech past, for they have been considered in some sense as Habsburg collaborators. Part of the problem may also stem from the fact that many have been frankly puzzled by the nature of this literature, which one scholar has called "a farrago of fantasy and erudition united only by a strong sense of local patriotism and loyalty to the church."[43] But if we place this material in the broader cultural context of the Catholic Reformation and see it as a response to a specific intellectual and confessional crisis in the Bohemian kingdom, these fascinating texts

---

[40] Pešina, *Prodromus Moravographiae*, b4r–v. For Pešina see V. V. Zelený, "Tomáš Pešina z Čechorodu," *ČMKČ* 58 (1884), 1–22, 250–69, 471–97; 59 (1885), 90–108, 226–43; 60 (1886), 102–21, 331–57, 554–82.

[41] Pešina, *Prodromus Moravographiae*, b2r–v.

[42] A. Fechtnerová, "Jiří Ferus a Jiří Plachý," in P. Pokorný, ed., *Pocta dr. Emmě Urbánkové* (Prague: Státní knihovna ČSR, 1979), pp. 427–59.

[43] Simon Ditchfield, *Liturgy, Sanctity and History in Tridentine Italy* (Cambridge: Cambridge University Press, 1995), p. 5. Here Ditchfield refers to the perception of this literature by nineteenth-century historians.

begin to make more sense. As opposed to many of their counterparts elsewhere, Bohemia's antiquarians had a narrower and more focused area of research. Theirs was a search not for ancient laws or a forgotten constitution, not for the legacy of barbarian tribes or even indigenous inhabitants, but for religious precedent and confessional origins.

The primary concern of these Catholic scholars was the catastrophic state of the church. The Hussites had almost destroyed the old faith while the Reformations of the following century nearly finished the task. By the end of the sixteenth century the Catholic church had virtually no infrastructure and could command the loyalties of only a small fraction of the populace. Though the Habsburgs worked to restore its institutional grounding, it would take time and significant effort before it could ever regain the power and prestige it had enjoyed in the years before Hus. In Rudolfine Prague, antiquarians like Jiří Pontanus looked back to that era when the church had been the bedrock of Czech society. In *Bohemia pia* he recalled the days when the Bohemian kingdom could boast of more than 150 monasteries.[44] Balbín and his colleagues expanded on the work of Pontanus and sought to bolster Catholicism's authority by remembering its former privileges. Much in the same way that Habervešl assembled documents to defend the traditional liberties of the Bohemian estates, they searched the kingdom's archives and libraries for material documenting the rights granted to the church. It is significant then that one of Balbín's earliest forays into historical research, what has been called the first historical monograph produced in the Czech lands, was a study devoted to Arnošt of Pardubice (1305–64), Bohemia's first archbishop.[45]

Written to commemorate the 300th anniversary of Arnošt's death, Balbín's life of the archbishop captures the essence of the Jesuit's antiquarian program. Though a search for origins, it was firmly anchored in the present and set forth an agenda for church reform. Most obviously, it was concerned with diocesan authority. Balbín called upon a second Arnošt, Archbishop Harrach, to continue the work of his predecessor by reaffirming episcopal rights and privileges.[46] The biography also illustrates the extent to which Balbín gave precedence to the sacred past. In this history that depicts the golden age of Charles IV, it is Arnošt who upstages Bohemia's most celebrated emperor. He becomes Charles's mentor and shapes the piety of

---

[44] G. B. Pontanus, *Bohemia pia* (Frankfurt: Apud Claud. Marnium & heredes Io. Aubrii, 1608), p. 53.
[45] Bohuslav Balbín, *Vita Venerabilis Arnesti* (Prague: Kastner, 1664); Kučera and Rak, *Bohuslav Balbín*, p. 121.
[46] Balbín, *Vita Venerabilis Arnesti*, p. 3.

the young prince whose later policies reflected the spiritual values of the archbishop. Balbín cited more than twenty manuscripts and letters where Charles expressed deep affection for Arnošt.[47] Thirteen years later Balbín followed this same pattern with the *Epitome historica rerum Bohemicarum*. In what is the first full survey of Bohemia's past, Balbín traced the kingdom's history from the Přemyslid dukes in the ninth century to the reign of Ferdinand II. But instead of focusing on critical battles or the expansion of the kingdom's territory and power, he highlighted an alternative set of events and developments. While historians today focus on powerful Přemyslid princes such as the swashbuckling Otakar II (1253–78) who for a short time made Bohemia the strongest state in central Europe, Balbín put greater emphasis on more obscure figures such as Boleslav II (972–99) who established the region's first bishopric or Břetislav I (1034–55) who invaded Poland and returned with the holy remains of St. Adalbert. Two of the book's seven sections, in fact, were exclusively devoted to a history of the Madonna of Stará Boleslav, one of the most venerated devotional objects in the Czech lands.

What Balbín accomplished on a larger scale with the *Epitome* was repeated many times over on the local level. While the church rebuilt its infrastructure with the restoration of burnt-out monasteries, ruined chapels and abandoned cloisters, the antiquarians reclaimed a similar landscape through the written word. Though Prague served as a general clearing-house for most of this ecclesiastical research, antiquarianism in Bohemia was not a centralized movement. It was much more of a grassroots phenomenon, a loose association of local Baronios intent on recovering the sacred heritage of their respective region, parish or monastic house. Not surprisingly, three of Balbín's earliest works were devoted to specific cults of the Virgin in the far-flung towns of Příbram, Tuřany and Warta.[48] Šimon Kapihorský recalled the glorious past of the Sedlec monastery, the oldest Cistercian house in Bohemia, while Jan Beckovský enumerated the many concessions princes had granted his religious order, the Crusaders with a Red Star.[49] For his part Jan Florián Hammerschmid investigated the ecclesiastical history of local communities such as Klatovy and Mladá

---

[47] See, for example, ibid., pp. 68–71; Kučera and Rak, *Bohuslav Balbín*, p. 122.
[48] Bohuslav Balbín, *Diva Wartensis, seu Historia originis, et miracula magnae Dei, hominumque matris Mariae* (Prague: Formis Caesareo-Academicis, 1655); Bohuslav Balbín, *Diva Turzanensis, seu Historia originis et miraculorum magnae Dei hominumque matris Mariae* (Olomouc: Typis V. H. Etteli, 1658); Bohuslav Balbín, *Diva Montis Sancti, seu origines et miracula magnae Dei hominumque matris Mariae* (Prague: Typis Universitatis Carolo-Ferdinandeae, 1665).
[49] Šimon Eustach Kapihorský, *Hystorya Klásstera Sedleckého* (Prague: Pavel Sessius, 1630); Jan Beckovský, *Poselkyně starých příběhů českých*, ed. A. Rezek, 3 vols. (Prague: Dědictví sv. Prokopa, 1879–80), vol. II, pp. 236, 238, 240, 407; vol. III, pp. 390, 471, 475, 478.

Boleslav.[50] Together, the antiquarians recreated the contours of a world that had been nearly destroyed in the fifteenth and sixteenth centuries.

Despite their best efforts to remember a vibrant ecclesiastical culture that had existed before Hus, the antiquarians were still confronted with a significant problem. There was a basic fact they could not alter. For over two centuries Bohemia had been a land of heretics. The taint of heterodoxy had become a reputation for heresy and was now almost a national stereotype. The antiquarians addressed this issue on a number of levels. The surest antidote to heresy was sanctity, and there was a concerted effort to bring the saints back into the mainstream of Czech culture. In the fifteenth and sixteenth centuries many of the region's saints had occupied a place on the margins of church and society. In response antiquarians produced a steady stream of literature that promoted these neglected cults. Leading the way, Balbín's *Bohemia sancta* highlighted the deeds of approximately 200 holy men and women of the Czech lands.[51] More importantly, the antiquarians cleverly reversed the perspective from which the Hussite period was traditionally viewed. They transformed Bohemia from a kingdom of heretics into a nation of martyrs. Working assiduously to create a culture of martyrdom, these clerics celebrated the bravery and constancy of a persecuted Catholic minority. Their books are full of stories detailing the courage of entire communities who refused to capitulate to Hussite armies or heroic individuals such as the seventeenth-century priest Jan Sarkander who was tortured and killed for his faith at the outbreak of the Thirty Years War. The most famous of these figures, the fourteenth-century priest John Nepomuk, was the only Bohemian canonized in the early modern period and one of only two martyrs to be elevated to sainthood between 1523 and 1767. Jan Florián Hammerschmid expressed a commonly held view when he proudly proclaimed that Bohemia could boast of more martyrs than any other nation.[52]

Perseverance through trial was a standard literary trope of the Catholic Reformation, one that was enthusiastically adopted by the Czech antiquarians. Sometimes they singled out specific individuals or regions that had

---

[50] J. F. Hammerschmid, *Hystorye Klattowská* (Prague: Archiepiscopal Press, 1699); *Krátký Weytah Slawy Swato-Swatého Králowského a Weyhradnjho Kostela* (Prague: Wolfgang Wickhart, 1700); *Historia ... monasterium S. Georgii* (Prague: Wolfgang Wickhart, 1715); *Descriptio Civitatis Neo Boleslawiae* (1722), manuscript history in NA, ŘPi, Inv. c. 678, Sign. B 128, Book number 488.

[51] Bohuslav Balbín, *Bohemia sancta* (Prague: Typis Georgii Czernoch, 1682). The text was published as part of Balbín's massive *Miscellanea historica regni Bohemiae*, decas I, 1–8; decas II, 1–2 (Prague, 1679–88).

[52] On Sarkander see František Hrubý, *Kněz Jan Sarkander, Moravský mučedník doby bělohorské a jeho legenda* (Prague: Nákladem vlastním, 1940); J. F. Hammerschmid, *Prodromus gloriae Pragenae* (Prague: Wolfgang Wickhart, 1723), p. 19.

kept the faith under great duress. Jan Kořínek went to great lengths to defend the miners of Kutná Hora whose allegiance to Rome had not wavered during the Hussite troubles.[53] Tomáš Pešina pointed to the stalwart souls of Plzeň. With pride he asserted that "from the time of its founding to the present day, none of its inhabitants had ever joined the heretics."[54] Balbín praised the Silesian nobility of Glatz, for they had also held firm to the old religion even in the darkest days of crisis.[55] The antiquarians were reminding their audience that Bohemian piety had deep roots. There had always been a remnant that had remained steadfast through testing. This message was intended at least in part for the kingdom's Habsburg rulers.

While the antiquarians directly and aggressively addressed the problems of a heretical past, their reaction to the post-White Mountain political situation and new power of the Habsburg family was more complex. In Bohemia there were outspoken imperial apologists as well as more cautious detractors. A number of Balbín's unpublished manuscripts contain scathing critiques of the regime such as his *Dissertatio apologetica pro lingua Slavonica, praeciupe Bohemica* which did not appear in print until the late eighteenth century. Generally speaking, however, the response of the antiquarians, including that of Balbín, was more restrained in tone and more sophisticated in nature. Representative was the approach taken by Jiří Pontanus. In *Bohemia pia* Pontanus recounted the story of the confrontation between St. Vitus and the emperor Diocletian. It goes without saying that Bohemia's patron saint ultimately bested the pagan *Kaiser* in this contest.[56] Pontanus's anecdote could certainly have been read as a subtle criticism of grasping imperial ambition. In the generation after 1620 there were many more attempts by the antiquarians to define Bohemian identity over and against a growing Austrian presence. Jan Beckovský reminded his readers that Habsburg power was built in part on a foundation of Czech piety. When in desperate financial straits, Archduke Ferdinand turned to the Cistercian cloister of Sedlec and received a loan that secured his family's fortunes at a

---

[53] Jan Kořínek, *Staré paměti kutnohorské* (Prague: Typis Georgii Czernoch, 1675); new edition Alexandr Stich, Radek Lunga and Jaroslav Kolár, eds. (Prague: NLN, 2000).

[54] Cited in Kučera and Rak, *Bohuslav Balbín*, pp. 194, 195; Plzeň inspired a significant body of antiquarian literature: see Václav Jan Fiklscher, *Slavná pověst královského krajského a starokatolického města Plzně* (Prague: Jan Václav Helm, 1710); Adam Kratochvile, *Nový koráb Noëmowý* (Prague: Jan Václav Helm, 1718); also note the undated manuscript history of Jan Tanner, *Historia semper catholicae semperque fidelis civitatis Plsnae in Regno Bohemiae* (Archiv města Plzně, inv. no. 158).

[55] Balbín, *Miscellanea*, decas I. Liber 3 (Prague: Typis Georgii Czernoch, 1681), p. 44.

[56] Pontanus, *Bohemia pia*, p. 48. To highlight the connection between St. Vitus and the Czech lands, Pontanus continued describing in some detail how the arm of the saint ended up in Prague.

particularly critical juncture.[57] The broad scope of local antiquarian studies is an important statement in itself validating regional traditions and practices against the potential encroachment of an Austrian ecclesiastical culture. Most intriguing in this respect is the work of the Jesuit Jan Tanner who in 1679 published the *Holy Way*, a tract publicizing an old pilgrimage route between Prague and Stará Boleslav, the site of Wenceslas's martyrdom. Tanner's text, though, was far more than a promotional brochure of a neglected holy site. Elaborating on the Wenceslas legend, he made the bold claim that before his death the Czech king had established the pilgrimage center of Mariazell in Styria.[58] Mariazell was the most important Austrian shrine of the seventeenth and eighteenth centuries and served a critical role in the fabrication of the family's Catholic image fashioned in this period. Tanner was now trumping the Habsburgs as he illustrated how a patron saint of Bohemia was actually the founder of the most Austrian of cults.

SHAPING A CATHOLIC IDENTITY

These then were the broad strategies developed by the Catholic antiquarians as they constructed a new identity for their troubled homeland after White Mountain. Their distinctive achievement was the product of a methodology that differed from an approach to the past adopted by the exiles. Stránský and his colleagues dissected the Czech past with a steely critical eye. Their political histories and martyrologies endeavored to expose the legal and doctrinal shortcomings of the present Habsburg regime. Focusing more closely on social and cultural issues, the Catholics, in contrast, sought to reconstruct a past that had existed before Hus. At the root of the antiquarian enterprise was a distinctly organic impulse. They saw themselves nurturing the delicate blooms of culture and custom that had been weakened but not completely destroyed by the storms of a long and difficult Hussite winter. The images that Balbín employed to describe Bohemia are very telling in this regard. In the opening chapter of his most important work, *Miscellanea historica regni Bohemiae*, he used the metaphors of a heart, navel and rose to characterize the kingdom. In the *Epitome* he included a map of Bohemia shaped in the form of a rose with

---

[57] Beckovský, *Poselkyně*, vol. I, p. 63.

[58] Jan Tanner, *Swatá Cesta z Prahy do Staré Boleslawě* (Prague: Typis Universitatis Carolo-Ferdinandeae, 1679); for a fuller discussion see M. E. Ducreux, "Der heilige Wenzel als Begründer der *Pietas Austriaca*: Die Symbolik der Wallfahrt nach Stará Boleslav (Alt Bunzlau) im 17. Jahrhundert," in Hartmut Lehmann and A. Trepp, eds., *Im Zeichen der Krise* (Göttingen: Vandenhoeck & Ruprecht, 1999), pp. 597–636.

each petal representing a district of the kingdom (Figure 9).[59] The past for the antiquarians was a living tradition that needed both nourishment and support.

Contrasting methodologies resulted in varying perceptions of Bohemian identity. Stránský maintained that the Czech lands had long been characterized by a plurality of cultures and confessions. The Catholics attacked this view relentlessly. From Pontanus to Beckovský, there was an almost constant refrain that religious innovations had left the nation dangerously divided, robbed it of a coherent identity, and allowed it to career uncontrollably towards fratricidal destruction. Balbín and his compatriots portrayed the Czech experience in a fundamentally different fashion. The project that may best capture this spirit is Balbín's wildly ambitious *Miscellanea historica regni Bohemiae*. Conceived originally as a compilation of thirty books that covered everything from a topographical survey of the kingdom to a detailed genealogical examination of Bohemia's leading families, the *Miscellanea* was the broadest and most thorough examination of Czech history, culture and society that had or for that matter has ever been produced.[60] Though Balbín spent a significant portion of his career collecting material for the undertaking, he managed to complete only half of it. Book One was published 1679. An outline of the region's natural history, it ranged from a discussion of Bohemia's wines and gems to that of its baths and bird songs. Balbín dedicated Books Four, Five and Six to ecclesiastical issues. Here he carefully enumerated the traditional rights and privileges of the kingdom's church which he supported with a broad sampling of primary documentation, including one of the earliest references to Christianity in the Czech lands, a ninth-century letter from Pope John VIII to the Byzantine missionary Methodius. Though the *Miscellanea* is full of digressions and fascinating anecdotes, Balbín's text is no aimless ramble through the Czech past. There is an order and coherence to this grand enterprise as reflected in Book Nine, posthumously published as *Bohemia docta* (1776–80). Saluted by modern scholars as the first comprehensive survey of Czech literary history, *Bohemia docta* clearly illustrates Balbín's methodology. In encyclopedic fashion, he systematically worked his way through the kingdom's literary heritage, beginning with general histories of the fatherland

---

[59] Balbín, *Miscellanea*, decas I. Liber 1 (Prague: Typis Georgii Czernoch, 1681), pp. 1–2. For a more general discussion of these organic motifs in the Catholic Reformation see Trevor Johnson, "Gardening for God: Carmelite deserts and the sacralisation of natural space in Counter-Reformation Spain," in Will Coster and Andrew Spicer, eds., *Sacred Space in Early Modern Europe* (Cambridge: Cambridge University Press, 2005), pp. 282–301; Jorge Cañizares-Esguerra, *Puritan Conquistadors* (Stanford: Stanford University Press, 2006), pp. 178–214.

[60] For a brief overview of this work see Kamil Krofta, *O Balbínovi dějepisci* (Prague: Melantrich, 1938), pp. 44–55. By Balbín's death, the first eight books of Part I and first two books of Part II had been published. Books nine and ten of Part I were published posthumously nearly a century later.

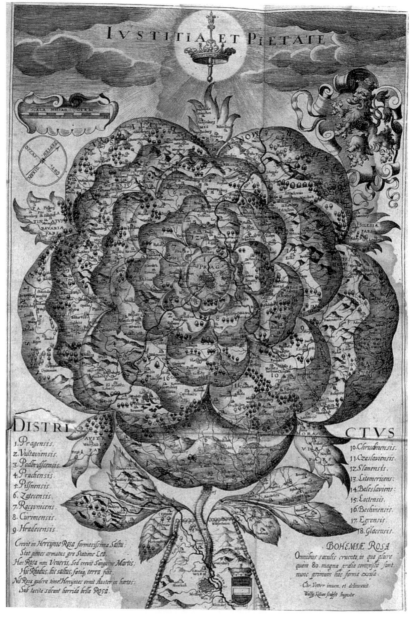

9. Rose map of Bohemia from B. Balbín, *Epitome historica rerum Bohemicarum*

before moving on to the memoirs of the nobility, the learned texts of doctors and philosophers, the writings of churchmen, and the work of orators and poets. He even included a section on women writers.[61]

The exile community never produced a text that could match the sprawling scope of the *Miscellanea*. Indeed, one of the great strengths of the antiquarian movement was its ability to incorporate such a broad range of source material in its reconstruction of the kingdom's past. Over time the Catholics even began to subsume elements of the dissenting tradition into a broader conception of Bohemian identity. In the *Epitome* Balbín included a favorable assessment of Jan Milíč of Kroměříž, an outspoken critic of the fourteenth-century church whom later Protestant historians viewed as a forerunner of Hus.[62] His judgment of Bohemia's Utraquist king, George of Poděbrady, was not only remarkably mild, but he actually defended the "heretic" prince from many of his detractors. Jan Beckovský later claimed that on his deathbed King George renounced his words against the pope.[63] Even a figure such as the controversial one-eyed Hussite general, Jan Žižka, occasionally merited praise. Though Hammerschmid had nothing but contempt for an individual who had supposedly murdered 500 Catholic priests with his own hands, Balbín was more circumspect. He saw Žižka as a product of a noble family that had slipped into decline while Tomáš Pešina even offered cautious words of praise for the indefatigable soldier.[64] Over time it became easier for Catholics to incorporate the Hussite heritage into their own. By the late eighteenth century František Pelcl could reasonably query:

Should not a Czech have the right to be proud of the heroism of his Žižka or his Prokop? True, they were Hussites, but even so they believed in Christ, and adored His Sacred Mother and Saint Wenceslas. Žižka even had a mass read to him every day in his encampment. Thus they are in this way superior to those heathen heroes whose deeds without regard to their idolatry are generally praised to high heaven.[65]

The antiquarians worked in other ways to incorporate the writings of their religious rivals into a broader literary heritage. Tomáš Pešina admired the

---

[61] Bohuslav Balbín, *Bohemia docta*, 2 vols. (Prague: J. C. Hraba, 1777); J. Hanuš, "Bohuslava Balbína *Bohemia Docta*," *ČČH* 12 (1906), 133–48, 298–311, 407–26.

[62] Bohuslav Balbín, *Epitome historica rerum Bohemicarum* (Prague: Typis Universitatis Carolo-Ferdinandeae, 1677), pp. 406–8.

[63] Ibid., p. 515; Jan Beckovský, *Poselkyně starých příběhů českých* (Prague: Jan Karel Jeřábek, 1700), pp. 935–6.

[64] Hammerschmid, *Prodromus gloriae Pragenae*, p. 19; Kučera and Rak, *Bohuslav Balbín*, pp. 318, 367.

[65] Cited in Frederick Heymann, "The Hussite movement in the historiography of the Czech awakening," in Peter Brock and Gordon Skilling, eds., *The Czech Renascence of the Nineteenth Century* (Toronto: University of Toronto Press, 1970), p. 229.

work of Pavel Skála, and it was primarily through his efforts that the great manuscript history was preserved. In *Bohemia docta* Balbín highlighted a literary legacy that crossed confessional and linguistic divides. He discussed texts of Catholics alongside those of Utraquists and exiles. Immediately after his consideration of Vilém Slavata, he saluted with no apparent sense of irony the writings of Kryštof Harant of Polžice, the chancellor's confessional opponent who was executed in June 1621.[66]

Antiquarians today are often seen as dilettantish eccentrics engaged in pursuits that have little relevance to the society around them. Such was not the case in the Catholic Reformation. From revising breviaries to promoting neglected cults of forgotten saints, scholars looked to the past as a means to instill piety in the present. Cesare Baronio's *Ecclesiastical Annals* actually began as an informal series of sermons delivered to the devout at Philip Neri's Oratory in Rome. Bohemia's antiquarians were religious reformers, priests who heard confessions, celebrated the Eucharist, led pilgrimages and delivered homilies. Mission work was frequently a central feature of their labors. In 1650, for example, Balbín participated in at least six different missions tramping from villages outside Prague to the mountains of northeast Bohemia, from the flatlands of the Elbe basin to the rolling hills of the kingdom's southern marches. He later boasted that he had converted 1,500 people without any threat of compulsion. This was his true ministry. Scholarship was merely its handmaiden. In a letter to Jan Tanner, Balbín specifically referred to the work of Baronio and the importance of antiquarian research in the daunting enterprise of rebuilding the Catholic church in Bohemia.[67] His early monograph on Archbishop Arnošt must be read in the light of the wider task of restoring episcopal authority while his life of John Nepomuk was an important contribution in the campaign to canonize the priest who had defied a paranoid king. Also instructive in this regard is the activity of Jan Jiří Středovský whose *Sacra Moraviae historiae* was published in 1710. An exploration of Moravia's Christian origins, the text focused on the missionary work of Cyril and Methodius. In his account Středovský gave an extensive description of the Slavic god Radegast and his loyal devotees. At the summer solstice these pagan worshipers climbed Radhošť mountain and there honored the god of fertility with human sacrifice. Středovský's excursus on the Radegast cult was more than a colorful incident from local folklore. In this remote region of eastern Moravia

---

[66] Skála, *Historie česká*, p. 18; Balbín, *Bohemia docta*, vol. I, pp. 53–4.
[67] Bohuslav Balbín to Jan Tanner, 11 February 1659. Reprinted in Kučera and Rak, *Bohuslav Balbín*, pp. 393–7; Rejzek, *Bohuslav Balbín T.J.*, pp. 110–15.

there were concerns that pagan practices and beliefs had not been completely eradicated. Středovský's work was part of a broader campaign to finish the task started by the Byzantine missionaries. After the publication of the text, a cross and a chapel were raised on the summit of Radhošť.[68]

Whether leading missions or digging through cloister archives, the primary goal of Bohemia's antiquarians was the restoration of a faith that had been sorely tested. In his correspondence with Jan Tanner, Balbín commented on a biography his friend was writing on Albrecht Chanovský, one of Bohemia's most effective missionaries. Tanner had originally intended to name his study, *Sacred Bohemia*, but Balbín, ever the realist, was somewhat critical of this proposal. With the task of reestablishing Catholicism far from complete, he argued that it would be more appropriate to use the title *Sparks of Czech Piety*.[69] The image of a spark, of a fire that has burned down to its embers and now needs to be carefully fanned back to life, captures an important aspect of Czech antiquarianism. Restoration was a central feature of these scholars' writings and research, and in this respect their understanding of the past and its relation to the present harkened back to the Middle Ages. Giles Constable once noted concerning the medieval understanding of the past:

> People [in the Middle Ages] lived the past in a very real sense, and the past, living in them, was constantly recreated in a way that made it part of everyday life. Sight, smell, hearing, and touch were all enlisted in the task of reconstructing the past. Even speech was a dramatic performance, and the actions that accompanied many rites and ceremonies helped to bring past people and events into the present, giving meaning to history and linking it to the future.[70]

Constable's observation neatly encapsulates the objective of the Czech antiquarians. For them the past was meant to be more than studied. It was to be recreated and brought into the present.

Balbín and his colleagues employed a number of strategies to accomplish that end. Their understanding of time and manipulation of chronology is typical in this regard and characteristic of the Catholic Reformation as a whole. In Rome in 1578 a workman busy digging a well came across the ancient tomb of Priscilla, an early Christian woman. His discovery led to a broader series of excavations that uncovered an entire network of Christian

---

[68] Jan Jiří Středovský, *Sacra Moraviae historia sive vita ss. Cyrilli et Methudii* (Sulzbach: Lehmann, 1710), pp. 37–43.

[69] Kučera and Rak, *Bohuslav Balbín*, pp. 396–7.

[70] Giles Constable, "A living past: the historical environment of the Middle Ages," *Harvard Library Bulletin* n.s. 1 (1990), 49.

catacombs. The discovery of a *Roma sotteranea* infused the Catholic world
with a remarkable energy from an earlier and more heroic age.[71] Time stood
still when the coffins of early martyrs such as St. Cecilia were opened, and
the body was found completely intact and free from decay.[72] This sense of
atemporality, of collapsing the past into the present, was a standard characteristic of Bohemia's antiquarian texts. Instructive here is Jan Beckovský's
Messenger of Old Czech Tales (1700). Organizing his text into chapters that
highlighted major occurrences of a specific year, Beckovský modeled the
Messenger on Hájek's popular *Czech Chronicle*. Unlike Hájek, however,
Beckovský filled his narrative with a strikingly high number of chronological interpolations. One short excerpt from the year 1621 includes references
to events of 936, 941, 1060, 1129, 1142, 1222 and 1343.[73] The *Sacri pulveres*
(1669) of Jiří Kruger functioned in a similar fashion. Kruger narrated the
principal events of the Czech past in the form of a historical calendar. On
2 May, for example, readers discovered that on this day John Nepomuk had
been thrown into the Moldau (1383), the town of Litomyšl had been
attacked by the Hussites (1421) and St. Norbert's translation had been
celebrated in Prague (1627).[74]

And then there are the ghosts. Antiquarian literature is full of stories of
spectral visitations and appearances. Balbín gave these phantoms an entire
chapter in the *Miscellanea*.[75] Nearly all the Catholic accounts of the
Calvinist regime in Prague include some reference to ghosts. When a sacred
site was threatened or a traditional liturgical rite in jeopardy, stories often
circulated of the appearance of an important Czech saint who issued a stern
warning concerning any religious innovation. When in 1619 the fiery court
preacher, Abraham Scultetus, instigated an iconoclastic riot in St. Vitus
Cathedral, Jan Tanner reported that St. Wenceslas himself called out from
his crypt with grave words of reproach for this brazen act of desecration.[76]
The ghosts of these tales were not just the most prominent saints of the
kingdom who miraculously appeared in the hour of greatest need. Specters

---

[71] Gisella Cantino Wataghin, "Roma sotteranea: Appunti sulle origini dell'archeologia cristiana,"
Ricerche di storia dell'arte 10 (1980), 5–14. Simon Ditchfield offers a concise overview of these
developments in *Liturgy, Sanctity and History*, pp. 86–91.
[72] Ditchfield, *Liturgy, Sanctity and History*, pp. 181–4.   [73] Beckovský, *Poselkyně*, vol. II, pp. 356–7.
[74] Jiří Kruger, *Maiales Triumphi* (Litomyšl: J. Arnolt, 1669), pp. 8–15.
[75] Balbín, *Miscellanea*, decas I. Liber 3 (1681), Chapter 15; more generally on phantoms and their
function in pre-modern society see Jean-Claude Schmitt, *Ghosts in the Middle Ages* (Chicago:
University of Chicago Press, 1998) and for the English perspective Peter Marshall, *Beliefs and the
Dead in Reformation England* (Oxford: Oxford University Press, 2001).
[76] See Tanner's story in *Trophaea sancti Wenceslai Bohemiae regis ac martyris* (Prague: Typis Universitatis
Carolo-Ferdinandeae, 1661). Cited in Robert Pynsent, *Questions of Identity: Czech and Slovak Ideas of
Nationality and Personality* (Budapest: Central European University Press, 1994), p. 197.

of more ordinary men and women also contributed to a general defense of old Czech traditions. Balbín related the story of a well-intentioned nobleman who had decided to refurbish a church after generations of neglect. Various craftsmen were brought in, and the church quickly became a confused and disorganized construction site. The project was interrupted, however, when a ghost appeared to the local lord. The unhappy apparition was the original founder of the church who was buried within its walls. Workers threatened his tomb, he claimed, and must be stopped. Needless to say, building plans were quickly altered.[77] Ghosts at times could offer more active resistance in defense of Catholic rituals. Johannes Miller told the story of a Protestant pastor in Glatz whose congregation occupied a church that housed an important votive image. In an effort to combat what he perceived as Catholic superstition he prepared a sermon against the Virgin and the saints. He never had the opportunity to deliver it, for before the service a ghost struck him down dead.[78] From the most stately cathedral to the village church, ghosts, then, were the spectral custodians of Bohemia's holy sites. As a literary device, these phantoms were an effective means for the antiquarians to suspend chronology and literally bring the past into the present.

These writers employed other strategies as well to restore the memories of a lost religious world. Pre-modern Europe was a memorial culture. Material images, ranging from the lowly tombstone to ornate public statuary, were constructed to retain and transmit important social memories. With a clever turn of phrase, Balbín once described the Protestant faith as one that had been stripped of all outward ornament. He continued by arguing that the true church should follow instead the example of Solomon, who took gifts of gold and silver to construct a brilliant and resplendent temple.[79] Antiquarian literature was a veritable feast for the senses. Apart from the handsome illustrations, the actual text of so many of these volumes was oriented towards the visual. Beckovský filled the *Messenger* with all sorts of intriguing digressions including a detailed excursus on the church of St. Barbara in Kutná Hora where he described the history and design of Bohemia's most stunning example of late Gothic architecture.[80] Jan Florián Hammerschmid recreated a virtual Prague for his reader in his *Prodromus gloriae Pragenae* (1723). From a detailed account of the nineteen altars of the Týn Church to an elaborate history and description of the Charles Bridge,

[77] Balbín, *Miscellanea*, decas II. Liber I (Prague: Georgii Laboun, 1687), p. III.
[78] Johannes Miller, *Historia Beatissimae Virginis Glacensis* (Glatz: Pega, 1690), pp. 175–6.
[79] Balbín, *Miscellanea*, decas I. Liber 3, p. 129.   [80] Beckovský, *Poselkyně*, pp. 464–8.

he described in painstaking detail the most important highlights of Prague's sacred topography.[81] By relating the history of a specific altar, religious image or statue, these clerics were helping the reader understand and appreciate a rich ecclesiastical heritage; a culture, though partially destroyed by the Hussites and invading Protestant armies, had emerged triumphant.

At the heart of the antiquarian project was the conviction that the recovery of the past would ultimately lead to the salvation of the present. Balbín in many ways saw himself as an archaeologist of a civilization that lay half-buried beneath the debris of the troubled Hussite era. Through his writings he was slowly removing the rubble and uncovering the cultural foundations upon which a renewed Catholic society could flourish. Perhaps nothing better captures the spirit of this work than an incident that occurred during a mission to northeast Bohemia. Here in the heartland of the Bohemian Brethren with their clear Protestant orientation, Balbín purportedly had amazing success. In one village, he visited the local church and found the discarded high altar, definitive proof in his mind that the building had originally belonged to an ancient monastic order. Excitedly, he displayed the altar and explained its significance to the townspeople who according to the Jesuit all promptly converted.[82] It was a simple equation for the antiquarians. The discovery of the past, the unearthing of a Christian antiquity, logically and ineluctably led to a Catholic *renovatio* of their society and culture.

A full consideration of antiquarianism is thus foundational for any further discussion of Catholic reform in Bohemia. The literary production of Balbín and associates was not the pursuit of bookish dilettantes. Though the task of finding a Catholic identity may have begun in the archives and was first expressed on the written page, these endeavors quickly spilled over into a wider arena. Arguably the greatest triumph of Bohemia's antiquarians was their success in bringing the past into the present and there firmly securing it in the popular imagination. In 1675 ordinary men and women were far more aware of their region's past than a century earlier, for the scope and influence of antiquarianism had expanded significantly. Tomáš Pešina served as an informal "curator" of St. Vitus Cathedral. His interests in its extensive relic collection became a focal point of his research. Amateur enthusiasts took the work of Pešina and Balbín into the field. Mikuláš Franchimont of Frankenfeld, a professor of medicine and rector of the university in Prague, boasted that his estates housed the remains of one of

[81] Hammerschmid, *Prodromus gloriae Pragenae*, pp. 31–3, 590–9.
[82] Rejzek, *Bohuslav Balbín T.J.*, p. 113.

the oldest Christian monuments in Bohemia, a tenth-century church now restored and refurbished. In western Bohemia a church sexton assumed the role of archaeologist and uncovered a medieval reliquary that had been hidden away for generations in a country church.[83] The visual nature of antiquarian scholarship also helped make the translation of their material to more popular media possible. Playwrights brought to life the stories of humble martyrs and miraculous relics while artists created lasting monuments commemorating critical moments of the kingdom's holy past. At its most basic level, then, antiquarianism provided Bohemia's Catholics with a mental map of their world. It not only showed them where they had come from, but it also furnished them with directions for the future as they looked towards the completion of the kingdom's reformation.

---

[83] Tomáš Pešina, *Thesaurus in lucem protractus, sive S. Mercurius, Maximus Orientis Martyr* (Prague: Typis Joannis Arnolti de Dobroslavina, 1675); Kučera and Rak, *Bohuslav Balbín*, p. 196; Johannes Miller, *Historia Mariascheinensis* (Prague: In der Academischen Buchdruckerey des Collegii S. J., 1710), pp. 163–5. More generally on the growing scope of antiquarianism see Woolf, *Social Circulation*, pp. 180–2.

CHAPTER 5

Reshaping the landscape: art and confessional identity

Despite the ravages of the Thirty Years War, there were unmistakable signs in the second half of the seventeenth century that new life and energy were returning to Prague. Though the city had lost more than half of its population during the war years, its demographic base was growing once more. The French doctor Charles Patin visited Bohemia two decades after the war and found in Prague a vibrant metropolis that was rapidly expanding thanks in large part to the patronage of the church, for as he noted, "they have cloisters here resembling palaces rather than the simple refuges of people who despise the vanities of the world."[1] A few years later the Englishman Edward Brown praised Prague's architectural monuments, comparing the city favorably to even Florence. From Brown's perspective the Moldau surpassed the Arno, and "the large, massy, long Stone-Bridge in Prague exceedeth any of, if not all, of the four bridges of Florence."[2] In the early eighteenth century three travelers from England were duly impressed by the marvels of Prague's ecclesiastical topography. They included a description of more than forty of the city's churches and cloisters in their travel account.[3] Indeed, there are few regions north of the Alps that can match the rich landscape of the Bohemian baroque. Leading an artistic and architectural makeover of unprecedented proportions, a host of painters, sculptors and craftsmen transformed the Czech lands in the seventeenth and early eighteenth centuries. Marian columns, wayside chapels, pilgrimage complexes along with new or restored churches, convents and monasteries sprung up across the region.

[1] Zdeněk Kalista, "Charles Patin a jeho návštěva v Čechách let sedmdesátých XVII. v.," *ČČH* 37 (1931), 358.
[2] Cited in R. Wellek, "Bohemia in English literature," in Wellek, *Essays on Czech Literature* (The Hague: Mouton, 1963), p. 119.
[3] "The travels of three English gentlemen, in the year 1734," in *The Harleian Miscellany* (London: White, 1810), vol. V, pp. 352–6.

These monuments, the most visible signs of Bohemia's new confessional identity, have been the subject of considerable study. From the statuary of Matthias Braun to the architectural production of the Dientzenhofer family, art historians have produced a formidable body of research on this period. In much of this literature, however, there has been a tendency to discuss aesthetic developments in isolation from the historical circumstances in which they are grounded. Though scholars of the Bohemian baroque would certainly acknowledge that the artistic activity of their period was a product of the new religious climate, they have often failed to integrate their work into a broader historical narrative. Artists and architects of the seventeenth and early eighteenth centuries played an essential role in the shaping of Bohemia's Catholic identity. Of all those engaged in this grand project it was the artist whose work had the widest reach and broadest impact. Though there were shortages of priests in the countryside, though ignorance of doctrine was widespread, though literacy rates remained low, this new Catholic art was everywhere. Painters and sculptors took the stories of the antiquarians and the sermons of the missionaries and made them real, tangible and accessible. At the beginning of the seventeenth century, however, the situation was substantially different. The role and function of religious art was a matter of significant debate and considerable controversy in Czech society and in the end became a fundamental issue in the military confrontation between King Frederick and Emperor Ferdinand.

BATTLING IMAGES IN BOHEMIA

Though Jan Hus had once commented, "It is as great a shame to destroy a valuable picture as a valuable book," the revolution that followed his death developed in an entirely different fashion.[4] Even before Hus's execution events were occurring that foretold a stormy future. On the last day of March 1414, a follower of Hus, who was worshiping in the monastery church of St. James in Old Town, drew close to the crucifix during the middle of a service in an attitude of apparent devotion. At the last moment, however, he suddenly darted forward and smeared the cross with excrement. This act of desecration was not an isolated occurrence. There were at least three such incidents in Prague that year, and the pace quickened after 1415. In Prague the firebrand Jan Želivský urged the faithful to action as he decried "the great idols" that had been erected in the churches. The

---

[4] Cited in Karel Stejskal, "Ikonoklasmus českého středověku a jeho limity," *Umění* 48 (2000), 206.

defenestration of 1419 was accompanied by riots where churches were looted
and pillaged. Two years later Želivský incited a mob to cross the river and
climb the hill to St. Vitus Cathedral and destroy some of the church's most
precious treasures. Outside Prague similar events were occurring. In the
southern Bohemian town of Prachatice, Hussites went on a spree of
destruction targeting religious paintings in particular. To the north in
Litoměřice they focused their attention on sacred statuary, hacking off the
noses of saints and martyrs. Hus's followers also took their iconoclastic zeal
abroad. During the sensitive negotiations at the Council of Basel, the
Hussites at one point were accused of throwing snowballs at a crucifix.
More serious was the damage they caused in Poland where they staged a
series of raids including an attempt to seize and presumably destroy the
kingdom's most famous religious object, the Black Madonna of
Częstochowa.[5]

It is difficult to underestimate the destruction that accompanied the
Hussite wars. The revolution unleashed an iconoclastic frenzy that could
not be matched even by the zeal of the Reformation's most ardent image
breakers. There were few churches or monasteries that were left untouched
by the great unrest, and all this took place in a region that boasted a rich
ecclesiastical heritage. This trauma and sense of loss had a devastating effect
on Bohemia's Catholics and continued to haunt the church in the post-
White Mountain period. So much of the art and architecture of the
seventeenth and eighteenth centuries either directly or indirectly reflected
back on this tumultuous era. Despite these long-lasting repercussions, this
first wave of iconoclasm was essentially over by the time Emperor
Sigismund reached an agreement with the Hussites at Jihlava in 1436. The
Hussite legacy, however, never completely disappeared. It lived on in
splinter groups that drew their inspiration from the more radical Hussite
wing. Occasionally there was an incident such as the one in 1504 when a
Prague tailor pulled down a statue of Christ and began whipping it with his
colleague.[6] But in general Bohemia's religious culture from the middle
decades of the fifteenth century forward was relatively conservative in
nature. Images, processions and a moderate Marian cult remained important elements of Czech ecclesiastical culture after the initial dislocations of
the Hussite revolution had passed. Even the Bohemian Brethren were later

[5] Thomas Fudge, *The Magnificent Ride: The First Reformation in Hussite Bohemia* (Aldershot: Ashgate,
    1998), pp. 110, 178, 252.
[6] J. Macek, "Bohemia," in R. Porter and M. Teich, eds., *The Renaissance in National Context*
    (Cambridge: Cambridge University Press, 1992), p. 211.

criticized for retaining papal elements in their celebration of the Eucharist. It was only when more radical notions reached Prague in the person of the Winter King that iconoclasm once more became a significant issue.

The relationship of the Reformation to the visual arts is of course a complicated issue. The Lutherans were generally conservative on this matter while the Calvinists assumed a more aggressive stance, but even Calvin did not advocate iconoclasm. He maintained that religious images should be removed from former Catholic churches in an orderly fashion under proper supervision. The problem arose when local authorities were resistant to these views. In regions such as France and the Low Countries Calvinist adherents frequently found no support from secular leaders and thus took it upon themselves to execute this commission. As a result, there were waves of violence when mobs ransacked churches and destroyed sacred art. The situation in Bohemia, however, was very different. With Frederick's election, the Czech estates installed a regime that vigorously promoted an iconoclastic agenda. The Winter King's *éminence grise* was his court preacher and adviser, Abraham Scultetus. Beginning his education at Wittenberg, Scultetus was part of the university's crypto-Calvinist faction. He eventually found a more congenial home in Heidelberg where he finished his theological education and ultimately became a professor. An earnest Calvinist, Scultetus helped Johann Sigismund, the elector of Brandenburg, implement a Reformed order of worship at his court. A far bigger challenge lay before him and Frederick in Bohemia.

Significant changes began in Prague on 15 October 1619 when St. Vitus was officially handed over to Frederick's entourage with plans to transform it into the new king's court church. The dean and the canons were promptly evicted and given three days to quit the premises while the cathedral itself was sealed and guarded by Frederick's men. Though the Palatine elector was crowned in the church a few weeks later, more substantial alterations were needed before St. Vitus was suitable for Calvinist worship. In the days surrounding the Christmas holiday Scultetus launched a thorough "cleaning" of the cathedral. To appreciate the bold and aggressive steps taken by Scultetus, we should note that those princes implementing a "second Reformation" in Lutheran territories during this period frequently met significant resistance from the populace when they attempted to remove religious images from the churches. In the Upper Palatinate these actions were often stealthily undertaken at night while in Berlin the decorating changes in the cathedral precipitated a riot in 1615 where Prince Johann Georg of Brandenburg-Jägerndorf was physically attacked.[7] Scultetus, in contrast, was not inclined to work furtively nor afraid of popular opposition. One of the German workers engaged to take down the images reported that Scultetus turned to the crew during their work and loudly exclaimed, "O you Lutherans, come to me and I will open your eyes, for you most assuredly stink of Rome."[8] At the center of this protracted operation at the cathedral was a celebrated sermon Scultetus delivered on 22 December.

Structuring his homily around the second commandment, Scultetus bluntly declared that God clearly forbids the portrayal of his likeness and the worship of images. He later related in his autobiography how disturbed he was when he saw a number of Frederick's Bohemian advisers kneeling before certain images in the cathedral.[9] To ensure that proper worship is restored, it is thus the prince's duty to remove all items that are offensive to God. Scultetus's subsequent remarks, however, indicate how sweeping his vision for reform actually was. In the Low Countries in those instances when the magistrates did support Calvinist reforms, religious art was often disassembled in an orderly fashion or returned to their original donors, and as we have just noted, Calvin himself did not support iconoclastic activity. Frederick's court preacher was of another mind altogether. He cited a series of examples from the Old Testament where the Israelites threw down and completely destroyed the idols and altars of the Philistines.[10] In his autobiography he elaborated further on this theme. God has called us to remove all idols from our heart, and as a sign of this inner conversion, outward action is necessary. The Lord enjoins all true believers to "take pictures away; that is, *to break them or consign them to the flames.*"[11]

This is exactly what occurred during the last two weeks of December. An eyewitness to the events, Šimon Kapihorský, reports that on the 21st Frederick began his "war against the altars, the images, and the tombs of the saints." The Winter King's followers started their work by taking down the large crucifix opposite the high altar before moving on to the tomb of John Nepomuk, which they quickly dismantled. Finally, they proceeded to the high altar itself. Apart from the images and the statues they also gathered

[7] Werner Troßbach, "Volkskultur und Gewissensnot: Zum Bilderstreit in der 'zweiten Reformation'," *Zeitschrift für Historische Forschung* 23 (1996), 477.

[8] V. Kramář, *Zpustošení Chrámu svatého Víta v roce 1619* (Prague: Artefactum, 1998), p. 118.

[9] G. A. Benrath, ed., *Die Selbstbiographie des Heidelberger Theologen und Hofpredigers Abraham Scultetus (1566–1624)* (Karlsruhe: Evangelischer Presseverband, 1966), p. 80.

[10] Abraham Scultetus, *Krátká, avšak na mocném gruntu a základu Svatých Písem založená zpráva o modlářských obrazích* (Prague: Daniel Karolides z Karlsberka, 1620), Diii. The text was most widely distributed in a German version.

[11] Benrath, ed., *Selbstbiographie*, p. 81.

together the chairs of the archbishop and canons and then burned them all in a heap. They returned the next day, and as Kapihorský relates, the heads and bones of the saints were trampled upon and burned. The iconoclasts continued their campaign two days after Christmas. We learn from another account that they focused their attention on the cathedral's stone altars, which they systematically reduced to rubble. Among the casualties that day was an altar painting of Lucas Cranach that had been commissioned by Ferdinand I.[12]

Unlike more typical incidents of Reformation iconoclasm in France, the Swiss lands and the Low Countries, the "cleaning" of St. Vitus Cathedral was not a movement with broad-based support. Even some of the men who had been hired to do the work had serious qualms about the business. When Jakob Hübel voiced his reservations, one of Frederick's advisers responded with a wry laugh, "We would like to do this to Rome as well."[13] The Catholics, of course, were the most vociferous in their opposition to Scultetus's program. The deans and canons saw the cathedral as one of the last Catholic redoubts in the city. When the directors had ordered the cathedral bells to be rung as Frederick entered his new capital, the dean had refused. The king responded in kind. When Frederick wanted to melt down the cathedral's silver plate, and it could not be found, it was suggested that they put the dean on the rack to learn where it had been hidden.[14] The canons wrote an impassioned letter to Archbishop Lohelius who was in exile in Vienna. They described the destruction of the cathedral furnishings and saw this as a token of the end of Catholicism altogether in Bohemia.[15] The resistance to Frederick's policies, however, extended far beyond the small Catholic community. The Utraquists, too, were concerned with his ecclesiastical innovations. Cooperating with the Catholics, they were able to preserve St. Wenceslas Chapel, far and away the cathedral's most important shrine with the tomb of the saint, the priceless gold reliquary, the inlaid walls of gemstones, the stunning frescoes and famous statue of the prince.[16]

Utraquist fears were heightened by a general suspicion that events in the cathedral were only the first step of a broader program of ecclesiastical reform. Though the king had publicly guaranteed religious freedom,

---

[12] Kapihorský's account is reprinted in Tomáš Pešina, *Phosphorus septicornis, stella aliàs matutina* (Prague: Joannis Arnolti de Dobroslavina, 1673), pp. 350–5; related is the pamphlet *Grewel der Verwüstung* (Prague, 1620) (KNM, 42 D 17).

[13] Kramář, *Zpustošení*, p. 117.

[14] C. A. Pescheck, *The Reformation and Anti-Reformation in Bohemia* (London: Houlston and Stoneman, 1845), vol. I, pp. 365–6.

[15] Reprinted in Pešina, *Phosphorus septicornis*, pp. 356–7.   [16] Ibid., p. 642.

developments in Prague indicated that Frederick may have had other intentions. He extended his campaign across the river into the former Jesuit domain of the Clementinum. The order had been expelled in 1619, and now Frederick appropriated their church and its belongings. With his eye on their furnishings, he requisitioned two large candelabras for his palace while two of its altars were carted off to nearby Protestant churches. In the second week of January, Frederick himself led a procession down from the castle for a ceremony to rededicate the building for Calvinist worship.[17] Back at St. Vitus we have a fascinating account of the Christmas service that took place while the images were coming down. To celebrate communion the Calvinists had set up a simple table with twelve seats in the choir as they prepared to eat what one sarcastic wag described as "cake" for "breakfast." Even more ominous were rumors of a new worship ordinance for the kingdom mandating the destruction of all religious images, the abolition of clerical vestments and a drastic simplification of the liturgy.[18]

After the St. Vitus incident Frederick turned his attention to another of Prague's famous landmarks. A cross had stood on the third pier of the Charles Bridge since 1361. Though Hussites had pulled it down in the early fifteenth century, once peace was restored, it had been re-erected and joined by two flanking statues. When Frederick arrived, his wife, Elizabeth Stuart, took offense at what she referred to as the "naked bath attendant" on the bridge. Shortly after Christmas 1619, Frederick conferred with his council concerning the fate of the object. They warned the king of a public outcry were it to be removed. Though no official steps were taken, some time later it mysteriously disappeared at night.[19] These examples suggest that Frederick was operating on a level very different than that of his subjects. For the Palatine prince his actions were based on well-defined theological principles. Religious objects, however, can possess a multiplicity of meanings, and what was merely a doctrinal issue for the Calvinist court was perceived as an attack on traditional Bohemian culture by the general populace.[20]

[17] Alois Kroess, *Geschichte der böhmischen Provinz der Gesellschaft Jesu*, 3 vols. (Vienna: Opitz, 1910–38), vol. II, p. 8.

[18] Pešina, *Phosphorus septicornis*, pp. 354–5; Kroess, *Geschichte der böhmischen Provinz*, vol. II, p. 9.

[19] Pešina, *Phosphorus septicornis*, p. 353. Though Pavel Skála downplayed public reaction to the disappearance of the cross, a legend later circulated that those who attempted to remove the cross were punished directly by God as in the case of Elizabeth who was forced to flee the city in 1620. Josef Svátek, *Pražské pověsti a legendy* (Prague: Paseka, 1997), pp. 107–8.

[20] For a comparative example see Joel Budd, "Rethinking iconoclasm in early modern England: the case of the Cheapside Cross," *Journal of Early Modern History* 4 (2000), 402.

The backlash against Frederick and Scultetus was substantial. Scultetus, himself, seemed somewhat surprised that his reform agenda had provoked such a violent reaction. In his autobiography he noted how his opponents accused him of being an atheist and a great persecutor of Catholics, Lutherans and even the Bohemian Brethren.[21] The St. Vitus incident immediately became a *cause célèbre* initiating a significant flurry of pamphlets. Both Catholic and Lutheran theologians jumped into the fray as strong denunciations of the action were quickly issued from Ingolstadt, Mainz, Tübingen, Wittenberg and Leipzig.[22] Pamphlets were also produced in Prague that attacked the policies of the Calvinist court. One fascinating tract appeared in the form of a dialogue between an Utraquist, Catholic and Lutheran. Distressed by Scultetus's zeal, the Utraquist remarked to his Lutheran colleague, "It would be better for you and me to follow the Jesuits than the Reformed, for they have never thrown such a big rock in our garden as the Calvinists have just done." At his turn the Lutheran passed on the rumor that a thousand English iconoclasts were even now preparing to descend on Bohemia and finish the business that Scultetus had begun.[23] In the end, all three individuals banded together and condemned the religious innovations that threatened the kingdom's spiritual and cultural heritage.

The issue of religious images primary to the pamphlet war remained a prominent feature of the struggle between Frederick and Ferdinand once the weapons changed from pen and ink to gunpowder and musket. In October 1620 Bavarian troops entered the southern Bohemian town of Strakonice. Forces loyal to the Czech estates had recently pulled back from the village. Dominicus a Jesu Maria, a Spanish Carmelite who accompanied the Bavarians and served as spiritual adviser to the duke, picked through the ruins of a building that had recently belonged to the Knights of Malta. In it he found the usual tokens of an army in quick retreat. Furniture was demolished, windows were smashed, and in this case images of the saints lay scattered and torn throughout the residence. The Carmelite realized that much of this disorder was merely the byproduct of an army in quick retreat, but he found one item in particular that indicated that not all of the destruction was random. In one corner he came across an Adoration of the Shepherds which lay before him ritually mutilated. The departing

---

[21] Benrath, ed., *Selbstbiographie*, p. 78.
[22] Specific publication details can be found in ibid., pp. 80–1.
[23] *Einfältiges Gespräch uber den kurtzen aber unschriffttmässigen Bericht von den ungötzen Bildern an die Christliche Gemein zu Prag* (Prague, 1620), pp. 1, 6.

soldiers had carefully sliced out the eyes of all in the scene save for the baby in the manger. A biographer later recounted the friar's stunned reaction:

Suddenly, our Father felt a pain as real as if he had been struck by a lance in the heart. Having seen with what impiety the Holy Mother of God and all the other saints had been treated, his disgust had become so great and his feelings had been so offended that on the spot he made a noble vow to dedicate all his attention and power to honor the image of the Holy Mother because of the great injury that had been done to it by the perfidious heretics.[24]

After this experience Dominicus a Jesu Maria placed images at the center of the struggle with the Winter King. Catholic illustrations of White Mountain featured the friar standing before the Duke of Bavaria and his troops mutilated painting in hand exhorting them to beat back the heretic and reclaim Bohemia for Rome. The soldiers who went into battle against Frederick's mercenaries carried images with them. Crucifixes, medals and small devotional pictures accompanied them into the fray. For pious Catholics the outbreaks of iconoclasm at St. Vitus, Strakonice and elsewhere surely recalled a longer history of image breaking in Bohemia and the earlier unsuccessful crusades against the Hussites. Now once more, the emperor and his allies had assembled an army to fight an old foe who had reappeared in new form. Even the Carmelite chaplain, the spiritual leader of this new military expedition, consciously styled himself after an old enemy of the Hussites, John of Capistrano. In one hand he carried the image of Strakonice, while in the other, like his predecessor, he held a large crucifix that he brought into battle.[25]

If images figured prominently in the war against Frederick, the victory of White Mountain was in large part celebrated as their triumph. The painting of Strakonice came to be seen as a relic of tremendous importance for all of Catholic Europe. As such, there was significant demand to install it in Rome itself. On 8 May 1622 it was placed on an elaborately decorated throne together with the imperial crown of Ferdinand II in the church of Santa Maria Maggiore. Its final destination, though, was a smaller church constructed only a few years earlier, Santa Maria della Vittoria. There it headed a festive procession that commemorated the victory of White Mountain a year and a half earlier. The image became the iconographic focus of the church. Gian Domenico Cerrini later painted the frescoes of the nave and cupola celebrating the victory of the Virgin over the heretics while sometime

---

[24] Cited in Olivier Chaline, *La Bataille de la Montagne Blanche* (Paris: Éditions Noesis, 1999), pp. 304–5.

[25] This comparison is made explicit in Georg Stengel, *Gloria bellica* (Ingolstadt: Haenlinus, 1623), pp. 378–9. My thanks to Trevor Johnson for this reference.

in the second half of the seventeenth century an anonymous painter depicted in the sacristy four large scenes of the battle outside Prague. Dominicus a Jesu Maria is shown in one detail fearlessly riding a charger into the fight while rays of divine energy stream forth from the image hung around his neck. A similar series of paintings was executed for the Monastery of the Discalced Carmelites in Munich. Within Bohemia the victory was celebrated primarily through a series of engravings and special medals minted to commemorate the event. A small pilgrimage complex was built at White Mountain at the beginning of the eighteenth century. Copies of the painting were executed both for a church in Strakonice and for Our Lady Victorious in the Lesser Town.[26]

Catholic preachers and writers proclaimed the same theme across the continent. The Bavarian Jesuit Jeremias Drexel wrote with great conviction, "Truly on the octave of the feast of All Saints, the saints of heaven avenged themselves on the injury inflicted on them in Prague by the Calvinists who had cut off their hands, lips, noses and even heads."[27] Texts and sermons poured out of Italy, France, the Low Countries, Germany and of course Bohemia itself linking the fall of Frederick to the blasphemy he committed in the cathedral.[28] Johann Bissel, another Bavarian Jesuit, wrote one of the most memorable accounts of the battle. In a creative adaptation of a passage from Isaiah he described in apocalyptic terms how Europe's most pernicious heretics had gathered at White Mountain: "Here were the factions of Geneva, the armed bands of Zurich, the Schwenkfeldian monsters, the Anabaptist plague, the four-headed Utraquist giants and the rest of the Taborites, Orphans, Procopians and Adamites."[29] In this cosmic struggle between good and evil the saints came down from heaven and fought against those who had desecrated their cathedral. Legends and stories also circulated that described how the images defended themselves against the Calvinists who sought to destroy them. Tomáš Pešina compiled many of these accounts and included them in his history of the cathedral. The

---

[26] On the medals and engravings see Čeněk Zíbrt, *Bibliografie české historie*, 5 vols. (Prague: Nákl. České akademie císaře Františka Josefa pro vědy, slovesnost a umění, 1900–12), vol. IV, pp. 412–14; on the Strakonice image and its copies see Jan Royt, *Obraz a kult v Čechách 17. a 18. století* (Prague: Karolinum, 1999), pp. 222–3.

[27] Cited in Chaline, *La Bataille*, p. 316.

[28] A. Miraeus, *De rebus Bohemicis liber singularis* (Lyon: Landry, 1621); L. Aureli, *Della ribellione de Boemi* (Milan: Malatesta, 1626); Johannes Labenus, *Prager Schlacht* (Augsburg: Aperger, 1621); Carlo Caraffa, *Commentaria de Germania sacra restaurata* (Aversa: Longhi, 1630); J. Placentius, *Victoria belli et deditio Pragensis* (Prague: Leopold, n.d.); C. Questenberg, *Lob und Danck Predigt Am Jahrtag der Gedenkwürdigen Siegreichen Victori* (Vienna: Formica, 1626).

[29] Johann Bissel, *Leo Galeatus* (Amberg: Burger, 1677), p. 19.

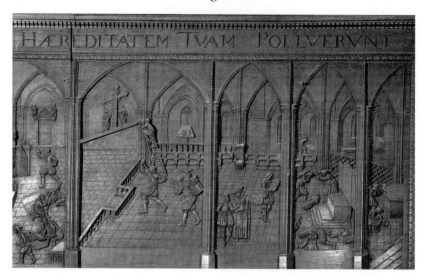

10. Wood panel depicting destruction of St. Vitus Cathedral, Caspar Bechteler

workman commissioned to demolish the tomb of St. Vitus was knocked senseless and lost the use of his hands for a significant period of time. Much worse, however, was the fate in store for those charged to remove the grill around the grave of St. John Nepomuk. A Hussite blacksmith who was initially sent in to do the job knew better and refused the assignment directly. The Saxon Lutheran who replaced him was knocked on his back when he tried to disassemble the railing. In a state of delirium and great pain, he was consumed by an internal fire that slowly killed him. As Pešina pointed out, these developments were in no way surprising, for there had long been a popular saying in Prague that whoever destroyed the cathedral would be promptly sent to hell.[30]

The memory of December 1619 became a permanent feature of St. Vitus itself. In the early 1620s the cabinet maker Caspar Bechteler carved four large and intricate panels that depicted these events for the ambulatory of the cathedral. The first two scenes illustrate the Calvinists at work destroying the furnishings of the church. One worker has climbed a ladder intent on bringing down the crucifix in front of the altar. Others are busy smashing or breaking objects with axes, hammers and mallets (Figure 10). Even the incident at Nepomuk's tomb is recorded. Through these two

---

[30] Pešina, *Phosphorus septicornis*, p. 633.

panels the artist and designer intended to recall the destruction of Solomon's Temple, and the connection with the biblical narrative was strengthened by one of the most prized possessions of the cathedral. According to the fourteenth-century *Chronicle of Dalimil*, the Jerusalem Candelabrum of the Ludmila chapel had originally come from the temple itself. Titus had carried it off to Rome, and then in the twelfth century it was brought across the Alps to Bohemia. The story is completed on the other side of the ambulatory. With an inscription recounting the destruction of Pharaoh's army at the Red Sea, Frederick and his entourage are shown crossing the Moldau in haste, confusion and fear after their unexpected defeat at White Mountain.

An ironic testament to the brief reign of the Winter King, the panels, which are themselves a beautiful work of religious art, memorialized the policies of an individual who attempted to remove all such images from the cathedral. The carving, however, was more than a clever joke at Frederick's expense, for all those who busied themselves restoring St. Vitus were making a broader statement concerning the nature of artistic activity. The Jerusalem Candelabrum, which had been badly damaged, was carefully repaired and returned to the cathedral with a new shaft topped by the Lamb Triumphant and surrounded by four of Bohemia's patron saints. For a time it was even placed atop the tomb of John Nepomuk. Emperor Ferdinand donated a new triptych for the altar to replace the one that had been destroyed by the Calvinists. Its central scene, now the focal point of the church, was St. Luke painting the Virgin. The apostle at work on his portrait became a common motif in this period. After the desecration of the Calvinists, the images had returned to St. Vitus victorious, and now the making of religious art was celebrated in and of itself as an act of orthodoxy.

JAN JIŘÍ BENDL AND KAREL ŠKRÉTA: FOUNDATIONS OF A CONFESSIONAL ART

The confrontation between Frederick and Ferdinand was of course only the first act in what was unfolding as a great tragedy in the Bohemian lands. Though the Thirty Years War affected all aspects of life in central Europe, it had a devastating impact on the arts in particular. The lament of the German painter Joachim von Sandrart perhaps best captured these feelings of loss and despair:

Queen Germania saw her palaces and churches decorated with magnificent pictures go up in flames time and again, whilst her eyes were so blinded by smoke and tears that she no longer had the power or will to attend to art … So art was forgotten and its practitioners were overcome by poverty and contempt.[31]

War, however, did not stop all activity. In the midst of the chaos and destruction painters and sculptors were at work quietly charting a new direction for the arts in the Bohemian lands. The careers of two individuals stand out in particular, the painter Karel Škréta (1610–74) and the sculptor Jan Jiří Bendl (*ca.* 1620–80). Together, they developed an aesthetic vocabulary that was used for the next century as they helped make the arts an effective marker of confessional identity.

Bendl and Škréta were both raised in the Czech lands in the early years of the seventeenth century. Bendl's father had come to southern Bohemia from Bavaria and worked as a sculptor for the Rožmberk family in the regional centers of Český Krumlov and Jindřichův Hradec before settling in Prague around 1630.[32] Škréta had a more distinguished Czech pedigree. His family had moved to Prague from Moravia in the middle of the sixteenth century. His enterprising grandfather had become a citizen of Old Town in 1559 and made a substantial fortune. Škréta's father worked as a royal clerk living in a handsome house off Old Town Square where the future painter was born in 1610.[33] In 1627, however, this Protestant family was forced to emigrate. The young Škréta returned in 1638 as a Catholic.

The seventeenth century, especially for painting, is one of the more problematic periods of central European art, and Škréta has often been interpreted out of context. In the nineteenth century, his work was debated in a narrower nationalist framework while in the middle of the twentieth his paintings were refracted through a simplistic Marxist lens.[34] Bendl, in contrast, has been the subject of far less study. Overshadowed by the brilliant careers of Matthias Braun and Ferdinand Maximilian Brokoff, Bendl's work a half century earlier is often passed by with little note. The contributions of both these artists, however, take on new significance if they are placed more squarely in the context of Catholic reform. The Council of Trent devoted considerable attention to artistic matters, and these issues

[31] Cited in Thomas DaCosta Kaufmann, *Court, Cloister and City: The Art and Culture of Central Europe, 1450–1800* (Chicago: University of Chicago Press, 1995), p. 235.

[32] O. J. Blažíček, "Jan Jiří Bendl, Pražský sochař časného baroku," *Památky archaeologické* 4–5 (1934–5), 55–91; O. J. Blažíček, "Jan Jiří Bendl," *Umění* 30 (1982), 97–116.

[33] Most recent on Škréta is Jaromír Neumann, *Škrétové: Karel Škréta a jeho syn* (Prague: Akropolis, 2000).

[34] On nationalism see G. E. Pazaurek, *Carl Screta (1610–1674)* (Prague: Ehrlich, 1889); for the Marxist perspective see the comments of Jaromír Neumann cited in Eberhard Hempel, *Baroque Art and Architecture in Central Europe: Germany, Austria, Switzerland, Hungary, Czechoslovakia, Poland* (Baltimore: Penguin, 1965), p. 85.

were actively debated in the Czech lands.[35] The delegates at Trent laid special emphasis on the didactic nature of art. Used properly, it could educate and support the mission of the church. Religious painting and sculpture had tremendous power to shape patterns of personal piety. Škréta and Bendl were trained in Italy and brought this influence back to Bohemia. Through his drawings and paintings the prolific Škréta supported specific cults of the church, helped create a Catholic martyrology and promoted Rome's renewed emphasis on episcopal authority.

Bendl's work followed a similar pattern. The sculptor's most important patrons were the Jesuits, who granted him four different commissions alone on their St. Salvator Church in the Clementinum. His second assignment for them was a series of massive figures decorating the façade of the building. Above the portal he completed six statues of the church fathers, five of them bishops. Along with Clement, Augustine, Gregory the Great, Ambrose and Jerome, Bendl included St. Adalbert (*ca.* 957–97), who as Bohemia's greatest bishop completed the Christianization of the region.[36] What most art historians consider his best work, though, was inside the church. One of the least studied features of Catholic art in this period is its place and function in the liturgical context, yet it was precisely in this area that Bendl had his greatest success. He first came to the attention of Ferdinand III when the visiting emperor marveled at his wooden pulpit in the Augustinian church of St. Wenceslas in Prague. In 1673, the Jesuits commissioned Bendl to carve a set of apostles for the confessional booths. Here his work should be viewed in conjunction with the church's recent reforms of penance.[37] A few years later, the Jesuits approached Bendl again, this time for work on the pulpit. They had always laid significant stress on sacred oratory, and the preaching at St. Salvator's had a high reputation. For thirty years, the legendary Jiří Ferus held forth here before crowds that often overflowed into the streets. When he was reassigned to the countryside, there was purportedly such an outcry that the Society was forced to bring him back

---

[35] See, for example, the proceedings of a 1605 synod convened in Prague. *Synodus Archidioecesana Pragensis* (Prague: Typis Nigrinianis, 1605), pp. 25–7. For a recent study that places Škréta in this context see Sylva Dobalová, *Pašijový cyklus Karla Škréty: mezi výtvarnou tradicí a jezuitskou spiritualitou* (Prague: Nakladatelství Lidové noviny, 2003).

[36] V. Novotný incorrectly identifies the final figure as Basil of Caesarea in "Účast Jana Jiřího Bendla na výzdobě Kostela sv. Salvátora v Praze," *Památky Archeologické* 5 (1937), 46. More reliable is the entry in Pavel Vlček, ed., *Umělecké památky Prahy, Staré město/Josefov* (Prague: Academia, 1996), pp. 109–14.

[37] Neils Krogh Rasmussen, "Liturgy and liturgical arts," in John O'Malley, ed., *Catholicism in Early Modern History: A Guide to Research* (St. Louis: Center for Reformation Research, 1988), pp. 285–8; W. David Myers, *"Poor, Sinning, Folk": Confession and Conscience in Counter-Reformation Germany* (Ithaca: Cornell University Press, 1996).

and allow him to resume his preaching.[38] Bendl, whose earlier work had so
moved Emperor Ferdinand, must have seemed the ideal craftsman to create
a pulpit that could emotively match and complement the oratory of Plachý
and the other Jesuit fathers.

Of all the concerns to occupy Bendl and Škréta, it was their promotion of
the Virgin that may have been most significant. The Marian cult was one of
the most important dynamics in Czech society after the Thirty Years War.
Catholic apologists had long acknowledged the critical role the Virgin had
played in the defeat of the Winter King, but Mary's contribution at the end
of the war may have been even more substantial. In July 1648, the Swedes
swept down over Castle Hill into the Lesser Town and laid siege to Prague's
Old and New Towns. In one of the most celebrated events in the city's long
history, a citizen militia held out under difficult circumstances until imperial troops relieved the beleaguered capital at the beginning of November.
The Jesuits credited the Virgin for this miraculous success, and when peace
and stability finally returned, there was a virtual explosion of Marian
literature and a swift expansion of her cult. During this period Bohuslav
Balbín wrote his trilogy popularizing the kingdom's Marian pilgrimage
routes. The promotional efforts of Balbín and others yielded impressive
results. The 1657 edition of the *Atlas Marianus*, a European gazetteer of
Marian devotion, listed only two Bohemian shrines. The second edition of
1672 included twenty-six.[39]

Growth of the Virgin's cult within the Czech lands was bolstered by a
broader Habsburg campaign championed by Ferdinand III. The Jesuits had
introduced new regulations at the universities in Vienna and Prague mandating adherence to the dogma of the Immaculate Conception. More
popular devotional literature was also produced in support of this teaching.[40] But what may have been the most effective means of doctrinal
advocacy was visual. In 1647, the emperor raised a Marian column in
Vienna, and back in Prague an imperial committee was organized to oversee
the erection of a similar monument. There was some debate concerning the
location of the memorial. The Jesuits submitted a petition arguing that it
should be placed outside the Clementinum, but in the end, and for very

[38] F. Pelcl, *Abbildungen böhmischer und mährischer Gelehrten und Künstler*, 4 vols. (Prague: Gerle,
1773–82), vol. III, pp. 110–18.
[39] Johanna von Herzogenberg, "Heiligtümer, Heiltümer und Schätze," in Ferdinand Seibt, ed.,
Bohemia sacra (Dusseldorf: Pädagogischer Verlag Schwann, 1974), pp. 467–8.
[40] *Laurea gloriae* (Prague: Typis Caesares. Acad., 1652); *Fons Marianus* (Prague: Typis Caesareo-
academicis, 1653); Jan Tanner, *Oratio de Immaculata Conceptione ... anno Domino 1685, 9 Decembris*
(NK 65 C 226).

important reasons, Old Town Square was selected.[41] Bendl won the commission, and preparatory work of clearing the ground and setting a foundation began in May 1650. By August the task was complete. Standing at sixteen meters, Bendl's Marian column was the most monumental of his sculptures. He decorated its base with a set of angels battling demons beneath them. At the top stood a gilded figure of the Virgin who triumphantly strode across the prone body of a dragon, a reference to her Immaculate Conception.

While the column was being raised in August, another important Marian celebration was occurring no more than fifty meters away at the Týn Church. The Madonna of Stará Boleslav, a small metal relief of Virgin and child, was one of the kingdom's oldest devotional objects. Various legends had it connected with Sts. Cyril and Methodius, Ludmila, Wenceslas, Adalbert and Procopius. It had been removed to Vienna for safety during the war but was now returning with great pomp and fanfare. Church officials had carefully planned its route from Vienna with frequent stops in major towns along the way. In late August it arrived in Prague where it made a triumphant circuit through the city's three most important churches: St. Vitus, the Vyšehrad complex and the Týn Church.[42] This image, saluting Mary as Queen of Bohemia, was complemented in the Old Town church with a new painting for the high altar. The previous year, Karel Škréta completed one of his largest and most ambitious works, an imposing canvas depicting the Assumption of the Virgin.

This crescendo of artistic activity represented in the work of Bendl and Škréta constitutes an important cultural and religious turning point. Thirty years earlier, the events that were staged in Old Town Square were of an entirely different nature. The execution of 1621 was a ritual of purification. Now at the end of the war, rites of punishment were giving way to a celebration of confessional victory as represented in Mary's defeat of sin and death itself. The Virgin, in the guise of the Immaculata, represented the definitive triumph of a pure and untainted Catholicism over the errors of Protestantism. In these three decades, Old Town Square was being carefully transformed from a symbol of resistance to an icon of orthodoxy. The old

---

[41] APH-AMKSV, Codex VI 9, 178v–179v; J. F. Hammerschmid, *Prodromus gloriae Pragenae* (Prague: Wolfgang Wickhart, 1723), p. 570; Peter Rigetti and Johann Christoph Pannich, *Historischer Nachricht* (Prague: Wittib, 1773), pp. 210–14.

[42] Hammerschmid, *Prodromus gloriae Pragenae*, p. 30. This object acquired the title, Palladium of Bohemia, in the seventeenth century. M. E. Ducreux, "Zum Thema Wallfahrt: das Beispiel Böhmens im 17. Jahrhundert," in R. Leeb, S. Pils and T. Winkelbauer, eds., *Staatsmacht und Seelenheil* (Vienna: Oldenbourg, 2007), p. 105.

Utraquist emblems of King George and the chalice that had hung on the gable of the Týn Church had been taken down and replaced by the Virgin and child. Ferdinand also ordered the removal of the gallows that had been a central feature of the square and a reminder of the recent unrest. The column, as well, took on a life of its own. A copy of the Madonna of Stará Boleslav had been installed in a niche at its base to unite the old pre-Hussite cult with the new form of Marian devotion. At the monument's formal dedication in 1652 the emperor donated funds to support regular celebrations on Marian feast days while the Jesuits organized their own series of ceremonies around the monument. There were weekly processions every Saturday during which regular market activities of the square were suspended, and all Jews were forbidden to enter the area.[43] Perhaps most importantly, however, this work of Bendl and Škréta in the heart of Old Town became a template for artistic activity across the kingdom. Marian columns were erected in virtually every city and town. Bendl, himself, executed another such commission for Louny in northwest Bohemia while Škréta made Bendl's column the centerpiece of a famous illustrated thesis sheet commissioned by future archbishop Johann Friedrich Waldstein. In similar fashion, the Assumption of the Virgin reappeared countless times in the many churches and chapels of the region. Škréta returned to this theme at least twice before the end of his career.[44]

One of the great strengths of early modern Catholicism was its ability to adapt to local cultures. Though Škréta and Bendl promoted general concerns of the church such as Marian devotion and penitential piety, there was also a regional side to their work. Bendl's career underwent a significant shift in this respect. While before 1660 less than 10 percent of his commissions included figures of the kingdom's patron saints, after this date they appeared in more than 40 percent of his work. Of all these figures one in particular comes to the fore, the martyr Wenceslas.[45] Though there was no similar transition with Škréta, Wenceslas was a subject to which he turned frequently. His largest project, in fact, was devoted exclusively to the national saint. Sometime before 1644, he completed a massive cycle of thirty-two paintings that highlighted the life and miracles of Bohemia's

[43] APH-AMKSV, Codex VI 9, 178v–179v; also Codices XXVII, XLIV; Susan Tipton, "'Super aspidem et basiliscum ambulabis…': Zur Entstehung der Mariensäulen im 17. Jahrhundert," in Dieter Breuer, ed., *Religion und Religiosität im Zeitalter des Barock* (Wiesbaden: Harrassowitz, 1995), vol. I, pp. 383–5.

[44] Antonín Šorm and Antonín Krajča (eds.), *Mariánské sloupy v Čechách a na Moravě* (Prague: Antonín Daněk, 1939); Blažíček, "Jan Jiří Bendl," 113; O. J. Blažíček, "Škrétova mapa evropy," *Časopis společnosti přátel starožitností* 60 (1952), 134–41; Neumann, *Škrétové*, pp. 90, 92.

[45] Blažíček, "Jan Jiří Bendl," 110–13.

saintly prince. Together, Bendl and Škréta developed what became the standard iconography of the Wenceslas cult in the seventeenth and eighteenth centuries.[46]

The two artists memorialized features of the saint's life that had special relevance for their society. The veneration of Wenceslas was, above all, a cult of the ruler. His relics figured prominently in the coronation rites. The king received the crown of the dead saint and was knighted with his sword. Thus, by its very nature this was a conservative form of devotion. The Wenceslas legend, in fact, was one of the earliest to unite royalty with sanctity.[47] If, as Peter Burke has argued, Cardinal Borromeo was the prototypical saint of the Catholic Reformation reinforcing a new emphasis on episcopal authority, within Bohemia Wenceslas was his secular counterpart, a reminder of the sacred nature of princely rule. The Habsburgs grasped this point immediately as reflected in their rivalry with the Winter King. While the Calvinist Frederick had little use for Wenceslas and sought to dismantle his shrine in the cathedral, Ferdinand assiduously cultivated the links between himself and his holy predecessor. In 1631 he commissioned Matthias Mayer to paint his family in the company of the duke. Catholic writers later claimed that a king's legitimacy depended on his relationship to "the family of St. Wenceslas."[48]

In the hands of seventeenth-century hagiographers, the life of Wenceslas became a *Fürstenspiegel*, a carefully defined model of the ideal prince. Whereas the duke's early hagiographers highlighted aspects of his life and devotion that corresponded to a monastic ideal, the archetype developed by Škréta and his colleagues coalesced with a new form of piety embraced by the Habsburgs, the so-called *pietas Austriaca*.[49] Škréta's cycle, which was reproduced in print form in at least three seventeenth-century biographies of Wenceslas, described in great detail the pious deeds of the saint.[50] Here Škréta highlighted a number of scenes that matched the devotional

---

[46] Jaromír Neumann, *Karel Škréta 1610–1674* (Prague: Národní galerie, 1974), pp. 65–83; Jindřich Šámal, "Barokní cykly svatováclavské. Jejich význam v obraze sv. Václava," unpublished Ph.D. thesis, Charles University (1945).

[47] Gábor Klaniczay, *Holy Rulers and Blessed Princesses* (Cambridge: Cambridge University Press, 2002), pp. 107–8.

[48] Jan Tanner, *Swatá Cesta z Prahy do Staré Boleslawě* (Prague: Typis Universitatis Carolo-Ferdinandeae, 1694), pp. 43–4.

[49] Klaniczay, *Holy Rulers*, pp. 103–4.

[50] Aegidius a s. Joanne Baptista, *Věnec blahoslavenému a věčně oslavenému knížeti českému* (Prague: Bylina, 1643); Aegidius a s. Joanne Baptista, *D. Wenceslao Bohemorum duci ac martyri inclyto* (Prague, 1643) [recte 1644]; Paul Krieger, *Fons Apollinis Oder Sonnen Brunnen, das ist: das Leben dess heil. Wenceslai Martyrers* (Prague: Goliasch, 1662); the original cycle of paintings has not survived in its entirety.

standards of the Catholic Reformation: the promotion of the Eucharist, the practice of pilgrimage and the translation of relics. These themes were picked up and elaborated by others such as the Viennese court preacher, Abraham a Sancta Clara, who in the early eighteenth century again pointed to Wenceslas as the ideal ruler.[51]

Though in life the duke was a devout and compassionate prince, in death he became a fierce warrior when the Christian cause was threatened. Škréta depicted Wenceslas's martyrdom at a point only two thirds of the way through the cycle. The final nine canvases were devoted to the saint's afterlife. In scene thirty, pagans gather on a hillside to destroy the rapidly growing Christian community. At this critical juncture the saint appears in the sky riding a white horse. With blasts of thunder and lightning, he kills many of his enemies while scattering the rest.[52] Like the cult of the Virgin, devotion to Wenceslas experienced a significant boost in Bohemia at the end of the Thirty Years War, for the saint, too, was credited with saving Prague's Old and New Towns from the Swedes in 1648. In a painting for the Emmaus Monastery commemorating the tenth anniversary of the siege, Škréta portrayed Wenceslas in full armor leading a detachment of angels into the conflict. Bendl also favored the motif of a bold and militant Wenceslas. His first free-standing statue of the saint, executed in 1662, was for the residence of the cathedral provost. Dressed in full armor, Wenceslas self-assuredly surveys his surroundings while in his right hand he grasps a standard that has been outfitted with the sharp end of a pike.[53] Bendl also fashioned the first equestrian statue of the saint that stood in what is today Wenceslas Square. A confident warrior astride his steed looks out on the field before him as he advances against his foes. This iconography was later reinforced by a famous legend that developed around this statue which stood in the square until 1879. At a crucial juncture in a last great battle, the horse and the rider would come alive. Wenceslas would summon his former knights who were lying asleep under Blaník hill and deliver his land from a foreign oppressor.[54]

Wenceslas was not only a ruler but also a missionary. Here his legend could be read as a parable of seventeenth-century Bohemia. The Christian duke came from a mixed family. While his grandparents, Ludmila and Bořivoj, were the first of Bohemia's princes to be baptized, his mother,

---

[51] Abraham a Sancta Clara, *Drey Buchstaben W, W, W. Das ist: Ein gering geschmidte Lob-Red von den Glorwürdigen Blutszeigen Christi Wenceslao* (Prague, 1703).
[52] Krieger, *Fons Apollinis*, E8v–F1v.   [53] Blažíček, "Jan Jiří Bendl," 76–7.
[54] Svátek, *Pražské pověsti*, pp. 16–17.

11. Drahomíra dragged to hell, Karel Škréta

Drahomíra, was a pagan. As Škréta illustrated in the fourth painting of his cycle, Drahomíra was a great enemy of the Christians. She persecuted the new converts and even ordered the murder of her own mother-in-law. Wenceslas endeavored to undo the damage of his mother and foster further Christian expansion. Škréta painted a number of important scenes saluting the young duke's work as missionary. He depicted Wenceslas demolishing the altars of his mother's priests and baptizing the children of pagan parents. The struggle between mother and son reached its climax in one of the most dramatic scenes of the series (Figure 11). Drahomíra has stopped outside a Christian shrine as her coachman, a secret believer, has entered the chapel to receive the sacrament from the priest. As she hurls curses at her servant, the ground suddenly opens beneath her, and at the moment of the Host's elevation, the devil grasps a wheel of her carriage and drags her to hell.[55] While Škréta captured this moment on canvas, Bendl and his colleagues memorialized the Wenceslas legend in stone. A cross was erected on the spot of Drahomíra's demise which supposedly occurred on Loreto square above the castle. Shortly thereafter, Matthias Braun commemorated the moment more theatrically with a statue depicting her unexpected departure to the netherworld. Bendl, for his part, produced a figure of Wenceslas to mark the

---

[55] Krieger, *Fons Apollinis*, C7v–D1r.

spot where a procession, led by the duke, miraculously crossed the swollen Moldau on its way to Castle Hill with the sacred remains of the martyred Ludmila.[56]

The parallels between the medieval legend and the recent past were not lost on Bohemia's Catholic commentators. Tomáš Pešina drew the comparison between Elizabeth of Bohemia and the godless Drahomíra. The impiety of both women cried out to the heavens, and the divine response that followed fully justified the Catholic cause.[57] There was another member of Wenceslas's family, however, who occupied a slightly different position. Boleslav, the duke's brother and later murderer, had been baptized a Christian. Unlike Wenceslas, who had been raised by his devout grandparents, Boleslav had remained with his mother and, not unexpectedly, the young prince had been led astray and in the end committed the crime for which he is infamously known. It is significant that though the pagan Drahomíra was damned, Boleslav was not. Škréta in fact portrayed Wenceslas as a type of Christ figure, whose personal suffering ultimately led to the redemption of his wayward brother and family. In the scene immediately before his death, Wenceslas is warned by a friend of Boleslav's plans. Well aware of his fate, the duke continued on his way and met his end composed and triumphant. Miraculous events after Wenceslas's martyrdom later convinced Boleslav of his brother's sanctity. This part of the Wenceslas legend spoke directly to a society that had been divided so long by confession. Like Boleslav's son, whom Balbín praised as one of Bohemia's great Christian princes, reconciliation and reunion were possible for those who had wandered from the true path of orthodoxy.[58]

THE CHARLES BRIDGE AND CONFESSIONAL IDENTITY

Škréta and Bendl fashioned the iconographic building blocks that were used by the next generation of artists. This tradition reached its high point in the early decades of the eighteenth century with the work of sculptors Ferdinand Maximilian Brokoff and Matthias Braun, painters Jan Jiří Heinsch and Petr Brandl, and architects Christoph Dientzenhofer and

---

[56] Jan Royt, "Kult a ikonografie sv. Václava v 17. a 18. století," in Jan Royt, ed., *Svatý Václav v umění 17. a 18. století* (Prague: Národní galerie, 1994), p. 9.

[57] Pešina, *Phosphorus septicornis*, pp. 622–56.

[58] Krieger, *Fons Apollinis*, D3v–D4r, D6v–D7r, E8v–F1v; the Boleslav-Wenceslas theme was also a popular pedagogical model in the seventeenth century. See for example the Jesuit plays *Cereus Iuventutis Animus* (Prague, 1674); *Bonae & malae educationis typus Wenceslaus, & Boleslaus fratres* (Vienna, n.d.).

Jan Blažej Santini-Aichel. The structure that may best encapsulate these aesthetic developments is Prague's most recognizable landmark today, the Charles Bridge and its flanking batteries of statues. In terms of collaborative effort, there is no other baroque monument in the kingdom that can match the Charles Bridge. Though it became the showplace of Brokoff and Braun, at least seven other artists produced statues for the span. Škréta had a hand with one of its earliest monuments, and both Brandl and Heinsch planned designs that sculptors later executed. The bridge, though, had a checkered past, and like Old Town Square, its entire character was transformed in the late seventeenth century.

The bridge itself, which did not acquire the name of its builder until the nineteenth century, had been constructed by Charles IV to replace an older structure that had been destroyed by floods in 1342. The new bridge quickly developed a rather dubious reputation. Even before its completion, local felons, often in the hire of a third party, found it a useful place to do away with their enemies. In the late fourteenth century, three important church officials, including a future saint, were hurled from its ramparts.[59] The fate of its first monuments also reflected the turbulent nature of this period. Though the stone bridge remained relatively free of decoration in these early centuries, a crucifix had been erected in 1361 to mark the spot where Martin Cink, a priest of the cathedral, had been flung into the river. The cross, which became an informal center of devotion, was first destroyed by the Hussites in 1419. Replaced in the second half of the fifteenth century, it was tossed in the river by a supporter of Elizabeth Stuart. It reappeared for a third time in 1629, only to be shot down by the Swedes in 1648. The bridge acquired other unsavory connotations over time. In its early days it had been used as an official place of execution. Across from the crucifix, a headsman had dispatched local felons where a column of Justice had stood.[60] More recently, the impaled heads of the prominent Czech rebels executed in 1621 were grimly displayed on its eastern tower while in 1648 the bridge actually served as the frontline in the Swedes' brief but bitter siege of the city. When the invading army finally withdrew, many must have wondered what new tragedy would next unfold on the span. For Bohemia's Catholics the Charles Bridge was thus an apt symbol of a faith that had been under siege for nearly three centuries. Those who worked on the bridge in the

---

[59] Hammerschmid, *Prodromus gloriae Pragenae*, p. 591.
[60] Jaroslaus Schaller, *Beschreibung der königlichen Haupt- und Residenzstadt Prag* (Prague: Gerzabeck, 1795), vol. II, p. 364.

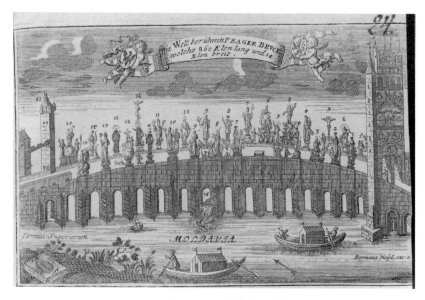

12. 1729 illustration of Charles Bridge

subsequent generation endeavored to transform a site of death, rebellion and heresy into a space that celebrated the triumph of orthodoxy.

The original inspiration for the decoration of Prague's stone bridge came from Rome and the statues created by Bernini for the *Ponte degli Angeli*.[61] But this relatively modest set of angels over the Tiber was soon surpassed by a virtual army of saints that quickly appeared across the Moldau (Figure 12). The first monument to go up was the crucifix that had been shot down by the Swedes. In 1657, the Bohemian Court Chancellery decided that a more permanent and dignified memorial should stand in the place of the old wooden cross. They sent Karel Škréta along with a goldsmith to Dresden where they purchased a large bronze replacement. The first of the statues, John Nepomuk, was raised in 1683. Though two more appeared in the 1690s, it was not until the first decade of the eighteenth century that the saints began arriving in significant numbers. In a frenetic flurry of activity, twenty-four of the original twenty-eight statues were erected between 1706 and 1714. No single individual, institution or religious order dominated this phase of construction. Commissions came from all corners. Of the twenty-eight monuments raised between 1659 and 1714, thirteen were sponsored by

---

[61] Karel Neubert, Ivo Kořán and Miloš Suchomel, *Charles Bridge* (Prague: Klas, 1991), p. 46.

individuals, nine by religious orders and six by other institutions.[62] Participation among the orders was particularly wide. The Cistercians, Dominicans, Jesuits, Premonstratensians, Augustinians, Theatines and Servites were all patrons.

These statistics are significant for a number of reasons. In the first place, they reflect a slow but general shift in patronage patterns that had been occurring over the seventeenth century. Bohemia's towns had been a dynamic center of cultural energy before White Mountain. The deprivations of war and the religious policies of the Habsburgs precipitated their decline. Though the vitality of these towns eventually recovered, the gap they initially left was quickly filled by the church and nobility, who between them redirected the confessional and cultural orientation of the kingdom. The Charles Bridge and its many saints may be the clearest expression of this new trend that was being replicated across the region. Equally important to note is the broad representation of the church. There was no master plan for the bridge, no centralized design of the archdiocese, no secret scheme of the Jesuits. In fact, quite the opposite occurred. Though the city council exercised some regulatory power, there was a certain entrepreneurial spirit to the entire enterprise. The Society of Jesus actually joined the building phase at a rather late stage. In 1709, one of their members described the order's reluctance to sponsor a monument as a matter of "shameful neglect."[63] Patrons, in the end, competed with each other as reflected in the statues. The later works on the bridge, the dramatic 1710 rendering of St. Luitgard, the 1711 commissions of Loyola and Xavier, the massive 1712 monument of Vincent Ferrer and Procopius, and the riotous 1714 celebration of the Trinitarian order, were increasingly expensive and correspondingly more extravagant.[64]

Those who created the statuary on the bridge did so with an audience in mind. The Jesuits were keenly attuned to this matter and noted in 1709 that though most passersby stared with curiosity at the statues around them, it was only Nepomuk and the crucifix that consistently elicited a pious response from the viewer.[65] The design of specific monuments thus became a matter of considerable importance to the Jesuits and others active on the bridge. Contemporary reports indicate that over time their efforts were successful. The bridge became an important locus of popular devotion.

---

[62] Data on dates and patrons furnished by Kamil Novotný and Emanuel Poche, *Karlův most* (Prague: Pražské nakladatelství V. Poláčka, 1947), pp. 88–112.
[63] NA, SM, J 20/17/11, 1v–2r.   [64] Novotný and Poche, *Karlův most*, pp. 88–112.
[65] NA, SM, J 20/17/11, 1v–2r.

Hats were removed, candles lit, prayers said, and heads bowed. In the early nineteenth century a young Arthur Schopenhauer cynically remarked "the bigoted inhabitants of Prague would consider it the worst sin to cross the bridge without at least doffing their hats."[66] More significantly, many of the models on Charles Bridge were replicated across the region. Jan Mayer's 1708 statue of the apostle Jude leaning on his cudgel helped initiate this saint's cult in Bohemia and set the pattern for many churches outside Prague. In his dramatic portrayal of the Cistercian nun, St. Luitgard, Matthias Braun evidently drew his inspiration from the graphic work of Johann Christoph Lischka in the monastery of Plasy in western Bohemia. The same theme was repeated by Petr Brandl for the Sedlec cloister in the eastern half of the kingdom. The most famous of these examples is the statue of John Nepomuk. Jan Brokoff's saint with hands clasping a crucifix to his chest, head slightly askew and eyes clearly fixed on the hereafter, became the prototype for the hundreds of Nepomuks that appeared in nearly every Bohemian village.[67]

The originality or novelty of the bridge's statuary was thus a matter of secondary importance. Patrons and artists were more concerned with producing effective and compelling models that could be replicated in other settings as aids to devotion. The Jesuits saw the two rows of saints as a type of outdoor theater. An interesting discussion occurred within the order concerning the design of the Francis Xavier statue. In the creation of this towering and complex memorial, the Jesuits drew from their experience with school theater to help compose a design that from their perspective would prompt the appropriate pious response from the viewer.[68] Older monuments were also restored and expanded, heightening both their dramatic effect and religious significance. The new bronze crucifix from Dresden was one such improvement, adding a greater sense of dignity and honor to the oldest monument on the bridge. In 1681, Karl Adam Říčanský provided funds for two lamps to remain constantly lit at either side of the cross. At the beginning of the eighteenth century a small Golgotha, complete with skulls, frogs and lizards, was added to the base of the crucifix.[69] The originally modest marker, which first had been intended

---

[66] Cited in Zdeněk Hojda and Jiří Pokorný, *Pomníky i zapomníky* (Prague: Paseka, 1996), p. 24.

[67] Neubert *et al.*, *Charles Bridge*, pp. 46, 58, 60, 64.

[68] One Jesuit commentator argued that trivial decorations such as crabs were wholly inappropriate for a monument that was designed for a more serious spiritual purpose. NA, SM, J 20/17/11, 1r–v.

[69] Joachim Kamenitzky, *Eigentlicher Entwurff und Vorbildung der vortrefflichen kostbahren und Welt-berühmten Prager Brucken* (Prague, 1716), pp. 54–7.

to commemorate the death of Martin Cink, was being transformed into a more prominent and permanent wayside shrine.

As work on the statuary drew to a close, the printers took over where the sculptors left off. More than half a dozen books on the new landmark quickly appeared, most of them with a practical religious agenda. Joachim Kamenitzky's *Eigentlicher Entwurff und Vorbildung der vortrefflichen kostbahren und Welt-berühmten Prager Brucken* (Prague, 1716) was a detailed guide to the structure with a decidedly spiritual orientation. Each chapter contained an edifying biography of the specific saint or saints along with a prayer "so that the physical eye of the viewer when observing the statue would illuminate the inner eye and refresh the spirit."[70] Joannes Müller's *Triginta devotiones ad Christum et Sanctos eius* (Prague, 1712) was an aid to quiet meditation and worship across the bridge, an informal type of pilgrimage that could be performed during the bustle of everyday life. Augustin Neuräutter's magnificent *Statuae Pontis Pragensis* (Prague, 1714) had no text at all, though his handsome quarto-size illustrations were certainly intended for devotional purposes. Even in the early nineteenth century this literature retained its pious character. W. F. Welleba's *Die beruehmte Prager Bruecke und ihre Statuen* (Prague, 1827) helped the passerby decode the often complicated iconography of the statuary.

The creation of this devotional art leads us to an important observation on the nature of religious painting and sculpture in this period. After Trent, Catholic theologians argued that it was essential for those who executed ecclesiastical commissions to be fervent believers themselves, for the artist's work was an important form of worship. In the context of central Europe and its fluid confessional landscape, it is difficult at first glance to take this injunction seriously. Scholars have noted how artists effectively trimmed their sails to the shifting winds of religious change. In Augsburg, for example, Protestant engravers produced a significant volume of Catholic images.[71] Scholars have made similar arguments about Bohemia. Most have seen Škréta, the former Protestant, as an opportunist whose conversion to Catholicism was based primarily on economic considerations. Others have contended more broadly that the art of this period was merely an ideological façade intended to bolster the hegemonic claims of the kingdom's new Catholic masters.[72] Though it is naïve to dismiss these materialist concerns

---

[70] Ibid., A6v.
[71] W. Seitz, "Die graphischen Thesenblätter des 17. und 18. Jahrhunderts," 109; R. J. W. Evans, "Cultural anarchy in the Empire," *Central European History* 18 (1985), 24.
[72] Jaromír Neumann, *Malířství XVII. století v Čechách* (Prague: Orbis, 1951).

completely, evidence suggests that we should be careful not to discount the strength of the religious conviction behind this art. Though we lack relevant biographical information, the devotional content of Škréta's work was remarkably consistent from his early paintings of the 1630s, his putative Protestant period, to his final passion cycle. Bendl, who from all accounts was a devout Catholic, made a pilgrimage to the Loreto shrine in Italy and later worked on one of its many replicas back in Bohemia.

Contemporary observers commented on the potentially transformative power of religious art. The Jesuit Jan Tanner related the story of a Protestant artist who had been asked by a local priest to work on a painting of the Virgin and child. He consented and began the commission, but during the project he spoke in blasphemous tones about the image. His painting hand was immediately struck by lightning though the fire from heaven left the picture untouched. The injured heretic converted on the spot.[73] Bohuslav Balbín highlighted a similar theme in his biography of the first archbishop of Prague, Arnošt of Pardubice. According to Balbín, it was Arnošt's encounter with the Virgin of Glatz that changed him from a frivolous adolescent to a serious believer. One day, while daydreaming in church, the boy turned to view the famous image. Mary's eyes suddenly came to life, confronted the bewildered student, and convicted him of his sin. A chastened Arnošt henceforth devoted himself wholeheartedly to God.[74] The most dramatic statement concerning the nature of this devotional art came from the sculptor Jan Brokoff and is directly connected to his work on the bridge. Brokoff came to Prague from upper Hungary as an ardent Lutheran. By his own admission he was frequently involved in heated theological arguments with his Catholic colleagues. A turning point came in the early 1680s when he began working on a small statue of St. John Nepomuk that served as the model for the larger monument on Charles Bridge. As Brokoff relates, it was through the many hours he spent carving the saint that "the grace of the Holy Spirit shone on me." He converted in 1682. Whether or not we accept the sincerity of Brokoff's testimony, it tells us a great deal about Bohemia's Catholic culture. This was a society where religious images were imbued with tremendous spiritual energy. They had the power not only to stir the viewer to contrition but to bring the artist himself to conversion.[75]

---

[73] Jan Tanner, *Vestigium Boemiae piae* (Prague: Hosing, 1659), pp. 20–1.
[74] Bohuslav Balbín, *Vita Venerabilis Arnesti* (Prague: Kastner, 1664), pp. 21–35.
[75] Jan Herain, *Karlův most v Praze* (Prague: Nákl. Umělecké besedy, 1908), pp. 44–5.

The iconography of the stone bridge reflected prominent themes of the Catholic Reformation. The Marian cult, Eucharistic devotion and an emphasis on martyrs were all featured, but these general concerns of the church were balanced with more local themes specific to the Czech context. On the bridge's eastern tower a plaque was installed that helped set the tone for the entire space, transforming a casual stroll across the river into a patriotic meditation of the city's recent past. Commemorating the 1648 siege of the city, this panel urged the traveler to wander slowly across the bridge, remembering the Old Town citizens who fought with "fire and sword" against the Swedish invader. This historical moment became indelibly etched into the public memory of the bridge. Kamenitzky's guide recounts in obsessive detail the events of the fourteen-week siege. During this period the Swedes launched six separate attacks on the bridge, fired 186 shells and spent 12,587 rounds of ammunition in their vain attempts to reach the river's eastern bank.[76] One of the most important features of the siege was the melding of patriotic concerns with religious sentiment. The Jesuits assumed critical positions both militarily and spiritually during this difficult period. On the night of 26 July, when the Swedes stole down from Castle Hill, it was supposedly Jiří Ferus who rallied a few citizens to man the barricades and hold the bridge until morning and the arrival of reinforcements. When the Jesuits were not coordinating student militias, they were calling the city to repentance. They instituted fasts, led prayer services and even organized processions of flagellants.[77] They also helped sacralize the events of the war, endowing the bridge with an even greater sense of sanctity. When a Swedish sharpshooter leveled the crucifix, they took Christ's intact head to the Clementinum where it remained for many years as a treasured relic.[78] There were other reminders of the heroic defense of the bridge. The iconography of the St. Vitus statue is particularly interesting. The kingdom's patron saint stands undaunted before three lions cowering before him, a likely reference to both the saint's bravery before the beasts loosed by Diocletian and the valor of the Catholic Czechs before the Protestant lion of the north. The figure was funded by Matěj Vojtěch Macht, dean of Vyšehrad. His father had been one of the students

---

[76] Kamenitzky, *Eigentlicher Entwurff*, p. 14.
[77] Significant here is the eighteenth-century manuscript history of Johannes Miller, *Historia Provinciae Bohemiae Societatis Jesu ab anno Domini 1555*, book 3, number 21, section 9, "Auxilia spiritualia, & militaria tempore obsidionis Pragensis anno 1648 a nostris pro bono communi praestita" (SK, DG III 19).
[78] Svátek, *Pražské pověsti*, p. 108. An 1891 painting of Karel and Adolf Liebscher features the 1648 struggle on the bridge with a specific reference to the incident at the cross.

on the barricades, and for his service the emperor had granted the family the title *Löwenmacht*.

Art historians have noted that the bridge and its statuary represent an important stylistic fusion of international trends with a more local tradition.[79] What is true in terms of aesthetics is also a significant aspect of its content. There are a number of monuments, in fact, that feature some rather strange pairings between a local saint and a figure of more international significance. Brokoff coupled the great missionary Vincent Ferrer with Bohemia's St. Procopius, the founder of the monastic community of Sázava. Slightly more jarring is the statue of the Trinitarian order that had been founded in 1198 to redeem Christian captives from the Muslims. Standing next to its founders, John of Matha and Felix of Valois, is the kingdom's most rustic of saints, the hermit Ivan. Though these juxtapositions of figures might strike our eye as odd today, they served an important function when they were erected. The statues of the stone bridge were in many respects an attempt to reintegrate Bohemia's problematic past into a broader ecclesiastical narrative of the church triumphant. It is significant that with both Vincent and the Trinitarians their Bohemian partner was a saint who predated them by nearly three centuries, perhaps a way to remind the kingdom's believers that they too shared an old and distinguished Catholic heritage. The bridge's martyrs mirror the same theme. Nepomuk and Wenceslas are balanced by Jude and the Jesuit martyrs of Nagasaki. By focusing on the victories of an earlier period, the designers of the stone bridge were trying to reach past the relatively recent troubles of the Winter King and Hus and reconnect Bohemia both to its earlier cultural traditions and the wider Catholic world.

If there is a characteristic common to all these monuments, it is victory and celebration. As noted at the outset, the Charles Bridge had a rather ambiguous past. Its history had been marred by the assassinations of priests, the machinations of a Protestant queen and the assaults of Swedish soldiers. But the political and religious climate was changing, and these changes were made manifest on the bridge. 1648, of course, was a critical turning point for Bohemia. Another moment came in the early 1680s when a bloody peasant revolt was suppressed, and the Turks were turned back at Vienna. The crisis of the early seventeenth century was passing and giving way to a new period of stability. From the Catholic perspective the church had been tried and had emerged triumphant. A number of the statues were built specifically to celebrate noteworthy events. Brokoff's Nepomuk commemorated the

---

[79] Kaufmann, *Court, Cloister and City*, p. 361.

300th anniversary of the saint's martyrdom. The Trinitarian memorial of 1714 marked John of Matha's death five centuries earlier. And then there were the statues themselves. Two of the tallest monuments on the bridge, the twin towers of Xavier and Loyola, are perhaps the best examples of this new sense of confidence. A theatrical Ignatius is perched on a laurel wreath that symbolizes the victory of the Catholic cause. The wreath itself is resting on a globe which in turn is supported by allegorical representations of the four continents. Scattered across the structure are emblems and inscriptions that announce the valiant work of the Jesuits in turning back heresy and reestablishing the true faith. The equally massive Xavier has a slightly different orientation. Gesturing to a cross that he holds in his left hand, the tireless missionary is proclaiming the gospel to a savage who is bowing at his feet while an engraving to his right informs us that the saint has baptized 1.2 million new believers.

The theme of conversion introduced here by Xavier is significant as it illustrates to what extent the bridge had become an identity marker for Bohemia's Catholics. Conversion is a process of interaction, a dialogue between two parties. On the one hand, it points to the ultimate triumph of one's own faith. Apart from Ignatius and Xavier the bridge was filled with missionary saints. There was Norbert, bringing the gospel to central Europe; Dominic, combating the Albigensians; Vincent Ferrer, working among the Turks and Jews; and even the usually mild Anthony of Padua, known in some quarters as the "hammer of heretics." All these figures reminded Czech believers on what side they stood. But conversion also points to the faith of the other, and it is this side of the dialogue that is often more important in the formation of identities. Conversion reminds us of whom we are not. It distinguishes our enemies and exposes their weaknesses. This dual dynamic of highlighting one's friends while recognizing one's foes may have been the most important social function of the bridge.

Czech Catholics recognized three sets of confessional opponents scattered across the bridge. The Muslims as Turks, Saracens or more vaguely described as Moors were well represented. Kamenitzky identified the four individuals supporting the Xavier monument as Muslims.[80] Thematically, they play a more central role in the statues of the Trinitarians and Vincent Ferrer. At the base of the Trinitarian monument is a prison where a seemingly bored Turkish jailor is guarding a group of believers who are beseeching God for deliverance. Vincent Ferrer, in contrast, is represented as an apostle to the heretics. Below him is a turbaned figure of a new Saracen

---

[80] Kamenitzky, *Eigentlicher Entwurff*, p. 129.

Christian who bears an inscription announcing the saint's conversion of 8,000 Muslims. More interesting are the multiple references to the only non-Catholic community that existed in late seventeenth-century Prague, the Jews. Next to the Muslim convert on the Ferrer monument is a rabbi who with hand on chest is admitting the errors of his faith. Evidently, Ferrer had greater success with the Jews, for the engraving below the rabbi informs us that he succeeded in bringing 25,000 to the Catholic faith. There is a more subtle allusion on the statue of the Dominicans. Originally, below Dominic was an inscription from I Corinthians, "We preach Christ crucified, unto the Jews a stumbling block." This reference takes on special meaning when we consider the monument immediately to its right, the famous crucifix (Figure 13). In the mid-1690s as a result of a blasphemy case, the Jewish community had been compelled to erect a gilded inscription proclaiming Christ's sanctity in Hebrew. At the bottom of the cross three plaques were installed that described the incident in Czech, Latin and German.[81] The last of these confessional enemies were the Protestants. How the stone bridge came to include these heretics is an intriguing story that illustrates the extent to which this structure had become an identity marker for Bohemian Catholics. The supporters of neither Luther nor Calvin were officially represented in the bridge's statuary. By the early eighteenth century, however, there was a popular legend concerning two figures that decorated the corner of Old Town Bridge Tower. A man with a lascivious smile has slipped his hand under the dress of a woman. The tale which circulated and was told to foreign travelers identified this indecorous couple as an earthy Luther and a lusty Katharina von Bora.[82]

The stone bridge reflected broader aesthetic patterns of the period. Expressions of confessional triumphalism as found on the bridge were a more general characteristic of Bohemia's religious art of the early eighteenth century. Though Protestant reformers such as Luther and Calvin were not frequently represented, Jan Žižka, the famous Hussite general, was a familiar subject for Czech artists who depicted the great enemy of Catholic believers in hostile fashion.[83] Jews, too, were singled out for scorn and abuse. In 1709, the sculptor Jan Jiří Šlanovský completed a statue of Christ before Pilate for the Karlov Church. To its side was a series of seven figures, all burlesques and caricatures of Jews. This work in fact

---

[81] Schaller, *Beschreibung*, vol. II, pp. 349–50; Alexandr Putík, "The Hebrew inscription on the crucifix at Charles Bridge in Prague," *Judaica Bohemiae* 32 (1997), 26–71.
[82] See for example the story told to three English travelers in 1734. "The travels of three English gentlemen," p. 349; Svátek, *Pražské pověsti*, p. 111.
[83] See the 1737 ceiling in Prague's Karlov Church where Žižka appears as a destroyer of churches.

13. Charles Bridge, Crucifix

became so well known that a popular proverb, "You look like a Jew at Karlov," developed around it.[84] The first and second decades of the eighteenth century, the interval of greatest activity on the bridge, also

---

[84] Růžena Baťková, ed., *Umělecké památky Prahy, Nové město/Vyšehrad/Vinohrady* (Prague: Academia, 1998), p. 139.

corresponded to the architectural high point of the Catholic Reformation in central Europe. Only a few paces from the western terminus of the Charles Bridge the Jesuits were renovating St. Nicholas Church, a complex that a popular guidebook describes as "the ultimate symbol of [the Jesuit] stranglehold on the country." Hyperbole aside, this magnificent architectural accomplishment of Christoph and Kilian Ignaz Dientzenhofer mirrored the confidence of Bohemia's Catholic church at its zenith. The ceiling paintings celebrating the miracles of St. Nicholas, the monumental statuary of saints gleefully spearing heretics and the imposing façade and soaring dome of the building itself were powerful testimony to the dramatic shift that had occurred with the arts over the past century.[85] The days of the Winter King were a rapidly fading memory, and now with Marian columns in market squares, roadside chapels along commercial thoroughfares and Nepomuks in nearly every village, religious art had expanded far beyond traditional ecclesiastical space and had become the most prominent sign of the kingdom's new confessional loyalties.

---

[85] Rob Humphreys, *Prague: The Rough Guide* (London: Penguin, 1995), p. 69. On St. Nicholas see Pavel Vlček, ed., *Umělecké památky Prahy, Malá Strana* (Prague: Academia, 1999), pp. 91–100.

CHAPTER 6

Formation of the faithful: Catholicism in the countryside

In late summer 1627 a certain Matouš Ulický, a secret Protestant pastor, had the misfortune of being arrested by imperial troops as he was passing through the forest of Kouřim in eastern Bohemia. There had been rumors of a peasant revolt, and though Ulický had no ties to the rebels who had long passed from the region, he was immediately handed over to the authorities in the town of Čáslav. They began a thorough interrogation of the unhappy pastor who was no doubt a suspicious character from their perspective. Non-Catholic clergy had been officially banished from the Czech lands in 1623. Ulický had been conducting a covert ministry and had only come out of hiding to visit his sick wife in Čáslav. Shortly after his apprehension, he was handed over to the executioner who repeatedly plied him with a series of tortures as his interrogators tried to gather as much information as they could regarding the extended congregation he served. He was put on the rack, and under severe physical duress he was given a chance to save his life if he renounced his faith. Though weakened and in great pain, Ulický remained resolute and refused to apostatize. The next day he was led to the gallows. The authorities allowed no one to accompany him, and when one young man offered Ulický a hymnal as he passed, this would-be supporter was driven back and roughly beaten by the soldiers who escorted the condemned pastor. Once Ulický was on the scaffold, the executioner prolonged the process. The pastor was first compelled to extend his right hand. After a moment's hesitation the headsman brought down the sword and hewed it off with a single swing. Now in great agony Ulický was taunted and assaulted with a variety of insults. Pointing to the severed hand, officials reminded the pastor that it was this limb that had so offended God by passing the chalice to the laity. He was then forced to his knees and bent over on the block to await the executioner's axe. The day's work, however, was not finished once the headsman had completed this part of the grisly task. Soldiers disemboweled and then quartered the body. They skewered the four sections of the corpse with sharp poles which were then erected for prominent display. As a final touch to this horrific scene, they carefully gathered up Ulický's bloodied head, impaled it on a separate post and raised it close to the gallows.[1]

This grim story from the Bohemian countryside is a sober reminder that coercion and violence were also tools of the Counter-Reformation. In this chapter we make the transition from the world of the antiquarians and their histories, the Jesuits and their theological disputes to the problems and challenges of everyday life after White Mountain. How was Catholicism reintroduced to the common folk after the victory of 1620? How was a largely illiterate population taught the rudiments of a half-forgotten faith? What strategies were pursued to create a Catholic identity among the peasantry? These questions sparked a serious debate concerning the ways and means of reestablishing Catholicism across the kingdom. In one camp was Archbishop Lohelius, now returned from exile, and the papal nuncio Carlo Caraffa. They favored a quick and uncompromising campaign of recatholicization. They were countered by a more pragmatic faction that included Karl von Liechtenstein and Adam Waldstein who advised a slower and more gradual strategy. They argued that swift and precipitous action could trigger a broad-scale rebellion that would threaten the emperor's recent gains. Though debate continued through the first half of the seventeenth century, it became clear after early imperial success on the battlefield that the faster and more radical approach would be adopted. The first confessional group to be directly affected were the Anabaptists. In what was a type of test case for the future expulsions, imperial authorities targeted this vulnerable and isolated community in southern Moravia, forcing them into exile in September 1622.[2]

Such drastic measures were not implemented immediately for the populace at large. Non-Catholics were subject instead to punitive legislation that like a slowly closing vice gradually increased in pressure. In 1624 the emperor ordered Liechtenstein to introduce a series of laws intended to convince the region's discouraged Protestants that the acceptance of Catholicism was in their best interest.[3] One set of rules mandated outward conformity to the rituals of the church: fasting on Friday, no work on saints'

---

[1] Josef Petráň, "Matouš Ulický a poddanské povstání na Kouřimsku a Čáslavsku roku 1627," *AUC* 7 (1954), 43–64; J. A. Comenius, *Historia persecutionum ecclesiae Bohemicae* (Amsterdam, 1648), chapter 57, pp. 259–61.

[2] Thomas Winkelbauer, "Die rechtliche Stellung die Täufer im 16. und 17. Jahrhundert am Beispiel der habsburgischen Länder," in Eveline Brugger and Birgit Weidl, eds., *Ein Thema – zwei Perspektiven. Juden und Christen in Mittelalter und Frühneuzeit* (Vienna: Studien Verlag, 2007), pp. 34–66.

[3] Reprinted in František Krásl, *Arnošt Hrabě Harrach* (Prague: Arcibiskupská knihtiskárna, 1886), pp. 29–30.

days and no slipping out to the tavern during mass. Any artwork prejudicial to the Catholic faith, a reference principally to the many representations of the Utraquist chalice, was to be destroyed and replaced with a crucifix or other appropriate substitute. Any criticism or public mockery of either the clergy or public rites of the church would be severely punished. Another series of laws focused on religious instruction. Students were to be withdrawn immediately from Protestant schools. Secret catechizing at home was strictly forbidden, and no young person was allowed to begin training in a profession until he learned the basics of the Catholic faith. Arguably the most effective of these regulations focused on economic activities. Those who were unwilling to convert were prohibited "from all business, trade and commerce." Foreshadowing the heavy-handed tactics of land confiscation, a regulation was also introduced that invalidated the wills of all Protestants. The Liechtenstein legislation was used as a model by some of Bohemia's great landowners who enforced similar rules on their estates.[4]

Making laws is one matter. Enforcing them can be an entirely different issue. To deal with this potential problem, new administrative structures were created, the most important of which were the so-called "reformation commissions." The first of these was formed in 1624 to review the conditions of Catholic parishes with a specific focus on the royal towns. In 1627 another commission was created with a wider purview. At its top was a central committee consisting of four members: Cardinal Harrach, Jaroslav Martinic, Friedrich von Talmberk and Kryštof Vratislav of Mitrovice. Below them was a subcommittee of clerics who circulated through the countryside while at the local level were individual nobles who were responsible for a specific district.[5] We find them admonishing the town council of Mladá Boleslav with a rather direct warning to suspend the commercial rights of all non-Catholics. They urge the local clergy of Litoměřice to exert full pressure on Pavel Stránský to "persuade" him to return to the church, and they remind the town of Kadaň that all orphans must be taken from Protestant guardians and placed in Catholic families.[6]

Harrach's committee also remained in close contact with its local commissioners whose powers were quite extensive as in the case of Gottfried Hertel of Leutersdorf, the *hejtman* of the German enclave of Loket

---

[4] See for example the 1628 edicts for the lands of Albrecht von Wallenstein. Reprinted in Jiří Mikulec, *Pobělohorská rekatolizace v českých zemích* (Prague: SPN, 1992), pp. 24–5.

[5] Best on these early commissions is Eliška Čáňová, "Vývoj správy pražské arcidiecéze v době násilné rekatolizace Čech," *SbAPr* 35 (1983), 486–560.

[6] A. Podlaha, ed., *Dopisy reformační komisse v Čechách z let 1627–1629* (Prague, 1908), 17 April 1627, pp. 2–3; 14 July 1627, pp. 17–18; 18 November 1627, pp. 60–3.

(Elbogen).[7] The *hejtman* was responsible for reviewing the Easter confessional certificates, which were regularly used for measuring the progress of recatholicization. Evidently, Hertel of Leutersdorf questioned the tallies that were passed on to him by the parish priests. His suspicion was commended by the committee who also shared a healthy skepticism of these certificates which could all too easily be falsified through bribery and corruption. The commissioner also kept close watch on the borders. One of the major powers of the reformation commission was control of emigration. Those families who left Bohemia for religious reasons first had to obtain an official travel pass through this office, but before one could obtain the proper documents, a final attempt was made to convert the prospective emigrants. If there was some hesitation on their part, they were offered a chance to receive religious instruction. In the Loket region the commission did grant the *hejtman* certain powers of repatriation. A religious exile could reenter the kingdom and potentially recover his property by submitting a written attestation of conversion. Though the commission sought to accomplish its mission without the use of violence, its threat was ever present. In one letter to Hertel of Leutersdorf the central committee mentioned the case of Johann Philipp Kratz of Scharffenstein whose estates harbored a significant Protestant population. The *hejtman* was to warn the count that if he did not enforce Catholic uniformity, they would intervene and accomplish this end by harsher means.

Harsher means inevitably meant brute force most often accomplished by the military or as the commission put it "with the use of soldiers for damage, ruin and misfortune."[8] Ever since White Mountain, there had been troops marauding the countryside and implementing their own version of Catholic Reform. In 1622 the Spaniard Don Baltazar de Marradas entered the old Hussite stronghold of Tábor. There with his soldiers and three Jesuit priests he oversaw the conversion of fifty of the town's most prominent citizens. A year later according to reports of the local clergy, Tábor was entirely Catholic.[9] One of the tactics consistently employed by the military was quartering. When entering a city or town, the captain frequently billeted his men in non-Catholic homes. For many families several weeks with over a dozen soldiers in one's house was reason enough to convert. The most effective of these militia units were the dragoons of Don Martin de Huerta. Originally from the Low Countries, the former tailor joined the forces of Buquoy and Marradas on their march north from Bavaria to Prague. After

[7] Ibid., 19 Sept. 1628, pp. 113–16.   [8] Ibid., 19 Sept. 1628, p. 115.
[9] Josef Hanzal, "Rekatolizace v Čechách – její historický smysl a význam," *SbH* 37 (1990), 56.

the battle of Písek in February 1619 he was promoted to captain and began more than a decade of rampage across the Czech lands. The reformation commission made full use of de Huerta, calling upon him when ordinary measures did not achieve the desired result. In 1635, for example, he lent military support to the missionary activities of Albrecht Chanovský. The notoriety of his exploits was reflected in a popular saying that de Huerta had converted more people in less time than Christ and his apostles.[10] Even when soldiers were absent, the methods used in this religious campaign were often cruel. The bakers of Jihlava were at one point forbidden from selling bread to Protestants. More devilish yet were a series of oak cages put to use in the Moravian town of Holešov. Local heretics were confined in these devices, which allowed them to neither sit nor stand, until they made a "voluntary" decision to join the Catholic church.[11]

Though these stories of coercion reached their climax with the expulsions of the late 1620s, such tactics of force and intimidation continued to be used through the eighteenth century, albeit more sporadically. The last major wave of persecution came during the reign of Charles VI (1711–40) when religious leaders at the local level often resorted to harsh methods in their struggle to enforce confessional uniformity. There are tales of beatings and whippings. There is the account of Tomáš Kazda of Cerekvice who was purportedly imprisoned for distributing Lutheran books and then subsequently poisoned for failing to cooperate with church authorities.[12] Though one needs to handle such evidence judiciously, it cannot be denied that violence played a substantial role in Bohemia's recatholicization from start to finish. With that said, there is a need to move beyond this narrative of repression that has long dominated Czech historiography, for it has skewed our understanding of the seventeenth and eighteenth centuries. Although recent historiography is promising, more work needs to be done to locate this period of Bohemia's ecclesiastical history within the general parameters of early modern Catholicism. One of the most distinctive features of the church in this era was its emphasis on mission. As Louis Châtellier has recently observed, "The years following the Thirty Years War were marked by a prodigious outburst of missionary activity ... From Scandinavia to Andalusia, from Brittany to Bulgaria, they [the missionaries] were

[10] See in particular the letter of 19 September 1628 where the commission encouraged de Huerta to make use of "nicht allein gütliche, sondern auch schärfere Mitel." Podlaha, ed., *Dopisy reformační komisse*, pp. 116–17.
[11] C. A. Pescheck, *The Reformation and Anti-Reformation in Bohemia* (London: Houlston and Stoneman, 1845), vol. II, p. 234.
[12] Hanzal, "Rekatolizace," 83.

everywhere."[13] The archives and libraries of the Czech Republic are filled with accounts of the missions that were dispatched to the kingdom's rural areas during this period. The Jesuits, Capuchins and Piarists along with members of the secular clergy scattered across the countryside as they sought to communicate the gospel and reestablish a Catholic identity among the peasantry.

THE PERSISTENCE OF TRADITIONAL RELIGION

In what is one of the more important studies of early modern religion in recent years, Eamon Duffy has argued in *The Stripping of the Altars* that the English Reformation was a violent caesura in the religious life of the kingdom. In reaction to a Protestant historiography that characterized England's late medieval church as archaic and decadent, Duffy described a rich and diverse religious culture that was neither decaying nor particularly corrupt and only suppressed with considerable effort. Whatever the merit of Duffy's revisionist thesis, the Bohemian situation is in many respects its inverse. Though in certain respects 1620 was a distinct break with the past, scholars have generally ignored to what extent there was a degree of continuity on the level of religious practice. Although Hus and his followers have often been cast as proto-Protestants, the Utraquist church which emerged in the early fifteenth century was in many respects a decidedly Catholic institution. Though the Hussite revolution generated its own set of religious radicals, the main body of believers adopted a confessional stance that was far more conservative. The seven sacraments were retained, and the mass was celebrated as a rite of sacrifice. The first general synod of the Utraquist church declared in 1421, "All members of the Church must believe and confess that our Lord Jesus Christ is truly present in the bread and wine of the Sacrament of the Altar."[14] The church stressed the importance of good works while the veneration of the saints remained part of their tradition. Clerical celibacy was upheld through the sixteenth century. Utraquist orthodoxy in fact led to a great leadership crisis. In 1431 after the death of Archbishop Konrad von Vechta, who had defected from Rome a decade earlier, the Utraquists chose Jan Rokycana (1435–71) as their new archbishop. He was never recognized by Rome but believed so firmly in the

---

[13] Louis Châtellier, *La religion des pauvres: Les missions rurales en Europe et la formation du catholicisme moderne, XVIe–XIXe siècle* (Paris: Aubier, 1993), p. 61.

[14] E. Molnar, "The Catholicity of the Utraquist Church of Bohemia," *Anglican Theological Review* 41 (1959), 261; Zdeněk David, *Finding the Middle Way* (Baltimore: Johns Hopkins University Press, 2003), pp. 224–5.

doctrine of apostolic succession that he refused to ordain any new Hussite priests. The church instead sent their candidates to Paris, Erfurt, Passau or most frequently Italy where friendly bishops performed the sacrament of ordination.

Apart from their use of the chalice, the celebration of Hus's martyrdom and a few other innovations, the Utraquists, who never ceased viewing themselves as Catholic believers, preserved traditional practices of the late medieval church. To what extent did this culture survive into the sixteenth and even early seventeenth centuries? Identifying the religious loyalties of the Bohemian populace in 1620 is not an easy task.[15] Best estimates indicate that Catholics represented 10–15 percent of the population, though Caraffa actually wondered at one point whether one could find more than 300 in the entire kingdom! At the other end of the spectrum, the Bohemian Brethren stood somewhere between 5 and 10 percent. Apart from small pockets of religious minorities such as Jews and Anabaptists, those remaining belonged either to the Utraquist or Lutheran communities. It is difficult to sort out the respective size of these two confessional groups with any degree of precision. Not unexpectedly, the Lutherans were strongest among the ethnic Germans who lived in the border regions. There were also a number of prominent Czech nobles who embraced Luther's teachings. Nevertheless, twentieth-century historiography has tended to overemphasize the Lutheran influence. With the Reformations of the sixteenth century lurking around the corner, ecclesiastical historians have too frequently viewed developments of the late medieval period as ineluctably heading to Luther.[16] Most scholars have assumed that in the Bohemian context the vigor of the Utraquist church waned as the fifteenth century wore on. Luther's coming, they claimed, precipitated a split in this dying body with many joining a so-called "neo-Utraquist" movement that quickly absorbed the German reformer's teachings. According to this narrative, the moribund Old Utraquists continued to decline until they were mercifully euthanized by Catholic authorities after White Mountain. Recent work suggests that this model needs to be

---

[15] Josef Pekař, *Dějiny československé* (Prague: Akropolis, 1991), 91–2; Jan Kapras, *Právní dějiny zemí koruny české* (Prague: Unie, 1913), vol. II, p. 436; M. E. Ducreux, "La situation religieuse dans les pays tchèques à la fin du XVIe siècle," *Études danubiennes* 2 (1986), 122.

[16] John van Engen, "The church in the fifteenth century," in T. Brady, H. Oberman and J. Tracy, eds., *The Handbook of European History* (Leiden: Brill, 1994), vol. I, pp. 307–30; Howard Kaminsky, "From lateness to waning to crisis: the burden of the later Middle Ages," *Journal of Early Modern History* 4 (2000), 85–125.

rethought.[17] Traditional religion in the Bohemian kingdom, especially in the countryside, may well have been more vibrant than many have realized.

There is an interesting body of evidence to support such an argument. The first is liturgical. Liturgics has all too frequently remained a specialized subfield ignored even by many historians of religion, and yet the liturgy organized the lives of everyday believers and helped shape their view of the world. The Hussite mass adopted all the basic forms of the Catholic liturgy: introit, the Kyrie eleison, the Gloria, the Epistle, Gradual, Alleluia, the Sequence, the Gospel, the Creed, the Offertory, the Preface and the Lord's Prayer, the Sanctus, the Canon of Consecration and the Agnus Dei.[18] What is even more significant is the extent to which these forms of Utraquist worship continued unchanged from the fifteenth into the sixteenth and seventeenth centuries. Liturgical specialists have demonstrated that Utraquist missals of this period did not incorporate Lutheran innovations but instead preserved the traditions of the earlier period. With a few exceptions the liturgical calendar remained unaltered. The vibrancy of Utraquism in the second half of the sixteenth century is attested by the fact that of the seventy graduals produced between 1538 and 1600 only 10 were Catholic. The remaining 63 were Utraquist.[19] We also have the evidence of foreign visitors to Bohemia who in many cases were somewhat surprised to find that Utraquist worship differed very little from the rites of Roman Catholicism. The English Protestant Fynes Moryson noted with mild astonishment in 1591 that the Utraquists believed in transubstantiation.[20] Conversely, a delegation from Catholic France was bemused by what they found in Prague in summer 1600:

The Hussites inhabit over two thirds of the city and the rituals of their mass are virtually the same as ours. On the Feast Day of Corpus Christi they even conduct processions through the city and carry the host in the streets. The Jesuits and the others of our faith judge that they should not be impeded in adoring the host because as far as known, it is touched by the hands of a genuine priest.[21]

---

[17] The revisionist position is best represented by Zdeněk David, *Finding the Middle Way*. Though problematic in some respects, David's arguments regarding the vitality of traditional Utraquism should be carefully considered.

[18] Z. Nejedlý, *Dějiny husitského zpěvu* (Prague: ČSAV, 1955), vol. V, pp. 177–298.

[19] Barry F. H. Graham, *Bohemian and Moravian Graduals 1420–1600* (Turnhout: Brepols, 2006), pp. 33–7; David Holeton, "On the evolution of the Utraquist liturgy," *Studia liturgica* 25 (1995), 51–67.

[20] Fynes Moryson, *An Itinerary Containing His Ten Yeeres Travell* (New York: Macmillan, 1907), vol. IV, pp. 332–3.

[21] Eliška Fučíková, ed., *Tři francouzští kavalíři v rudolfínské Praze* (Prague: Panorama, 1989), pp. 44–5.

There is also anecdotal evidence indicating that many Utraquist communities actively resisted changes in worship and religious practice that reformers hoped to implement. We have already noted the reaction to the Calvinist reforms proposed by the Winter King. Resistance to Lutheran modifications could be equally fierce. The most famous incident was that of the Czech Lutheran, Jiří Dykastus. In 1614 he was appointed pastor of Prague's Týn Church, the most prominent and important Utraquist house of worship in the city. There he introduced a Protestant liturgy that caused considerable controversy. The more conservative congregation demanded a return to the traditional ceremonies, and the dispute was only solved by the appointment of an Utraquist chaplain who worked alongside Dykastus and carried on with the older rituals.[22] Finally, there are the reactions of Catholic authorities. A letter of instruction sent from Rome to Nuncio Caraffa in April 1621 characterized the majority of Bohemian dissidents not as Lutherans or Calvinists but as *Hussiti*. It is clear from contemporary documents that the term *Hussiti* was a specific reference to Utraquist believers. As such, they were viewed from the Catholic perspective more as schismatics than heretics. Significantly, an Utraquist could rejoin the Roman church with relative ease. Simple confession and the acceptance of the Eucharist *sub una specie* were alone sufficient, practices that stood in contrast to more complicated rites of conversion that a full Protestant was compelled to undergo. In similar fashion Utraquist clergy could be reaccepted by the church as Catholic priests, for all of their clergy were originally ordained by Roman Catholic or occasionally Orthodox bishops.[23] Though scholars today have generally overlooked this issue of continuity, this point was certainly not lost on missionaries and other contemporary observers. Many of the missionaries carefully adapted their message and ministry to local culture and traditions. In a number of cases new converts officially proclaimed their allegiance to the Catholic church on the feast day of St. Wenceslas, a patron whose cult had remained popular through the Hussite period.[24] Interestingly enough, some of these Catholic reformers looked back to Augustine's famous confrontation with the Donatists as a model to follow. Like the church father, they were critical of those misguided "religious zealots" whose rigorist approach risked alienating

---

[22] Zdeněk David, "The integrity of the Utraquist church and the problem of neo-Utraquism," *Bohemian Reformation and Religious Practice* 5 (2002), 338.

[23] Ibid., 342–3.

[24] Podlaha, ed., *Dopisy reformační komisse*, 26 August 1628, p. 109; 29 August 1629, p. 201. Zdeněk Uhlíř, *Literární prameny svatováclavského kultu a úcty ve vrcholném a pozdním středověku* (Prague: National Library, 1996). Wenceslas was recognized as a national saint.

those who were likely to convert if more sensitive and compassionate means were used.[25]

CATECHESIS IN THE COUNTRYSIDE

Let us return now to the fundamental problem of this chapter. How was Catholicism reintroduced to the Bohemian populace after 1620? In particular, what role did education play in this process? Any consideration of this question inevitably begins with the Jesuits. Though they established the Clementinum in 1556, it is often forgotten that their first mission to Prague nearly ended in failure. Ignatius's associate, Jerónimo Nadal, remarked that of the original twelve sent to Bohemia, less than half were truly competent and suitable for the task. They did persist, however, and over time they learned to accommodate themselves to the local situation. They allowed non-Catholics to attend the school, and though Protestants were exempt from certain religious obligations, the Jesuits began to have a significant influence on this population and sought to expand their activities. Allied with the Catholic nobility, they opened colleges in other Bohemian towns. At the height of their influence in the early eighteenth century, the Jesuits controlled a network of schools that annually served more than 10,000 students.[26]

Less well known are the educational activities of the Piarists. The order was founded in the early seventeenth century by the Spaniard Joseph Calasanz (1556–1648) and recognized by Pope Gregory XV in 1621. Calasanz had arrived in Rome in the 1590s and was concerned with the plight of the urban poor. In 1597 he opened a school for destitute children. The Piarists established their first house outside of Italy in the Moravian town of Mikulov in June 1631. Mikulov, a former Anabaptist center, became in these early years a hub of their operations north of the Alps. From there they eventually established outposts in Austria, Hungary and Poland. Their success was dependent on the support of the local nobility. Cardinal Dietrichstein stood behind their work in Mikulov while it was Francesco Magni, the brother of Valerian, who allowed them to take over the former grounds of the Bohemian Brethren in Strážnice. The convert Michael Adolf

[25] Matthias Tanner, *Societas Iesu apostolorum imitatrix* (Prague: Typis Universitatis Carolo-Ferdinandeae, 1694), 741–2.
[26] A. Podlaha, "Dějiny kolleji jesuitských v Čechách a na Moravě od r. 1654 až do jich zrušení," *SbHKr* 10 (1909), 73–88, 158–74; 11 (1910), 64–78; 12 (1911), 84–94, 161–8; 13 (1912), 57–75; 14 (1913), 195–209; 15 (1914), 105–7; 26 (1925), 1–4, 83–95; 27 (1926), 145–53; Kateřina Bobková-Valentová, *Každodenní život učitele a žáka jezuitského gymnázia* (Prague: Karolinum, 2006), p. 248.

von Althan enthusiastically supported their efforts in Oslavany. Gundaker von Liechtenstein assisted them in Moravský Krumlov, and the Pernsteins brought them to Bohemia proper with their mission in Litomyšl.

At their height, the Piarists ran more than thirty colleges in the kingdom.[27] While the Jesuits tended to work with the more privileged, the Piarists, who competed and at times clashed with the Jesuits, focused their energies on the lower classes and smaller towns. Their most important work was with the three-year primary schools. Boys could begin at the age of seven with the stipulation they arrive for their lessons clean and neatly attired. Instruction was in the mother tongue with emphasis on the basic skills of reading, writing and arithmetic. Religious training was an essential part of the program. There was mass each morning while in the afternoon the children gathered for the Litany of Loreto, one of the most popular forms of Marian devotion in the Counter-Reformation. In the secondary schools that the Piarists ran, the students learned their Latin through the catechism of the Jesuit Peter Canisius. Though they also struggled through Cicero and Seneca, each year they were expected to memorize long sections of Canisius's religious manual.[28]

Though between them the Jesuits and Piarists created a significant network of schools, their reach was obviously limited. The most basic form of religious training came at the parish level, and here the situation was at best troubling. Arguably, the greatest problem facing the Catholic church after White Mountain was the crisis of the parish. Though Harrach and others sought to strengthen the church's infrastructure and implemented a series of administrative reforms, in the end they confronted the same fundamental issue – too few priests for too many parishes. A number of stopgap measures were tried. An appeal for priests went out to Poland. Polish authorities responded by sending a rather motley assortment of clergy who in the end caused more harm than good by their purportedly dissolute lifestyles.[29] In the 1640s well over half of Bohemia's churches lacked priests. The situation did not improve in the following decade. Of the ninety-one parishes of Mladá Boleslav county in central Bohemia fifty-eight of them were vacant! While in the fifteenth century there were on average 850 parishioners for every parish in the

[27] Josef Svátek, "Organizace řeholních institucí v českých zemích a péče o jejich archivy," *SbAPr* 20 (1970), 572; V. Bartůsek, "Šíření piaristických kolejí a škol v Čechách, na Moravě a ve Slezsku v 17. a 18. století," *Paginae historiae* 11 (2003), 32–68; M. Zemek, J. Bombera and A. Filip, *Piaristé v Čechách, na Moravě a ve Slezsku 1631–1950* (Prievidza: Patria, 1992); G. L. Moncallero, *La fondazione delle Scuole degli Scolopi nell'Europa centrale al tempo del Controriforma* (Alba: Edizone domenicane, 1972).

[28] Zemek *et al.*, *Piaristé v Čechách*, pp. 95–124.

[29] Georg Holyk, *Blutige Thränen des höchst bedrängten und geängsten Böhmer Landes* (Wittenberg: Meyer, 1673), J7v–J8r; Krásl, *Arnošt Hrabě Harrach*, p. 35.

archdiocese, in the early eighteenth century that number had risen to nearly 2,000. In northern and eastern Bohemia some of these parishes could be as large as 9,000! French parishes during the same period averaged little more than 200.[30] Clearly, parishes were insufficiently equipped to meet the needs of the local inhabitants. In this light it is important to remember that the parish was not only the center of local religious life. Schools were often attached for the most basic educational needs. Though we have reports of various parish schools operating in the second half of the seventeenth century, it is difficult to determine how much learning actually took place. Music was a central feature of these schools, often at the expense of more elemental skills. One applicant for a position noted that he "could play the violin, viola, violincello, and trumpet, sing tenor and bass and also knew some arithmetic."[31]

Despite the best efforts of the Jesuits and Piarists the overall state of education in the Bohemian countryside was poor. The structures for learning and religious formation were simply not sufficient for the demand. The war had taken a heavy toll with large swaths of the landscape completely devastated. The expulsion of the Bohemian Brethren and the destruction of their schools also contributed to the gutting of the educational infrastructure. The result was widespread ignorance, not only in terms of letters, but more importantly from the church's perspective a disconcertingly high rate of doctrinal illiteracy and confessional ambiguity. Many were ignorant of basic Catholic teaching. This problem persisted well into the eighteenth century. We have reports of visitations where individuals were unaware of important Catholic rituals and confused the Trinity with the sacraments.[32] Though the Bohemian case may be extreme, the Catholic world at large was faced with a similar challenge during this period. There was in response a general campaign for basic religious education at the parish level. Many recognized, especially in central Europe, that religious loyalty and confessional identity were quite fragile. The rapid religious changes of the past century often caused by the fluctuating fortunes of war had left many communities confessionally confused. To combat this problem the church initiated an aggressive program

---

[30] R. J. W. Evans, *The Making of the Habsburg Monarchy 1550–1700* (Oxford: Clarendon Press, 1979), pp. 123–4; Eduard Maur, "Problémy farní organizace pobělohorských Čech," in Zdeňka Hledíková, ed., *Traditio et Cultus* (Prague: Karolinum, 1993), pp. 163–76; Jean Bérenger, "The Austrian church," in W. Callahan and D. Higgs, eds., *Church and Society in Catholic Europe of the Eighteenth Century* (Cambridge: Cambridge University Press, 1979), pp. 89, 91.
[31] Cited in Janet Berls, "The elementary school reforms of Maria Theresa and Joseph II in Bohemia," unpublished Ph.D. thesis, Columbia University (1970), p. 55; Josef Hanzal, "Nižší školy v Čechách v 17. a 18. století," *Muzejní a vlastivědná práce* 10 (1972), 152–70.
[32] M. E. Ducreux, "Lire à en mourir. Livres et lectuers en Bohême au XVIIIe siècle," in Roger Chartier, ed., *Les usages de l'imprimé* (Paris: Fayard, 1987), p. 284.

of missions that far exceeded any of its previous efforts. A team of priests would descend on a series of villages and conduct an intense program of preaching, teaching and administering the sacraments.[33] Jesuits such as Nicolaus Cusanus crisscrossed areas like the rugged Eifel and the duchy of Luxembourg instructing the local populace in the basic tenets of Catholicism using simple religious manuals. The missions quickly became one of the church's favorite tools in the task of solidifying the confessional norms of the hinterlands. Indeed, they proved so successful that they were expanded to the cities and more populated regions.

The church's emphasis on pedagogy and mission in seventeenth-century Bohemia has been overshadowed by the dominant narrative of force and repression. Though the fear of heresy was not inconsequential, ecclesiastical authorities were concerned with the more elemental task of teaching essential Christian truths and fundamental Catholic beliefs. Led by the Jesuits, significant numbers of missionaries wandered the byroads of the kingdom providing simple instruction in the faith for many who lacked the ministry of a resident priest. From Prague the archdiocese organized visitations on a regular basis to assess the conditions of the local parishes. The emphasis on evangelism was so great in fact that Bohemia provided nearly 200 priests for the missionary enterprise abroad.[34] Any understanding of the work of these itinerant priests must take full account of an immense body of sources that has been traditionally ignored by historians of the Czech lands, sources that have been normally relegated to the subfields of baroque literature, musicology or even folklore studies. In their quest to communicate Catholicism's core beliefs, reformers utilized a wide range of approaches and techniques. Songs and sermons, catechisms and devotional literature, religious drama and even the production of folksy nativity scenes were part of this broad program of religious education spearheaded by the missionaries who roamed the countryside in the century after White Mountain.[35]

---

[33] B. Duhr, "Zur Geschichte der deutschen Volksmissionen in der 2. Hälfte des 17. Jahrhunderts," *HJ* 37 (1916), 593–623.

[34] On visitations see NA, APA, B11/7–13/4b; B13/4a–14/24; Alfred Karasek and Josef Lanz, *Krippenkunst in Böhmen und Mähren vom Frühbarock bis zur Gegenwart* (Marburg: N. G. Elwert Verlag, 1974), pp. 10–11; Z. Kalista, *Cesty ve znamení kříže* (Prague: Evropský literární klub, 1941); R. Grulich, *Der Beitrag der böhmischen Länder zur Weltmission des 17. und 18. Jahrhunderts* (Königstein: Institut für Böhmen, Mähren, Schlesien, 1981).

[35] Though there is scattered material on the mission movement within Bohemia, there is no comprehensive treatment of the phenomenon. One can begin with A. Podlaha, "Z dějin katolických misií v Čechách," *SbHKr* 4 (1895), 104–31. Of additional use is Jiřina Kubíková, *Křesťanská misie v 16.–18. století* (Brno: Marek, 2001), pp. 87–115; M. E. Ducreux, "La mission et le rôle des missionnaires dans les pays tchèques au XVIIe siècle," in *Transmettre la foi, XVIe–XXe siècle* (Paris: Ministère de l'éducation nationale, 1984), vol. I, pp. 31–46.

The most important weapon in this pedagogical arsenal was the catechism which truly came of age in the sixteenth century. Though the
catechism is of course an old genre, it had long been on the periphery of
Christian society, popular with certain elites or used by select confraternities. Its status changed dramatically with the advent of the printing press.
Quickly entering the mainstream, catechisms became the favored means of
both Catholics and Protestants for teaching the basic truths of the faith.
They also became more standardized, generally adapting a simple question
and answer format.[36] Initially composed for missionary work in central
Europe, the most important catechisms in the Catholic world were those of
the Jesuit Peter Canisius. His *Small Catechism* of 1558 had the greatest
impact and was widely used in Catholic lands. During Canisius's lifetime
alone, his catechisms ran through more than 200 editions. As opposed to
their late-medieval antecedents, Canisius's catechisms presented the
Christian message in a more positive light. Emphasis on sin and judgment
was replaced by a framework organized around the twin virtues of wisdom
and righteousness. The Apostles' Creed, the Lord's Prayer and the Ten
Commandments were taught under the rubric of faith, hope and love.
Though his catechisms were certainly a response to those of Luther, their
polemical character was generally muted.[37] These catechisms enjoyed a
broad popularity in the Czech lands. Though initially written in Latin,
translations quickly followed. A 1563 German edition appeared in Dillingen
while nine years later a Czech version was published in Prague. More than
twenty Czech editions were produced between the late sixteenth and the
mid-eighteenth century often with simple woodcuts illustrating specific
teachings.[38]

Canisius's catechisms were frequently modified to meet the specific
needs of a local population. A 1588 hymnal transposed portions of the
small catechism into musical verse while several decades later the Belgian
Jesuit Jacques des Hayes (1615–82), who worked for a number of years on
the Bohemian estates of Count Lamboy, produced a paraphrase of
Canisius's text which was later translated into a colorful Czech idiom by

---

[36] John O'Malley, *The First Jesuits* (Cambridge, MA: Harvard University Press, 1993), pp. 115–18. For
Germany see Karl Schrems, "Der 'modus catechizandi' der katholischen Kirchenkatechese in
Deutschland im 16. und 17. Jahrhundert," in Willi Kessel, ed., *Beiträge zur bayerischen und deutschen
Geschichte: Hans Dachs zum Gedenken* (Regensburg: Historischer Verein für Oberpfalz und
Regensburg, 1966), pp. 219–41.
[37] O'Malley, *The First Jesuits*, pp. 123–4.
[38] On Canisius in the Czech context see Josef Vašica, *České literární baroko* (Prague: Vyšehrad, 1938),
pp. 128–37. This first Czech translation, *Katechismus katolický* (*Knihopis*, 1432), has not survived. The
first extant Canisius catechism in Czech is a 1584 edition of his small catechism (*Knihopis*, 1442).

Šimon Hlína.[39] A wide variety of other catechisms were also produced in this period. František Rozdrażewski wrote his handbook, *The Dispute of the Chalice* (Roudnice nad Labem, 1626), to combat the central tenet of Utraquism. In the early eighteenth century the Jesuit Johann Kraus composed a number of texts to counteract a Lutheran revival.[40] Antonín Koniáš's *Golden Morningstar* (Prague, 1727) borrowed from a variety of earlier catechetical works in his quest to refute the doctrinal errors of the Hussites, Calvinists and Bohemian Brethren. One of the most intriguing catechisms of this era came from a parish priest of eastern Bohemia, Jiří Antonín Hanuchna. His *Dialogue between Vitus and Wenceslas regarding Matters Necessary for Salvation* (1695) laid out in rhyming verse basic teachings of the church.[41] One of the more popular genres that developed in this period was a series of texts with the title *Duchowní Pohádky* (*Spiritual Tales*). An early modern trivia game, these were compilations of riddles and puzzles intended to entertain while addressing the widespread problem of religious illiteracy. Readers were asked who lost his head over wine (Holofernes) or the identity of the world's most beautiful women (Job's daughters).[42] In the countryside individual clergy composed their own material for a broad range of situations. The most creative of these figures was the Premonstratensian Evermod Jiří Košetický who for twenty years served as a rural missionary and compiled a massive collection of such material known as the *Quodlibeticum*.[43]

The range of catechetical material was matched by an equally broad approach to instruction. While in regions such as the Low Countries the Jesuits were able to organize catechism classes on a massive scale, the weak ecclesiastical infrastructure and chronic shortage of clergy made such an undertaking often unfeasible in Bohemia. Bohemia's missionaries responded to these challenges with inventive solutions. There were of course traditional catechism classes where the circumstances permitted, and standard texts such as the *Spiritual Exercises* were utilized by individual priests such as the Jesuit Jiří Pelinga on his travels through the Moravian

---

[39] Vašica, *České literární baroko*, p. 132.
[40] See for example his *Lutherischer Scrupulant…* (Prague: Wickhart, 1714); *Alte und neue Irr-Geister* (Prague: Wickhart, 1714).
[41] A small portion is reprinted in Vašica, *České literární baroko*, pp. 272–3.
[42] *Duchowní Pohádky* (Hradec Králové: V. J. Tybely, 1723). For a fuller list of such titles see *Knihopis*, 14074–14083a.
[43] Jan Pařez, "Dílo Evermoda Jiřího Košetického jako zrcadlo lidových Čech druhé poloviny 17. století," *Kuděj* 2 (2000), 3–13. Košetický's manuscript is preserved in five volumes in the Strahov Monastic Library (SK, DG II 4–8).

countryside.[44] More often than not, however, the clergy was forced to employ rather unconventional methods to meet their goals. In his mission to the Giant Mountains in 1679, Kašpar Dirig faced the problem of weather. Extreme winter cold made the use of large, unheated church buildings impracticable. Instead he sought warmer and more comfortable domestic confines as he moved his catechism class from house to house in the villages through which he passed.[45] The most resourceful of these missionaries was Albrecht Chanovský who spent nearly his entire career wandering through the remote corners of the kingdom (Figure 14). When encountering children, he often engaged them by posing basic questions of the faith in forms of riddles – What is together three but also one? *The Holy Trinity.* Who are those who want to die but cannot? *The damned in hell.* He frequently went out to the fields and led the women harvesting crops through a series of hymns. He met men in the tavern and there conducted an impromptu catechism class. As for the mass, he taught the meaning of the liturgy, the vestments and the sacrament itself through a series of simple games. From these experiences Chanovský eventually compiled his own catechism.[46] Many of these missionaries were multilingual as well. When Jiří Pelinga worked in rural districts, he used the regional dialect. Valentin Bernard Jestřábský composed his *Household Catechism* in a Moravian variant with the observation that there were many in this district who did not know German. Written in the form of a dialog between a mysterious wayfarer and an innkeeper, Jestřábský's catechism illustrates that this priest was not only attuned to linguistic matters but also sensitive to cultural issues. The innkeeper who represented the common person is both entertained and edified by a series of stories from the traveler who used anecdotes from the peasant world to teach the Ten Commandments, the Apostles' Creed, and the Lord's Prayer in a very local idiom.[47]

Any discussion of catechetical activity in this period must eventually include a discussion of the Jesuit missionary Fridrich Bridel (1619–80). One of the most celebrated literary figures of the Bohemian baroque, Bridel was born into a non-Catholic family that suffered much in the aftermath of the

---

[44] Tanner, *Societas Iesu apostolorum imitatrix*, p. 746.
[45] See Dirig's account published as A. Podlaha, "Missie P. Kašpara Diriga v horách Krkonošských vykonaná r. 1679–80," *VKČSN*, 1900 (18), 7.
[46] Jan Tanner, *Muž apoštolský aneb život a ctnosti ctihodného pátera Albrechta Chanovského* (Prague: Typis Universitatis Carolo-Ferdinandeae, 1680), pp. 105–8; A. Chanovský, *Správa křesťanská* (Prague, 1676).
[47] Tanner, *Societas Iesu apostolorum imitatrix*, p. 748; Valentin Bernard Jestřábský, *Katechysmus Domácý* (Olomouc: Jan Adam Avinger, 1723), A3v. See in particular Jestřábský's discussion of honoring the Sabbath which is told through the adventures of a dissolute but ultimately repentant peasant boy, pp. 31–45.

14. Albrecht Chanovský, missionary of the peasants

kingdom's rebellion.[48] Emotionally scarred by these tumultuous early years, the sensitive young man entered the Society of Jesus at the age of eighteen. After the completion of his studies he taught rhetoric for four years and later directed the Jesuit press at the Clementinum. Honing his obvious gift for language during this period, Bridel left behind a significant corpus of religious poetry and prose which has been the subject of considerable study. His early biographers, however, made little mention of his literary accomplishments. Instead they focused on his missionary activity. We learn in his funeral oration that he was involved in mission work for more than two decades. For fifteen of those years he led a traveling ministry through the counties of central and eastern Bohemia. According to Bridel's eulogist, the Jesuit's evangelistic efforts were memorialized by one of his converts who created an informal monument to him in the forest of Hrádek. Literally marking his encounter with Bridel, the former heretic carved the following inscription on a tree, "Here I had a quarrel with Father Bridel. He convicted me by the Word of God."[49]

Books were an aid to his ministry, and throughout his career he translated texts that assisted him in instructing children and adults in the basics of the Christian faith. He placed a particularly high value on catechisms. His 1656 Czech paraphrase of Nicolaus Cusanus's *Gulden Kleynodt* with its inventive rhyme scheme, clever word plays, popular proverbs and folksy sayings was an early indication of his considerable talent. Bridel's most important work in this regard was his *Christian Teaching Composed in Verse*, an epic poem of more than 5,000 lines. Based on years of mission work, the catechism was a massive undertaking.[50] Although the text covers a tremendous amount of material, *Christian Teaching* is no stale recitation of Catholic dogma. Cognizant of his audience, Bridel used simple rhyming verse along with a selection of entertaining anecdotes from the Bible, history and legend to illustrate and teach specific articles of belief.

As John O'Malley has recently argued, the Jesuits saw themselves principally as teachers of *Christianitas*, essential Christian belief and practice. Less concerned with abstract doctrine, *Christianitas* for the Jesuits was an ideal

---

[48] Zdeněk Kalista, "Bedřich Bridel," *Annali dell' Istituto Universitario Orientale, Sezione slava* 14 (1971), 13–46; Antonín Škarka, *Fridrich Bridel nový a neznámý* (Prague: Universita Karlova, 1969); Vašica, *České literární baroko*, pp. 25–45.

[49] *Elogium P. Friderici Bridelii, Kuttenbergae in obsequio pestiferorum in Domino defuncti*, reprinted in Škarka, *Fridrich Bridel*, pp. 25–41. Here see pp. 25–6, 28.

[50] Fridrich Bridel, *Křesťanské učení veršemi vyložené*, in Bridel, *Básnické dílo* (Prague: Torst, 1994), pp. 243–397. The original was published posthumously in 1684 in Kutná Hora.

primarily oriented towards a more basic goal of Christian living.[51] Bridel clearly constructed *Christian Teaching* from this perspective. Although he was not hesitant to confront "Protestant error" in the text, the catechism is neither defensive nor overtly polemical. Bridel's foremost priority was the formation of Christian character within the framework of Catholic belief. Though *Christian Teaching* encompasses the fundamental points of Catholic doctrine from purgatory to penance, there is a consistent emphasis on practical application. His discussion of the fifth petition of the Lord's Prayer was typical in this regard. Here Bridel dealt with everyday issues of forgiveness and reconciliation including a story of a priest who attempts to reunite two feuding neighbors who stubbornly refuse to relinquish their mutual grievances, ready to suffer in hell before pardoning the other.[52] His treatment of the Ten Commandments followed a similar pattern. The injunction against murder is expanded to crimes of the tongue where spiteful words are as deadly as a double-edged sword. For adultery he described a typical peasant debauch which culminates with a visit from the devil. The sin of theft is brought to the village market and the very real temptation of using false weights and measures. Even his treatment of the sacraments retained this moral edge. He discussed not only the sanctity of marriage but like a contemporary counselor dispensed advice on how spouses should best handle their anger.[53] The distinctiveness of *Christian Teaching* stands out all the more when compared to typical Protestant catechisms where the emphasis was laid more squarely on dogma. Catholic identity for Bridel was more complex. Though doctrine was certainly not unimportant, it was only one element of a more comprehensive process of spiritual and moral formation.

Throughout *Christian Teaching* Bridel placed significant weight on what we might call markers of identity, specific actions and behavior that distinguish Catholic from Protestant. He in fact began the catechism with the query, "By what is a true Catholic recognized?" Interestingly enough, his answer was the cross. By making the sign of the cross, the Catholic identifies himself as a true believer.[54] Outward signs and public actions were essential components of Catholic identity for Bridel, and their absence among Lutherans and Calvinists weakened these communities. When Protestants mocked such rituals, God often intervened directly. Bridel related the story of a Protestant who sought to provoke the ire of his orthodox neighbors by eating meat on Friday. As he was poised to consume the first piece, his jaw

---

[51] O'Malley, *The First Jesuits*, pp. 86–7. [52] Bridel, *Křesťanské učení*, pp. 304–7.
[53] Ibid., pp. 346, 353–6, 396–7. [54] Ibid., pp. 243–7.

was suddenly paralyzed in an open position. Unable to close his mouth, the thwarted heretic became a sign himself of Catholicism's veracity.[55]

Utilizing more than a millennium of church history, Bridel filled his catechism with anecdotes that highlighted the antiquity and solidity of the Catholic church. Not surprisingly, he made special use of the Czech past. Illustrative was his treatment of St. Ivan, a ninth-century holy man and the spiritual mentor of Bohemia's first Christian princes, Duke Bořivoj and his wife Ludmila. Bridel enlisted the rustic Ivan as a means to bolster the cult of the holy cross. Living in seclusion, Ivan was tormented by a series of diabolic visitations. Divine assistance arrived in the form of John the Baptist who came to the hermit and demonstrated how through the use of the cross the evil one could be driven off.[56] Such a story underscored the antiquity of this form of devotion in the Bohemian lands. More generally, Bridel's use of Czech history and legend served as an interesting analog to the work of the antiquarians. While they sought to recover the memories of a *Bohemia sacra*, the literary Bridel exploited the past for more devotional purposes. He extolled Wenceslas for his devotion to the Eucharist, praised Procopius as the ideal priest and elevated Ivan as the earnest pilgrim.[57]

Apart from the catechism missionaries made use of other tools in their travels through rural areas. The sacred lecture and sermon, a theme I will return to in the following chapter, were also part of this program of basic Christian education. Pelinga and Chanovský were purportedly masterful preachers who regularly brought their audiences to tears.[58] Music was also an important part of their ministry. When Chanovský first entered a village, he often initiated his mission by singing a Czech hymn. As his biographer noted, he quickly gathered an audience, for "the inquisitive common folk are most addicted to song."[59] Music and especially song had long been an important part of Czech popular culture. In an effort to demoralize their enemies, the Hussites marched into battle lustily singing their famous war songs. Hymns became a central part of worship for the Bohemian Brethren, a tradition that was carried on by John Amos Comenius. Apart from their religious use, songs, especially after White Mountain, could also be exploited subversively. They were one of the few means in this period for expressing dissent. Košetický recorded several of these ballads in his compendium of folk culture. One of the most popular of these songs, "On the

---

[55] Ibid., pp. 366–7.   [56] Ibid., pp. 244–5.
[57] *Stůl Páně* (Prague: Jezuitská tiskárna, 1660); *Sláva svatoprokopská* (Prague: Jezuitská tiskárna, 1662); *Život svatého Ivana, prvního v Čechách poustevníka vyznavače* (Prague: Jezuitská tiskárna, 1657).
[58] Tanner, *Societas Iesu apostolorum imitatrix*, p. 749; Tanner, *Muž apoštolský*, p. 121.
[59] Tanner, *Societas Iesu apostolorum imitatrix*, p. 716.

peasants and their difficulties," spoke of the burden of forced labor, the corruption of local officials, and the calloused indifference of the land-owners. There were others that challenged the Habsburg regime more aggressively. The anthem "Arise, O Czechs" became a rallying cry in the Bohemian revolt. After 1620 versions of this song continued to circulate, albeit in a less open fashion.[60]

In the seventeenth century Catholic authorities recognized the power of song and sought to harness it in the service of the church. Bohemian presses busily produced Catholic hymnals throughout the seventeenth and early eighteenth centuries. In the second edition of his *Czech Hymnal*, Matěj Šteyer observed, "Our Bohemian forefathers adopted the lovely and praise-worthy custom of meeting before the church early on Sundays and other holidays. There before the mass and sermon began, they gathered in large numbers and piously sang sacred anthems."[61] These practices continued after White Mountain as the Bohemians developed a great reputation as hymn singers. Those who compiled the new Catholic songbooks cleverly responded to the musical orientation of their audience. They carefully sifted through the older songs of the Hussites, Utraquists and Brethren including many of the most popular ones in their anthologies. One of the most important composers of this period was the town organist of Jindřichův Hradec, Adam Michna of Otradovice (1600–76). Setting his own poetry to music, Michna produced two hymnals, *Czech Marian Music* and *Music for the Liturgical Year*. Both of these texts were written for churches with limited musical resources. The simple four- and five-part homophonic settings of Michna's verse were appropriate for the most humble of parishes. Sensitive to his social context, he also incorporated folk motifs into many of the melodies.[62] Košetický's massive *Quodlibeticum* contained literally hun-dreds of hymns. Translated from the Latin into the vernacular, these songs which worked through the liturgical year were a type of theological primer. There were musical versions of the Ten Commandments, Lord's Prayer and Hail Mary along with hymns celebrating major Marian holidays and the feast days of Bohemia's patron saints. Fridrich Bridel also used music as part of his catechetical program. His "Fourteen secrets of the Christian faith,"

[60] Evermod Jiří Košetický, *Quodlibeticum*, SK DG II 5, 23r–24r; Josef Petráň, "Píseň 'Vzhůru Čechové' a její varianty," *SbH* 3 (1955), 166–78; Zdeňka Tichá, ed., *Verše bolesti, posměchu, i vzdoru* (Prague: ČSAV, 1958).
[61] Matěj Šteyer, *Kancyonal Cžeský* (Prague: Jan Karel Jeřábek, 1687), unpaginated letter of dedication.
[62] Adrienne Simpson and Jiří Sehnal, "Adam Václav Michna z Otradovic," *The New Grove Dictionary of Music and Musicians* (New York: Grove, 2001), vol. XVI, pp. 600–1.

which was set to a popular melody, summarized the major points of his longer catechism.[63]

Over time music assumed an ever greater importance in the actual educational process. As Catholicism reestablished itself across the kingdom, the demand for musicians consequently increased. With music a substantial part of each service, the need for competent choristers and instrumentalists was not insignificant. Musical instruction was a high priority in both Jesuit and Piarist academies.[64] The musical orientation of the village schools was even more pronounced. The town magistrates entrusted basic pedagogical responsibilities to an individual who was known as the *kantor*. The cantor was also normally the organist and director of church music. Besides the weekly mass he was charged with readying the musicians for the many feast days, processions, funerals and weddings of the parish. Not unexpectedly, the educational priorities of his classroom were more often than not primarily directed towards his musical obligations. This system produced some of the finest musicians of early eighteenth-century Europe. Both Jan Dismas Zelenka, the court composer of Dresden, and Johann Stamitz, the director of instrumental music in Mannheim, came from distinguished families of cantors. But at the same time this musical emphasis frequently came at the expense of more basic pedagogical skills. We have stories such as the German organist of Litoměřice who applied for a position in the Czech-speaking region of Louny. It seems that he believed his qualifications as musician outweighed his inability to communicate to the students in their own tongue.[65] As late as the 1770s, there are reports indicating that many of these village schools were still more concerned with music than with literacy and arithmetical competency.[66] Thus, music played a dual role in the formation of a Czech religious identity. On the one hand, it was a popular and effective means of communicating fundamental beliefs of the church. But as religious music slowly grew to occupy an increasingly larger place in the culture of the day, it became in and of itself an important marker of Bohemian identity.

---

[63] Košetický, *Quodlibeticum*, SK DG II 4, pt. 2, 1r–260r; Bridel, *Básnické dílo*, pp. 397–8.
[64] Jiří Sehnal, "Pobělohorská doba (1620–1740)," in Jaromír Černý, ed., *Hudba v českých dějinách* (Prague: Editio Supraphon, 1983), p. 162. On the Jesuits and Piarists see Jaroslav Bužga, "Musiker und musikalische Institutionen im Zeitalter des Barocks," in Elmar Arro, ed., *Beiträge zur Musikgeschichte Osteuropas* (Wiesbaden: Steiner, 1977), pp. 351–9.
[65] Bužga, "Musiker und musikalische Institutionen," pp. 337–8.
[66] See the account of the Englishman Charles Burney published as P. Scholes, ed., *An Eighteenth-Century Musical Tour in Central Europe and the Netherlands* (London: Oxford University Press, 1959), vol. II, pp. 131–8.

The example of music points to a more general approach followed by these missionaries. They sought to reintroduce Catholicism through tactile and expressive forms of piety. They were convinced that the faith could be learned and appropriated most effectively through the active engagement of the senses. When Albrecht Chanovský entered a new region, he initiated a whole series of different activities. From singing in the fields to organizing plays, from renovating church buildings to designing processional banners, he enlisted an entire village in projects intended to strengthen the faith and religious identity of local communities. When actually teaching, he often employed some type of prop, an image of the infant Jesus, a crucifix or rosary. His own catechetical text, *The Christian Rule*, also reflected this orientation. He used physical objects such as pictures, bells, crosses and even church doors to teach basic Catholic doctrine. It was during the Christmas season, however, that Chanovský's ingenuity was put to its greatest test. After a year of slowly collecting the appropriate items or even traveling back to Prague for last-minute purchases, he painstakingly assembled an elaborate nativity scene in the village church where he was working.[67]

These early crèches which Chanovský and others constructed quickly grew in popularity, and Bohemia eventually became one of the most important centers of their production. Though folklorists have devoted significant attention to these objects, they have paid relatively little attention to their original function and purpose in the Czech lands.[68] In the sixteenth century it was the Jesuits who initially recognized the potential of the crèche for mission work. During their early days in Prague, their church of St. Clement became a type of laboratory for evangelistic experimentation. In 1559 over Easter week, they set up a tomb scene which attracted tremendous crowds. Archduke Ferdinand was so impressed that he visited the scene twice in the same evening. Pointing to the Jesuit's innovative work, he later reproached the staid canons of St. Vitus: "You should follow their example. Why don't people see similar things in your church? Why are you depriving them of a spectacle that can inspire so much piety?"[69] In 1562 the Jesuits applied this same creative spirit to the Christmas season and installed what is reported to have been the first crèche north of the Danube. Like its Easter counterpart, the St. Clement nativity scene attracted

---

[67] Tanner, *Muž apoštolský*, pp. 51, 58–9; Chanovský, *Správa křesťanská*. See chapters 75, 83 and 85.
[68] See for example the work of Vladimír Vaclík (*Chrámové betlémy v Čechách a na Moravě* [Prague: Vyšehrad, 1990]; *České betlémy* [Prague: Integra, 1994]).
[69] Cited in Oscar Teuber, *Geschichte des Prager Theaters* (Prague: A. Haase, 1883), vol. I, p. 15.

significant notice and became an annual tradition. Children of the high nobility would assemble before it and sing carols in Czech, German and Latin. Distinguished visitors including Empress Maria journeyed to Prague to view the order's celebrated handiwork. The collection's exquisitely carved Christchild was in fact a gift of the dowager empress.[70] The popularity of the nativity scene convinced the Jesuits that it could be an effective tool for evangelism. In the 1570s they regularly dispatched a team of priests to accompany the Clementinum's crèche on a tour through the surrounding countryside. Parish priests and missionaries were soon constructing their own simpler versions of this Christmas spectacle. Between 1560 and 1772 there are more than 3,000 references in the Jesuit records to crèches built in the Bohemian lands. Indeed, results were so impressive that Czech clergy quickly adapted it for mission work abroad. Their nativity scenes eventually appeared in the steamy jungles of southeast Asia.[71]

During the Christmas season the crèche was only one part of a broader didactic program recalling the mystery and significance of the incarnation. These displays were often used in conjunction with some form of religious drama. In Bohemia the Jesuits took the lead in fitting theater to the needs of the church. They used drama aggressively to confront their confessional opponents. The polemical edge of their plays was so strong in fact that in 1609 the Utraquists submitted a petition to the emperor demanding that the order cease performing productions that defamed their church.[72] Evidently, the supplication had little effect, for the following year the Jesuits in yet another attack on their rivals produced with spectacular pyrotechnics a play highlighting Elijah's confrontation with the prophets of Baal.[73] The situation did not alter substantially after White Mountain. In cities such as Cologne the clergy often utilized drama as an adjunct to the catechism. Students assumed the roles of Lutherans and Calvinists whose doctrinal errors were succinctly refuted by a Catholic apologist.[74] A genre similar to these catechism plays also developed in Bohemia. The former presence of religious schismatics actually helped the Catholic orders employ drama pedagogically. By using their confessional opponents as a foil, they could more easily contrast heretical and orthodox belief. Hus, Žižka and

[70] Karasek and Lanz, *Krippenkunst*, pp. 21–2. [71] Ibid., p. 12.
[72] František Černý, ed., *Dějiny českého divadla* (Prague: Academia, 1968), vol. I, p. 135; more generally on their activities see Bobková-Valentová, *Každodenní život*, pp. 86–119.
[73] *Summa hry o s. Eliášovi proroku* (Prague, 1610) (UK 54 E 2726).
[74] Theo van Oorschot, "Die Kölner Katechismusspiele. Eine literarische Sonderfom aus der Zeit der Gegenreformation," in J. M. Valentin, ed., *Gegenreformation und Literatur* (Amsterdam: Rodopi, 1979), pp. 217–43.

even the Winter King made frequent appearances as devious but fatally flawed enemies of the true church and its teaching.[75] The 1659 production of *Vinea Ecclesiae* used the story of Naboth and his vineyard to explain the mystery of the Eucharist. In the second act of the play a Lutheran, Calvinist and Hussite discuss the nature of the sacrament. Arguing heatedly with each other, they are in the end interrupted by the figure of *Ecclesia* who exposes their errors and then teaches them the proper use and meaning of the Eucharist.[76]

This religious drama was not only intended to inculcate proper belief. Perhaps more importantly, it was designed to foster specific practices of piety. Prague's Marian congregations frequently mounted plays as part of their Holy Week processions. Members of the confraternity carried a portable stage on which a short morality story was enacted. In one such performance Christ's sufferings were compared to the Christian's struggle against the seven deadly sins. In a 1703 procession a confraternity transformed a carriage into a type of penitential float where five costumed figures, who represented the Savior's victory over the will, the intellect, the body, death and the darkness of purgatory, encouraged the faithful to mortify the desires of the flesh.[77] The feast of Corpus Christi was another festival that lent itself to this type of devotional drama. Entire villages participated in elaborately orchestrated ceremonies. A Corpus Christi procession that included forty children dressed as angels was one of the highpoints of Kašpar Dirig's mission to the Giant Mountains.[78] Eucharistic plays were frequently a central part of these observances. At the last station of a 1690 Corpus Christi procession in Tábor, church leaders staged a dramatic dialog between a Catholic and a Lutheran who launched a spirited debate on the Eucharist. Presented in both Czech and German, the discussion concluded with the Protestant acknowledging his error and accepting the faith of his neighbor. One creative cleric adapted the Adam and Eve narrative for the festival. In rhyming verse he set forth the story of the fall, the expulsion from Eden and the murder of Abel. With Abel's death prefiguring Christ's ultimate sacrifice, the performance concluded by

---

[75] *Comedia Jesuitica contra Fridericum Bohemiae regem* (1620) (ÖNB, HSS, 8852, 254r–266v); *Všech sedm planet* (Jindřichův Hradec, 1655) (UK 52 B 44, no. 76); *Antitheton boemicum Joannis Huss* (Litomyšl: Kamenický, 1710).

[76] *Vinea Ecclesiae per vineam Naboth adumbrata* (Prague, 1659) (UK 52 B 44, no. 5).

[77] *Jesus Christus ein Obsieger sieben Haupt-sünden* (1683) (UK 52 B 44, no. 87); *Dominus Exercitum, vir Bellator* (1703) (UK 52 A 39, no. 2); Černý, ed., *Dějiny českého divadla*, vol. I, pp. 179–81.

[78] A. Podlaha, "Missie P. Kašpara Diriga," p. 16.

calling the faithful to action. Only through frequent communion could the sin of the first parents be overcome.[79]

How effective was this campaign to teach basic Catholic doctrine? Were the missionaries, teachers, parish priests and village cantors able to bring real change in the post-1620 period? Gerald Strauss, in what may be the fullest examination of religious education in the Reformation era, considered this issue in the Lutheran context. His conclusion was decidedly negative:

A century of Protestantism had brought about little or no change in the common religious conscience ... Given people's nebulous grasp of the substance of their faith, no meaningful distinction could have existed between Protestants and Catholics – a distinction arising from articulated belief, conscious attachment, and self-perception.[80]

Does Strauss's contention hold true in Bohemia? Though this question could only be answered with a thorough examination of visitation records and other similar sources, on one level his assessment may not be far off. Theological illiteracy remained a significant problem through the eighteenth century. This type of analysis, however, is of limited utility in Czech lands, for it does not fully consider the ways in which Bohemian Catholics constructed their identity.

In a recent study of catechetical patterns among Magyar Calvinists, Graeme Murdock has concluded that Hungary's Reformed community defined itself almost exclusively through words. Suspicious of visual images, they articulated their identity through a system of beliefs recorded on the printed page.[81] The contrast with Bohemia could not have been greater. Missionaries used a variety of media to both express and ultimately define the Catholic experience. Music, art and architecture all became important manifestations of confessional identity. Though doctrine was not unimportant, being a Bohemian Catholic was as much about public rites and rituals as specific articles of belief. Missionaries also endeavored to link individual Catholic identity to a broader and deeper sense of communal identity reflected in their emphasis on processions and other social forms of piety. By identifying the faith with traditional signs or symbols of community, the missionaries attempted to secure their teaching to a firm cultural foundation. In this sense, then, the program of catechesis was not

---

[79] Košetický, *Quodlibeticum*, SK DG II 6, 473r–482r, 490r–504v.
[80] Gerald Strauss, *Luther's House of Learning* (Baltimore: Johns Hopkins University Press, 1978), p. 299.
[81] Graeme Murdock, "Calvinist catechizing and Hungarian Reformed identity," in M. Crăciun, O. Ghitta and G. Murdock, eds., *Confessional Identity in East-Central Europe* (Aldershot: Ashgate, 2002), pp. 81–98.

without success. By the beginning of the eighteenth century church leaders had clearly laid out the markers of a corporate Catholic identity.

BOHEMIAN CATHOLICISM AND RURAL CULTURE

Recent scholarship on early modern Catholicism has demonstrated in convincing fashion both the flexibility and adaptability of the faith to local circumstances. Post-Tridentine Catholicism underwent a profound transformation during the period of missionary activity that we are examining. A more intellectual and doctrinaire version of the faith gave way to softer and more reassuring forms of confessional expression where basic problems of the human condition played a central role. Jean Delumeau has described a religious culture where ordinary believers sought comfort and protection in a hostile world through a broad range of public rituals and private devotional practices. A city such as Naples which had seven patron saints overseeing its municipal welfare at the beginning of the seventeenth century sought further security and busily added twenty-one over the next hundred years. Early modern Catholicism responded to human weakness and insecurity and developed new forms of piety and spirituality to address these fundamental needs. The rural missions were part of this general shift in religious sensibilities.[82]

The missionaries who scattered throughout the countryside after White Mountain centered their attention on the peasant population. Though they certainly did not ignore larger towns and cities, it was the rural areas that they most frequently visited, and their biographers focused on this aspect of their ministry. Adam Kravařský supposedly spent so much time among the peasants that he was eventually adopted as one of their own. During his mission trips Fridrich Bridel regularly scoured the fields for shepherds and searched the forest for heretics. Albrecht Chanovský consistently refused the more elaborate meals prepared in his honor and instead shared the humbler fare of the poorer farmers.[83] Even when we discount the obvious hagiographical excess of these accounts, it does seem clear that the missionaries worked diligently to reach the lower strata of Czech society. As opposed to Gerald Strauss's Lutheran preachers who "tended to talk above the heads of their flock," the Catholic message was more carefully tailored to its rustic audience.[84] The former Utraquist, Václav František Kocmánek (1607–79),

---

[82] Châtellier, *La religion des pauvres*; Jean Delumeau, *Rassurer et protéger* (Paris: Fayard, 1989), p. 245.
[83] Tanner, *Societas Iesu apostolorum imitatrix*, p. 865; Tanner, *Muž apoštolský*, pp. 60–1.
[84] Strauss, *Luther's House of Learning*, p. 306.

wrote his plays with the hardships of the peasants in mind. In one of his Christmas dramas the poor shepherds recite the grievances they have suffered under Herod's tyrannical regime, a not-so-thinly veiled critique of the contemporary regime.[85] The music and poetry of Adam Michna was also oriented towards Bohemia's rural society. Unlike the work of many of his contemporaries, Michna's religious verse did not recreate an idealized pastoral world that drew its inspiration from antiquity. Instead, he filled his poetry with scenes from the woods and meadows of his homeland. Michna, who also owned an inn in southern Bohemia, incorporated regional idioms and figures of speech in his devotional poetry. God "waves to me" from heaven. The Virgin has "applied rouge to her cheeks from the heavenly apothecary," and "the soup which Adam gladly cooked in paradise was eaten by the Lord to his fill."[86] In a more didactic fashion the Moravian cleric Valentin Bernard Jestřábský wrote *The Many Visions of a Simple Peasant* as a basic primer of Christian behavior and belief for the country farmer.[87] Finally the songs, plays and prayers recorded by Jiří Košetický are ample testimony of the extent to which Bohemian Catholicism had absorbed the peasant culture of its day.

The church also worked hard to advance a cult connected closely to peasant life. 1622 was a year of celebration across Catholic Europe with the canonization of four great heroes of the Counter-Reformation: Ignatius Loyola, Francis Xavier, Teresa of Avila and Philip Neri. Alongside this august quartet of spiritual luminaries, Pope Gregory XV also celebrated the elevation of a fifth but decidedly more obscure figure. Isidore, the farmer, was an eleventh-century Spanish peasant who purportedly lived a model life of hard work and Christian charity. Significantly, he was the only layperson canonized between 1588 and 1665.[88] In central Europe the cult found fertile ground. One of the first confraternities devoted to the new saint was in Poland, and it did not take long before it spread to Bohemia. The Jesuits were particularly active in this regard, and brotherhoods of the farmer-saint tended to develop in close proximity to their colleges. An early rule of one of these confraternities reflected the church's efforts to address

---

[85] Černý, ed., *Dějiny českého divadla*, vol. I, pp. 162–5.

[86] Adam Michna z Otradovic, *Das dichterische Werk: Česká mariánská muzika, Loutna česká, Svatoroční muzika*, ed. A. Škarka (Munich: Fink, 1968), pp. 19–22.

[87] Valentin Bernard Jestřábský, *Vidění rozličné sedláčka sprostného* (Opava: Schindler, 1719); for a modern edition see Milan Kopecký, ed., *Vidění rozličné sedláčka sprostného* (Uherský Brod: Nakl. Muzea J. A. Komenského, 1973).

[88] Simon Ditchfield, "Tridentine worship and the cult of the saints," in R. Po-Chia Hsia, ed., *The Cambridge History of Christianity*, vol. VI: *Reformation and Expansion 1500–1660* (Cambridge: Cambridge University Press, 2007), p. 215.

typical vices of peasant communities. Strict regulations were laid down against drunkenness, laziness, brawling and sexual immorality. Superstition and magic were censured while members of the brotherhood were to commit themselves to the godly education of the young.[89] Though the cult remained primarily a rural phenomenon, church officials continued to promote it throughout the period. Devotional tracts and short biographies were distributed, and statues of the saint including one executed by Jan Jiří Bendl began to appear across the region. In the eighteenth century preachers such as Bohumír Bílovský saluted the Spanish farmer as the ideal laborer while Dominik Stehlik elevated the patient Isidore as a model for overtaxed and overworked peasants.[90]

In light of all this activity it is important to note that the interaction between the church and Bohemian society was not unidirectional. Ecclesiastical authorities did not construct a folk Catholicism from the bits and pieces of popular culture they found useful and then simply impose it on the populace. Religious identities are never created in this fashion. They are negotiated as compromises are struck and accommodation is found. Though Protestantism had to be quashed, the church was hesitant to attack many forms of popular culture. Many customs, even from the pre-Christian era, were allowed to survive. From the blessing of colored Easter eggs to the burning of straw effigies on Laetare Sunday, a whole array of these activities were actually condoned and incorporated into church life.[91] Though Kašpar Dirig encountered some hostility when he set up a crèche during his mission, he was far more successful organizing a procession on St. John's Day. This holiday, which was originally a fertility rite celebrating the summer solstice, had been superficially adapted by the church to honor its saint. Older practices, such as the lighting of bonfires, had persisted and, as Dirig's account illustrates, they contributed to the appeal of his procession through the mountains.[92]

The use of sacramentals also illustrates how compromises between church and peasant cultures were found. Along Bohemia's western border in the Upper Palatinate, the Jesuits had great success distributing so-called

---

[89] *Regule neb Ustanoweni Bratrstwa Swatého Izydora* (Mikulov, 1635); Jiří Mikulec, "Kult svatého Izidora sedláka v českých zemích," in Z. Hojda, ed., *Kultura baroka v Čechách a na Moravě* (Prague: Historický ústav, 1992), pp. 65–83; Janusz Tazbir, "Die gesellschaftlichen Funktionen des Kultus des heiligen Isidor des Pflügers in Polen," *Acta Poloniae Historica* 20 (1969), 120–37.

[90] Johannes Eusebius Nieremberg, *Žiwot a Zázrakowé Sv. Izydora* (Prague: Jezuitská tiskárna, 1673); B. Bílovský, *Doctrina christiana animabus inservitura* (Olomouc: Jan Adam Avinger, 1721), part I, pp. 124–5; Dominik Stehlik, *Sedlák Urozený Sprostý a Bohu milý Swatý Isidorus* (Znojmo: Anna Terezie Svobodová, 1726).

[91] Bérenger, "The Austrian church," pp. 104–5.   [92] Podlaha, "Missie P. Kašpara Diriga," 16.

Xavier water, a liquid that had been touched with a relic from the missionary-saint and was credited with thaumaturgic properties.[93] It seems that sacramentals played a similar function in the Czech lands. Though in his catechism Fridrich Bridel unequivocally stated, "The first commandment forbids magic," he continued by affirming the great practical benefits of holy water. While regulations of a St. Isidore confraternity condemned folk magic, the miraculous virtues of holy water were extolled for all in the community.[94] Prayers and charms were written on pieces of paper known as "lengths" and worn as amulets to ward off all kinds of dangers. Songs and poems of supplication were chanted to protect farm animals. Though the situation in Bohemia may not have been as extreme as what David Gentilcore describes in southern Italy, a shared "system of the sacred" did develop that cut across lay and clerical divides and provided common folk with direct access to sacred power.[95] The church was in some ways so willing to accommodate to popular culture that it is often difficult to tell whether Bohemian Catholicism was actually assimilating these folk customs and beliefs or was itself being amalgamated into the peasant world. Over time, certain forms of cultural expression, such as the nativity scene, which had been introduced as an evangelistic tool, slowly lost their distinctly confessional character and became a more general feature of regional identity with only a secondary religious function.

After White Mountain, Catholicism also responded to the economic and social conditions of the peasant. It is hard to exaggerate the chaos and upheaval of the Czech countryside in the post-1620 period. The nineteenth-century historian Antonín Rezek described this world in rather blunt terms: "The generation that came of age in 1648 grew up for the large part without religion, education and the oversight of any governmental structure. For their whole life they knew only blood, looting, pillaging and other forms of corruption and criminal activity."[96] The destruction of war, regular outbreaks of the plague and the reimposition of what Czech scholars

[93] Trevor Johnson, "Blood, tears and Xavier-water: Jesuit missionaries and popular religion in the eighteenth-century Upper Palatinate," in R. Scribner and T. Johnson, eds., *Popular Religion in Germany and Central Europe, 1400–1800* (New York: St. Martin's Press, 1996), pp. 183–202.
[94] Bridel, *Křesťanské učení*, pp. 328–32; *Regule neb Ustanowení Bratrstwa Swatého Izydora*, a IIv–a I2r.
[95] *Píseň Prosební k Swatým Patronům, Proti Pádu Dobytka welkým v Boha Orodowníkům na Swětlo wydaná* (n.p., n.d.) (KNM, 27 H 131); V. Vlnas, ed., *The Glory of the Baroque in Bohemia* (Prague: Paseka, 2001), p. 483; David Gentilcore, *From Bishop to Witch: The System of the Sacred in Early Modern Terra d'Otranto* (Manchester: Manchester University Press, 1992).
[96] Cited in Jaroslav Kadlec, *Přehled českých církevních dějin* (Rome: Zvon, 1987), vol. II, p. 142. More recent economic and social assessments are offered in Markus Cerman and Hermann Zeitlhofer, eds., *Soziale Strukturen in Böhmen* (Munich: Oldenbourg, 2002); Markus Cerman and Robert Luft, eds., *Untertanen, Herrschaft und Staat in Böhmen und im "Alten Reich"* (Munich: Oldenbourg, 2005).

have referred to as the "second serfdom" made living conditions unimaginably grim. The sufferings of the peasants culminated in the cathartic outbursts of the 1680 rebellions. Though it is difficult to make generalizations concerning the role of the church in this context, a few points should be noted. The Jesuits in particular had a significant ministry among the sick, especially those suffering from the plague. In his massive compendium of Jesuit lives, Matthias Tanner specifically singled out their work with the dying. Not surprisingly, his text is full of heroic stories: the priests of the Jičín college who with steely resolution refuse to flee the disease-ravaged region, the efforts of Andreas Nigrinus to secure medicine for the stricken inhabitants of Opava and the stoic deportment of Melchior Kaukal who after ministering to others calmly awaits his own death from the plague. This anecdotal evidence is supported statistically as well. In the plague year of 1680 the mortality rate of the Jesuits of the Bohemian province rose by nearly 400 percent. Their commitment to work with plague victims in towns such as Kutná Hora did have a substantial impact on their general reputation.[97] Although it would be naïve to claim that the Jesuits and other missionaries were uniformly embraced as champions of the common folk, their identification with the poor and dying surely must have had some impact at the local level.

The homiletic literature of the period offers another perspective on the church and its relationship with the peasant world. On the one hand, priests railed against the vices of rural society. Drunkenness, sexual immorality and indolence were targets of their social critique. But at the same time they lashed out against the frequent brutality and cruelty of the landowners. Though the most famous of these baroque preachers, Bohumír Bílovský, acknowledged that peasants needed to be governed with a firm hand, he also recognized the often inhumane circumstances under which they worked and lived. Šebastián Berlička noted acerbically that the game on many noble estates received better treatment than the agricultural laborers. Bohuslav Balbín spoke of the sweat and blood of the wretched farmers that was extracted through extortionate taxes. Valentin Bernard Jestřábský began *The Many Visions of a Simple Peasant* with a preface defending the honor and dignity of this estate.[98]

---

[97] Tanner, *Societas Iesu apostolorum imitatrix*, pp. 639, 727–30, 872–7; Martin Svatoš, "Jezuitské *litterae annuae* a jejich podání náboženského života v Kutné Hoře v morovém roce 1680," *LF* 124 (2001), 85, 87; Jiří Havlík, "The Jesuits and plague epidemics (1562–1713)," in A. Richterová and I. Čornejová, eds., *The Jesuits and the Clementinum* (Prague: NK, 2006), pp. 37–44.

[98] For a sample of some of this literature see Eduard Maur, "Pobělohorské poddanské poměry a Bohuslav Balbín," in Z. Pokorná and M. Svatoš, eds., *Bohuslav Balbín und die Kultur seiner Zeit in Böhmen* (Cologne: Böhlau, 1993), pp. 13–22; Jiří Mikulec, *Poddanská otázka v barokních Čechách* (Prague: Historický ústav, 1993), pp. 79–89; Jestřábský, *Vidění rozličné sedláčke sprostného*, p. 24.

While the church as an institution was hesitant to interfere directly in the affairs of the great landowners, individual clergy were often more sympathetic to the plight of the peasants such as the priest of Kostelní Bříza in western Bohemia who complained to his superiors that unjust agricultural demands were prompting many of his parish to flee to Lutheran Saxony. There were others who challenged the system more directly by marrying peasants without the sanction of their respective landowners.[99] The most famous of these peasant advocates was the Jesuit Jacques des Hayes, who apart from his catechetical texts composed a controversial reform proposal.[100] Aimed specifically at his patron Count Lamboy, des Hayes's memorandum did not mince words. The Jesuit warned the count that his very soul was in jeopardy if he failed to reconsider the management of his estates. Des Hayes continued with a long list of grievances that detailed the various ways in which the nobleman had exploited his workforce. Concluding with a series of bold recommendations, he put forward his own scheme of agricultural reorganization aimed at boosting productivity while easing the burden of the peasantry. Des Hayes's proposal was obviously not greeted with universal approbation, but when one critic noted that a number of his suggestions were actually economically counterproductive, Karel Grobendonq, a Jesuit professor at the university, rose to des Hayes's defense by arguing that moral concerns held precedence over financial considerations.[101] Again it is naïve to view the church as a firm and constant ally of the peasant. There were priests who cared little for society's lowest orders and were as rapacious as many of the nobility. Spiritual and secular authorities were not afraid to employ force against a presumed Protestant threat. Nonetheless, when considering the confessional transformation of the Bohemian kingdom, we should not underestimate the dynamism of early modern Catholicism. Culturally, socially and economically it was able to identify with major concerns of rural society, thus helping the faith take root and grow of its own accord in the Czech countryside.

---

[99] Mikulec, *Poddanská otázka*, pp. 71, 76–9.
[100] Reprinted in A. Rezek, "Dva příspěvky k dějinám selských bouří a selského povstání v XVII. století," *VKČSN* (1893), 18–28. Substantial portions are also reproduced in M. Kovář, "Considerationes…," *SbHKr* 3 (1894), 73–87.
[101] M. Kovář, "Considerationes…," 87.

CHAPTER 7

Sermons, songs and scripture: reforming believers by the word

Of all the negative stereotypes that have emerged from the post-White Mountain period, the activities of the Jesuit priest Antonín Koniáš (1691–1760) loom particularly large. Though Koniáš was a favorite target of nationalist historians lamenting the loss and destruction of Czech culture under the Habsburg yoke, it may have been the nineteenth-century novelist Alois Jirásek who most successfully formulated the popular image of this controversial figure. In his historical novel *Temno* (*Darkness*), Jirásek depicted Koniáš as a half-crazed burner of books whose mission trips to the countryside culminated with the construction of a great pyre of forbidden manuscripts. Adding to the effect were the illustrations of Jirásek's collaborator Adolf Kašpar (Figure 15). In one scene the skeletal figure of the missionary priest is flanked by two columns. To the left an unfortunate prisoner, presumably a religious dissident, is bending his head to the executioner's sword while to the right a martyr's stake is ablaze with leaping flames. With the grim face of fanatical resolution, Koniáš slowly rips the pages of a confiscated book and tosses them into a fire that is burning vigorously at his feet.

The image of book-burning Koniáš has contributed to another stereotype that has dogged the Catholic lands of central Europe during the seventeenth and eighteenth centuries, a division between the visual and the verbal. As early as the Reformation era, printmakers portrayed Protestants as people of the book while representing their Catholic counterparts as believers who expressed their piety through physical forms of ritual devotion. This generalization has persisted in modified form to the present day.[1] Those studying print culture in central Europe have traditionally focused on Protestant areas and material written in the vernacular. While in most cases censorship and book production were more restrictive in Catholic

---

[1] See for example James Melton, "From image to word: cultural reform and the rise of literate culture in eighteenth-century Austria," *Journal of Modern History* 58 (1986), 95–124.

15. Antonín Koniáš as burner of books

lands, scholars working in this area have long faced an additional problem, a Whiggish historiography that has tended to construe the region's literary history as a slow but gradual process of secularization. Religious literature produced in the Catholic lands of this period has been frequently passed over as merely a minor road stop on the way to the Enlightenment. As Dieter Breuer has observed in the German context, the seventeenth century is one of the most problematic periods of this region's literary tradition in large part for confessional reasons.[2] But whatever the sources of neglect, the presses were definitely not idle in Bohemia after 1620. As we noted earlier, the printed word was one of the tools used by the missionaries in their travels across the kingdom. But what exactly was being sung in the pews, preached from the pulpit and read at home? What was the nature and impact of this new religious literature?

The printing industry had grown slowly in the Bohemian kingdom.[3] Although there were presses in Plzeň, Kutná Hora, Prague, Olomouc and Brno before 1500, the first half of the sixteenth century was overall a rather stagnant period for book production, especially in Bohemia proper. The industry established itself during the reigns of Maximilian II and his son Rudolf. Leading the way were the presses of the Melantrich and Veleslavín families. Jiří Melantrich had studied with Melanchthon in Wittenberg before moving to Basel and an apprenticeship with the man who revolutionized that city's printing industry, Johann Froben. Returning to Prague in the 1540s, he set up his own business with the Swiss scholar-printer as his model. The new enterprise did remarkably well, eventually producing texts that represent the literary high point of Czech humanism. The work was taken over by his son-in-law, Daniel Adam of Veleslavín. A former professor at the university, Veleslavín kept the high standards of his predecessor. While Melantrich and Veleslavín published for the elites, there were many other successful printers in Prague who marketed their wares for more popular audiences. The religious literature of Jiří Nigrin, the calendars of Michael Peterle and the news sheets of Jiří Jakubův Dačický all found avid readers. Outside Prague there were lively publishing hubs in smaller towns such as Hradec Králové, Litomyšl and Mladá Boleslav. Moravia, too, enjoyed a brisk trade with activity in Olomouc, Prostějov and, most importantly, the Brethren center of Ivančice. The booksellers, who normally worked independently of the printers, also prospered. More than 100 were doing business in Prague by the end of the sixteenth century. Importing books from abroad while selling Czech products at the fairs of Frankfurt and Leipzig, these busy entrepreneurs helped create a vibrant intellectual network between Bohemia and its neighbors.

There is no question that the events of 1620 led to a broad transformation of Bohemia's literary world. The new regime quickly identified the book as

---

[2] Dieter Breuer, *Oberdeutsche Literatur 1565–1650* (Munich: Beck, 1979). See especially pp. 1–21.
[3] For an overview of printing see Čeněk Zíbrt, *Z dějin českého knihtiskařství* (Prague: Typografia, 1913); Josef Volf, *Dějiny českého knihtisku do roku 1848* (Prague: Novák, 1926); Zdeněk Tobolka, *Dějiny československého knihtisku v době nejstarší* (Prague: Nákladem Československé společnosti knihovědné, 1930). More recent is Mirjam Bohatcová, *Česká kniha v proměnách staletí* (Prague: Panorama, 1990).

one of the chief causes of the revolt. Parallel to the harsh tactics employed by de Huerta and de Marradas, Karl von Liechtenstein took strong and immediate measures to regulate and control the kingdom's print culture.[4] Even before the execution of the prisoners in Old Town Square, he had decreed that all printers were forbidden from publishing any material without the permission of his office. In the first decade after White Mountain the busy governor issued a whole series of edicts that radically restructured the book trade. In 1623 he implemented legislation stipulating that only Catholic printers were allowed to produce the popular astrological calendars and banning the import of all foreign texts. Three years later he sought to regularize these new ordinances by establishing a commission to oversee the industry. Printing houses were placed under the authority of the new institution which was charged with confiscating materials that were deemed harmful to both church and state. In addition, the commission was empowered to enter private homes and carry off any offensive books. The following year Liechtenstein expanded the responsibilities of this body to the activities of booksellers who were now burdened with even more restrictions. The pattern in Prague was followed around the region. Non-Catholic texts were burned or carted off to specially designated libraries. In rural areas the local priest was instructed to examine the books of his parishioners. The actual mechanics of censorship were also hammered out in this period. Liechtenstein initially ceded substantial authority to the Jesuits, a decision that prompted a power struggle between the order and the archbishop. By the middle of the seventeenth century a compromise had been reached. In line with Trent, the archbishop retained his traditional powers as censor, though the Jesuits were allowed to control the publications of their own members as well as the right to review the texts of Bohemia's Jewish printers.

The post-1620 changes should be seen as a continuation of policies that had been initiated nearly a century earlier with the accession of Ferdinand I. Though there had been piecemeal legislation restricting the anti-Catholic texts of the Bohemian Brethren, in 1530 Ferdinand issued a more comprehensive decree against any heretical literature dangerous to Rome. After the uprising of the 1540s he moved more aggressively against the printers whom

---

[4] On censorship see Ferdinand Menčík, "Censura v Čechách a na Moravě," *VKČSN* (1888), 85–136; Klára Homerová, "Tisková cenzura v Čechách, 1621–1660," *SbNMP* 42–3 (1997–8). For the eighteenth century and broader ettempts to control reading material see M. E. Ducreux, "Le livre et l'hérésie, modes de lecture et politique du livre en Bohême au XVIIIe siècle," in H. E. Bödeker, G. Chaix and P. Veit, eds., *Le livre religieux et ses pratiques* (Göttingen: Vandenhoeck & Ruprecht, 1991), pp. 131–51.

he saw as the fomenters of revolt. He initially banned printing altogether in the kingdom, but he eventually relented and allowed books to be produced in Plzeň and Prague. Plzeň, which had remained loyal during the war, had no active presses, and in Prague Ferdinand's close ally, Bartoloměj Netolický, had a virtual monopoly of the industry. Though Ferdinand slowly loosened these restrictions and gradually licensed some of the older printing houses, he kept a close eye on the book trade and in 1562 signed an order that granted the newly installed archbishop substantial powers of censorship. In a certain respect, then, the more tolerant or perhaps negligent regimes of Maximilian and Rudolf, which allowed Bohemia's printing industry to flourish, were aberrations in a longer pattern of growing state control.

It is also important not to overestimate the effectiveness of censorship policies after White Mountain. The actual procedure of expurgating texts in the Bohemian kingdom was often executed in a haphazard or even careless fashion. The case of liturgical literature is particularly illustrative. In the fifteenth and sixteenth centuries the Utraquist church produced their own graduals, liturgical texts that contain the sung parts of the mass. Evidence indicates that in most cases church officials did not begin to examine these texts until the late seventeenth or even early eighteenth century, and once they started their work, review procedures were far from systematic and comprehensive. The censors normally singled out Czech-language graduals despite the fact that their Latin counterparts often contained problematic passages from Rome's perspective.[5] The clear objective of these clerics was the removal of any mention of Hus while other portions that may have been more offensive were frequently passed over. A gradual of the well-known Utraquist scribe Jan Táborský (1500–72) is an important case in point.[6] For the feast day of Sts. Peter and Paul he included a lengthy commentary on the alleluia verses for the day (Mt. 16:18–19). Here he elaborated on the famous passage that Catholic leaders had traditionally used to affirm the papacy, "You are Peter, and on this rock I will build my church." Táborský explicitly denied Peter's special status explaining that the rock upon which Christ would build his church was not a reference to the papacy but to the

---

[5] It is often difficult to distinguish whether a gradual was of Catholic or Utraquist origin. The surest marker for sixteenth-century Utraquist texts was the inclusion of the feast of Hus. After 1538, Utraquist graduals were nearly always produced in Czech though the Utraquists also continued to use older Latin versions. The following discussion on liturgy and censorship is drawn from the research of Barry Graham who generously shared many of his findings. Of the sample he examined, over 80 percent of the Czech graduals were censored while slightly over 40 percent of the Latin volumes were censored.

[6] For Táborský see *OSN*, vol. XXV, p. 16. Karel Konrád, *Dějiny posvátného zpěvu staročeského od XV věku do zrušení literátských bratrstev* (Prague: V. Kotrba, 1893), pp. 75–8, 89–91.

work of the Savior.[7] In at least three other graduals where antiphons and sequences for the feast of Hus were expunged, a rather questionable rubric designating the Marian feast of the Assumption was allowed to remain, "For the day of the burial of the Blessed Virgin Mary!"[8] In another a full-page illustration with the inscription SOLA FIDES IUSTIFICAT in block capitals was simply passed over.[9] It seems likely that many of the older Utraquist liturgies were simply carried over unaltered into the post-White Mountain period.

Censorship, then, should be seen neither as a new phenomenon in the Bohemian lands nor as the magic bullet that effectively eliminated heretical literature. Although we should not discount the efforts to control Protestant books and pamphlets, it makes more sense in many respects to examine the opposite side of the coin. It was not the celebrated bonfires of Koniáš that shaped a new confessional identity as much as a printing industry that was restructured and transformed after 1620. Books for our entire period remained a critical battlefield for wandering missionaries, parish priests and clerical administrators. The Czech exiles developed the so-called *špalíčky*, miniature editions of religious texts that were frequently smuggled back into Bohemia. In the eighteenth century Jakub Firmus claimed, "Heretical books, old and new, read and sung in private, are the cause of the persistence of heresy."[10] Such a threat helped stimulate the growth and spread of a new Catholic literature. Koniáš's father had been a printer, and the priest himself wrote more than half a dozen religious texts. Archbishops such as Sobek of Bílenberk and Johann Friedrich Waldstein devoted substantial attention to the printing industry as they recognized the book as a powerful tool in the fight against heresy. The book was even seen by some as a means to help establish new social patterns that would reinforce the kingdom's Catholic identity.[11]

After White Mountain major publishing activity was at first essentially limited to Prague, and it was the Jesuits who assumed the leading role. The masters of the university, they controlled the Academic Press which dominated the publishing trade for well over a century. Also important was the

---

[7] B. F. W. Graham, *Bohemian and Moravian Graduals 1420–1600* (Turnhout: Brepols, 2006), no. 132 (209r–210r).

[8] Ibid., nos. 20 (383v), 23 (10v), 126 (235v, 370v).   [9] Ibid., no. 18 (118v).

[10] Cited in Augustin Neumann, *Prostonárodní náboženské hnutí dle dokladů konsistoře královéhradecké* (Hradec Králové: Družstevní knihtiskárna, 1931), p. 161.

[11] See for example the efforts of Koniáš to popularize a set of greetings that were purely Catholic in nature. M. E. Ducreux, "Reading unto death: books and readers in eighteenth-century Bohemia," in Roger Chartier, ed., *The Culture of Print* (Oxford: Polity Press, 1989), p. 234.

rival establishment of the archdiocese founded by Ernst von Harrach in 1630. Over time more printers appeared, and the industry once again began to fan out across the region. The widow Judita Bylinová took over the old Veleslavín house. The ambitious Jan Arnolt of Dobroslavín established a press in the city in the 1660s. Jiří Černoch, the former manager of the Academic Press, started his own shop shortly thereafter, while the enterprising Jiří Laboun prospered printing religious literature and the popular St. Wenceslas calendars.

One of the most important resources to promote the publication of Catholic literature was established in 1669. The St. Wenceslas Endowment was the inspiration of the Šteyer family. Maria Šteyerová, a proprietor of a successful bakery, was a wealthy citizen of New Town. Her son, the Jesuit Matěj Václav, was an influential figure in the publishing world of late seventeenth-century Bohemia. Working with his mother, he set up a foundation that had a significant impact on the production and distribution of Czech religious literature well into the nineteenth century. The scope and activity of the endowment were carefully delimited in Šteyerová's 1669 will.[12] Books, she observed, were an effective means of fostering devotion. They brought sinners to repentance while spurring the devout to greater love and piety. But while such texts were readily available in both Latin and German, there was a pressing need for similar material in Czech. It was her wish, then, to establish a foundation that supported the publication of literature exclusively in this language. Furthermore, these books and pamphlets were to be distributed without cost, for the country was full of destitute peasants and poor townspeople. To manage this ambitious undertaking Šteyerová turned to the Jesuits of Prague's New Town. They were to administer the trust with her son as the estate's executor.

Financially, the St. Wenceslas Endowment was supported with an initial grant of 1,300 Rhenish gulden that Šteyerová provided. From the invested capital, the annual interest was to support the publishing activities of the foundation. In her will Šteyerová noted that she hoped her contribution would be matched by others who also understood the importance of this undertaking. The foundation's very name had been strategically chosen to inspire feelings of patriotic piety and loosen the purse strings of potential donors. Small gifts did come during those early years, and these amounts quickly grew. Within four years the foundation doubled its capital.[13] The real turning point, however, came in 1692. Archbishop Waldstein had taken

---

[12] NA, SM, J20/17/17/1, 1–9. [13] NA, SM, J20/17/17/1, 18.

an active interest in Šteyerová's trust and contributed more than 2,000 copies of the new Catholic translation of the New Testament to help increase the foundation's endowment. At the same time the ambitious prelate issued a decree that expanded the scope of its activities. He envisioned an active role for the St. Wenceslas Endowment in the Catholic reconquest of east central Europe with the distribution of religious literature not only in Bohemia but also in lands recently liberated from the Turks.[14]

The trust rarely supported an entire print run of a specific text. Working with a variety of presses, the foundation's administrators typically financed a portion of the run which it then distributed free of charge. More than 800 texts were given out in 1670, approximately 1,500 in 1671, and nearly 3,500 in 1673. According to the estimate of an eighteenth-century rector of the Jesuits' New Town college, in the first eighty years of its existence the St. Wenceslas Endowment distributed more than 80,000 books.[15] In many respects the foundation functioned as a catalyst for the entire industry of religious literature. The authors it supported frequently went on to enjoy tremendous success even without its subventions as in the case of Martin von Cochem (1634–1712), a German Capuchin who spent three years in Prague in the 1690s. In 1698 he published a life of Christ with support from the endowment. The popularity of his work was so great that there was soon no need to provide any further assistance.[16] The 1698 text was used as a model for passion plays across the Bohemian countryside. His prayer book, *The Key of Paradise*, went through an astounding seventy-nine printings by 1800. The text was so popular in fact that a prayer book was typically known in the region as a *Nebeklíč*, the Czech title of the Capuchin's work.[17]

By 1700, then, the publication of religious literature in the Bohemian kingdom was a well-established and thriving business. Though the St. Wenceslas Endowment had been founded to support the publication of Czech texts, significant material was also rolling off the presses in German and Latin. The issue of language has been problematic for scholars of this period who have often considered it part of a larger debate on Czech

[14] Jan Sedlák, "Dějiny Dědictví sv. Václava (1669–1900)," *ČKD* 42 (1901), 154–8.
[15] Ibid., 154, 250.
[16] Ibid., 253; J. C. Schulte, *P. Martin von Cochem 1634–1712* (Freiburg i.B.: Herdersche Verlagshandlung, 1910).
[17] *Knihopis*, 5237–5316; Jan Kvapil, *Ze zahrádky do zahrady aneb Od Hortulu animae k Štěpné zahradě Martina z Kochemu: utváření modlitební knihy barokního typu* (Ústí nad Labem: Univerzita J. E. Purkyně, 2001), p. 218. Further on devotional books see M. E. Ducreux, "Livres d'hommes et de femmes, livres pour les hommes et pour les femmes: Réflexions sur la littérature de dévotion en Bohême au XVIIIe siécle," in J. Pánek, M. Polívka and N. Rejchrtová, eds., *Husitství-Reformace-Renesance III* (Prague: Historický ústav, 1994), pp. 915–44.

nationalism. The fortunes of the Czech language after White Mountain have often been equated with the "fate of the nation." Was the language cruelly suppressed or did it tenaciously survive? Such discussions have frequently obscured a basic characteristic of this literature. The literary landscape of seventeenth- and eighteenth-century Bohemia was decidedly multilingual. In 1675 during an official visitation to the Bohemian Province, the Jesuit priest Nicolaus Avancinus insisted that all candidates to the order learn both languages. When the Premonstratensian priest Jiří Košetický roamed the countryside collecting material for his massive compilation of popular literature, he included contemporary texts in Czech, German and Latin.[18] Furthermore, the linguistic question should not overshadow the more fundamental issue of content. Whether sermons for ethnic Germans, simple devotional texts for Czech-speaking peasants or Latin songs and litanies for pilgrims, this vast body of literature was united by a common religious purpose. Towards that end we will focus on three specific genres that more than any other contributed most substantially to the transformation of Bohemia's confessional identity.

SCRIPTURE

The greatest literary achievement of the post-White Mountain period was the St. Wenceslas Bible (1677, 1712, 1715), a Czech translation of the Scriptures. At first glance it may seem somewhat peculiar that the publication of a vernacular Bible was such a high priority for Bohemia's Catholic reformers. From Rome's perspective bibles were a key element of the kingdom's problems. It was an encounter with Scripture that transformed Hus from a frivolous university master to an earnest reformer. Hussite Bohemia boasted a high degree of biblical literacy. Prague was famous for its theologically astute tavern keepers. In his history of Bohemia, Aeneas Sylvius Piccolomini noted that peasant women knew their Bible better than most Italian priests. Many of the common folk had committed long passages of the Scriptures to memory.[19] This phenomenon, though, was not entirely new. Vernacular bibles had long occupied an important place in this society. Their origins could be traced back to the ninth-century missionaries Cyril and Methodius who began to translate the liturgy and

---

[18] Evermod Jiří Košetický, *Quodlibeticum*, SK DG II 4–8; Martin Svatoš, "Zur Mehrsprachigkeit der Literatur in den böhmischen Ländern des 17. und 18. Jahrhunderts," *WSJ* 46 (2000), 33–42; best reference for literature in German and Latin is the CD database, Anežka Baďurová, *Bibliografie cizojazyčných bohemikálních tisků z let 1501–1800* (Prague: Knihovna Akademie věd České republiky, 2003).

[19] Ducreux, "Reading unto death," p. 219.

portions of the Bible from Greek into Old Church Slavonic. Their work was taken over by the clerics of the Sázava monastery, which became a prominent center for Church Slavonic during the eleventh century. The first entire translation of the Bible into Old Czech dates from the 1350s. The first printed version, the so-called Prague Bible, appeared in 1488 and exerted an important influence on other Slavic translations of Scripture. This tradition culminated in the second half of the sixteenth century with the Kralice Bible of the Bohemian Brethren, one of the great landmarks of the Czech language.[20]

This then was the situation that confronted Bohemia's Catholic leaders after White Mountain, and the manner in which they responded to the issue of Czech-language bibles speaks to the nature of Catholic Reform in the kingdom. The challenge of vernacular bibles was a pressing matter for the post-Tridentine church as a whole. One of the results of Trent was a standardized version of the Vulgate, the so-called Sixto-Clementine Bible. Vernacular versions of Scripture were more problematic. The fourth rule of Pius IV's 1564 Index stated that only learned and devout scholars, who were authorized by a bishop or inquisitor, could use such bibles. In 1593, however, Clement VIII rescinded this privilege. How these papal pronouncements were actually applied, however, varied from region to region.[21] The Iberian peninsula and Italy were the most restrictive of the Catholic lands. It was not until the 1757 bull of Benedict XIV, which allowed the use of vernacular bibles, that new translations of the Vulgate began to appear. The first translation into Spanish was not completed until 1793. The activities of the French Jansenists were at the other end of the spectrum. In the second half of the seventeenth century, their presses at Port-Royal were churning out translations of the liturgy and the Bible at an alarmingly quick rate. Critics such as François Fénelon noted that the proliferation of these texts diluted the authority of the church as "today everyone is his own casuist, everyone his own instructor."[22]

Fénelon's critique accurately captured the Catholic fear of vernacular bibles, and there were few regions in all of Europe that had as great a reason as Bohemia in clamping down on the production of these texts. It was precisely the lack of ecclesiastical oversight, a vacuum of authority and a consequent proliferation of theological opinion that had created the wide

[20] Vladimír Kyas, *Česká bible v dějinách národního písemnictví* (Prague: Vyšehrad, 1997).
[21] See the discussion of Dominique Julia, "Die Gegenreformation und das Lesen," in Roger Chartier and Guglielmo Cavallo, eds., *Die Welt des Lesens* (Frankfurt: Campus Verlag, 1997), pp. 359–70.
[22] Cited in ibid., p. 370.

range of schismatic groups that had plagued the kingdom for two centuries. It is somewhat surprising then that Bohemian Catholics were as open as they were to the use of vernacular bibles. In the sixteenth century Archbishop Brus had been involved in one such project, and after the conclusion of the Thirty Years War, the church aggressively promoted a new translation of the Vulgate. Archbishop Matouš Ferdinand Sobek of Bílenberk (1669–75) commissioned the Jesuits to oversee this venture. Three competent linguists, Jiří Konstanc, Matěj Šteyer and Jan Barner, toiled on this task for nearly fifty years.[23] All three Jesuits were active translators and brought into Czech some of the most popular texts of the Catholic world. Their work on the Bible must be seen in conjunction with this broad body of devotional literature that was so eagerly consumed in the second half of the seventeenth century. The St. Wenceslas Endowment actually sponsored the translation project and gave its name to the new Czech Bible.

Confessional historiography has obscured the extent to which Konstanc, Šteyer and Barner were following in the footsteps of earlier sixteenth-century scholars who have been saluted as much for their work systematizing Czech grammar as for their translations of Scripture. Konstanc and Šteyer had published important texts on grammar and orthography before undertaking the project.[24] The linguistic orientation of the Jesuits underscores the importance the church assigned to the production of religious literature in the vernacular. Their completed translation of the Scriptures in some ways even surpassed the Kralice Bible. The three main portions of the project represented three different traditions of written Czech. For the New Testament the translators used a clear and mature idiom that followed the standard established by the Bohemian Brethren. The Old Testament, in contrast, was composed in an elevated and slightly archaic Czech that expunged many of the Germanisms that had been included in the Kralice Bible. Finally, the commentary, which came at the end of each chapter, was written in a more colloquial form of the language.[25] Turning the tables on the Hussites, the translators, in fact, cleverly used the language issue against their confessional opponents. In the introduction to the 1715 edition of the Old Testament (Genesis–Psalms), they argued that the earliest Czech

[23] Hedvika Kuchařová and Pavel Pokorný, "Die St. Wenzels-Bibel im kulturhistorischen Zusammenhang," in Hans Rothe and Friedrich Scholz, eds., *Svatováclavská bible* (Paderborn: Schöningh, 2001), vol. II, pp. 563–6.

[24] Jiří Konstanc, *Lima linguae Bohemicae* (Prague: Jezuitská tiskárna, 1667); Matěj Šteyer, *Výborně dobrý Způsob Yak se má dobře po Česku psáti* (Prague: Jezuitská tiskárna, 1668).

[25] J. Vintr, "Jazyk české barokní bible Svatováclavské," *WSJ* 38 (1992), 209–10.

translations closely followed the Vulgate. Errors began to creep in through the textual innovations of the Hussites and their successors. The St. Wenceslas Bible, then, was truly a restoration of the earliest versions of the Czech Scriptures![26]

Like so many other activities in seventeenth-century Bohemia, there was a concerted effort to control, direct and regulate reading practices. In the eyes of the Catholic church, the unbridled license of both printers and readers had been one of the chief causes of the kingdom's confessional crisis. The St. Wenceslas Bible may be the best example of how ecclesiastical leaders sought to master this theological chaos by reconstructing reading habits. The first volume of the project, the New Testament, was published in 1677. In the foreword Archbishop Waldstein referred back to the efforts of his predecessor initiating the grand undertaking. Citing Ambrose, Waldstein noted that Sobek of Bílenberk, ever the faithful shepherd, had realized that "the books of Holy Scripture are the good meadows in which through daily reading we pasture, and by which we are refreshed and strengthened. We taste that which is written, and after we have tasted, we reflect back on these matters more deeply."[27] He continued by observing that such reading needed to be conducted in a supervised fashion. Faulty translations of the New Testament were the foundation upon which the Hussites and other heretical sects had constructed their false teachings. Once the text had been cleared of error, however, a clear understanding of the truth would again emerge.[28]

The most important means by which theological errors were corrected was of course the thick commentary that accompanied the translation. The extensive gloss that followed each chapter normally highlighted some distinctive feature of church doctrine, attacked a specific Protestant practice or defended a Catholic institution such as the papacy.[29] Though appended comments were common with many Catholic translations of the period, the length and scope of the Czech commentary stood in decided contrast to its closest counterpart, the Mainz Bible (1662). This standard text for German Catholics did not include a substantial commentary. The combative Czech translation was more similar to Catholic bibles composed during the height of confessional tensions in the late sixteenth century such as the English Rheims-Douai New Testament (1582) and the 1599 Polish

---

[26] *Svatováclavská bible*, vol. II, A1r.   [27] *Svatováclavská bible*, vol. I, pp. 3–4.

[28] *Svatováclavská bible*, vol. II, pp. 4–5. Similar sentiments are expressed in the introduction of the 1715 volume of the Old Testament. *Svatováclavská bible*, vol. II, A1r–A3r.

[29] See for example the commentary on Revelation 13, a list of ten reasons explaining why the pope could not possibly be the Antichrist. *Svatováclavská bible*, vol. I, p. 495.

translation of Jakub Wujek. The actual commentary of the Wenceslas Bible directly addressed the matter of reading. The notes on Isaiah 20 included a discussion on the most basic form of Hussite heresy, communion in both kinds. According to the gloss, Peter of Dresden had misunderstood Christ's injunction to eat his flesh and drink his blood (John 6:53). His improper reading of the passage had led to the start and spread of this heterodox practice in Bohemia.[30] Therefore as the commentators observed in Acts 19, the control of reading material was essential for the health of the church. As new Christian converts publicly burned their scrolls on sorcery and magic, so the church today had the responsibility to limit access to Protestant material and in some cases destroy texts harmful to Catholic believers.[31]

Many of these themes concerning the reading of Scripture were reiterated by Antonín Koniáš in what might have been the most infamous book of the post-White Mountain era, *Clavis haeresim claudens et aperiens*. The main body of the *Clavis*, a lengthy list of heretical Czech literature, eventually formed the basis of a Bohemian Index. Though Koniáš's work has been frequently cited as an example of the blunt repression of the Catholic regime, the actual text of the *Clavis* is more nuanced in tone. The first section deals generally with the dangers of Protestant books with Koniáš repeating many of the typical caveats of the Tridentine church. The second part specifically considers the problem of Scripture. Turning to 2 Peter, the Jesuit reflected on the apostle's injunction that "no prophecy of Scripture is a matter of one's own interpretation" (2 Peter 1:20). The Bible in the hands of unlearned individuals could easily be misused and distorted.[32] To support his argument he included an extensive list of Scriptural passages that Protestants had twisted through mistranslations to promote their own theological agenda. Obsessed with the notion of *sola fide*, Luther had purposefully excluded a reference to good works in Philemon 6. Protestants also sought to denigrate the Virgin's status by weakening the language of Jesus's encounter with Mary and Martha (Luke 10:42). Attacking the doctrine of transubstantiation, Lutherans had substituted the phrase "this is my body given to you" with "this is my body broken for you" (I Cor. 11:24).[33] In a 1736 letter to Count Sporck, Koniáš contrasted the Wenceslas Bible with Luther's 1522 German translation. Critical of the reformer's decision to reorder the books of the New Testament by placing

---

[30] Kyas, *Česká bible*, p. 222.
[31] See a similar critique in the gloss of I Thessalonians 5 and Deuteronomy 15 as noted by Josef Vintr. J. Vintr, "Komentář v české barokní bibli Svatováclavské," *LF* 117 (1994), 88, 91.
[32] A. Koniáš, *Clavis haeresim claudens et aperiens* (Hradec Králové: V. J. Tybely, 1729), pp. xlv, xlvi.
[33] A. Koniáš, *Clavis*, 2nd edn (Hradec Králové: J. K. Tybely, 1749), pp. 62, 70, 76.

Hebrews and James with Jude and Revelation, Koniáš contended that Luther was attempting to create a subset of deuterocanonical texts within the New Testament as he disagreed with James on the importance of good works and the author of Hebrews on regular confession. In like manner, Koniáš argued that Luther rejected the books of the Apocrypha as they supported the church's teachings on purgatory and indulgences. In terms of precision he averred that the Wenceslas Bible and even the Brethren's Kralice Bible were more accurate vernacular translations than Luther's freer paraphrase.[34]

Apart from the translation itself, Catholic readers of the Wenceslas Bible had the commentary to guide them. One of its most obvious features was its aggressive defense of church doctrine and practice. Konstanc, Šteyer and Barner often pirouetted creatively from a specific passage in Scripture to a more general Catholic teaching. A discussion on the "cross of Christ" in Philippians 3:18 eventually led to the injunction that all good Catholics should regularly make a sign of the cross on their foreheads.[35] The account of Christ's triumphant entry into Jerusalem (Mt. 21) became an occasion to defend public processions of the Host, such as that of Corpus Christi. In militant language the commentator declared that the celebration of such festivals in Bohemia reflected the church's definitive victory over those who denied the doctrine of transubstantiation.[36] A theological discussion of Romans 5 and the problem of original sin concluded with a vigorous defense of the Immaculate Conception.[37] A consideration of Luke 16 and the story of Lazarus and Dives eventually led to an excursus on the topography of the afterlife. Unlike Protestants who only accepted the existence of heaven and hell, Catholics properly acknowledged both purgatory and limbo.[38]

To help bolster the sense of Catholic community, Konstanc, Šteyer and Barner exploited opportunities to incorporate the kingdom's ecclesiastical heritage into the biblical narrative. They searched for Scriptural precedents that spoke to the particularities of the Bohemian situation. Using the story of Elijah and the ravens as a starting point, they launched into an excursus of God's miraculous provision for hermit saints. Here they considered not only the experiences of the apostle Paul and St. Anthony, the most famous exemplar of the Christian eremitic tradition, but also

---

[34] Cited in Kuchařová and Pokorný, "Die St. Wenzels-Bibel," p. 609.
[35] *Svatováclavská bible*, vol. I, pp. 367–8.
[36] Ibid., p. 38. Related is the commentary on Luke 22, ibid., p. 148.
[37] Ibid., p. 271. See also the related commentary of Gen. 3:15, *Svatováclavská bible*, vol. III, pp. 7–8.
[38] *Svatováclavská bible*, vol. I, p. 134. Relevant also is the commentary of 2 Macc. 12: 43–6, *Svatováclavská bible*, vol. II, pp. 464–5.

Bohemia's own anchorite, St. Ivan. In similar fashion they used the explanatory comments of Acts 5 as an opportunity to celebrate Bohemia's best-known pilgrimage sites. As early Christians had journeyed to Jerusalem to be healed by the apostles, so Bohemian Catholics had long traveled to the grave of St. Wenceslas in Prague, the place of his martyrdom in Stará Boleslav, or to the Holy Mountain of Příbram to find God's special blessing.[39]

The biblical narrative could also be used as a means to contrast the errors of the stubborn Hussites with the true teachings of the often beleaguered but faithful Catholic community. The proper administration of the Eucharist was not surprisingly a frequent point of discussion. The comments on Acts 20 included a lengthy critique of the Hussite celebration of the sacrament. Their practices were not only heretical. They also constituted a serious break with Bohemia's own ecclesiastical tradition. Denying Utraquist assertions, the Jesuits contended that for over five centuries Czech Catholics had received the Eucharist in one kind. It was not until the late date of 1414 that this dangerous innovation had been introduced. Iconoclasm was also highlighted as another aberration. Like the children of Israel who had eagerly contributed to the decoration of the tabernacle, Bohemian Catholics had constructed some of the most beautiful churches in all of Europe. Decidedly out of step with both Scripture and tradition, Hussites razed these buildings while Calvinists later created barren houses of worship.[40] Finally, there was the issue of language. The liturgical use of Czech over time became one of the most important markers of Hussite identity. As justification, the Utraquists could point back to the initial mission of Cyril and Methodius. With pride they looked at the early accomplishments of the Sázava Monastery where the liturgy was celebrated in Church Slavonic until 1097. Ambitious Roman authorities eager to impose a Latin hegemony on the Bohemian church prohibited the use of the older language and expelled the Slavic-speaking monks. Obviously a delicate issue for Czech Catholics, the Jesuits addressed this matter in their comments surrounding Paul's discussion of tongues in I Corinthians 14. Noting that their opponents construed these verses as a justification of the liturgy in Czech, they argued that Paul's injunction to speak intelligibly (i.e. the vernacular) pertained to preaching, teaching and admonition. On this point they agreed with their confessional opponents. These forms of instruction should be undertaken in the vernacular. The mass, however, was

---

[39] *Svatováclavská bible*, vol. II, pp. 671–2; vol. I, p. 212.
[40] *Svatováclavská bible*, vol. I, p. 148; vol. II, p. 198.

altogether different. Furthermore, with the proliferation of popular religious literature alongside frequent sermons that explained the church's various ceremonies including the Eucharist, this problem had been effectively addressed. A linguistic dispensation had been granted to those early Moravian priests who did not know Latin, but now such exceptions were certainly unnecessary.[41]

SERMONS

The St. Wenceslas Bible had its greatest impact from the pulpit. Preachers frequently drew from its commentary in the weekly sermons they composed and delivered. Sacred oratory of this period, however, has long been on the margins of scholarly research in Bohemia. And yet it was the church that played the central role in communal life, and it was the sermon that apart from its spiritual value was the community's main source of news and entertainment. The best of these preachers became regional celebrities such as the dynamic Silesian priest, Bohumír Bílovský (1659–1725).[42] Always in high demand, Bílovský attracted huge crowds wherever he went. In the villages where he preached, the churches were packed to overflowing with eager listeners outside the building pressing their ears to the wall and lining up ladders and benches to get a glimpse of him through the window. He rarely disappointed. He was attuned to his audience, and his homilies were full of local proverbs and fables, popular folk songs and entertaining stories including at least one from Boccaccio's *Decameron*![43] At times irascible and always outspoken, Bílovský, a former Jesuit, had withdrawn from the order after quarreling with its members. He brought this feisty spirit to the pulpit and played up to his audience. He railed against the Jews and their riches. At times he spoke out against the nobility and their reluctance to use their wealth to help the poor. He championed the cause of the underdog, and noted as in the case of Judith and Holofernes, God often uses the weak of this world to execute his judgment. He composed homilies that his rural parishioners could understand and relate to. Avoiding complicated discussions of doctrine, he crafted messages that had a strong moral component and often included a clever word scheme or mnemonic device to help his listeners remember the major points of the sermon. He

---

[41] *Svatováclavská bible*, vol. I, p. 313.

[42] Milan Kopecký, *Staří slezští kazatelé* (Ostrava: Profil, 1970), pp. 92–135; Josef Vašica, *České literární baroko* (Prague: Vyšehrad, 1938), pp. 189–99; K. Kadlec, "Bohumír Hynek Bílovský," *SbHKr* 3–4 (1921), 65–76.

[43] B. Bílovský, *Pia quadragesima* (Opava: Jan Kašpar Braüer, 1721), p. 93.

approached Scripture inventively and transformed a story such as Moses striking the rock in the wilderness into a discourse on domestic relations, reproving wives for beating their husbands while encouraging men to speak more gently to their spouses.[44]

Printers published these homilies at an astounding rate, and the sheer volume of these texts is in many respects overwhelming. A figure such as the forgotten Jesuit, Fabián Veselý (1684–1729), produced more than 3,000 pages of Czech sermons in a mere seven years! These printed texts appeared in different forms and were intended for a variety of uses. The most basic genre was the postil.[45] Following the church calendar, the postil normally included the day's Gospel reading along with an exegesis of the passage. Particularly popular among Bohemia's Protestants, this genre was retooled by Czech Catholics in the second half of the seventeenth century. The most famous of these publications was Matěj Šteyer's *Catholic Postil* (1691), which was supported by the St. Wenceslas Endowment and ran through seven editions by 1737. The primary function of the postil was devotional. In the introductory letter to Šteyer's 1736 edition, the archbishop of Prague noted that this text was intended to serve as an antidote to the dangerous Protestant literature that illicitly circulated through the kingdom.[46] Antonín Koniáš, who somewhat later in the century published his own postil, was even more explicit in his preface. He noted, "On Sundays and feast days it is not enough to hear the Word of God proclaimed in public in church. One must, at the hour of rest, read oneself or hear the reading of salutary books ... in order that the reading or the hearing of His divine discourse may sow in our hearts the seed of his Word."[47] A second major genre was the large-scale sermon collection, a literary form that reached its height in Bohemia during the early decades of the eighteenth century. These massive volumes were generally too expensive for most households, though at times the St. Wenceslas Endowment underwrote some of the costs. Normally, they were generally intended for the clergy who drew from them when crafting their own homilies. Finally, there was the single sermon that was printed for a specific occasion: a saint's feast, a funeral eulogy or a

---

[44] B. Bílovský, *Víno ze svadby v Káni a potřebnost roucha svadebního*, ed. J. Vašica (Ve Staré Říši, 1932), pp. 25–8.

[45] Franz Eybl, *Gebrauchsfunktionen barocker Predigtliteratur* (Vienna: W. Braumüller, 1982), pp. 105–13.

[46] Matěj Šteyer, *Postylla Katolická* (Prague: Archiepiscopal Press, 1737), unpaginated; also illustrative is the republication of Šebestián Vojtěch Scypio's postil originally published in 1618. See his *Yak Kostelnj tak Domácý Postilla* (Prague: Jezuitská tiskárna, 1667). My thanks to M. E. Ducreux for this reference.

[47] Cited in Ducreux, "Reading unto death," p. 202.

celebration of a confraternity. In Bohemia the publication of these individual homilies culminated with the 1729 canonization of John Nepomuk.[48]

One of the major priorities of these Catholic preachers was the proper ordering and regulation of society. Three decades of war, waves of mass emigration and a radical redistribution of wealth had taken their toll on this region. The kingdom's new Catholic identity was undeniably fragile. The sermon was a means to help shape and define the Bohemian community in such an unsettled context. Not unexpectedly, preachers laid significant stress on the maintenance of proper relations between the emerging classes. With the 1680 peasant uprising as yet another reminder of the weakness of the social order, clerics such as Jestřábský, Bílovský and Damascen Marek devoted substantial attention to this theme. Marek's often caustic view of human nature was reflected in a series of sermons he delivered on servants and agricultural laborers. The world was full of lazy and deceitful peasants who like Elisha's domestic Gehazi held back goods that were properly due their masters. Sadly there were few who followed the example of Joseph and faithfully discharged their responsibilities.[49] Bílovský was somewhat more evenhanded as he considered the obligations of both servants and masters. In his *Doctrina Christiana* he developed acrostics from the words *servus* and *dominus* to elaborate on the duties of obedience and submission that God had entrusted to domestics and those of justice and compassion granted to their masters.[50] A substantial portion of Bílovský's celebrated oratory focused on the social concerns of his day: the struggles of parents and children, the problems of husbands and wives and the unresolved tensions of peasants and landowners. Such an emphasis was of course typical of the period and could be found across Catholic Europe.[51] What may be a more distinctive feature of sacred oratory in the Czech lands was the attention given to relations of the clergy and the laity, a justifiable concern for a people who had stubbornly resisted papal leadership for over two centuries.

---

[48] For a sample of this vast literature see three recently published collections of sermons: B. Lifka, ed., *Medotekoucí sláva na hůře Libanu* (Kostelní Vydří: Karmelitánské nakladatelství, 1995); M. Kopecký, ed., *Žena krásná náramně* (Žďár nad Sázavou: Společnost Cisterciana Sarensis, 1998); M. Horáková, ed., *Nádoba zapálená* (Žďár nad Sázavou: Společnost Cisterciana Sarensis, 2000).

[49] Damascen Marek, *Trojí chléb nebeský* (Prague: Hraba, 1728), pp. 1047–54.

[50] Bohumír Bílovský, *Doctrina christiana animabus inservitura* (Olomouc: Jan Adam Avinger, 1721), part 1, pp. 127–33.

[51] On the general social order see ibid., part 2, pp. 93–8; on parental obligations, part 1, pp. 70–104; on spousal relations, part 1, pp. 39–51. For further Bohemian examples see Karel Račín, *Operae ecclesiasticae. Robota Cýrkewnj* (Prague: Vojtěch Jiří Koniáš, 1706), pp. 490–502; Daniel Nitsch, *Berla královská Jezu Krista* (Prague: Vojtěch Jiří Koniáš, 1709), vol. I, p. 150; Matěj Šteyer, *Postylla Katolická* (Prague: Jezuitská tiskárna, 1691), vol. I, part I, pp. 44, 70–82; vol. II, pp. 59–60.

On one memorable Sunday in Prague's Týn Church, Fabián Veselý thundered from the pulpit on the righteous anger of God. When the supporters of Emperor Henry IV had challenged the sacred authority of Rome in the eleventh century, a series of supernatural disasters quickly followed. Blizzards, earthquakes and even a deluge of bloody rain were the unmistakable signs of God's wrath. This lesson, however, was lost on a prosperous Prague, for three centuries later this city, too, revolted against the pope. Punishment was swift. During one siege Prague was bombarded by more than 18,000 rounds of shot, and when there was no external enemy, the populace turned their weapons on themselves. Even now the chastening was not complete. The plague had visited as recently as 1713.[52] This theme also featured prominently in Bílovský's homiletics. His first collection of published sermons spoke to the issue of episcopal authority in a cycle honoring St. Liborius, a fourth-century bishop of Gaul.[53] In *Doctrina Christiana* he built on the account of Christ's cleansing of the temple exhorting his congregation to render proper respect and reverence to the church and its leaders. Before attending mass, worshipers should carefully examine their hearts, and make sure that, unlike Nadab and Abihu, they did not enter God's sanctuary with an unworthy offering of "strange fire" which would lead to their own destruction.[54] A sermon of the aptly named Chrysostom Xaver Ignác Táborský was more explicit in its defense of ecclesiastical authority. Táborský turned to the life of Norbert of Xanten and argued that the saint's chief virtue was his unquestioning loyalty and unswerving obedience to the church. Where there was chaos and disorder, Norbert had restored clerical authority. Through his leadership the heretical Tanchelm had been suppressed, the restive archbishopric of Magdeburg had been reorganized, and a potential schism that would have divided Christendom had been averted.[55]

Táborský, a Moravian Premonstratensian, concluded his sermon on Norbert with a rather curious genealogy that elucidated the archbishop's relationship to Olomouc. Although Norbert had never directly worked in this region, he had helped establish Strahov as one of Bohemia's most

---

[52] Fábian Veselý, *Lehr-Geist- und Eyfer-volle Sonntags Predigen auf das gantze Jahr* (Augsburg: Veith, 1739), vol. II, p. 339.

[53] Bohumír Bílovský, *Salus sanctuarii anebo šestka duchowní swatému Liboriowi* (Olomouc: Ignác Rosenburg, 1713); related is Jan Václav Mezlecký z Palmolevu, *Thymiana pietatis Pij V* (Prague: Jan Václav Helm, 1713).

[54] Bílovský, *Doctrina christiana*, part 3, p. 321; Bohumír Bílovský, *Cantator Cygnus* (Olomouc: Jan Adam Avinger, 1720), pp. 208, 217.

[55] Chrysostom Xaver Ignác Táborský, *Erschallende Lob-Stimm* (Olomouc: F. A. Hirnle, 1737), pp. 399–422.

important monastic houses. Strahov, in turn, provided Olomouc with many of its first bishops. Although the influence of Norbert was then at best derivative, Táborský's enthusiastic promotion of this connection reflected a more general characteristic of this homiletic literature. Reminding the kingdom's Catholics of their true spiritual heritage, preachers balanced admonitions from the recent past with the consolation and encouragement of an even earlier history. The search for a *sacra Bohemia*, which was such a preoccupation with the antiquarians Balbín, Pešina and Kruger, had a distinctly pastoral character with Bílovský, Táborský and Veselý. Bílovský's dramatic retelling of Methodius's conversion of the Bulgarian prince Boris became a call for personal repentance.[56] Closer to home, sermons on St. Ludmila were particularly useful as pious object lessons. Jan Ignác Libertin held her up as the ideal widow. Tomáš Xaverius Laštovka used the death of Moravia's seventeenth-century martyr Jan Sarkander as an example of persecution that Christians should expect from unbelievers.[57] Ondřej František de Waldt mined Bohemia's history as a rich source of didactic metaphors. Through his deft manipulation of language, de Waldt illustrated that Bohemia's Catholic identity was literally engraved on its historical narrative. Illustrative in this regard was a 1709 homily on St. Wenceslas.[58] In the first half of the sermon de Waldt played a series of word games with Bohemia's early princes to help chart the progress of Christianity in the region. The first Christian duke was appropriately named Bořivoj, for he destroyed the vanguard (*bořil voj*) of Satan's kingdom in Bohemia, while his grandson, Boleslav, would be remembered by the painful shame (*bolest sláv*) he had brought upon himself through the murder of his brother Wenceslas. The second part of the homily focused specifically on the life of Wenceslas. Coupling Bohemia's past to the salvation narrative, de Waldt patterned his treatment of the martyred duke on the passion of Christ as he considered the betrayal, death and afterlife of Bohemia's most important patron saint.

Focusing on the past and its relationship to the present was one of the ways these orators helped define the contours of a Czech confessional identity. In this respect one of the most important preachers of the period was the Jesuit Fabián Veselý. A native of Moravia, Veselý ultimately came to Prague and held forth from the pulpit of Old Town's prestigious Týn

---

[56] Bílovský, *Doctrina christiana*, part 1, pp. 17–27.
[57] Jan Ignác Libertin, *Diva Ludmilla vera vidua* (Kutná Hora: Jiří Vojtěch Kyncl, 1718), A4v; Tomáš Xaverius Laštovka, *Čtvrtý článek víry katolické* (Trnava: Jezuitská tiskárna, 1748), p. 296.
[58] Ondřej František de Waldt, "Kázání o svatým Václavu, v městě Písku dělané 1709," in *Chwálo-Řeč, neb kázánj na některé Swátky* (Prague: Archiepiscopal Press, 1736).

Church. In the 1720s he published four major homiletic collections including the five-volume *Friday's Fast Sermons during Lent* (1723–8).[59] His reputation extended well beyond Bohemia as there were calls for translations of his work. A Latin version of his sermons appeared in 1727 while a massive two-volume German edition was printed in Augsburg twelve years later. Despite his substantial output and contemporary popularity, Veselý has been virtually ignored by both historians and literary scholars. The passing comments that have been made generally characterize his work as empty Jesuit bombast.[60] Viewed from another perspective, however, Veselý's wit and colorful rhetoric were the perfect tools to help shape the boundaries of communal identity from the pulpit. Though his theological training was thorough, he carefully avoided more theoretical discussions of doctrine. Instead, he drew from a wide range of sources to craft messages that were engaging and accessible to the congregation as a whole. When discussing the sins of gluttony and drunkenness, he quickly pointed to Luther and his followers as a prime example of fleshly living. Describing the excesses of Luther's favorite drinking game, Veselý was able simultaneously to praise moderation as a Catholic virtue and characterize his confessional opponents as inebriated buffoons.[61]

One of the more interesting dynamics to consider with Veselý was the actual venue of his sermons. The Týn Church was of course the Hussites' most important house of worship with the famous chalice and statue of Utraquist King George prominently displayed on the building's façade. Nearly a century after White Mountain, Veselý still acknowledged the power of these old religious symbols, and in 1719 on the feast day of St. James the Elder, he began his homily with the bold claim that he was a renewed Hussite. Continuing with a series of rhetorical questions, he elaborated on this provocative introduction. Did he mean to reintroduce the celebration of the Eucharist *sub utraque*? Did he intend to commemorate the chalice which had hung above the portal until 1623? Did he seek to honor the demolished tomb of the great Utraquist leader Jan Rokycana still present in the church? Not in the least, he averred. The chalice that he spoke of was the cup of Christ's suffering that had been poured out for every Catholic believer. True Hussite communion was the acceptance of the bread of sorrow and the wine of contrition.[62]

---

[59] For a full bibliography see *Knihopis*, 16503–16505a.
[60] Hynek Hrubý, *České postilly* (Prague: NKČSN, 1901), p. 267; *OSN*, vol. XXVI, p. 608; Jaroslav Vlček, *Dějiny české literatury* (Prague: Československý Spisovatel, 1951), vol. II, p. 16.
[61] Veselý, *Lehr-Geist- und Eyfer-volle Sonntags Predigen*, vol. II, p. 473. [62] Ibid., pp. 239–44.

If in this sermon Veselý reworked old religious symbols into a more orthodox framework, on the third Sunday after Epiphany he attempted to redefine the actual parameters of Bohemia's Catholic community.[63] Through the homily the Jesuit sought to transform the perception that many Catholics had of their recent past, that of a persecuted minority under Utraquist domination. No, he assured them, they had never been a minority. Working through a quick calculation of all the churches that were meeting that day in the three towns of Prague, he reminded his congregants that they were joined by nearly 20,000 believers. More important, though, was the testimony of the past. Like Abraham, who was promised that his descendants would be as numerous as the stars of heaven, they too were joined by an unseen multitude of silent witnesses. In a later sermon Veselý reconstructed Prague's sacred topography, noting that scarcely outside the church door, Drahomíra, Wenceslas's pagan mother, had soaked the streets with the blood of Christian martyrs. These saints were living members of their community, and their number extended far beyond those murdered by Drahomíra. They included the 170,000 who were martyred by Diocletian and the 600,000 who died under Jan Žižka's tyrannous regime. All told, Veselý assured his listeners that they were joined by well more than 11 million holy martyrs. As his fellow Jesuit Matěj Šteyer had argued, Catholic believers had always understood that they belonged to a broader community. Christ had set the pattern long ago when he had dispatched the disciples to work in the countryside not singly but in groups. The true church remained united through time and space, not disunified like feuding Protestants who continued to splinter into increasingly smaller sects.[64]

The manner in which Veselý, Šteyer and others construed community raises a broader issue concerning a Catholic conception of time. One of Veselý's more dramatic presentations was given on All Souls' Day.[65] Relating the story of Lazarus from the gospel of John, he told his audience that he was speaking to them not as a preacher but as an advocate and intercessor for the dead. He developed a series of parallels between the bound and buried Lazarus and the souls of the deceased. Neither could use their hands to help themselves, move their feet to enter heaven, or even raise their eyes to regard God's countenance. It was the responsibility of those present to aid those suffering in purgatory. Through their prayers and pious activities the

---

[63] Veselý, *Lehr-Geist- und Eyfer-volle Sonntags Predigen*, vol. I, pp. 61–8.
[64] Veselý, *Lehr-Geist- und Eyfer-volle Sonntags Predigen*, vol. II, p. 371; Šteyer, *Postylla Katolická* (1737), part 1, p. 242.
[65] Veselý, *Lehr-Geist- und Eyfer-volle Sonntags Predigen*, vol. II, pp. 428–34.

community of the living could assist the community of the dead. One of the most significant legacies of the Reformation were new attitudes to death that developed in Protestant regions. The cult of the dead, which was such a central feature of late medieval religious life, was violently disrupted by the reformers who were attacking far more than an abstract theological doctrine. The critique of purgatory was, as one scholar has put it, an attempt "to redefine the boundaries of human community ... to limit the claims of the past, and the people of the past, on the people of the present."[66] Although conservative Utraquists did acknowledge the existence of purgatory, it is not surprising that after White Mountain Catholic clerics devoted tremendous energy to rehabilitate this doctrine. The songs of Michna, the poetry of Bridel, the sculpture of Brokoff, the writings of Jestřábský and the commentary of the St. Wenceslas Bible all focused on this critical issue. Homiletic literature was equally concerned with this matter.[67] Purgatory expanded the community of the faithful and helped bring the past into the lives of ordinary Catholics in a real and tangible manner.

Though community may have transcended time for Veselý and his colleagues, they continued to emphasize its visible and public nature. In the intriguingly titled sermon, "Nicodemus, the light fleer," Veselý argued that the wise of the world are often ashamed and worship in secret.[68] He continued by relating the story of a learned friend who visited him privately. Somewhat embarrassedly, he told Veselý that he would like to hear him preach but was hesitant to be seen at his service. One Sunday he did come but instead of sitting with the main body of the congregation, he stood in a shadowed corner afraid to admit that an accomplished lawyer needed the same spiritual encouragement as others. Veselý concluded that such behavior was typical of the heretics. The ceremonies and celebrations of the church, the processions, the sacraments and other devotional practices, were for them a matter of shame. For Catholics, on the other hand, these public displays of piety were the fullest expression of their community.

SONGS

The reading and preaching of Scripture was complemented by its singing. The power and potential of song to shape confessional identities was quickly

---

[66] Eamon Duffy, *The Stripping of the Altars* (New Haven: Yale University Press, 1992), p. 8.
[67] See for example Šteyer, *Postylla Katolická* (1737), part I, pp. 314–24; Bartholomaeus Possl, *Der Beliebte Jedoch Kranck Ligende Lazarus* (Wiener Neustadt: Müller, 1727).
[68] Veselý, *Lehr-Geist- und Eyfer-volle Sonntags Predigen*, vol. II, pp. 154–63.

grasped by sixteenth-century reformers. Martin Luther observed, "Next to the Word of God, the noble art of music is the greatest treasure in the world. It controls our thoughts, minds, hearts, and spirits." Calvin argued that few things had greater impact on human emotions than words set to music. John Jewel, the bishop of Salisbury, attributed the success of England's Reformation to the formative power of song.[69] It should not be surprising, then, that immediately after White Mountain, the papal nuncio Carlo Caraffa sought permission from Rome to allow children and the "simple folk" to continue singing old hymns in the Czech language.[70] The St. Wenceslas Endowment later targeted hymnals as an important genre to promote. The prolific Matěj Šteyer may have had the greatest impact in this field. His massive *Czech Hymn Book* went through six editions between 1683 and 1764. In the introduction to the first edition Šteyer ran through a brief history of sacred song outlining its origins with Jubal in the Old Testament, carrying it through the New Testament and concluding with its development under the church fathers.[71] A casual survey of the preface would leave the reader with the impression that hymns had always been a critical part of Bohemian church life, and though this was true enough, Šteyer's comments did not indicate the extent to which the kingdom's Catholic hymnals were a relatively new phenomenon. To appreciate the rapid growth and development of this genre in the late seventeenth and early eighteenth centuries, it is necessary to backtrack and briefly highlight the history of sacred song in the Czech lands.

The Slavonic liturgy, introduced by Cyril and Methodius, did not survive the missionary brothers. At the death of Methodius in 885, Pope Stephen V promptly interdicted the Slavic rites. Though singing in Old Church Slavonic did persist, its use in the churches was finally prohibited in the eleventh century. Therefore, the earliest Czech songs, while religious, were not liturgical. It was the Hussites who reclaimed Czech as a liturgical language, and in the fifteenth century they began to produce hymn collections in manuscript form.[72] The most important of these Utraquist

---

[69] Walter Buszin, "Luther on music," *The Musical Quarterly* 32 (1946), 83; Francis Higman, "Music," in Andrew Pettegree, ed., *The Reformation World* (London: Routledge, 2000), p. 499; Horton Davies, *Worship and Theology in England* (Grand Rapids: Eerdmans, 1996), vol. I, p. 386.

[70] T. V. Bílek, *Reformace katolická* (Prague: F. Backovský, 1892), p. 7.

[71] Matěj Šteyer, *Kancyonal Cžeský* (Prague: Jiří Černoch, 1683), unpaginated preface.

[72] For Czech hymnology see Josef Jireček, *Hymnologia Bohemica* (Prague: NKČSN, 1878); Konrád, *Dějiny posvátného zpěvu staročeského*; Antonín Škarka, "Kapitoly z české hymnologie," in *Půl tisíciletí českého písemnictví* (Prague: Odeon, 1986), pp. 190–302. For the Catholic period see M. E. Ducreux, "Hymnologia Bohemica. Cantionnaires Tchèques de la contre-réform, 1588–1764," unpublished Ph.D. thesis, Université de Paris – III (1982).

compilers and composers was Václav Miřínský (d. 1492) whose work was published posthumously. In Bohemia the sixteenth century was the great age of the Protestant hymnal (*kancionál*). Between 1500 and 1620 more than 100 of these *kancionály* appeared in print. During this period it was the Bohemian Brethren in particular who appropriated this medium as a means to promote their church and its teachings. Their use of contrafacta, new lyrics set to old melodies, was strategically implemented as they believed that people would be led to "the truth more easily through the familiar sounds."[73] In one of their early songbooks, the editor noted that, though musical notation was included, his audience was free to set these hymns "to prettier and more beautiful melodies."[74] In contrast to the Utraquists, the hymns of the Brethren had a strong dogmatic emphasis. From the sacraments to Scripture, the songs expressed the basic teachings of the church. There were also simple woodcuts reinforcing this doctrinal content. In one such illustration, the elaborate but empty rituals of the Catholic Eucharist are contrasted with the Brethren's simple but sincere celebration of the Lord's Supper.[75]

These developments concerned many in the Catholic community, and it was not long before there was a response. The Jesuit Václav Šturm (1533–1601) led the counter-offensive as he wrote a series of tracts against the Brethren including a weighty indictment of their most important hymnal.[76] More important, though, were the Catholic songbooks that began to appear in the late sixteenth century. Bohemia's first Catholic hymnal was actually published in Plzeň in 1529. Following an Utraquist model, its confessional tones were muted. In like manner, the two Catholic hymnals of the poet Šimon Lomnický, which appeared more than a half century later, did not have a distinct doctrinal edge.[77] The first songbook that broke this pattern was issued in 1588. As indicated by its title, "New songs containing a brief teaching of the Christian religion," this relatively modest collection of hymns (92 songs) was more dogmatic in nature.[78] In the introduction, the editor, most probably Alexander Voyt, the Jesuit rector of the Clementinum, noted the desperate need for basic Christian education. The new hymnal was intended to serve in large part as a Catholic primer.

---

[73] From the foreword of their 1575 German hymnal, *Gesangbuch der Brüder in Behemen und Merherrn.* Cited in Rebecca Wagner Oettinger, *Music as Propaganda in the German Reformation* (Aldershot: Ashgate, 2001), p. 5.

[74] *Ein schön new gesang Buch* (n.p., 1570), A3v. [75] Ibid., 143r.

[76] Václav Šturm, *Rozsouzení a bedlivé uvážení Velikého kancionálu* (Prague: Burián Valda, 1588).

[77] Šimon Lomnický, *Písně nové* (Prague: Jiří starší Melantrich z Aventýna, 1580); *Kancionál, aneb písně nové historické* (Prague: Jiří Černý z Černého Mostu, 1595).

[78] *Písně nové, krátké naučení Křesťanského náboženství v sobě obsahující* (Prague: Burián Valda, 1588).

The first section was a cycle of catechetical songs ranging from a discussion of the individual sacraments to an exposition of the seven deadly sins. For these songs Voyt created an elaborate cross-reference system that matched doctrinal statements with passages from Scripture. For just one song of sixty-nine lines, there were thirty-five notes highlighting the Catholic teaching on justification.[79]

Though dogmatic, Voyt's hymnal was not overtly polemical. Thirteen years later, however, the Moravian priest Jan Rozenplut published his own songbook that was far more aggressive in tone. In his letter of dedication to Cardinal Dietrichstein, an impassioned Rozenplut denounced the work of the Brethren. He argued that this Protestant sect had seduced the souls of many by perverting Bohemia's great tradition of sacred song. They had kept many ancient tunes to entice unwary Christians but then had deviously changed the words to promote their heretical innovations. It was Rozenplut's objective to restore these songs that had been twisted and deformed. In so doing, he would recover the original teachings of Christianity and lead many back to the church, for "sacred song is genuine spiritual medicine for human souls composed by ardent lovers of true religion against the poison of the heretics."[80] Many of the actual hymns shared this polemical character. Some defended specific doctrines or Catholic rituals such as apostolic succession or the use of devotional images. Others attacked Protestants directly. In a section entitled "Songs against the false church" there were hymns that compared heretics to wolves or argued that Protestants were worse than Turks.[81]

After White Mountain there was a substantive change in tone of Catholic hymnals. The strident polemical rhetoric of Rozenplut faded and was replaced by songs that were less dogmatic and more devotional in character. Instrumental in this shift was Adam Michna of Otradovice. His two important hymnals *Czech Marian Music* (1647) and *Music for the Liturgical Year* (1661) reflect this intriguing transition. His most famous composition, "Wanting him to sleep," a popular Christmas carol in the Czech lands, is a quiet reflection on the birth of the Savior. More revealing are the series of metaphors he develops in his songbooks. Christ is the lover of our soul. He is

---

[79] Ibid., B1r–E6v; Ducreux, "Hymnologia Bohemica," vol. I, pp. 286–96; Antonín Škarka contends that it was the Jesuit Voyt who compiled the hymnal. Adam Michna z Otradovic, *Das dichterische Werk: Česká mariánská muzika, Loutna česká, Svatoroční muzika*, ed. A. Škarka (Munich: Fink, 1968), pp. 35–6. The cross-referenced hymn is found on B5v–B8r.

[80] Jan Rozenplut ze Švarcenbachu, *Kancionál aneb Sebrání zpěvův pobožných* (Olomouc: Jiří Handl, 1601), *viir; Ducreux, "Hymnologia Bohemica," vol. I, pp. 303–22.

[81] Rozenplut, *Kancionál*, pp. 543–7, 592–4, 598–600, 707–9.

the hunter, who carefully stalks us and then inflicts painful but tender wounds of loving compassion. We, on the other hand, are lost in the holy labyrinth of his love or like Mary Magdalene, who despairs at the empty tomb, are not able to live without the presence of our Lord.[82] Michna's devotional verse culminated with his *Czech Lute* (1653/66), a song cycle describing the soul's union with Christ which Michna intended ordinary believers to use as a devotional aid.

These trends popularized by Michna soon became characteristic of Catholic hymnals in general.[83] One can actually chart this devotional shift in the later versions of Šteyer's *Czech Hymn Book*. Seventeen new songs for Lent were added to the final four editions of the hymnal. Alongside choruses that retold the passion story and other standard themes of this liturgical season were a handful of new motifs. The contemplation of Christ's bloodied body before the tomb, the final parting of mother and son, and the despondency of Mary Magdalene were all expressions of this emphasis on inward piety.[84] The clearest representation of this new orientation was the *Heavenly Nightingale* (1719) of Jan Josef Božan. Božan was a simple parish priest who for many years served the rural district of Chroustovice in eastern Bohemia. Although biographical information on him is scarce, he evidently collected, wrote and edited a large collection of hymns that were published posthumously through the patronage of Count Franz Anton Sporck.[85] Božan explicitly stated that his hymnal was not directed towards professional musicians. It was written instead for ordinary believers, especially those who for whatever reason could not attend church regularly.[86] The most distinctive feature of the *Heavenly Nightingale* are the devotional passages scattered throughout the collection. Working through

---

[82] Michna, *Česká mariánská muzika*, hymns 3, 8, 9, 12, 19; *Svatoroční muzika*, hymn 37. Here his mystical language is similar to his Silesian contemporary, Angelus Silesius; M. E. Ducreux, "'Novost' hymnologického umění Adama Michny z Otradovic stručně naznačena," *Hubební věda* 38 (2001), 48–57.

[83] Note the parallel phenomenon in German with the work of Friedrich Spee. Theo van Oorschot, "Neue Frömmigkeit in den Kirchenliedern Friedrich Spees (1591–1635)," in Dieter Breuer, ed., *Frömmigkeit in der frühen Neuzeit* (Amsterdam: Rodopi, 1984), pp. 156–70.

[84] M. E. Ducreux, "L'hymnologie catholique tchèque de la Contre-Réforme," *Jahrbuch für Liturgik und Hymnologie* 30 (1985), 175. These songs were not composed by Šteyer but were taken from the earlier work of Fridrich Bridel.

[85] Jaroslav Bužga, "*Slavíček rájský* Jana Josefa Božana," *Časopis Slezského musea* 5 (1956), 31–41; Camillo Schoenbaum, "Jan Joseph Božans *Slavíček rajský* (*Paradiesnachtigall*, 1719) und die tschechischen katholischen Gesangbücher des XVII. Jahrhunderts," in Zofia Lissa, ed., *Studia Hieronymo Feicht septuagenario dedicata* (Kraków: Polskie Wydawn. Muzyczne, 1967), pp. 252–68. Most recent is a new partial edition of the actual hymnbook, Jan Josef Božan, *Slavíček rájský*, ed. Jan Malura and Pavel Kosek (Brno: Host, 1999).

[86] Jan Josef Božan, *Slavíček rájský* (Hradec Králové: V. J. Tybely, 1719), unpaginated introduction.

the liturgical calendar, Božan begins each section of his hymnal with an introductory meditation. For the feast of St. Stephen he discusses the necessity of forgiving one's enemies. For Lent he highlights ascetic disciplines modeled on the life of Christ. After Easter he turns to the practice of prayer.[87] The theme, however, which most occupied Božan was that of the afterlife.

The devotional crescendo of the *Heavenly Nightingale* reached its climax in a series of passages and songs that contemplated the length of eternity, the seriousness of sin, the pains of purgatory and the ultimate torment of hell.[88] Such an emphasis was characteristic of nearly all the hymnals of this period. Even the sensitive and usually mild Michna devoted an entire section of his *Czech Marian Music* to matters of death and eternity. In a song describing the soul in the fires of purgatory, he wrote with graphic detail, "First the cheeks turn red. Then defiled, they become black. Pus and the brain flow over them. Worms eat the lips. They find in them a rich pasture."[89] Numerous songs of this genre were translated into Czech. The most famous of these was Peter Franckh's *Der grimmig Tod mit seinem Pfeil*, which first appeared as "O cruel death, o dreadful death" in Jiří Hlohovský's *Catholic Songs* (1622) before being adopted and paraphrased in the respective hymnals of Šteyer, Božan and Koniáš.[90] Closely connected were the many devotional texts that were produced on the same theme. The most notorious of these tracts was Giovanni Battista Manni's *Eternal Jail of Hell* translated into Czech by Matěj Šteyer and published with support of the St. Wenceslas Endowment. The book describes in twenty-seven short chapters the various torments of hell which are also neatly depicted in a series of accompanying engravings luridly illustrating the sufferings of the condemned souls (Figure 16).[91] This attention to death and the pains of the hereafter corresponded naturally enough to developments in the broader Catholic world. It was a typical feature of Spanish asceticism which had long been an undercurrent in Bohemia's religious culture fully emerging in the late seventeenth century. More importantly, it represented a popularization of spiritual disciplines, such as the *Spiritual Exercises*, that had heretofore been practiced in more limited circles. As such, it addressed the issue of

---

[87] Ibid., pp. 69, 149–51, 227.

[88] Ibid., pp. 714–31, 750–7. Appropriately, one of the longest songs in the entire collection is entitled "Grimace, o mouth of hell" (pp. 757–9).

[89] Michna, *Česká mariánská muzika*, hymn 64.   [90] Vašica, *České literární baroko*, pp. 92–109.

[91] NA, SM, J20/17/17/1, 46r; Giovanni Battista Manni, *Věčný pekelný žalář* (Prague: Jezuitská tiskárna, 1676); Vašica, *České literární baroko*, pp. 113–27. For a modern edition see Alena Wildová-Tosi and Martin Valášek, eds., *Věčný pekelný žalář* (Brno: Atlantis, 2002).

16. Image of hell from G. B. Manni, *Věčný pekelný žalář*

confessional formation though on a deeper level than that of the dogmatic Rozenplut who highlighted the obvious doctrinal differences between Catholic and Protestant. The focus on punishment and suffering was not simply a morbid fascination with death intended to titillate the senses. It was a serious call for repentance in the present life, an appeal for a more profound conversion and a renewed commitment to follow the path of salvation marked out by the church.

Apart from his devotional emphasis, Michna was also instrumental in reviving a regional tradition. Aside from the language, there was little that was distinctively Czech in the songbooks of Voyt and Rozenplut. Though both contained short hymns to Wenceslas, Bohemia's patrons were generally absent.[92] In contrast, Michna's *Music for the Liturgical Year* was a collection of songs in praise of the saints. Here he gave significant attention to the kingdom's patrons, including a hymn to the neglected St. Sigismund. He singled out St. Hippolytus and celebrated the martyr's connection with the composer's hometown, Jindřichův Hradec. He also developed figures of speech based on patriotic motifs such as the metonymic pairing of Christ and the Virgin with the Bohemian Lion.[93] Božan's *Heavenly Nightingale* and Holan Rovenský's *Capella regia musicalis* (1693–4) were also distinguished by a similar emphasis highlighting both patron saints and local pilgrimage sites. More significant, though, was the fashion in which these later songbooks responded to the kingdom's long tradition of sacred song.

Reacting against the popular *kancionály* of the Bohemian Brethren, Jan Rozenplut recognized the dangers of singing in the vernacular. It was easier for heretics to twist the original teachings of the church through songs in their mother tongue. Nonetheless, he considered it important to continue the practice of singing in Czech.[94] In the latter half of the century, Rozenplut's sentiments were echoed by many who consciously saw themselves reclaiming a distinguished musical tradition that had been subverted by the Protestants. Most interesting in this regard is the *Capella regia musicalis* of Václav Karel Holan Rovenský (1644–1718). Though from a Brethren family, Holan Rovenský was sent to a Jesuit college where he eventually converted to Catholicism. A gifted musician, he later became the organist of the St. Peter and Paul Church of Prague's Vyšehrad and an active composer in his own right including a popular hymnal.[95] Holan Rovenský's patron and Prague's suffragan bishop, Jan Ignác Dlouhoveský, wrote an introduction to the *Capella regia musicalis* that may best encapsulate the sentiments of those who worked to reconfessionalize Bohemia's musical heritage. Dlouhoveský began by noting that all regions of the world were distinguished by a special characteristic. India was known for its precious gems, France for its fine silks, Italy for its palaces, Germany for its military

[92] *Písně nové*, K4v–K5r; Rozenplut, *Kancionál*, pp. 427–30.
[93] *Svatoroční muzika*, hymns 42, 75; *Česká mariánská muzika*, hymns 23, 44. Relics of St. Hippolytus had been given to the town in 1637 and 1639. Three years after the publication of *Česká mariánská muzika* Michna would also rework one of the hymns, "Rejoice, O Czechs," to celebrate the Madonna of Stará Boleslav which after the war passed through Jindřichův Hradec on its return from Vienna to Stará Boleslav.
[94] Rozenplut, *Kancionál*, *4r.
[95] Jaroslav Bužga, "Holan-Rovenský představitel měšťanské hudební kultury koncem 17. století," *Hudební věda* 4 (1967), 420–39; J. Bužga, "Capella regia musicalis Václava Karla Holana Rovenského," *Časopis Národního musea* 224 (1955), 154–70; Bohumil Malotín, "Holan Rovenský a jeho kancionál," *Miscellanea oddělení rukopisů a vzácných tisků* 4 (1987), 85–118.

fortifications. Though the Czech lands could boast of beautiful cities and bountiful natural resources, it was the riches of its ecclesiastical culture that set it apart from other European lands. Foremost was the love of sacred song. This tradition had begun with Bohemia's great missionary and martyr, St. Adalbert (956–97), who had composed the very first hymns in Czech. Though the ancient songs and melodies had been misused and distorted by Hussites and Protestants, this proud heritage was now being restored. Its church music was once more the envy of Europe. Its composers were in demand, the songs of its pilgrims were praised in Rome, and its many hymns were being translated and adapted by Catholics in other countries.[96]

The most intriguing aspect of this reclamation project was the manner in which these hymnals incorporated non-Catholic material. Holan Rovenský, who may have been influenced by his Brethren background, included a surprisingly high number of Utraquist and Protestant songs in the *Capella regia musicalis*. More striking still is Jan Josef Božan's *Heavenly Nightingale*. The more than 800 hymns of Božan's collection represent a broad cross-section of Bohemia's musical past. Apart from his own compositions, Božan brought in songs from the pre-Hussite and Utraquist periods including the famous "Hospodine pomiluj ny," Bohemia's oldest vernacular hymn. From the sixteenth century he incorporated both Brethren and Lutheran compositions. Songs of Lukáš of Prague, Jan Blahoslav and Jan Augusta, a leader of the Brethren who had been tortured by the Habsburgs, were all part of the *Heavenly Nightingale*. In fact more than 20 percent of the hymns in this collection were of Protestant origin.[97] From the seventeenth century he took the songs from early Catholic hymnals (Rozenplut and Lomnický) as well as those from the later period (Michna, Šteyer, Bridel and Holan Rovenský). Finally there were the so-called *kramářské písně*. These popular ballads, printed on single sheets and sold in the markets, traditionally recounted tales of forbidden love and tragic romance or perhaps news of contemporary events. After White Mountain this genre was adapted by the

---

[96] Václav Karel Holan Rovenský, *Capella regia musicalis* (Prague: Georg Labaun, 1693), A2r–v. Barbara Ann Renton calculates that more than sixty Bohemian composers found employment outside the Czech lands in the late seventeenth and eighteenth centuries. Barbara Ann Renton, "The musical culture of 18th-century Bohemia with special emphasis on the music inventories of Osek and the Knights of the Cross," unpublished Ph.D. thesis, CUNY (1990), pp. 477–85.

[97] Božan, ed. Malura, *Slavíček rájský*, p. 24. In some parts of the *Heavenly Nightingale* more than 40 percent of these songs are Protestant. See for example his section "hymns for the morning," 403–37. M. E. Ducreux has estimated that more than 30 percent of all songs from Catholic hymnals of this period were of Protestant origin. M. E. Ducreux, "Kniha a kacířství, způsob četby a knižní politika v Čechách 18. století," *Literární archív* 27 (1994), 61–87. Šteyer's hymnbooks actually include a greater number of Protestant songs than Božan's collection! My thanks to M. E. Ducreux for this reference.

church and frequently employed to tell the stories of early Christian martyrs or other pious subjects. Božan made liberal use of this popular trove of musical literature. The extent to which many of these Catholic hymnals incorporated their region's musical heritage is best reflected visually in the title page of Michna's *Music for the Liturgical Year*. For this purpose his Jesuit publishers borrowed a woodcut from Jan Roh's 1541 Brethren hymnal. A figure of the lamb triumphant is at the top of the page while at the bottom a large group of choristers sing before an open hymnal. There in the right-hand corner somewhat apart from the larger group is a man singing heartily from his own songbook. In one of the great ironies of Catholic publishing, the Jesuit press had included an image of Bohemia's most recognizable religious leader, Jan Hus (Figure 17)![98]

In most general terms, these songbooks were an attempt to co-opt religious dissent. It should not be forgotten that Protestant hymnals were regularly smuggled in from Saxony. The devotional emphasis of their Catholic counterparts was a close match to the spirituality of Paul Gerhardt and other Lutheran hymn writers. An individual such as Jan Božan was very clever in his adaptation of Protestant material. On the one hand, there was a type of ecumenical spirit to his enterprise. He used Lutheran hymns praising Scripture to prepare the congregation for the weekly homily.[99] On the other hand, he subtly subverted the original meaning of a Protestant hymn by embedding it in a traditional form of Catholic piety. The Brethren's foremost theologian, Lukáš of Prague, would have been horrified to learn that his song, "Christ the model of humility," was now being deployed to support Catholic devotional practices during Lent. Even more extreme was the use of a Brethren hymn to celebrate the Corpus Christi festival.[100] Such patterns underscore one of the great strengths of Bohemian Catholicism – its ability to take the traditions of the past and reshape them in an orthodox manner for the needs of the present.

The three genres that I have examined in this chapter, bibles, sermons and hymnals, certainly complemented and reinforced each other. But of course there were also substantive differences between them, and it may well have been the song that had the greatest reach. Michna, Šteyer and Božan emphasized that their hymns were to be sung anywhere and at any time. Dissolving the walls of church and cloister, the sacred song brought Catholic piety into the everyday lives of ordinary people. The range of these hymns also grew over time as the scope of the songbooks slowly

---

[98] Observation of Antonín Škarka in the introduction of Michna, *Das dichterische Werk*, p. 32. The same illustration was also used for his *Česká mariánská muzika*.
[99] Božan, *Slavíček rájský*, pp. 416–17.   [100] Ibid., pp. 102, 344.

17. Title page of Adam Michna of Otradovice, *Music for the Liturgical Year*

expanded. The early Catholic hymnals were relatively modest undertakings. Voyt's collection contained less than 100 songs, and even Michna's work was comparatively short. It was Šteyer who began compiling the mammoth hymnals that became so common in the late seventeenth and early eighteenth centuries, and while these songbooks generally followed the liturgical year, there were hymns for nearly every occasion. From the perils of lightning to the threat of famine, Božan's *Heavenly Nightingale* covered a broad range of human activity.[101] Considered together, these later hymnals created a web of piety that helped sacralize the most mundane aspects of life.

---

[101] Ibid., pp. 261–3, 274.

When assessing the impact of these hymns in Bohemian society, it is important to realize that they represented a powerful fusion of what might be described as high and low musical cultures. As noted earlier, these hymnals frequently adapted popular material such as the ballad. Indeed on the popular level, the boundary between sacred and secular was often quite permeable. Peasants occasionally borrowed hymn melodies for songs of satire and protest.[102] At the other end of the spectrum, musicians such as Michna and Holan Rovenský were also serious composers. Michna was known for his elaborate liturgical works while Holan Rovenský composed two important passion cycles. His *Capella regia musicalis* with its polyphonic arrangements and short cantatas with instrumental accompaniment was a significant musical achievement in itself. This synthesis of high and low produced an expressive and vibrant genre that helped create a sense of belonging and community among Czech Catholics that could mediate other social differences. It is all the more significant, then, that this synthesis which propelled the hymn into the forefront of Bohemia's musical culture began to unravel as the eighteenth century progressed. Fewer new hymns were written. The later editions of Šteyer's *Czech Hymn Book* and Koniáš's *New Testament Lyre* (1752) tended to recycle older songs and their melodies. Unlike the days of Michna and Holan Rovenský, serious ecclesiastical music was moving away from the hymnal. Even Božan's *Heavenly Nightingale* began to reflect this lack of musical innovation.[103] What had once been an effective means of uniting a community, an enterprise that embraced a broad range of Bohemian society, was becoming a narrower cultural phenomenon. Spurned by the elites and gradually restricted to the countryside, these Catholic hymns were over time seen as quaint cultural artefacts sung by peasants.

---

[102] Jaroslav Bužga, "Musiker und musikalische Institutionen im Zeitalter des Barocks," in Elmar Arro, ed., *Beiträge zur Musikgeschichte Osteuropas* (Wiesbaden: Steiner, 1977), p. 348.

[103] Ducreux, "L'hymnologie catholique tchèque," 175–6; Jiří Sehnal, "Die Entwicklungstendenzen und Stilschichten im tschechischen barocken Kirchenlied," *Musica antiqua* 3 (1972), 127–60; Jiří Sehnal, "Lidový duchovní zpěv v českých zemích v době klasicismu," *Hudební věda* 22 (1985), 248–58.

CHAPTER 8

Pilgrimage and popular piety

Sometime at the beginning of the seventeenth century Samuel Andrýsek, an ambitious merchant from Lower Silesia, moved his family from their rural home to the more prosperous setting of Olomouc, the commercial hub of central Moravia. It was a wise decision, and Andrýsek and his son Jan quickly established themselves in the local wine trade. As their business began to grow, they frequently found themselves on the road between Moravia and the Austrian lands to the south. These were perilous times, however, and the family knew that a prosperous business could be destroyed literally overnight by raiding soldiers or roaming ruffians. Jan was a particularly pious youth, and on one of these trips south he made a short detour to seek divine protection for the family's commercial interests. He and his business associates had stopped for the night in the tiny village of Luleč. Rising early the next morning, he climbed a small hill outside the hamlet to the church of St. Martin. There he made a vow to the Virgin in the presence of his traveling companions. It was a simple transaction. If she would secure his fortune, he would build a chapel in her honor in the hills just east of Olomouc. In the years that followed the family business prospered, and when the estate of Jan's wealthy brother-in-law passed to him, it was clear to all that Mary had answered the vintner's request.

The Virgin did not allow Jan to forget his promise. She began appearing in his dreams with pointed reminders of her assistance. Andrýsek, ever the astute businessman, had no intention of cheating his heavenly partner, but he did have a problem. Though he was ready to fulfill the vow, he was not sure where he should raise the chapel. This issue occupied him for many months as he traipsed the countryside around his home. But the answer was soon to come. One winter night in February 1629 he left Olomouc in a snowstorm and headed for the ridge of hills east of the city. The journey was initially difficult as he struggled through the steep drifts that were quickly piling up along the road, but as he entered a thick wood not far from his home, the snow let up dramatically and opening before him was a clearing that was surrounded by a great arc of light. It was the divine response for which he had been searching. Marking the spot with branches, he returned home and began to make inquiries regarding the land. He discovered that the plot belonged to the local Premonstratensian community. He made an appointment with the abbot and related the entire story. Once the monks heard his report, they had a difficult time refusing the request of the very insistent merchant. They allowed him to build a small pilgrimage church on the site of the clearing, and there he served as an informal custodian during the difficult years of war and the Swedish occupation. His involvement with the new shrine had a profound impact on his family. His son Ignác became a Jesuit while his two daughters, Anna and Kateřina, entered nearby cloisters. But more significant was the effect on the local area. Shortly after the dedication of the chapel in 1633 reports began to circulate of a blind man who had been miraculously healed at the site. Soon there were stories of other miracles, and this new shrine of the "Holy Knoll" (Svatý Kopeček) along with its votive image quickly became a popular destination for pilgrims across the region. Crowds became so large in fact that an overwhelmed Andrýsek passed the administration of the chapel to the Premonstratensians, who in turn expanded the complex as visitors came in ever greater numbers. In the course of a generation the modest chapel was transformed into a major baroque church. By the end of the century more than 100,000 pilgrims annually ascended the hill to visit the shrine and receive the Eucharist.[1]

The story of Svatý Kopeček with its miracles and visions was repeated scores of times across Bohemia and Moravia in the century after White Mountain. Yet historians of the Czech lands have generally paid scant attention to this rich body of material. To borrow a phrase from an eminent scholar of nineteenth-century Germany, such accounts have "occupied a kind of historical limbo."[2] Pilgrimage, however, offers one of the best entry points to the popular religious culture of the era. Though the Middle Ages are often remembered as the great age of pilgrimage, quantitative evidence indicates that the highpoint of this phenomenon actually occurred in the post-Reformation period. In central Europe, in particular, the expansion of pilgrimage sites was far and away most rapid during this period.[3] The Jesuit

---

[1] For numbers see Thadeus Schrabal, "Ortus et progressus Sacri Montis in Marchionatu Moraviae prope Olomucium," 342 r–v, SK, D J I 15. Andrýsek's account can be found in *Krátké Wypsánj o Nalezenj Téz Sto-Letní Slawnosti* (Hradec Králové: V. J. Tybely, 1733).
[2] David Blackbourn, *Marpingen: Apparitions of the Virgin Mary in Bismarckian Germany* (Oxford: Clarendon, 1993), p. 13.
[3] Mary Lee Nolan and Sidney Nolan, *Christian Pilgrimage in Modern Western Europe* (Chapel Hill: University of North Carolina Press, 1989), pp. 86–114.

Johannes Miller boasted in his history of one such shrine that Bohemia was a kingdom of pilgrims. "No city," he wrote, "no market town, not even the smallest village can be found where there is not annually some type of pilgrimage."[4] Ranging from rustic wooden chapels hidden deep in the woods to magnificent baroque churches in busy urban centers, these shrines attracted the faithful in ever-increasing numbers.

Though pilgrimage could certainly be an expression of personal piety, as a public form of devotion, it became in the course of the seventeenth century one of the most prominent features of Bohemia's confessional identity. This had not always been the case. Although the tradition of Christian pilgrimage in the Czech lands could be traced back to the era of Wenceslas and Ludmila, it became a more established practice several centuries later. During the Crusades a number of prominent Bohemians made the trip to the Holy Land including the bishop of Olomouc, Jindřich Zdík, who returned with a trunk full of relics. To commemorate his trip he established the Strahov Monastery in Prague which he named Mount Zion. In the fourteenth century the peripatetic Charles IV amassed a veritable trove of relics and along with his ally Archbishop Arnošt of Pardubice strategically deployed them to help establish what became a thick network of shrines within the kingdom. These developments, however, were dramatically interrupted at the end of the century. Reformers such as Matěj of Janov began to question the cult of the saints. Jan Hus spoke out against the fraudulent claims of unscrupulous priests promoting miraculous cures, while two decades later Hussite soldiers destroyed many of the shrines that had been erected only a few generations earlier.[5] Though pilgrimage would not disappear, it was generally a more sluggish and stagnant phenomenon during the Jagiellonian period and the first years of the Habsburg regime. All this of course changed after 1620 with the dramatic rebirth and rapid spread of this form of corporate devotion.

PILGRIMAGE AND PEOPLE

Studies of Catholic devotional patterns in the Habsburg lands have traditionally focused on the elites. It has often been assumed that practices popularized by the imperial family were copied by the nobility, adapted

---

[4] Johannes Miller, *Historia Mariascheinensis* (Prague: In der Academischen Buchdruckery des Collegii S.J., 1710), p. 34.
[5] Jan Royt offers a general survey of pilgrimage in the Bohemian lands in "Křesťanská pouť po barokních Čechách," *ČL* 79 (1992), 323–39. For the Hussite critique of the cult of the saints see Ota Halama, *Otázka svatých v české reformaci* (Brno: L. Marek, 2002).

by townspeople, and modified by the peasants. In related fashion, scholars have frequently "instrumentalized" religion, isolating it and treating it as yet another tool the Habsburgs had at their disposal in their ongoing quest to solidify their control of their disparate territories. From this perspective, then, pilgrimage was an especially useful practice to exploit. Recent scholarship on the upper Styrian shrine of Mariazell has demonstrated how this site attracted believers from all corners of central Europe and helped unify a divided region.[6] To what extent do these models work in the Bohemian context? Should we view pilgrimage from this top-down perspective? Is it helpful to consider it as another form of social discipline? More generally, what does this phenomenon tell us about the new religious sensibilities of the region?

The kingdom's elites did play an integral role in this process. Ferdinand II helped bring the bones of St. Norbert to Strahov. The Pernsteins, Martinics and other prominent families promoted the new shrine of the Infant Jesus of Prague, and the network of Loreto chapels that stretched across the region was essentially a product of the nobility. Simply put, the aristocracy was indispensable in the reconstruction of Bohemia's pilgrimage infrastructure. But of all the shrines they helped establish or rebuild, one more than any other stood out as a monument of elite piety – the pilgrim route between Prague and Stará Boleslav.[7] This village northeast of Prague had a special place in Bohemia's religious tradition. It was both the site of Wenceslas's martyrdom and home of one of the kingdom's most treasured relics, the Madonna of Stará Boleslav. This miraculous object attracted the interest, devotion and ultimately patronage of the Habsburg rulers. At the insistence of Empress Anna, construction of a new church for the relic was begun in 1617. In his first visit to Bohemia after White Mountain, Ferdinand II took part in an elaborate procession to Stará Boleslav. In 1638 the metal relief, which had been seized by Saxon troops, was ransomed as a prisoner of war and brought to Vienna where it could be more closely guarded by its imperial patrons. It accompanied Ferdinand III on his travels

[6] Anna Coreth, *Pietas Austriaca*, trans. William Bowman and Anna Maria Leitgeb (West Lafayette: Purdue University Press, 2004); Karl Vocelka, "Habsburská zbožnost a lidová zbožnost," *FHB* 18 (1997), 225–39; Thomas Winkelbauer, *Ständefreiheit und Fürstenmacht: Länder und Untertanen des Hauses Habsburg im konfessionellen Zeitalter* (Vienna: Ueberreuter, 2003), vol. II, p. 221; Laura Kinsey, "The Habsburgs at Mariazell: piety, patronage, and statecraft, 1620–1770," unpublished Ph.D. thesis, University of California at Los Angeles (2000).

[7] Foundational here were the efforts of the Jesuit Jan Tanner in popularizing the site. Jan Tanner, *Swatá Cesta z Prahy do Staré Boleslawě* (Prague: Typis Universitatis Carolo-Ferdinandeae, 1679) (German edn, 1680; Latin edn, 1690; Czech 2nd edn, 1692); M. E. Ducreux, "Symbolický rozměr pouti do Staré Boleslavi," *ČČH* 95 (1997), 585–620; Winkelbauer, *Ständefreiheit und Fürstenmacht*, vol. II, pp. 221–3.

and his wife insisted that it be brought into her room when she was giving birth to the future Leopold I. Though captured by the Swedes during the late stages of the war, it was restored to the Habsburgs as part of the peace settlement and returned triumphantly to Bohemia in 1650. In the future, all of Bohemia's kings and queens undertook a pilgrimage to Stará Boleslav as part of the coronation ritual. Leopold I made this trip numerous times. The nobility also left their mark on this site. One of the most distinctive features of the route was a series of forty-four chapels that were constructed between the city and village. Each of these wayside shrines was sponsored by a patron. Thirty-three of the kingdom's most important families along with eleven high-ranking prelates participated and financed their construction.

Apart from the secular elites, the religious orders were also influential in reestablishing the pilgrimage network. Not unexpectedly, the Jesuits were quite active in this regard, illustrative in their mission at the Moravian shrine of Tuřany. According to legend, the missionary brothers Cyril and Methodius had brought a statue of the Madonna and child to Moravia in the ninth century but left it hidden in the woods. Almost 200 years later it was discovered and became the focal point of a pilgrimage shrine.[8] The cult had suffered during the Hussite period and the Reformation, and though Cardinal Dietrichstein considered the restoration of this site an important priority, he had little success initially. The turning point came when the Jesuits took over the administration of the pilgrimage church in 1666. In an effort to promote the shrine Bohuslav Balbín had written a history of the miraculous statue.[9] The efforts of Balbín and his colleagues eventually yielded handsome dividends. When the Jesuits began their work, the church was attracting approximately 3,000 pilgrims annually. Just one year into their mission, 10,000 visited Tuřany. By 1699 the number had purportedly grown to 100,000. The Jesuits, of course, had no monopoly on pilgrimage sites. In the Czech lands the Spanish Benedictines developed two shrines to the cult of the Black Madonna of Montserrat. The Dominicans were active in northern Bohemia, and their community was influential promoting the cult of St. Barbara in the tiny village of Dubice. In eastern Bohemia the Carthusians were responsible for recovering an important relic that had been lost during the Hussite period. Their discovery in 1627 of a wooden cross that had been carved by Arnošt of Pardubice helped restore

---

[8] Zdeněk Kalista, "Diva Turzanensis," in *Česká barokní pouť* (Žďár nad Sázavou: Cisterciana Sarensis, 2001), pp. 31–70.
[9] Bohuslav Balbín, *Diva Turzanensis, seu Historia originis et miraculorum magnae Dei hominumque matris Mariae* (Olomouc: Typis V. H. Etteli, 1658).

the pilgrim route to the hilltop shrine of Tábor. The Paulists constructed shrines in southern Bohemia and Moravia (Klášter and Vranov). The Cistercians maintained complexes in Mariánska Týnice and Vyšší Brod, while apart from Strahov the Premonstratensians also controlled the ancient monastery of Teplá which housed the remains of the blessed Hroznata.

Confraternities also contributed to the growth and spread of pilgrimage. These organizations first appeared in Bohemia in the fourteenth century though their development was stunted by the Hussite disturbances.[10] Originally a more urban phenomenon, after 1620 confraternities spread rapidly across the entire region. Between White Mountain and their dissolution by Joseph II in 1783, more than 650 were active in the kingdom. From shoemakers to cooks, from nobles to high government officials, they were theoretically open to all ranks of society. Membership numbers of individual sodalities could range from barely a dozen to more than a thousand. In the countryside or in the city, these organizations helped inculcate Catholic devotional patterns across a broad social spectrum. Over 40 percent of these confraternities were dedicated to the cult of the Virgin.[11] In southern Bohemia one of these sodalities had been founded to promote the Habsburg shrine of Mariazell. Most, however, were oriented towards pilgrimage sites within Bohemia. The brotherhoods of the scapulary maintained a series of six chapels that housed devotional images of Our Lady of Mount Carmel.[12] Confraternities dedicated to the rosary supported shrines in Česká Kamenice and Dolní Újezd while a brotherhood of the Sacred Family kept the pilgrims coming to the lonely chapel of Svéraz in the foothills of the Šumava mountains.

Finally, there were communities or even single individuals whose efforts were critical for the success of a specific shrine or chapel. In southern Bohemia during the difficult years of the late sixteenth century the simple but tenacious priest Martin Strakonický fought off the Protestants and preserved the site of a Marian apparition at the remote settlement of Strašín.[13] It was a local woman, the feisty Zuzana Veselá, who was the driving force behind a shrine in the border town of Domažlice nearly a

---

[10] The best overview is offered by Jiří Mikulec, *Barokní náboženská bratrstva v Čechách* (Prague: Nakladatelství Lidové noviny, 2000). More recently see Tomáš Jiránek and Jiří Kubeš, eds., *Bratrstva: světská a církevní sdružení a jejich role v kulturních a společenských strukturách od středověku do moderní doby* (Pardubice: Univerzita Pardubice, 2005).

[11] Mikulec, *Barokní náboženská bratrstva*, p. 32. Jiří Mikulec, "Poutníci a sodálové. Barokní pouť v životě náboženských bratrstev," unpublished conference paper, Poutnictví v evropské kultuře, May 2004.

[12] Jan Royt, *Obraz a kult v Čechách 17. a 18. století* (Prague: Karolinum, 1999), pp. 257–8.

[13] Zdeněk Kalista, "Madona lesů, studánek a poustevníků ve Strašíně," in *Česká barokní pouť*, pp. 167–99.

century later. Though a town council had decided to build a pilgrimage chapel in honor of St. Lawrence after a fire had destroyed a significant portion of their village, their corporate vow was conveniently forgotten until Zuzana Veselá took it upon herself to fulfill the promise. She credited the saint for curing her melancholia during the time of the fire, and in 1695 the church for which she aggressively campaigned was officially consecrated.[14] In northern Bohemia during the late seventeenth century a butcher's apprentice was responsible for the establishment of the popular site of Křešice. In 1679 the devout lad purchased a clay relief of Our Lady of Passau. That same year he claimed that the image had saved him from a great danger. Convinced that an item of such power should not be kept to himself, he took it out to a nearby wood and attached it to a large alder tree not far from a well. Stories began to circulate, and before long a steady stream of pilgrims was coming to see the image and drink from the well that was now supposedly blessed by the Virgin. They returned home cured of a variety of ailments and convinced of the water's curative properties. The informal shrine became so popular that in 1704 the bishop of Litoměřice established a commission to investigate the site. The committee affirmed many of these reports, and four years later a chapel was built around the alder with its miraculous image.[15]

One of the most intriguing of these communal shrines was the pilgrimage Church of the Visitation in the Giant Mountains. The tiny town of Bozkov had been a destination for pilgrims since the fourteenth century, but with the arrival of the Hussites, the parish priest buried the small statue of the Virgin that had been the center of the local cult, and the church was abandoned. When the villagers later decided to build a new chapel at some distance from the original site, the construction materials were miraculously transported back to the first location while a mysterious July snowstorm left a clear outline of the forgotten church which lay in ruins. A new chapel was raised on that spot while the statue was rediscovered during its construction. The most interesting aspect of this shrine, however, was its continued success without substantial support from either the local nobility or clergy. The lands around Bozkov passed to the Protestant Smiřickýs whose most famous member, Albrecht Jan, was one of the ringleaders of the 1618 rebellion. After White Mountain this backwoods region was not able to secure the services of a permanent priest. Nevertheless, with the support of

[14] Zdeněk Boháč, *Poutní místa v Čechách* (Prague: Debora, 1995), p. 249.
[15] J. Košnář, *Poutnická místa a památné svatyně v Čechách* (Prague: V. Kotrba, 1903), pp. 218–27; Royt, *Obraz a kult*, p. 246; Boháč, *Poutní místa*, pp. 271–2.

the local populace this Marian cult survived and even flourished during this period. Furthermore, it is not completely clear whether all the residents of the immediate area were Catholic. It seems most likely that this was an Utraquist community up to White Mountain. Even in 1651, the faithful sacristan of the pilgrimage church, a certain Matěj Košťál, was classified as a "heretic" during a church visitation. Košťál, in fact, declared that he would rather leave his property than deny his convictions. His heterodox beliefs, however, did not affect his devotion to the Bozkov Madonna.[16] In Bohemia, Marian veneration could cut across confessional boundaries. The devotional statue in the church of Česká Kamenice had been carved by the Lutheran Christian Ulrich, a resident of the border town of Zittau where Marian holidays were still celebrated.[17]

In most cases the success of a specific shrine was dependent not on the efforts of a single individual or group but on a variety of parties who worked together. Svatý Kopeček began through the efforts of Jan Andrýsek, but it would not have grown without the full cooperation of the resident Premonstratensian community. The renewal of Tuřany was initiated by Cardinal Dietrichstein and supported by a confraternity before the Jesuits arrived on the scene. This pattern is also reflected at one of Bohemia's most popular pilgrimage sites. The origins of the Holy Mountain of Příbram (Svatá Hora) purportedly date back to the thirteenth century.[18] A local knight built a small chapel to fulfill a vow he had made the Virgin for her assistance against a band of thieves. Archbishop Arnošt of Pardubice made frequent visits here the following century and allegedly carved a small statue of the Virgin that became the center of the shrine. The Holy Mountain, however, would not assume major significance until after White Mountain. In 1632 Jan Procházka, a blind beggar from Prague, had a vision during the Easter season. For years he had lived on alms, but according to his dream, he would be able to provide and care for himself if he traveled to the shrine at Příbram. There he went and was promptly healed. Procházka's miraculous

---

[16] Zdeněk Kalista, "Bozkov čili Maria na hory putující," in *Česká barokní pouť*, pp. 125–66; J. V. Dolenský, *Starší paměti farní osady Bozkova zvláště poutního chrámu Panny Marie* (Bozkov: Šolc, 1888).

[17] Boháč, *Poutní místa*, pp. 258–9.

[18] František Holas, *Dějiny poutního místa mariánského Svaté Hory u Příbramě* (Prague: Nákl. Matice svatohorské, 1929); J. Koláček, *Jezuité na Svaté hoře* (Velehrad: Refugium Velehrad-Roma, 1988); Markéta Holubová, "Svatá Hora u Příbrami v obraze barokní doby," unpublished Ph.D. thesis, Charles University (2002). M. E. Ducreux argues that the Holy Mountain did not become a significant pilgrimage center until the seventeenth century. Claims of an earlier provenance were made by enthusiastic Jesuits. M. E. Ducreux, "Zum Thema Wallfahrt: das Beispiel Böhmens im 17. Jahrhundert," in R. Leeb, S. Pils and T. Winkelbauer, eds., *Staatsmacht und Seelenheil* (Vienna: Oldenbourg, 2007), p. 102.

cure opened the floodgates. So great was the response that even Ferdinand II undertook the journey that same year. The sudden influx of pilgrims overwhelmed the local clergy who traditionally oversaw what had been a more modest chapel. To manage the new situation, a call was sent out to the Jesuits who arrived in 1647.

Once the Jesuits assumed control of the complex they devoted substantial resources to the promotion of its cult. In 1655 Jiří Konstanc, a translator of the St. Wenceslas Bible, wrote a brief history of the shrine. The following decade Bohuslav Balbín wrote his own study of the Holy Mountain. Both focused on the miracles connected to the site.[19] As at many shrines of the period, the Jesuits systematically recorded the various miracles the pilgrims reported. Apart from a brief description of the actual event, each entry included basic biographical data of the person involved, helping us recreate the social background of those who journeyed to Příbram. The results are remarkably balanced. Slightly over 25 percent were from the nobility while the clergy represented 17 percent. Thirty-three percent came from larger towns while nearly 23 percent were from smaller villages.[20] It seems that the Jesuits were also impressed by this broad spectrum of involvement. As they continued to expand the complex over the years, they celebrated this feature of the growing cult in the actual design of the site. In the early eighteenth century they began decorating the shrine's inner courtyard with a series of paintings depicting the various miracles that pilgrims had attributed to the Virgin of the Holy Mountain. By the time the project was completed, the arcades were covered with 100 scenes initially documented in the miracle book. There was the nobleman, Peter of Říčany, who was saved from a potentially fatal throw from a horse. There was a priest from northern Bohemia who while returning from Příbram was preserved during a violent thunderstorm, and then there was the simple mason, Jan Luňáček, who was miraculously saved in a construction accident.[21] This visual encyclopedia of the Virgin's mercies reflected the reach and appeal of this cult in the Bohemian lands.

[19] Jiří Konstanc, *Succurre miseris* (Prague: Archiepiscopal Press, 1655); Bohuslav Balbín, *Diva Montis Sancti, seu origines et miracula magnae Dei hominumque matris Mariae* (Prague: Typis Universitatis Carolo-Ferdinandeae, 1665) (Czech edn, 1666; German edn, 1668; 2nd Czech edn, 1692).
[20] Holubová, "Svatá Hora u Příbrami," part IV. The remaining 1.2 percent were soldiers. Data drawn from the miracle book recording these events between 1639 and 1751. NA, Historie Swato-Horská, Kniha třetí, ŘR, P-118, # 152.
[21] NA, Historie Swato-Horská, Kniha třetí, ŘR, P-118, # 152, 55, 64, 130–1. For the actual cycle at Svatá Hora see Markéta Holubová, "Textové a obrazové zaznamenání svatohorských zázraků ve světle barokní doby," *Podbrdsko* 8 (2001), 68–75.

As this brief survey of the Holy Mountain suggests, religion cannot be reduced to a mere tool of social discipline. Though ecclesiastical rituals could be harnessed for a specific end as with the translation of St. Norbert, the religious impulse of this period was far broader in scope. It could be directed and shaped to some extent, but as a whole, it exceeded the grasp of any individual or corporate body including the institutional church. Pilgrimage in early modern times defies simple attempts of classification. It was a complicated and capacious phenomenon that incorporated an entire range of religious sensibilities. As such, it needs to be located in a broad social context. Historians of modern Europe have observed that the great wave of Marian apparitions in the nineteenth century occurred during periods of political crisis, social upheaval or economic distress.[22] It is thus not surprising that so many of these sites in Bohemia developed or were revived in an age of unprecedented social dislocation. The toll of unrelenting war, the repercussions of dramatic demographic change, and the consequences of economic and agricultural crisis created a climate in which the appeal of divine immediacy was undeniable. At a pilgrimage shrine the supplicant could approach a supernatural patron directly and through a simple vow cement a relationship with a heavenly ally. As William Christian has observed in the Spanish setting, these devotional acts or "bargains with the gods" were a basic human response to a world that was beyond their control.[23] What could be more natural than raising a chapel to the Virgin for her protection from the plague as happened in the village of Přelouč in 1680?[24] When the rains did not come, peasants could turn to Our Lady of Vyšehrad. Pregnant women could appeal to the Virgin of Karlov. Jesuit records from the Holy Mountain list more than a thousand miracles and divine assistance for over seventy different types of disease, accident or other forms of calamity.[25] Though the elites may have been spared from some of life's rigors, they were all too aware of their own mortality. Leopold I made ten trips to Mariazell, two to the Holy Mountain, and a further two to Bavaria's Altötting. For both emperors and peasants, pilgrimage was a natural response to life's crises and an acknowledgment of humanity's ultimate impotence in a hostile world.

Central, then, to a proper understanding of pilgrimage in the Czech lands is an acknowledgment of the strength and depth of these basic religious

[22] Blackbourn, *Marpingen*, pp. 7, 399.
[23] William Christian, *Local Religion in Sixteenth-Century Spain* (Princeton: Princeton University Press, 1981), pp. 175–6.
[24] Boháč, *Poutní místa*, pp. 114–15.
[25] Holubová, "Textové a obrazové zaznamenání svatohorských zázraků," 70.

convictions. That is not to deny that pilgrimage could serve a variety of social functions. Recent studies have illustrated how peasants could use these popular processions to promote a specific political or economic agenda.[26] From Émile Durkheim to Victor and Edith Turner, scholars have long debated the political and social uses of pilgrimage. One theme that is common in much of this literature is inversion. If only temporarily, pilgrimage suspended or even overturned the traditional order of society. Children and women, the poor and the sick assumed central roles in the development of these sites. The classic example is that of Lourdes. Here, Bernadette Soubirous, an illiterate shepherdess and daughter of a destitute miller, became the focus of a worldwide cult. In nineteenth-century Bohemia, Magdalena Kade, a sickly spinster who had long been the butt of local jokes, turned the tables on her critics once the Virgin began to visit her. Kade's miraculous recovery pushed her into the spotlight and for a short time made the village of Philippsdorf (Filipov) one of central Europe's most important centers of Marian devotion.[27]

These accounts of inversion were also common for the earlier period. In 1710 a young servant girl was making a long trip on foot from České Budějovice to her home in Jihlava. On this dangerous journey she passed through a thick wood where two thieves set upon her. Terrified, she began to pray aloud to the Virgin. This open display of piety unsettled the ruffians to such a degree that they turned heel and left their intended victim in peace. The grateful domestic credited the miracle to a devotional image in the Dominican church of České Budějovice. There she returned and made a copy of the Marian icon which she hung from a tree at the place of the thwarted assault. Her action, however, precipitated a conflict with the uncooperative monks of a nearby Augustinian cloister who endeavored to suppress the new cult. In the power struggle that ensued the simple servant ultimately faced down the abbot himself who was not able to deny the miraculous power of the Marian image.[28] Indeed, many of the stories that developed around these Bohemian shrines are reminiscent of fairy tales that were collected by folklorists in later centuries. The popular site of Hejnice in northern Bohemia allegedly had its origins with an impoverished net maker whose wife and children were seriously ill. While napping under a linden tree, he had a dream where he was instructed to proceed to the market town,

---

[26] David Luebke, "The seditious uses of 'naïve monarchism' and Marian veneration in early modern Germany," *Past and Present* 154 (1997), 71–106; Rebekka Habermas, *Wallfahrt und Aufruhr: Zur Geschichte des Wunderglaubens in der frühen Neuzeit* (Frankfurt: Campus, 1991), pp. 35–44.

[27] Blackbourn, *Marpingen*, p. 28.   [28] Shrine of Mláka near Třeboň; Boháč, *Poutní místa*, pp. 174–5.

purchase a small wooden statue of the Virgin and hang it from the branches of the tree. This he did, and once he led his family to the linden, they were miraculously healed.[29]

By reversing the social order, by embracing the underdog, pilgrimage in the world of desperate peasants and impoverished townspeople could act as a type of safety valve, a temporary release from the hardships, pressures and concerns of everyday life. As such it served the needs of both state and church in a region slowly recovering from the wounds of confessional conflict and war. It should be remembered, however, that this form of popular piety was an unstable and uncertain force. During the late Middle Ages reports of a bleeding host transformed the north German town of Wilsnack almost overnight into a major pilgrimage destination while a Marian apparition in Niklashausen turned this sleepy village into the center of a significant religious revival. But both Wilsnack and Niklashausen served more than the needs of the pious and devout. They also attracted the poor and rootless and became sites of significant social and economic unrest. Visionaries, too, were potential threats to the established religious and political order. The fates of Joan of Arc and Girolamo Savonarola are of course well known, but there were many others like Hans Böhm, the so-called Drummer of Niklashausen, and the Spanish teenager Lucrecia de León, who in the end met resistance and hostility from authorities all too sensitive to the subversive undertones of their revelations.[30]

Although Bohemia's disaffected may have cloaked a mild critique of their society in these pilgrimage rituals, none of the kingdom's shrines became the focus of widespread protest, dissent and disorder. What explains the relatively conservative nature of this phenomenon in the Czech lands? Despite the genuinely popular appeal of these shrines, the broad network of pilgrimage sites would not have developed without the assent and support of those who mattered most: the nobles, the church and even the emperor. In similar fashion, though the initial stimulus and subsequent patronage of these sites may have come from a wide cross-section of society, the regulatory arm of the church was usually never far behind once a shrine had gained a popular following as was the case with Křešice and its miraculous alder. When pilgrims began arriving in significant numbers, the bishop stepped in to investigate the matter. The archives give ample

---

[29] Ibid., pp. 264–5.
[30] Jonathan Sumption, *Pilgrimage* (London: Faber & Faber, 1975), pp. 282–8; Klaus Arnold, *Niklashausen 1476* (Baden-Baden: Koerner, 1980); Richard Kagan, *Lucrecia's Dreams* (Berkeley: University of California Press, 1990).

testimony to the ecclesiastical oversight of these affairs.[31] The visions, too, that were connected to the sites were local and conservative. Mary's command to Jan Andrýsek to build a chapel in a deserted woodland was hardly revolutionary. Though scholars have debated the extent to which pilgrimage created a sense of collectivity or *communitas* that erased boundaries of social status and economic difference, pilgrimage within Bohemia normally functioned as a unifying force. The custodians of the sacred sites worked hard to efface pragmatic differences such as language.[32] More generally, the promotion of Marian devotion harmoniously fused a state-sponsored cult with the popular sensibilities of local religion. Finally, human frailty and suffering helped unite those who traveled to these chapels and churches for healing or thanksgiving.

PILGRIMAGE AND THE PAST

When viewed as a whole, one of the key features of Bohemia's Counter-Reformation was its emphasis on the past. Through their research the antiquarians recovered the memories of a vibrant ecclesiastical culture that had existed before Hus. Painters, sculptors and musicians surrounded believers with reminders of this sacred heritage while preachers recreated this world through their Sunday homilies. But it was pilgrimage that made the past come alive in a way that none of the other media could replicate. At these shrines the past was immediate and tangible as it transported the faithful back to an earlier and more heroic age. There were four types of sites that specifically celebrated the kingdom's *sacra historia*. The first group consisted of shrines connected to the early evangelists of the Czech lands. Though the diocese of Regensburg had sent monks to Christianize the region in the first half of the ninth century, it was the more famous mission of Cyril and Methodius that captivated the imagination of Bohemia's ecclesiastical historians. With their Byzantine origins, the missionary brothers were somewhat problematic for the post-White Mountain church. Nevertheless, there were attempts to develop a cult around the brothers. Flush from the success of the Norbert translation, Archbishop Harrach

---

[31] See for example the archbishop's investigation of the cult of the Virgin of Karlov in the early eighteenth century. NA, AZK, Fond Karlov, 2535, no. 1141; Royt, *Obraz a kult*, pp. 56–60.

[32] The liminality thesis is best articulated by Victor and Edith Turner in their *Image and Pilgrimage in Christian Culture* (Oxford: Blackwell, 1978). For an important critique of this model see John Eade and Michael Sallnow, eds., *Contesting the Sacred: The Anthropology of Christian Pilgrimage* (London: Routledge, 1991), esp. pp. 3–9. For an example from Bohemia see the efforts of the Jesuits who worked to minimize linguistic differences at the shrine of Tuřany in Moravia. Kalista, "Diva Turzanensis," pp. 61–2.

sought to persuade the Bohemian estates to finance a trip to Italy in 1629 to secure the remains of St. Cyril, but prying his bones free from Rome and Urban VIII was a task even too difficult for the capable Harrach.[33] The contributions of Cyril and Methodius, however, were celebrated by their connection with some of the kingdom's most important relics. In Stará Boleslav they were honored through their relationship with the Madonna of Stará Boleslav, in Tuřany through the miraculous Madonna and in Hradec Králové through the relics of St. Clement that Cyril had supposedly brought to the city from his earlier travels among the Khazars.

It was Wenceslas and the second major wave of Christianization which of course received the greatest attention during this period. Though the martyred saint was interred in St. Vitus Cathedral, the two most important centers of his cult were Stará Boleslav and the monastery of Zderaz (Prague), for here were sites directly connected to his life. After 1648 the cloister of Zderaz and a nearby well supposedly used by the duke became an important destination for pilgrims including Ferdinand III who visited the complex in 1655 and left a handwritten inscription in Czech, "Saint Wenceslas, Bohemian King, pray for me."[34] At Stará Boleslav the devout could retrace Wenceslas's final steps to the church and his fatal encounter with his brother Boleslav. Nearby one could remember the death of his faithful servant, the blessed Podiven, for a chapel had been raised at the spot where according to local legend he had been hung by Boleslav's supporters. Although overshadowed by her grandson, Ludmila was also the beneficiary of renewed attention after 1620. Her birthplace in Mělník, the site of her murder at Tetín, and her final resting place in St. George's Basilica (Prague) drew increasingly larger crowds of pilgrims.

A second group of pilgrimage sites were dedicated to Bohemia's early hermits: St. Günther at Břevnov and his retreat in the Bohemian Forest, St. Procopius at Sázava and his tomb on Castle Hill, and St. Ivan in the cave complex in the wooded hills southwest of Prague. These sacred places served a number of important functions. From the time of Constantine, the anchoritic holy man had occupied an honored position throughout the Christian world. In a region whose rural areas were better known for producing a broad assortment of schismatics and heretics, renewed attention on the kingdom's godly hermits was yet one more way of resanctifying

---

[33] Alessandro Catalano, *La Boemia e la riconquista delle coscienze: Ernst Adalbert von Harrach e la Controriforma in Europa centrale (1620–1667)* (Rome: Edizioni di storia e letteratura, 2005), p. 168.

[34] František Ekert, *Posvátná místa král. hl. města Prahy* (Prague: Nákl. Dědictví sv. Jana Nepomuckého, 1883), vol. II, p. 221.

Bohemia's ecclesiastical heritage. Predating the Hussites by several centuries, all three of these ascetics were reminders that the kingdom had a distinguished sacred past. Holy men are also significant as they have voluntarily rejected power and privilege to pursue a life of poverty and piety. Günther was the cousin of Emperor Henry II (1014–24). Ivan was purportedly the son of a Croatian prince, and though Procopius came from yeoman stock, he gave up both a family and promising career at the Vyšehrad in Prague. As such, Catholics used them as a foil to the lowborn heretics of the Hussite period whose illegitimate seizure of power brought ruin to the kingdom. Despite their rejection of worldly values, however, holy men have traditionally exercised significant influence as in the case of Byzantium's famous stylite sitters who were sought out by emperors, clerical leaders and ordinary people for advice and counsel on a broad range of issues. Bohemia's anchorites fit the same pattern. Living in a cave without human contact for over a decade, Ivan became the confidant of Bohemia's first Christian duke, Bořivoj, and his wife Ludmila. Prince Oldřich († 1034) met Procopius during a hunting expedition and was so impressed with this saint who had reputedly battled hundreds of demons in the Sázava valley that he asked him to become his confessor. Günther was a veritable hermit diplomat advising Emperor Conrad II (1027–39) during the Burgundian war and helping the Přemyslid princes settle rivalries within their family.

This old tradition was reestablished in the second half of the seventeenth century. Leopold I and Archbishop Sobek of Bílenberk became Ivan's new patrons with a high-profile campaign to renovate his decaying shrine.[35] Though the elites rallied round this undertaking, the new complex they sponsored made pilgrimage on a larger scale possible. Now the assistance of these ascetics which had been restricted to the few was available to a far wider audience as clerical authorities endeavored to popularize the cults of the other two anchorites as well. Abbot Otmar Zinke oversaw the translation of Günther's bones back to the Břevnov monastery and their final resting place in the new Dientzenhofer church of St. Margaret, a short trip for those living in Prague. At the same time there were efforts promoting his hermit refuge in the Šumava mountains.[36] Though Procopius's remains

[35] Ivo Kořán, "Legenda a kult sv. Ivana," *Umění* 35 (1987), 219–39; Viktor Kotrba, *Svatý Jan pod Skalou* (Prague: Vyšehrad, 1944); A. Podlaha, *Posvátná místa Království českého* (Prague: Nákl. Dědictví sv. Jana Nepomuckého, 1907–13), vol. II, pp. 47–61.
[36] Jiří David, *Des Königreiches Böhmens heilsamer Waldarzt* (Prague: Academische Buchdruckerei bei St. Clemens, 1713); Jiří David, *Medicus Hercinius* (Prague: Jezuitská tiskárna, 1713); J. A. Mansfeld, *Heylsames Brünnlein* (Prague, 1745).

were brought to Prague in 1588, Sázava remained an important pilgrimage site and experienced a new period of expansion after the Thirty Years War. Those who journeyed there could see important relics that had been preserved from Procopius's time. A cup that he had supposedly carved and from which he had served Oldřich was now used as a chalice for the Eucharist, a tangible reminder of the saint's presence and the grace he dispensed to those who properly honored him. Procopius's Slavic roots also endeared him to pilgrims. A supporter of a Slavonic liturgy, he was especially revered by ploughmen and miners.[37]

A third category to be considered are the sites connected to the clerical elites who helped solidify the gains of Bohemia's first missionaries. Bishops in particular received special attention. St. Adalbert's cult was revived at Břevnov. The second bishop of Prague was instrumental in establishing this monastic community, the Benedictines' oldest house in Bohemia. St. Wolfgang, the reform-minded bishop of Regensburg, was also remembered, for he, more than any other church official, was responsible for the creation of an independent Bohemian diocese in 973. At Chudenice in western Bohemia a chapel was raised atop a small hill to mark the spot where the saint turned and blessed the new bishopric during his last visit to the region. Other Bohemian towns (Zelená Lhota, Kájov and Kladruby) memorialized Wolfgang's work with small shrines of their own. The final member of this trio is Bohemia's first archbishop, Arnošt of Pardubice, whom the Jesuits were promoting as a candidate for canonization after White Mountain. Though the campaign ultimately failed, pilgrimage sites connected with his life (Příbram, Tábor, Glatz) once more became popular destinations. The efforts of seventeenth-century reformers to burnish the legacy of individuals who created the kingdom's ecclesiastical infrastructure ran parallel to their own attempts to restore Catholicism at the level of parish and diocese and more generally reflected the church's renewed emphasis on episcopal authority.

The kingdom's martyrs comprise a final grouping to investigate. Martyrs of course have always played a significant role in the life of the church, but during the Protestant and Catholic Reformations they assumed an even greater importance as these heroes of faith helped solidify the identities of competing confessional communities. For the antiquarians the witness and death of these devoted Catholics was an indispensable element in their

---

[37] Jaroslav Kadlec, "Svatý Prokop," in J. Kadlec, ed., *Bohemia Sancta* (Prague: Česká katolická charita, 1989), pp. 126–39; A. Podlaha, *Posvátná místa*, vol. I, pp. 117–26. Miners derived their connection to the eleventh-century hermit by his name. The verb *prokopat* means to dig or tunnel.

construction of Bohemia's sacred past. But martyrs can also serve as a link between time and space. For ordinary believers the story of Wenceslas's betrayal and death could take real and material form through a journey to Stará Boleslav where they could walk in the duke's footsteps to the very door of his assassination. Here the sacred past was transformed into sacred space. In Bohemia martyrs were also a means by which the church could illustrate the continuous and unbroken nature of the Catholic community, for their shrines spanned Bohemia's entire Christian era.

The earliest days were memorialized by the pilgrim routes dedicated to Wenceslas and Ludmila. There were considerably fewer martyrs in the following centuries when the church faced little opposition, but after the death of Charles IV, they once more became a regular feature of the kingdom's ecclesiastical tradition. Foreshadowing the troubled years ahead, John Nepomuk, the confessor of Queen Sophie, allegedly met his end during the reign of Charles's problematic son, Wenceslas IV. Then there were sites that recalled those who were martyred during the Hussite period. The Benedictines of the Ostrov Monastery, the Cistercians of the Sedlec community and the Catholic townspeople of Chomutov were all honored after 1620. Clerical victims of the Reformation period were also remembered including fourteen friars who were killed by an angry mob in Prague during the 1611 "Passau incident." A small cult developed around these Franciscans and the place of their martyrdom, St. Mary of the Snows. For many years visitors to the church were shown bloodstains of the fallen heroes. In 1677 Archbishop Waldstein set up a commission to initiate the process of their beatification.[38] Finally, there was the recent past and sites connected to the martyrs of the Bohemian rebellion. Noteworthy here is the pilgrimage chapel of the Moravian priest Jan Sarkander in Olomouc. Sarkander was arrested, tried and executed for his suspected collaboration with Polish mercenaries who had been summoned to help suppress the 1619 uprising in the margravate. His death and grisly torture was a frequent subject of contemporary hagiographical literature. In 1672 a portion of the prison where these events took place was turned into a pilgrimage chapel and attracted such visitors as Jan Sobieski and Maria Theresa who would have been able to see the rack and other instruments of torture that had been used on the priest.[39] By appealing to the collective witness of a persecuted

[38] Ekert, *Posvátná místa*, vol. II, pp. 58–62; K. Minařík, *Čtrnácte ctihodných mučedníků pražských z řádu sv. Františka* (Prague: Nákl. Dědictví sv. Jana Nepomuckého, 1911).

[39] František Odehnal, *Poutní místa Moravy a Slezska* (Prague: Debora, 1995), pp. 80–2; František Hrubý, "Kněz Jan Sarkander, moravský mučedník doby bělohorské a jeho legenda," *ČČH* 95 (1939), 236–71, 445–78.

church, the holy sites of Czech martyrs redefined the nature of time for those who visited them. At these sacred places the past was folded into the present as pilgrims were reminded that they too were members of a community that extended from the valiant Wenceslas to the mutilated but ultimately triumphant Sarkander.

Although the shrines of martyrs may have been one of the more dramatic means of pulling the believer into the church's living tradition, there were other ways in which the pilgrimage phenomenon brought the past into the present. The miracles of these sacred places, be it a mysterious light emanating from St. Mary of the Snows or healings at the tomb of John Nepomuk, were reminders that the community of saints continued to intervene in the lives of faithful Catholics. The use of relics, such as Procopius's chalice in the Eucharist, linked the worshiper to an earlier era. The songs that pilgrims sang en route to various shrines often recapitulated the history of these holy places highlighting the miracles of the past in anticipation of the blessings of the future.[40] The most visible way of appealing to the past, however, was through the actual design of these churches, shrines and chapels. Though the seventeenth and eighteenth centuries were central Europe's great age of the baroque, the use of Gothic architecture continued during this period as well. The prince bishop of Würzburg, Julius Echter von Mespelbrunn (1573–1617), built or renovated more than 100 churches in this style as part of his aggressive program of recatholicization.[41] In Bohemia the Gothic tradition was kept alive and reinvigorated by one of the most original and intriguing architects of all central Europe, Jan Blažej Santini-Aichel (1677–1723).

Santini, the grandson of an architect who had immigrated to Bohemia from northern Italy, was particularly sought after by the kingdom's older monastic orders.[42] The Cistercians, Benedictines and Premonstratensians all entrusted him with significant commissions, for his creative use of space and design was an effective means of expressing a sense of continuity with the past. One of his most remarkable accomplishments was the pilgrimage church of John Nepomuk in Žďár nad Sázavou. Construction on this site

[40] Jiří Fiala and Marie Sobotová, "Vznik kultu Panny Marie Svatokopecké a jeho reflexe v kramářských písních," *ČL* 86 (1999), 61–79; Zdeněk Kalista, "Na cestu poutníkům," in *Česká barokní pouť*, pp. 71–94.

[41] Ludger Sutthof, *Gotik im Barock* (Münster: Lit, 1990), pp. 29–37. For the case of Olomouc see Ondřej Jakubec, *Kulturní prostředí a mecenát olomouckých biskupů potridentské doby* (Olomouc: Memoria Artis, 2003), p. 113.

[42] There is a significant body of literature on Santini though substantially in Czech. Most recent is Mojmír Horyna, *Jan Blažej Santini-Aichel* (Prague: Univerzita Karlova, 1998). For an English summary see Thomas DaCosta Kaufmann's entry in the *Macmillan Encyclopedia of Architects* (New York: Free Press, 1982), vol. III, pp. 660–3.

began shortly after the discovery in 1719 of what was thought to be the miraculously preserved tongue of the priest. Caught up in this great flurry of activity that culminated ten years later with Nepomuk's canonization, the Cistercian abbot, who was the driving force behind this project in Moravia, wanted to use this commission to demonstrate the connection between his community and the original Cistercian monastery in southwest Bohemia where Nepomuk had gone to school as a boy. That monastery had been destroyed by the Hussites, and the Cistercians of Žďár considered their house to be the legitimate heir of the earlier settlement. Santini was asked to make that connection explicit in the church's architectural scheme. His adaptation of the Gothic accomplished that end through a complicated iconographic program that included the use of a statue that had been brought from the original monastery.[43]

Santini was also involved in a project in western Bohemia where he had been charged by the Benedictine community of Kladruby to restore their abbey church. Kladruby was a pilgrimage site associated with St. Wolfgang, who according to legend predicted that this town would one day be home to a great monastery.[44] In the early twelfth century Duke Vladislav I († 1125) did establish a Benedictine cloister here, and pilgrims were later drawn to the site by a miraculous Marian statue. This church did not fare well during the Hussite period. It was destroyed in 1421, and though it was rebuilt in the late sixteenth century, it sustained further damage in the Thirty Years War. In the early eighteenth century Abbot Maurus Finzguth initiated its renovation and selected Santini as his architect after rejecting a proposal by Bohemia's great baroque architect, Christoph Dientzenhofer. At Kladruby one is immediately struck by the Gothic vocabulary Santini employed: the fanciful flying buttresses, the pointed arches and windows, and the stunning climax of the dome that masterfully combined elements of the older style with the newer baroque (Figure 18). The interior with its complicated scheme of ribbed vaulting inventively matched the exterior. Even the church furnishings, the confessional booths, the choir stalls, the tomb of Vladislav I and the exceptional high altar, were created in a Gothic idiom and effectively complemented the building's architectural motifs.

---

[43] Jaromír Neumann, "Das ikonographische Programm der Wallfahrtskirche St. Johannes Nepomuk auf dem Grünen Berg," in *Festschrift Kurt Rossacher* (Salzburg: Verlag des Salzburger Barockmuseums, 1983), pp. 241–63.

[44] Jaromír Neumann, "Ikonologie Santiniho chrámu v Kladrubech," *Umění* 33 (1985), 97–136; Thomas DaCosta Kaufmann, "'Gothico More Nondum Visa': the 'Modern Gothic' architecture of Jan Blažej Santini Aichl," in S. Mossakowski and A. Rottermund, eds., *Artes atque Humaniora* (Warsaw: Instytut Sztuki Polskiej Akademii Nauk, 1998), pp. 317–31.

18. Abbey church of Kladruby, Giovanni Santini-Aichel

Kladruby's architectural scheme, however interesting in itself, speaks more generally to the issue of sacred time and its understanding in the Bohemian setting. For both Santini and Abbot Finzguth, the Gothic of the reconstructed church did not merely represent a revival of an older style. Both architect and patron clearly saw their work as a continuation and evolution of an old and venerable building tradition. As a point of reference, it may be useful to compare this project with a similar undertaking along the Danube at Melk. During this same period another Benedictine abbot, Berthold Dietmayr, was supervising the construction of what became one of the great masterpieces of the Austrian baroque. Aware of each other's work, a type of friendly rivalry developed between Finzguth and Dietmayr as they began exchanging letters. The contrasting architectural styles of these two Benedictine establishments are instructive. The triumphant baroque of Melk matched the Austrian church's relatively easy victory over its Protestant opponents. The Gothic, in contrast, served an entirely different purpose. In the disputed religious landscape of early modern Europe, it spoke to the authority of the past and its claims on the present. Such a style fit the needs of Kladruby, where after two centuries of fierce confessional conflict, an appeal to the past emphasized both the antiquity and continuity of the kingdom's Catholic community.

PILGRIMAGE AND PLACE

Pilgrimage can only grow and prosper in a region where the ground has been properly prepared. In early modern Bohemia this preparatory work was undertaken by a series of clerics and antiquarians who recorded the histories and legends of these holy sites. To use another metaphor these individuals first mapped the contours of the kingdom's sacred geography. This work properly began in the late sixteenth century during those years when pilgrimage was much more of a contested phenomenon. Instrumental here were the efforts of the dean and later provost of St. Vitus Cathedral, Jiří Barthold Pontanus of Breitenberg. Pontanus wrote a biography of St. Ivan to commemorate the dramatic discovery of his remains in 1589. Towards the end of his career he composed his encyclopedic *Bohemia pia* which provided a more extensive overview of "the innumerable saints who have either lived in Bohemia or whose patronage the kingdom celebrates."[45] Pontanus's

---

[45] G. B. Pontanus, *Vita beatae Hroznatae* (Prague: Typis Georgii Nigrini, 1586). G. B. Pontanus, *Vita S. Ivan* (Prague: Typis Georgii Nigrini, 1591); G. B. Pontanus, *Bohemia pia* (Frankfurt: Apud C. Marnium & heredes Io. Aubrii, 1608), p. 48.

successor at the cathedral, Kašpar Arsenius of Radbuza, contended that the very survival of Catholicism in the years before White Mountain was due to the miraculous relics of the kingdom's many saints. His promotion of the Madonna of Stará Boleslav was so effective that even non-Catholics journeyed to Stará Boleslav to see the relic.[46]

After 1620 there was a veritable explosion of this topographical literature. There were the antiquarian surveys of Pešina, Kruger, Beckovský and others whose histories of the kingdom included an examination of its holy places. There was also a more specialized literature that focused on specific shrines as represented by Bohuslav Balbín's trilogy popularizing the Marian sites of Warta, Tuřany and Příbram. Though Balbín's work may be the best known of this genre, throughout the seventeenth and early eighteenth centuries the kingdom's presses were busy producing tracts for even the smallest and most rustic of these chapels.[47] Finally, there was a group of texts that were part of a newer literary form emerging in central Europe. So-called Marian atlases began to appear at the end of the Thirty Years War. Foundational were the publications of the Jesuit Wilhelm Gumppenberg. The first edition of his *Atlas Marianus* came out in Ingolstadt in 1655. Gumppenberg's initially modest undertaking outlined the principal sites of Marian devotion in the Catholic world, but over time the project was expanded. A second edition was issued in 1672 which was later adapted and translated for a Czech audience.[48] Gumppenberg inspired local imitators who composed more than half a dozen atlases specifically for Bohemia.[49] By the centenary of White Mountain this topographical literature had reached its height with its many gazetteers mapping a world of miraculous shrines, holy tombs and wonder-working images. What was happening in print was being matched with developments on the ground, for a series of individual shrines and chapels scattered across the countryside was becoming a more integrated and comprehensive network of pilgrimage sites.

---

[46] From his *O blahoslavené Panně Marii* (Prague: Kašpar Kargesius, 1613) cited in *České nebe* (Prague: National Gallery, 1993), p. 4. A second edition of the text, dedicated to the three survivors of the Prague defenestration, was published in 1629. For the comments of a Protestant professor at the Charles University on the Madonna of Stará Boleslav see Adam Rosacius z Karlsperka, *Oratio Panegyrica de Boemiae reviviscentia* (Prague: Paulus Sessius, 1615), p. 56.

[47] Many of these texts have not survived. For a sample of this literature see those works listed in Josef Jungmann, *Historie literatury české* (Prague: Řiwnáč, 1849), pp. 318–22.

[48] Wilhelm Gumppenberg, *Obrowisstě Maryánského Atlanta*, trans. Antonín Frozín (Prague: Jiří Laboun, 1704); A. Sartorius, *Marianischer Atlas* (Prague: Beringer, 1717). Royt gives an exhaustive overview of this literature in *Obraz a kult*, pp. 28–55.

[49] See for example the work of Georg Castulus, *Peregrinus Mariana Bohemiae tempae obiens* (Prague: Typis Universitatis, 1665), *Hortulus Mariae* (Prague, 1686) or the anonymous tract *Maria Lust-Garten* (Prague, 1704).

The focal point of this landscape was an intriguing set of devotional objects. Many of them had been imported. Václav Plescher, the parish priest of Manětín in western Bohemia, returned from Italy in 1700 with a silver image of the Madonna of the Loreto. It was shortly credited with a number of miracles and became the focus of a local cult. In similar fashion, Daniel Schindler, the Premonstratensian abbot of Želiv and an imperial delegate at the peace negotiations of Utrecht, returned from the Low Countries with a statue of Our Lady of Foy. He, in turn, donated it to the nearby church of Vojslavice where it quickly attracted crowds of pilgrims.[50] Among the many items imported from Spain was the so-called Caravaca cross, a popular devotional object valued by Spanish peasants for its miraculous properties. A cross of this kind had been carried by Dominicus a Jesu Maria into battle at White Mountain. Shortly thereafter, they began appearing on church spires, chapels and columns to ward off the dangers of storms and lightning.[51] There was even a fascinating import from England. A wooden *Pietà*, originally constructed for a church in London but then cast off during the Reformation, eventually surfaced in seventeenth-century Bohemia and was installed in the new pilgrimage church of Liberec in northern Bohemia. Apart from these replicas of statues and icons, there were also reproductions of entire pilgrimage chapels. Alongside the kingdom's many Loretos were copies of Catholic Europe's most famous shrines: Switzerland's Einsiedeln (Ostrov nad Ohří), Bavaria's Altötting (Nová Včelnice) and Austria's Mariazell (Chlum u Třeboně).[52]

Despite the proliferation of these imported models, this new pilgrimage network did not simply reflect the aspirations of an aggressive Catholic church eager to impose standard forms of piety across its territory. Bohemia's new confessional culture took the more universal concerns of the church and creatively blended them with regional traditions. In Prague, for example, chapels dedicated to the Virgin of Altötting and Einsiedeln were balanced with the local cults of Our Lady of St. Stephen and the Virgin of Karlov. Foreign images were successfully domesticated and made part of local religious life. Illustrative in this regard is the pilgrimage complex that developed in Jičín around the Vladimir Madonna. The Jesuits brought a copy of this famous devotional image from Russia to the town in 1637. The

---

[50] Podlaha, *Posvátná místa*, vol. III, pp. 41–55; Boháč, *Poutní místa*, pp. 129, 228; Royt, *Obraz a kult*, pp. 119, 254, 266.
[51] A. K. Huber, "Iberische Kulteinflüsse im Barock der böhmischen Länder," *Königsteiner Studien* 15 (1969), 107–8.
[52] Boháč, *Poutní místa*, pp. 273–4; Vít Vlnas, ed., *The Glory of the Baroque in Bohemia* (Prague: Paseka, 2001), p. 20.

transplantation of this cult in Catholic Europe was generally not successful. In Bohemia, however, the Orthodox icon was well received. Legends of miraculous healings and rescues from danger began to circulate shortly after its arrival while its centenary was celebrated with significant fanfare. A tract written for the occasion chronicled the ever increasing number of miracles that occurred at the site. So popular was the image that a further copy was made for the parish church of Vilémov, creating yet another shrine.[53] Pilgrimage centers could also be constituted on a temporary basis for extraordinary occurrences. When the plague struck Prague in 1680, a Polish Jesuit appealed to Silesia. The Blessed Mother of Piekar, one of the most venerated images in Poland today, was dispatched to the Bohemian capital where it was prominently displayed in St. Salvator Church before returning home with devotional pit stops in Hradec Králové and other towns along the way. The memory of its visit was preserved through votive images commemorating the events of 1680 along with copies of the actual icon.[54] The adaptable nature of pilgrimage culture facilitated the creation of a confessional identity that while strengthening Bohemia's connection with the broader Catholic world reaffirmed its local practices, customs and traditions.

This expanding pilgrimage network also transformed the religious landscape within the kingdom by rebalancing the relationship between the metropole and the periphery. Inversion was a phenomenon that not only reordered social relationships at these shrines, it was also a dynamic that affected geography. Lourdes, Knock and Fátima, the great pilgrimage sites of modern Europe, were far from centers of power and wealth. Marian apparitions, in particular, have tended to occur in rural and isolated locations. From the remote mountaintop of Hostýn in Moravia to the mining town of Příbram, this pattern holds for many of the most important shrines of the Czech lands. Pilgrimage lent supernatural prestige to traditionally marginalized communities and allowed them for a brief period to outshine their more urban and sophisticated rivals. A new geography was being created that dictated importance not by political and economic significance but by divine appointment. Even the smallest shrines with a local and limited audience were part of a broader network united by a common source of grace. These routes also created new links between the hinterland and city. Cults dedicated to Wenceslas, Ludmila, Adalbert and Procopius had multiple sites, shrines which took the pilgrim from rustic hamlets to the hustle and bustle of Prague.

[53] Josef Lauritsch, *První věk rodičky Boží Rušánské* (Hradec Králové: V. J. Tybely, 1743), esp. pp. 72–188.
[54] Vlnas, ed., *The Glory of the Baroque*, pp. 94–5.

Pilgrimage by its very nature is an expression of celebration and victory. From the private space of churches and monasteries, religion is literally moving out of doors and claiming new territory as sacred. In Bohemia this theme of victory was arguably more pronounced than in most other regions of Catholic Europe. Two centuries of confessional conflict had provided the church with a usable past. Through their shrines they could exploit a heritage of persecution and miraculous preservation. This tradition had begun with the wounded image of Strakonice and its supernatural power at White Mountain. The image was copied many times and became the focal point of at least four pilgrimage centers. Its thaumaturgic powers continued long after the actual battle as pilgrims reported scores of miracles well into the eighteenth century.[55] Throughout this period there were many other stories of miraculous icons thwarting the enemies of the church. There was the bleeding Chrudim Christ, an image slashed by Swedish soldiers but later credited with saving an entire town from the plague.[56] At the Franciscan monastery of Bechyně, not one but three images successfully withstood a series of sacrileges by looting Protestants during the Bohemian revolt and subsequently became objects of veneration.[57] Whether it was Hussites (Bohosudov), Bohemian Protestants (Nicov), Hungarian soldiers (Ústí nad Orlicí), Swedish infantry (Dvůr Králové) or simply looters and thieves (Mláka), the story of the victorious icon was one of the most common pilgrimage motifs of the post-White Mountain period.[58]

The theme of confessional victory manifested itself in a variety of other forms at these shrines. Of the many miracles recorded at Příbram's Holy Mountain one category merits special notice. Though supernatural healings or dramatic rescues from danger were certainly attestations of this cult's validity, there was another type of miracle that spoke directly to the power of its heavenly patron. One of the most famous incidents connected to the shrine occurred in 1629. Town authorities in Příbram had commissioned a Protestant artist to paint a devotional image. In the middle of his work the irreverent heretic uttered a few blasphemous remarks against the Virgin. His

[55] *Compendiosa Relatio Thaumaturgae Imagines Virginis. Mariae de Victoria* (Prague: Typis Universitatis Carolo-Ferdinandeae, 1672); *Kurtzer Bericht v.d. wunderthätigen Bild unser Lieben Frauen Maria de Victoria* (Prague, 1706); Z. Wirt, *Klášter a poutní kostel na Bílé Hoře* (Prague: A. B. Černý, 1921). For the many copies of the image and its popularity see Royt, *Obraz a kult*, pp. 222–3.

[56] See in particular the writings of the devout Chrudim physician Václav Petržilka, *Nebeský Lékař Krystus Gežiss* (Prague: Beringer, 1709); 2nd edn (Hradec Králové: V. J. Tybely, 1735); *Fons Ruber, Aneb Czerwená Studánka* (Hradec Králové: J. K. Tybely, 1744).

[57] Jindřich Labe, *Trias Sacra, seu Historica Narratio de Tribus Devotissimis Imaginibus* (Prague: Daniel Michalek, 1685).

[58] Royt, *Obraz a kult*, p. 87.

comments were quickly met with a bolt of lightning dispatched directly from the chapel atop the mountain.[59] In similar fashion there was an account of a cleric who was leading a group of pilgrims home after their trip to the Holy Mountain. During the journey a cynical member of the delegation publicly mocked the Virgin. Once more the response from heaven was prompt. A terrible wind drove the frightened travelers on to an open field where they were overtaken by a violent thunderstorm. All, however, were preserved from injury save for the scoffer who was struck dead by lightning.[60]

Shrines themselves could also become symbols of confessional victory. The small parish church of Zbynice in southwestern Bohemia had been an isolated Catholic outpost during the sixteenth century. Just to its east was an important community of the Bohemian Brethren. The focal point of the church, a statue of the Virgin, helped rally the region's Catholics and later became a memorial of her definitive triumph over the heretics.[61] In the hills further to the south was the forest chapel of Strašín. Long a site of Marian devotion, the Hussites had unsuccessfully tried to suppress this cult. Both Albrecht Chanovský and Bohuslav Balbín highlighted the missionary activity of its local priest, Martin Strakonický, who used this pilgrimage church as his base in the late sixteenth century. Strakonický, who supposedly slept outside the shrine in a simple shelter with a rock as his pillow, spearheaded a devotional revival that was centered on a wonder-working statue of the Virgin. A century later Strašín's parish priest pointed to this ministry and the renewal of the chapel as a critical turning point in the confessional battle for this area.[62] Even more dramatic was the development of the shrine of Votice south of Prague. Before White Mountain a group of the Brethren lived in the area, and its major landowner was the imperial rebel Kašpar Kaplíř, executed in Old Town Square in 1621. The entire character of this community was transformed by the founding of a Franciscan cloister in 1627. The legacy of the Protestant Kaplíř and the *Unitas Fratrum* was quickly replaced with an alternative set of confessional heroes. In 1631 the remains of two Irish Franciscans, who were murdered by Saxon troops entering Prague, were ceremoniously translated to Votice. The new martyrs were soon joined by a miraculous devotional image that was credited with saving the town from marauding Swedish troops in 1645.[63] For faithful

[59] Jan Tanner, *Vestigium Boemiae piae* (Prague: Hosing, 1659), pp. 20–1.
[60] NA, Historie Swato-Horská, Kniha třetí, ŘR, P-118, # 152, 130v, 131r.
[61] Boháč, *Poutní místa*, p. 203. [62] Kalista, "Madona lesů," p. 181.
[63] Severin Vrbčanský, *Nucleus minoriticus* (Prague: Hraba, 1746); Podlaha, *Posvátná místa*, vol. VI, pp. 176–92.

Catholics these pilgrimage centers were powerful sources of divine energy and grace. Here the most obstinate and militant of heretics could not prevail. The Premonstratensians who oversaw Svatý Kopeček reflected this attitude in the records they kept for the shrine. The diligent fathers noted not only the count of annual communicants. They also tallied the numbers of those whose experience at the site ultimately led to their conversion.[64]

This general mood of triumph and victory culminated in the early eighteenth century with a series of major ecclesiastical celebrations focusing on the kingdom's most significant pilgrimage sites. In 1737 the Jesuits of Jičín marked the centennial of the Vladimir Madonna with an elaborate festival that included a procession route lined with 1,500 linden trees. In 1740 the Paulists of Vranov celebrated the five hundredth anniversary of their shrine, an event for which they had been preparing many years.[65] Of greater significance, however, were a series of coronation ceremonies that were new to central Europe. In the early Middle Ages popes had begun to honor famous Marian images or statues by crowning them with small but exquisite coronets. Though this custom had been practiced sporadically, it was revived and supervised with greater oversight in the seventeenth century. Similar to the process of canonization, a specific object had to meet a number of tests before it was accorded this honor. Its antiquity and miraculous nature had to be proven. It must have a long and consistent history of veneration and its cult a broad geographic base. Even if an image met these requirements, the procedure by which one secured final approval from Rome was a complicated bureaucratic affair.[66]

Not surprisingly, official coronations were infrequent occurrences north of the Alps. It is all the more significant, then, that three such ceremonies took place in the Czech lands during the span of four years: Holy Mountain (June 1732), Svatý Kopeček (August 1732) and St. Thomas of Brno (May 1736). All three of these events were elaborate and demanding undertakings. In preparation for the coronation at Svatý Kopeček, an entire forest was leveled while the actual celebrations lasted two weeks. At Příbram over 500 masses were celebrated with nearly 16,000 participants. More than 5,000

[64] Schrabal, "Ortus et progressus," 342r–343v.

[65] Lauritsch, *První věk rodičky Boží Rušánské*; *Aula Dominae Wranovii quingentis annis perpetuo portensis, et gratis celebris* (Brno: M. C. Swobodin, 1740).

[66] Stephan Beissel, *Wallfahrten zu unserer lieben Frau in Legende und Geschichte* (Freiburg i.B.: Herder, 1913), pp. 169–76; Johanna von Herzogenberg, "Zur Krönung von Gnadenbildern vom 18. bis zum 20. Jahrhundert," in F. Büttner and C. Lenz, eds., *Intuition und Darstellung* (Munich: Nymphenburger, 1985), p. 281.

people were confirmed during the festival.[67] The expenses, too, were immense. Religious orders, the nobility and city councils shared the bulk of these not insignificant costs. The crown for the Madonna of St. Thomas with over 400 diamonds, seventy-two rubies, two sapphires and one emerald was financed completely by local resources.[68] Finally, there was the actual lay-out and iconography of these ceremonies. Though ecclesiastical celebrations of the baroque were traditionally elaborate affairs, the complexity of these designs reached new heights. In Brno, for example, a wall between the two major arches of the processional route had been transformed by its eighty-seven illustrations into a veritable encyclopedia of Marian symbolism. In Příbram the 25-meter arch of the town square was illuminated by 800 lamps. To commemorate these events lengthy tracts, often with illustrations, were published describing the iconography of the festivities down to the smallest detail.[69]

These events of the 1730s represent the climax of the church's campaign to promote the kingdom's pilgrimage sites. The coronation of Příbram, in fact, was the first such ceremony in the Empire officially sanctioned by Rome.[70] The metamorphosis of the Holy Mountain from a sleepy regional shrine into one of the most important pilgrimage centers of central Europe speaks to the more general process by which clerical elites were transforming the Bohemian countryside. In Balbín's *Diva Montis Sancti* (1665) an artist chose to superimpose a biblical landscape on the title illustration. A small figure of the Virgin displays a map of the holy sites of the Příbram region while a larger representation of the Holy Mountain is encircled by the hills of Palestine. This illustration highlights a broader dynamic of historicizing or perhaps more accurately "biblicizing" the Czech landscape. This was not an entirely new phenomenon. In the twelfth century Bishop Zdík and Vladislav II established the Premonstratensian house of Mt. Zion in Strahov. Charles IV founded the Emmaus Monastery. Even the Hussites had their Tábor in southern Bohemia. After White Mountain, however,

---

[67] NA, ŘR, sign. P-7, Diarium Residentiae in Sacro Monte, 29.6.1732. My thanks to Markéta Holubová for this reference.

[68] Royt, *Obraz a kult*, p. 158.

[69] For Příbram: *Regina Caeli Corona Gloriae & Majestatis* (Prague: Typis Academicis, 1732); *Wiederbrechung des Glantzes von der durch ihren Sohn...gekrönten...Jungfrauen Maria auf dem heiligen Berg* (Prague: Hraba, 1732); *Refractio splendoris a sanctiss. Virgine et Matre Maria in coelis coronata* (Prague: Hraba, 1732). For Svatý Kopeček: *Krátké vypsání o nalezení* (Hradec Králové: V. J. Tybely, 1733); *Athenaeum sive Universitas Mariae* (Olomouc, 1732); *Der Grossmächtigsten Durchläuchtigsten Kayserin Himmels* (Olomouc, 1733). For Brno: *Gemma Moraviae Thaumaturga Brunensis* (Brno: Typis Jacobi Maximiliani Swoboda, 1736); *Conchylium Marianum* (Brno: M. B. Svobodová, 1736).

[70] Stephan Beissel, *Wallfahrten zu unserer lieben Frau*, p. 321.

there was a more systematic effort to reshape a landscape marred and blighted by heresy. The subsequent architectural *reconquista* followed both biblical and Tridentine models. Apart from the many Loreto chapels, many towns had Calvaries and Holy Sepulchers. The Moravian shrine of Štramberk was consciously styled as a new Mount of Olives while the eccentric Count Sporck created a Bethlehem retreat on his extensive estates of eastern Bohemia. Three pilgrimage chapels were planned for the cloister of Zderaz: one representing the Holy Land of Palestine, another the hallowed city of Rome and a third the sacred kingdom of Bohemia.[71] One of the intriguing features of this architectural program was a near obsession for measurement and detail. The pilgrimage complex of Římov in southern Bohemia featured stations of the cross modeled on the original route in Jerusalem. According to local legend the Jesuits had sent a Capuchin monk to visit the Holy Land and return with the exact dimensions of the route Christ had followed to Golgotha.[72] Architectural historicism captured the imagination of many influential people in seventeenth-century Bohemia including the busy builder and bishop of Hradec Králové, Jan František Kryštof of Talmberk (1676–98), and the kingdom's grand burgrave, Bernard Ignác Martinic (1651–85), who commissioned precise reproductions of Loretos and Altötting chapels.[73]

In similar fashion, many Marian columns sprung up across the country-side. Bendl's famous monument was raised in Prague's Old Town in 1650. By the accession of Maria Theresa in 1740 nearly 200 others could be found across Bohemia and Moravia.[74] Prominently displayed in town squares, these public monuments were a type of victory column. There was a distinct apocalyptic character to many of these memorials as well. The Mary standing atop these columns is not the sweet and gentle mother of Jesus. Perched on a crescent or crushing a dragon, this is the Virgin of St. John's vision on Patmos, the militant Immaculata whose purity was a sign of Catholicism's definitive triumph over Protestant error.[75] These columns, though, were

---

[71] Matěj Tanner, *Hora Oliwetská* (Nisa?: Josef Schlögl, 1704); Ivo Kořán, "Santini a Brokof na Zderaze," *Umění* 45 (1997), 202–8.
[72] Other pilgrimage sites (Votice, Mníšek pod Brdy, Jaroměřice u Jevíčka) also developed stations of the cross following the same model. *České nebe*, p. 17.
[73] Ivana Panochová, "Biblicismy v české architektuře 17. století," *Umění* 52 (2004), 198–217.
[74] See the data of A. Šorm and A. Krajča, eds., *Mariánské sloupy v Čechách a na Moravě* (Prague: Antonín Daněk, 1939), pp. 84–7.
[75] Coreth, *Pietas Austriaca*, pp. 45–50; Franz Matsche, *Die Kunst im Dienst der Staatsidee Kaiser Karls VI* (Berlin: de Gruyter, 1981), vol. I, pp. 142–58; Susan Tipton, "'Super aspidem et basiliscum ambulabis …': Zur Entstehung der Mariensäulen in 17. Jahrhundert," in Dieter Breuer, ed., *Religion und Religiosität in Zeitalter des Barock* (Wiesbaden: Harrassowitz, 1995), vol. I, pp. 385–6.

19. Marian Column, Prague; thesis sheet of J. F. Waldstein (1661)

not only a symbol of Mary's victory over Bohemia's heretics. They also spoke to her triumph over nature itself. A substantial number of these memorials were erected to commemorate her protection from the plague, which swept through the region in 1680 and 1714.[76] The extent to which many Catholics saw these monuments as markers of a new sacred landscape is reflected in the 1661 thesis sheet of the future archbishop Johann Friedrich Waldstein (Figure 19). Designed by Karel Škréta, this detailed illustration features an oversized copy of Prague's Marian column centrally positioned on a map of the European continent. In the heavens are the patron saints of various countries all paying tribute to the Czech Virgin. Radiating from the column itself are a series of lines indicating the distance from different locations on the continent to the Prague column. From the gondoliers of Venice to the Dutch merchants of the Atlantic, from the hunters of

---

[76] Of the 47 columns raised in Moravia (including those dedicated to the Trinity), 34 percent of them were raised in the five-year period following the 1714 plague. Nearly 20 percent of those erected in Bohemia were constructed in the same period.

Scandinavia to the grandees of Spain, all of Europe is irresistibly drawn to its new spiritual center in Bohemia.[77]

This fascination with Bohemia's sacred geography so evident in Škréta's map and the Marian atlases was also present in the pilgrimage shrine itself. After White Mountain a distinctive form of pilgrimage architecture developed in the Czech lands. Initially inspired by Italian models, builders constructed a central sanctuary and then enclosed it with a cloister-like structure. Though there are scattered examples of this style in Franconia and Bavaria, this design scheme is essentially unique to Bohemia where more than thirty shrines were built in this fashion.[78] As opposed to pilgrimage centers with an open architectural plan, the enclosed model effectively marked out a sacred space that was protected from the outside world. Many of these structures, including Příbram's Holy Mountain with its imposing gate and squat towers, seem at first glance more akin to fortresses than chapels. This model of an enclosed sanctuary was on the one hand a means to demarcate the sacred from the profane while on the other it provided artists with an architectural form on which they could physically chart Bohemia's sacred geography. In many of these shrines the visitors were surrounded by illustrations of the kingdom's most important devotional images. At Příbram, for instance, small statues of *putti* decorating the balustrade of the inner courtyard held shields that featured these miraculous objects. When visiting these complexes, then, pilgrims were entering a broader world of Catholic sanctity. Circling the rustic shrine of Řimov in southern Bohemia, they were reminded of the Vladimir Madonna of Jičín, the Virgin of Bohosudov or the wounded image of Strakonice. This self-referential system of mapping was yet one more way to remind the believer that they truly lived in a landscape marked by God's special grace.[79]

Catholic apologists were quick to note, however, that the kingdom's terrain was transformed not only by human activity. Nature itself participated in the process. When the Hussites sacked the Cistercian monastery of Zbraslav in 1420, its famous Madonna was presumed lost or destroyed. Two hundred years later, however, a bird pulling a silken thread in the cloister

---

[77] NK, inventory number 463; O. J. Blažíček, "Škrétova mapa Evropy," *Časopis společnosti přátel starožitností* 60 (1952), 134–41.

[78] Josef Morper, "Zur Geschichte des osteuropäischen Wallfahrtskirchentypus. Heilige Berge und Marianische Gnadenburgen in Böhmen und Mähren," *Die christliche Kunst* 22 (1926), 121–42; Franz Matsche, "Wallfahrtsarchitektur – die Ambitenanlagen böhmischer Wallfahrtsstätten im Barock," in Lenz Kriss-Rettenbeck, ed., *Wallfahrt kennt keine Grenzen* (Munich: Schnell & Steiner, 1984), pp. 352–67.

[79] Johanna Herzogenberg, "Marianische Geographie an böhmischen Wallfahrtsorten. Der Weisse Berg-Rimau in Südböhmen-der Heilige Berg," *Alte und moderne Kunst* 114 (1971), 9–21.

ruins led monks to the popular devotional image that had been miraculously preserved. Deep in the Ore Mountains at the chapel of Bohosudov, a snake indicated where a statue of the Virgin was buried, and it was a miraculous July blizzard that disclosed the location of the original chapel of Bozkov.[80] Though the sanctity of many of these sites was confirmed through the intuition of animals or abnormal weather patterns, natural phenomena did more than merely corroborate the sacred nature of a specific shrine. They spoke to the actual character of the landscape. In the Christian world holy spaces have been traditionally created through human agency. A building is constructed, a votive image is painted, or a relic is dedicated. Reminiscent of ancient nature religions where sanctity was connected to a specific site, holiness in Bohemia was often revealed as part of the landscape. One of the motifs that recurs in Czech pilgrimage literature is the return of an object to its location of origin. A devotional image appears in a tree, and when local authorities attempt to place it in the parish church, it disappears and wondrously reappears back on the tree. Unlike a relic where holiness is portable, these images indicate that a specific location is sacred. Churches at sites such as Hejnice and Křešice actually incorporated holy trees in their architectural design. There were also springs and distinctive rock formations that according to local legends were created on the spot where the Virgin had once appeared. The soil, too, yielded spiritual treasures. While plowing, a peasant uncovered the Madonna of Stará Boleslav, which had been hidden for centuries. More dramatic is the account of a miner in the Giant Mountains who far underground came across a statue of the Virgin that became the focus of the chapel of Nová Paka.[81] These stories of holy rocks, wells and trees remind us how deep and profound the confessional changes within Bohemia were intended to be. While pilgrimage chapels dedicated to the region's many saints reaffirmed the kingdom's holy past, these sites connected to some wonder of nature reminded the believer that the very landscape had been redeemed and now reflected God's glory and truth.

---

[80] Miller, *Historia Mariascheinensis*, pp. 5–6; *The Glory of the Baroque*, p. 37. See more generally Christian, *Local Religion*, p. 208.

[81] Royt, *Obraz a kult*, pp. 86–7; Boháč, *Poutní místa v Čechách*, pp. 110, 264, 271.

CHAPTER 9

Making Bohemia holy: Christian saints and Jewish martyrs

The revival of pilgrimage in Bohemia that reached its highpoint in the early eighteenth century was part of a broader pattern playing out across the Habsburg lands. The mood of celebration at these shrines was matched by a more general spirit of victory and confidence that culminated during the reign of Emperor Charles VI (1711–40). Indeed from start to finish, Bohemia's Counter-Reformation needs to be viewed in tandem with developments shaping both the Habsburg family and the lands they controlled. Though in hindsight Ferdinand II (1619–37) may be remembered for his achievements consolidating his family's holdings, it must not be forgotten that the first half of the seventeenth century was marked by an impending sense of crisis. Ferdinand came within inches of losing Vienna in 1619. His son, Ferdinand III (1637–57), was forced to evacuate Vienna as late as 1645 when the Swedes nearly entered the imperial capital. Even with the successful conclusion of the war matters were far from stable. The Turks were on the move again with their military activity culminating in the dramatic siege of 1683. The peasants remained restless with memories still fresh from the recent uprisings across the Austrian lands. The situation in Bohemia was in some respects even more precarious. For a significant portion of the war, the Swedes moved with impunity across this region. Prague had fallen to the Saxons in 1631. Seventeen years later the Swedes had their turn with the occupation of Prague's left bank and subsequent siege of Old Town. Even when peace had been reestablished, unrest in the countryside remained, reaching a climax with the peasant revolts of 1680.

Though the withdrawal of the Swedes from Prague in 1648 was a critical moment for Bohemia, the real turning point for the Habsburg lands as a whole came in the 1680s. A dashing young soldier who caught Emperor Leopold's attention in 1683 led the Austrians to undreamed of military success. Prince Eugene's campaigns against the Turk resulted in a dazzling series of victories that forced the Ottomans to cede large portions of Hungarian and Transylvanian territory back to the Habsburgs at the peace of Karlowitz (1699). In the west he helped break the hegemony of Louis XIV during the War of the Spanish Succession (1701–14). These accomplishments on the battlefield assisted the Habsburgs in their quest for confessional uniformity. Following a pattern set by Louis XIV with the expulsion of a Huguenot minority and the suppression of a Jansenist opposition, Catholic princes of central Europe took advantage of a propitious moment to settle old religious scores. The most celebrated event was the decision of Salzburg's Archbishop Firmian to send 20,000 Lutherans into exile in 1731. On a far smaller scale the Toruń (Thorn) incident of 1724 put Copernicus's city back on the European map when Polish royal officials executed more than a dozen Lutheran leaders of the city. During this period Charles VI was busy formulating confessional guidelines that would essentially direct Habsburg religious policy until the Edict of Toleration in 1781. Isolating the Protestants of his territories from their co-religionists abroad, the emperor sought their conversion through the combined strategies of evangelization and force. Those communities that resisted the pleas of the missionaries were to be broken up and their inhabitants were to be relocated in the new frontier regions of the east.

Though he faced a number of real limitations, Charles VI was in many respects the last of the Counter-Reformation emperors. After the settlement of the Rákóczi rebellion in 1711, Charles labored diligently to reinvigorate Hungary's Catholic church while restricting its Calvinist rival. It was during his reign that Bohemia's Protestants suffered the last major wave of persecution. The draconian imperial mandates of 1721, 1723 and 1724 were specifically aimed at the secret non-Catholics of the kingdom's eastern region.[1] Charles worked equally hard to project the image of a zealous Catholic prince. The most Spanish of the Austrian Habsburgs, he implemented a strict court protocol that followed the well-established model of the now extinct Spanish branch of the family. As a builder, he revived an imperial iconography that harked back to the days of Charles V. His renovation and expansion of the *Hofburg* with its magnificent library, the Winter Riding School, and the Imperial Chancellery all spoke to the family's dynastic pretensions. But it was his ecclesiastical commissions that may best capture the character of the fervent Habsburg. Up the Danube at nearby Klosterneuburg, Charles had ambitious plans to transform the modest cloister into an Austrian version of the Spanish Escorial. The palace/monastery was to feature nine cupolas in the shape of the

---

[1] A. Gindely, *Die Processierung der Häretiker in Böhmen unter Kaiser Karl VI* (Prague: Verlag der königl. böhm. Gesellschaft der Wissenschaften, 1887).

Austrian crown. Though the full plan was never realized, back in Vienna the emperor was able to push through the construction of the famous *Karlskirche*. Under the direction of Fischer von Erlach and his son, this votive church became the city's most important baroque monument. With its complex iconographic program that united the secular claims and sacred mission of the Habsburg family, the *Karlskirche* is perhaps the clearest representation of Charles's grand view of himself as central Europe's Catholic champion.

As king of Bohemia, Charles made liberal use of an extensive iconographic arsenal in his efforts to memorialize his family's achievements transforming the rebel kingdom. It was under his watch that Fischer laid out the plans of the Bohemian Court Chancellery in Vienna, a building whose architectural scheme embodied the kingdom's recovery through the wise leadership of the Habsburgs. Even more spectacular was the coronation festival of 1723 in Prague to celebrate Charles's accession to the Bohemian throne. Though he had actually assumed the crown twelve years earlier, the occasion had been timed to correspond with the millennium of the city's founding. This milestone event demanded meticulous planning. Nearly every carpenter of central Bohemia was enlisted in the construction of temporary theaters, triumphal arches and elaborate pavilions. The local nobility were compelled to lend furniture, tapestries, carpets and other furnishings to fill the royal castle. For the occasion the city also received its first public lighting system. The celebrations themselves were characterized by an ostentation unmatched by any previous imperial visit. From the actual ceremony in St. Vitus Cathedral to the elaborate coronation opera, *Costanza e Fortezza*, Habsburg propagandists made every effort to portray Bohemia's new prince as the kingdom's hero and illustrious heir of Charles IV.[2]

It is in this setting of dynastic triumph and confessional victory that we find the highpoint of Bohemia's Catholic revival. Only six years after Charles's coronation Prague witnessed its greatest celebration of the baroque era, the canonization of John Nepomuk. The flurry of activity that culminated in the 1729 festivities is a convenient bookend to close our consideration of Bohemia's confessional transformation. We began with a similar though decidedly smaller celebration, the 1627 translation of St. Norbert. Though a modest following for the kingdom's new patron did emerge, Norbert's cult never gained widespread support despite the

[2] Franz Matsche, *Die Kunst im Dienst der Staatsidee Kaiser Karls VI* (Berlin: de Gruyter, 1981), vol. I, p. 315; Vít Vlnas, ed., *The Glory of the Baroque in Bohemia* (Prague: Paseka, 2001), pp. 64–5.

determined efforts of the church. He was a translated saint, an outsider who had been brought to Prague to meet the pressing needs of a beleaguered church. The canonization of John Nepomuk a century later is a stunning indication of the extent to which Bohemia's confessional climate had changed. Emergency assistance from the outside Catholic world was no longer needed. The once heretic kingdom could now produce its own saints. Nepomuk, in fact, became Bohemia's most successful export in the eighteenth century. His cult was propagated from Portugal to Poland, from Mexico to the Philippines. In the broader Catholic world Nepomuk's canonization during the pontificate of Benedict XIII (1724–30) may have been one of the last expressions of a baroque Catholicism that was slowly passing from the scene. The ascetic pope who busily made saints during his short reign was decidedly out of touch with the political realities of his day. His more worldly and pragmatic successors would refrain from Benedict's strident rhetoric that so alienated both Catholic and Protestant princes. But in 1729 a mood of confessional triumphalism still held sway in Rome and central Europe.

MAKING A NATIVE SAINT

John Nepomuk was an unlikely saint, an ecclesiastical bureaucrat who rose from obscurity to become one of central Europe's great celebrities of the eighteenth century. The son of a minor noble, Nepomuk was born *circa* 1345 in a small village in southwestern Bohemia. Though we know little of his early life, he eventually came to Prague and began a career in the church. There he studied at the university before heading south and completing his academic training in Padua. Once he returned to Prague in the late 1380s, he quickly worked his way up the church hierarchy. His career culminated with his appointment as vicar-general of the archdiocese. Upward mobility had its price, for as principal aide of the archbishop, the strong-willed Jan Jenštejn, Nepomuk had his fatal encounter with King Wenceslas IV. Like the famous confrontation between England's Thomas Becket and Henry II, the relationship between Jenštejn and Wenceslas also degenerated into a deadly power struggle. As tensions escalated and tempers flared, a parley was arranged between the two parties in March 1393. The meeting quickly broke down, however, when a stormy Wenceslas peremptorily arrested the archbishop's delegation. Though Jenštejn escaped, Nepomuk did not. He was imprisoned, tortured and executed. When the king's henchmen had finished their task, they threw his body into the Moldau.

Legends quickly developed around the unfortunate priest. Jenštejn, who fled to Rome, wrote to the pope that Nepomuk had died a saintly martyr's death. Similar stories began to circulate in Prague. The archbishop's confidant and later biographer, Petr Klarifikátor, described a miraculous aura of light that surrounded the tortured priest once he had been thrown from the bridge. The body itself had initially been laid to rest in a church adjacent to the river, but popular sentiment was such that only three years later Nepomuk was moved up the hill and interred in St. Vitus. As time passed, chroniclers would draw sharp contrasts between the saintly Nepomuk and the tyrannous king. In his history of the Great Schism, Ludolf von Sagan vilified Wenceslas as a second Nero while praising the priest as a holy martyr.[3] Thomas Ebendorfer in the fifteenth century added another critical component to the Nepomuk legend. The Viennese scholar contended that Nepomuk had been the confessor of Queen Sophie and that his refusal to betray the secrets of the confessional to her jealous husband had ultimately led to the priest's torture and death.[4] In the following century Václav Hájek compiled a number of these accounts in his *Czech Chronicle* which was later copied and modified by antiquarians of the baroque era.

It was not, however, until the end of the sixteenth century that there was a more concerted effort to promote the Nepomuk cult. Antiquarians and artists, musicians and missionaries, preachers and playwrights all collaborated on the project of transforming Jenštejn's unlucky lieutenant into a saint with a worldwide following. The antiquarians initiated the process. Though Hájek was a Catholic, the appeal of his chronicle cut across religious boundaries and was especially popular with many in the Utraquist community. The real turning point, though, came late in the century with the work of that tireless promoter of Czech saints, Jiří Pontanus. Pontanus was among the first to recognize Nepomuk publicly as one of Bohemia's patrons. His 1599 prayer book, published in both Latin and Czech, included petitions to the martyr and unofficial saint. Three years later he highlighted Nepomuk again, this time in a collection of hymns.[5] After White Mountain the slow trickle of publications on Nepomuk gradually developed into a steady stream. Most significant of

[3] Petr Klarifikátor, "Vita Joannis de Jenczenstein," KNM XIV E 19; Ludolf von Sagan, *Tractatus de longevo schismate*, ed. Johann Loserth, *AÖG* 60 (1880), 345–561.

[4] Thomas Ebendorfer, *Chronica regum Romanorum*, ed. H. Zimmermann (Hannover: Hahnsche Buchhandlung, 2003), pp. 627–1249.

[5] *Spirituale Regni Boemiae jubilum* (Prague: Georgius Nigrinus, 1599); *Duchovní obveselení Koruny České* (Prague: Jiří Černý z Černého Mostu, 1599); *Hymnorum sacrorum … Libri tres* (Prague: N. Straus, 1602).

these early texts was the 1641 Latin treatise, *Fama posthuma Ioannis Nepomuceni*, the first full synthesis of the Nepomuk legend. Appearing simultaneously in Latin, Czech and German, the three editions were part of a campaign to erect a church dedicated to Nepomuk on the site of the saint's birthplace.[6] Two decades later Jan Ignác Dlouhoveský began work on an influential biography of Nepomuk while also publishing a popular prayer book that promoted the cult. In 1669 Jiří Kruger included an entry on Nepomuk in a short devotional work. Kruger, in fact, concluded his text by calling upon the pope to begin the formal process of canonization.[7] It was Bohuslav Balbín, however, who became Nepomuk's greatest champion. Pulling from a variety of sources including Dlouhoveský's unpublished biography, Balbín stitched together a life of the fourteenth-century martyr that he presented to the cathedral chapter in 1671. By this time the Nepomuk legend had assumed elements that were markedly similar to hagiographical accounts of Bohemia's other patrons. Though Balbín was forced to revise portions of the text, the amended version was published by the Bollandists in 1680 as part of the *Acta sanctorum*. Two years later Balbín adapted it for *Bohemia sancta*, his mammoth study of official and unofficial saints of the Czech kingdom.[8]

A group of artists collaborated with the antiquarians to promote the Nepomuk cult on the visual level. The first woodcut of Nepomuk, a depiction of the priest hearing the confession of Queen Sophie, was produced for Pontanus's 1602 hymnbook while the first known painting of the martyr was executed seven years later as a votive image for the Bendectine abbot of Broumov, Wolfgang Zelender.[9] The early biographies of Nepomuk were not only important for their printed content but also for their illustrations. *Fama posthuma* included five engravings based on the work of Karel Škréta, designs that helped shape the emerging iconography of Bohemia's new patron. The artistic celebration of the Nepomuk cult, which quickly spread around the world, began at St. Vitus Cathedral in the immediate aftermath of White Mountain. Nepomuk's tomb had been dismantled as part of the iconoclastic program of the Winter King.

---

[6] *Fama posthuma Ioannis Nepomuceni* (Prague: Typis Academicis, 1641); V. Vlnas, *Jan Nepomucký, česká legenda* (Prague: Mladá fronta, 1993), pp. 76, 78–80.

[7] J. I. Dlouhoveský, *Koruna Cžeská* (Prague: Jiří Cžernoch, 1673); Jiří Kruger, *Maiales Triumphi* (Litomyšl: J. Arnolt, 1669), pp. 8–10.

[8] The biography would also appear in three handsome posthumous editions that were produced in the years surrounding Nepomuk's beatification and canonizaton: *Vita B. Joannis Nepomuceni martyris* (Augsburg: Typis J. J. Lotteri, 1725); *Das Leben des seligen Joannis v. Nepomuck* (Augsburg, 1725); *Vita S. Joannis Nepomuceni* (Augsburg: Pfeffel, 1730).

[9] Jan Royt, *Der Hl. Johannes von Nepomuk* (Munich: Schnell & Steiner, 1993), p. 13.

Arguably the most important aspect of the cathedral's subsequent renovation was the new emphasis that was devoted to the veneration of the martyred priest. In May 1621 intricate new grillwork was erected around Nepomuk's tomb to replace what had been carted off by the Protestant workmen. In a solemn ceremony the following July, Archbishop Lohelius dedicated a new altar to the kingdom's patrons including "the glorious martyr, the holy John Nepomuk." About the same time Caspar Bechteler carved the panels of the ambulatory that depicted the destruction of Nepomuk's tomb and God's swift punishment of the Saxon ironsmith who had foolishly desecrated the holy site. In 1630 the cathedral chapter commissioned Bechteler to add a relief of Nepomuk to the main door of the church. Shortly thereafter, one of the cathedral's most precious relics, the Jerusalem Candelabrum, was redeployed and used to decorate the priest's tomb. This artistic activity at St. Vitus culminated in 1736 with a massive baroque sepulcher designed by Joseph Emanuel Fischer von Erlach.[10]

In the midst of this artistic and antiquarian activity, church leaders had initiated a diplomatic and legal process to secure Nepomuk's canonization. The first steps were taken by Archbishop Sobek of Bílenberk. The archbishop was an eager promoter of the kingdom's saints. He had renovated the major shrine of St. Ivan, popularized the Wenceslas cult, and in 1673 he initiated discussions with Rome regarding the Nepomuk case.[11] For assistance he turned to the university, seeking the counsel of the school's theologians. They warned the archbishop that the process could be long and complicated. The new guidelines for canonization set in place by Urban VIII were rigorous, and the Nepomuk campaign did languish after the archbishop's death in 1675. It was briefly revived by Leopold I in 1699 though there were still significant hurdles to clear. The antiquity of the cult had to be authenticated, and after initial inquiries it was discovered that there were substantial holes in the archival records. Somewhat discouraged by this disappointing news, Archbishop Breuner (1695–1710) did not move forward quickly.

The turning point came in 1714 with the accession of Ferdinand Khünburg as Prague's eighteenth archbishop. He made Nepomuk one of the highest priorities of his administration. Hearings on his beatification began in spring 1715. Three tribunals gathered oral testimony in Prague,

---

[10] Franz Matsche, "Das Grabmal des hl. Johannes von Nepomuk im Prager Veitsdom," *Wallraf-Richartz-Jahrbuch* 38 (1976), 92–122.

[11] For an overview of the proceedings see Vlnas, *Jan Nepomucký*, pp. 98–127; Johanna von Herzogenberg, "Zum Kult des heiligen Johannes Nepomuk," in *Johannes von Nepomuk* (Munich: Schöningh, 1973), pp. 25–35.

Olomouc and Vienna. Working through the libraries of the St. Vitus
Cathedral chapter, the Strahov Monastery, and the archiepiscopal palace,
a subcommittee collected written evidence that affirmed the antiquity of the
cult. The climax of these proceedings came in April 1719 with the opening of
Nepomuk's tomb. Here examiners found what they believed was the
miraculously preserved tongue of the martyred priest.[12] News of this discovery buoyed the hopes of many, and to further Nepomuk's cause with
Rome an extensive lobbying campaign was initiated. Both Charles VI and
his wife Empress Elizabeth, a former Lutheran from Saxony, sent letters to
Clement XI pleading for Nepomuk's speedy beatification. The Empire's
leading princes, including a descendant of the Winter King, sent letters as
well. Within the church there was also a massive mobilization of support.
From the archbishops of Mainz and Cologne to the local Bohemian bishops
of Hradec Králové and Litoměřice, nearly every diocese of the Empire sent
enthusiastic letters to the pope.[13]

The matter was finally put before the Congregation of the Holy Rites. As
a part of the official process, the church turned to one of its most astute
canon lawyers, Prospero Lambertini, who had been appointed "devil's
advocate" in 1712. It was Lambertini's job to challenge the evidence that
was put forward. But though the future pope had substantial misgivings,
Nepomuk's cult was officially confirmed on 31 May 1721. Beatification,
though, was only the first step. Once more, evidence was gathered in Prague
with further depositions and new forays into the archives.[14] A shift in papal
politics also assisted the Nepomuk campaign. In 1724 the ascetic Cardinal
Orsini was elected Benedict XIII. Out of place in the more worldly
surroundings of palace and court, the austere Orsini was something of a
medieval throwback with his forceful assertions of papal authority and his
enthusiastic support of frequent canonization. When the case was earnestly
pressed in Rome and accompanied with sizeable financial contributions
from both the emperor and the Bohemian church, it was only a matter of
time before Archbishop Khünburg's long-awaited dream would be realized.
Once the question of miracles had been addressed, the final issue had been

---

[12] For the deposition see *Acta utriusque processus in causa canonisationis beati Joannis Nepomuceni martyris* (Vienna: Schilgen, 1721), pp. 363–82.
[13] APH-AMKSV, Codex LXI; *Acta utriusque processus*, pp. 247–96.
[14] See the following holdings of the NA: Acta Processus Canonisationis seu Declarationis Martyrii B. Joannis Nepomucni, APA I, B 60/1; Jura Compulsata in Processu Canonisationis B. Joannis Nepomuceni, APA I B 61/1; ČDK, IV B 1, Kart. 341, Jednání o kanonizaci Jana Nepomuckého: 1710–1731.

laid to rest. Nepomuk's canonization was officially celebrated in the Basilica of St. John Lateran in March 1729.

The celebrations in Bohemia that accompanied Nepomuk's canonization were the most elaborately produced festivals the kingdom had ever witnessed. Far exceeding the festivities that had honored the translation of St. Norbert a century earlier, the primary celebration took place in Prague on 9–16 October. Though special events and processions were staged throughout the city, the focal point was the cathedral. Before the church craftsmen erected a massive four-tower structure that memorialized Nepomuk's ministry in Prague. In front of the doors of St. Vitus was a stage flanked by two fountains representing the river of Nepomuk's birthplace, the Úslava, and that of his martyrdom, the Moldau. The cathedral, itself, was specially decorated for the occasion. Fourteen tapestries depicting the major scenes of Nepomuk's life had been shipped north from the original celebration in St. John Lateran. The pilgrims who flooded the city for the octave doubled if not tripled Prague's population. For that period over 30,000 masses were said in St. Vitus while the Eucharist was reportedly served to more than 200,000 at Nepomuk's tomb alone.[15]

The church organized festivities celebrating Nepomuk's canonization in nearly every major city of the Habsburg domains. Even smaller towns such as the mining community of Kremnica in Upper Hungary staged ceremonies to honor the new saint. At first glance, then, it would seem as if Nepomuk's cult had a broad following across central Europe. But upon closer examination it is clear that the situation was actually more complex. In Salzburg, for example, the archbishop canvassed his territory in 1701 and found that, though the cult was known to the nobility, the common folk had little knowledge of Nepomuk. Within the Czech kingdom the situation was only marginally better. Reports from the 1690s indicate that in times of crisis residents of Nepomuk's hometown turned not to the martyred priest but directed their prayers to the Virgin and St. Adalbert. When nearly two decades later Archbishop Khünburg initiated the process of beatification, he surveyed his parishes only to discover that many under his care knew little to nothing of the prospective saint.[16] What then are we to make of the widespread activities celebrating Nepomuk's canonization and the subsequent spread of the cult? Was he another Norbert, a new patron for the kingdom

---

[15] For a sample of the significant body of ephemeral literature describing the events see *Agnus Dei e Cera Virgine* (Prague: Typis Academicis, 1729) (NK, 51 A 14, #6); also useful are the tracts in SK, BS I 53; BX II 12; Vlnas offers a brief overview in *Jan Nepomucký*, pp. 159–68.

[16] Leopold Schmidt, "Die volkstümliche Verehrung des heiligen Johannes von Nepomuk," in *Johannes von Nepomuk* (Passau: Passavia, 1971), p. 98; Vlnas, *Jan Nepomucký*, pp. 104, 106.

who would never have more than a limited following? Or worse, was he a second Joseph, a patron saint essentially imposed by the Habsburgs in 1654 only to be generally forgotten by the people?

At its very base, the cult of John Nepomuk was a phenomenon of the elites. The archbishop and the emperor were the two individuals most responsible for Nepomuk's canonization. Supporting their efforts was a dedicated group of nobles who helped transform the cult of a relatively unknown priest into one that eventually stretched from Asia to the Americas. Two families merit special notice. In Rome Khünburg's case for Nepomuk's canonization had critical inside support. Instrumental was the work of Cardinal Michael Friedrich von Althan. While visiting Rome in 1721, Althan's nephew, Count Michael Karl, narrowly escaped serious injury at a musical performance when a dilapidated stage on which he was standing suddenly gave way. The cardinal attributed his nephew's miraculous preservation to Nepomuk and continued by doggedly pushing the case forward despite the growing skepticism of Lambertini and others. Back in Bohemia another family was responsible for popularizing the cult. As the story was later recounted, while crossing the Charles Bridge in 1646 Matthias Wunschwitz saw an image of a cross marking the spot of Nepomuk's martyrdom. Considering this vision a divine commission, Wunschwitz pledged that his family would do all in their power to propagate devotion to the future saint. True to their word, the family soon had a proprietary interest in Nepomuk. They commissioned the statue for Charles Bridge, and the clan's next generation supported the renovations of his tomb in the cathedral. Even their private veneration of Nepomuk had an important public dimension. Once the bronze monument of Nepomuk had been cast for the bridge, the original statue of Jan Brokoff was requisitioned by the family and housed in their private chapel, first in their castle outside Prague and then after 1718 in their city palace in Old Town. Opened at times to the public, the chapel became an informal site of pilgrimage with devotees bringing flowers, candles and other votive gifts.[17]

It was not just in Bohemia where the elites took the lead as Nepomuk's principal promoters. In Styria, for example, devotion to Nepomuk can be traced back to Countess Elise Rosine von Herberstein who in 1694 brought a small votive picture of the priest back from Prague and donated it to the

---

[17] Most important for the Wunschwitz family is the so-called *Gedächtnus-Monument* compiled by Johann Anton Cajetan Wunschwitz (SK, D II 22); on the Nepomuk statue and the yearly feast day celebrations organized by the family see *Wunschwitziana Miscellanea. Anniversariis honoribus sancto Joanni Nepomuceno sacris* (SK, AO XI 14).

Church of the Holy Blood where it became the focus of a local cult. Nepomuk also had significant exposure in Poland thanks in large part to Augustus II, who was a strong advocate of his canonization. His successor, the unfortunate Stanisław Leszczyński, would further the cause, and once he had lost his throne for a second and final time he would bring Nepomuk to France. As the Duke of Lorraine, he eventually donated his personal collection of the saint's relics to the Blois cathedral. With the marriage of his daughter to Louis XV, the cult was transported to Versailles itself.[18]

The religious orders were also instrumental in propagating the Nepomuk cult. In the months leading up to his beatification, at least a dozen were involved in the general lobbying campaign.[19] After his canonization they continued their efforts. While the Premonstratensians, Theatines and Benedictines focused their energies primarily in Bohemia, the Franciscans and Capuchins were especially important in promoting the new saint in Italy. The Jesuits, however, were the most active and effective of all these groups. With an extensive network of colleges and missions, they were well equipped to spread this new form of devotion. Particularly important were their literary activities that now broadened out from the narrower antiquarian studies of a previous generation to include works intended for a more general audience. In southern Italy they used Latin epics and even a baroque novel to popularize his cause. In Brazil they produced plays celebrating his virtues. A few years later in Mexico, Juan Antonio de Oviedo wrote a well-received popular biography. Even a small island in the Gulf of California was named in his honor. In the Pacific, a life of Nepomuk was translated into Tagalog in 1741 while a Chinese study of the saint was prepared at approximately the same time. Back in Europe the Flemish Jesuit, Joseph Wielens, wrote what became the most influential biography of Nepomuk for the late eighteenth and nineteenth centuries.[20]

[18] *Acta utriusque processus*, pp. 252–3; H. J. Mezler-Andelberg, "Bemerkungen zur Verehrung des hl. Johannes von Nepomuk," in H. Wiesflecker and O. Pickl, eds., *Beiträge zur allgemeinen Geschichte* (Graz: Akadem. Druck- u. Verlagsanst., 1975), p. 33; Anton Pinsker, "Die Gesellschaft Jesu und der hl. Johannes von Nepomuk," in *250 Jahre Hl. Johannes Nepomuk* (Salzburg: Dommuseum zu Salzburg, 1979), p. 60.

[19] APH-AMKSV, Codex LXI, 40r–41v, 50r–51r, 54r, 66r–67v, 72r–73r, 78r–v, 96r–97v, 102r–103v, 104r.

[20] F. M. Galluzzi, *Vita di San Giovanni Nepomuceno* (Rome: Komarek, 1729); Juan Antonio de Oviedo, *Vida admirable y triunfante muerte de S. Juan Nepomuceno* (Mexico City: Por Joseph Bernardo de Hogal, 1727); Joseph Wielens, *Histoire de saint martir Jean de Nepomuc* (Antwerp, 1759). Useful on the spread of the Nepomuk cult is Zdeněk Kalista, "Čeští světci v cizině barokní," in V. Mathesius and J. Štyrský, eds., *Co daly naše země Evropě a lidstvu* (Prague: Evropský literarní klub, 1939), pp. 197–9. Most exhaustive is Yves Lasfargues, "Le culte mondial de Saint-Jean Népomucène aux XVIIe et XVIIIe siècles," unpublished Ph.D. thesis, Université de Paris (1965).

Despite their considerable influence it was not just lay and clerical elites who were responsible for propagating this new form of devotion. Confraternities were also involved. Evidence from the canonization hearings indicates that in Prague a group of townspeople began informally to promote the Nepomuk cult as early as the 1680s. A chapel dedicated to the future saint was built next to the Emmaus Monastery in 1691 while five years later the first Nepomuk confraternity was organized here. Eventually, there would be more than twenty Nepomuk confraternities scattered across the archdiocese, the most dedicated to any saint save that of Barbara. The Nepomuk brotherhoods promoted the cult through a variety of means. They wore rings or medals of the saint's image. They helped organize the annual celebrations honoring his feast of 16 May. The confraternities sponsored the construction of one of Prague's most beautiful churches, the exquisite St. John Nepomuk on the Rock. There on his feast day some of the city's most famous preachers climbed to a platform atop the façade and beneath an obelisk capped with a golden image of Nepomuk's tongue spoke to huge crowds assembled outside the church.[21]

The new saint's most active patrons employed a broad range of means to transform the cult from a phenomenon of the elites to a devotional form with genuine popular support. Undoubtedly, the most important tool at their disposal was the sermon. It was from the pulpit that most learned the basic contours of the Nepomuk legend. There are in the libraries of the Czech lands today at least 130 extant eighteenth-century homilies extolling the virtues of the martyred priest. Of these sermons, approximately 60 percent were composed in Czech while the remainder were produced in either German or Latin. This was a saint, then, who easily crossed linguistic and ethnic boundaries.[22] The production of this literature was not centered exclusively in Prague. Brno, Hradec Králové, Kutná Hora and Litomyšl all had their presses busily printing sermons. Especially worthy of note were the efforts of the Cistercian abbot Václav Vejmluva who in the tiny village of Žďár nad Sázavou, the home of Santini's remarkable pilgrimage church, established an important center for the publication of these texts.[23] In the hands of a skillful orator Nepomuk could serve a variety of homiletic uses. His story was one that could be creatively shaped and molded to meet an ever-changing series of needs. At times he was portrayed

[21] NA, Náboženská Bratrstva, Inv. c. 627, Sign. XVII/26, Kart. 128; Vlnas, *Jan Nepomucký*, pp. 173–6.
[22] Michaela Horáková, "Italský přínos svatonepomucenské homiletice na českém území," in Vilém Herold and Jaroslav Pánek, eds., *Baroko v Itálii – baroko v Čechách* (Prague: Filosofia, 2003), pp. 357–8.
[23] See chapter 7, fn. 48. On the entire Žďár complex see Zdeněk Kalista, *Česká barokní gotika a její žďárské ohnisko* (Brno: Blok, 1970).

as a symbol of Bohemia's Catholic revival while in other instances he was used as a polemical foil against crypto-Protestants or elevated as an example of Christian charity.[24]

Drama was frequently used in conjunction with sacred rhetoric. Its reach, in fact, was often even greater. From Protestant audiences in the Baltic to Orthodox crowds in Russia, plays on the life of Nepomuk were presented across the continent in the eighteenth century. These dramatic productions, though, varied significantly. There was a series of performances that were connected directly to his canonization and almost liturgical in nature.[25] Of greater impact was the use of Nepomuk in school drama. As early as 1689, the Jesuits were staging performances with their students at the Clementinum. Jesuit instructors creatively used Nepomuk's life story to teach a variety of moral and devotional lessons. Antonín Machek, who wrote a series of plays on Nepomuk in the early eighteenth century, was particularly adept at tailoring his material for the spiritual needs of his students.[26] Nepomuk also made the jump to a new popular form of theater that was beginning to develop in central Europe. In 1724 Josef Anton Stranitzky produced a dramatization of the saint's martyrdom in Vienna. Stranitzky's Nepomuk was more solemn than most of his plays that featured the sly Hanswurst, and over time the martyred priest became a more frequent subject in this type of popular drama. Inventive playwrights combined more serious themes from the saint's life with scenes of mild comic relief.[27]

Music was a prominent feature of many of these theatrical performances. The use of song helped draw the audience more directly into the drama unfolding before them and heightened its effect. More generally, songs, as one contemporary observer noted, were one of the most effective means of spreading the Nepomuk cult. Singing pilgrims crossed borders disseminating news of Bohemia's saint.[28] Throughout this period the kingdom's

---

[24] Matěj Bartys, *Růže Nad potoký Wod wsazená* (Prague: Matěj Höger, 1733); J. T. A. Berghauer, *Apologia oder Schutz-Schrifft für den Heiligen Joanne Nepomuceno* (Dillingen: Schwertlen, 1730).

[25] Most notable in this regard was the elaborate musical allegory of the Moravian Jesuit Antonín Saletka staged in October 1729 as part of the broader canonization festivities in the Bohemian capital. *Fama sancta sub sacram S. Joannis Nepomuceni Apotheosim in erigendo* (UK, 51 A 14, nos. 17, 18). Also see the synopsis of the drama produced for his beatification, NA, ČDK, IV B 1, Kart. 341, *Jednání o kanonizaci Jana Nepomuckého: 1710–1731*, unpaginated synopsis.

[26] NA, SM, J 20/17/18, Kart. 998–1000.

[27] Fritz Homeyer, ed., *Stranitzkys Drama von "Heiligen Nepomuck"* (Berlin: Mayer & Müller, 1907); František Černý, ed., *Dějiny českého divadla* (Prague: Academia, 1968), vol. I, p. 315; Leopold Schmidt, "Volksschauspiele vom hl. Nepomuk. Sammlung volksdeutscher Legendenspiele," *Volk und Volkstum. Jahrbuch für Volkskunde* 2 (1937), 239–47.

[28] APH-AMKSV, Codex LXI, 90r–v.

presses busily produced hundreds of songs in Nepomuk's honor. During the eighteenth century, new hymns to Nepomuk in fact exceeded those dedicated to Wenceslas by nearly a factor of twenty.[29] The growth and spread of this music was not restricted by language. The earliest German songs to Nepomuk can be dated to the beginning of the eighteenth century. This genre developed quickly, and hymns to Nepomuk were soon sung throughout the German Catholic world. These songs, in fact, were so ubiquitous that it was not long before irreverent wits were producing clever parodies of them.[30] For the more pious, songs served a variety of purposes. A hymn to Nepomuk in Jan Josef Božan's *Heavenly Nightingale* spoke of the saint's power to convert the most stubborn sinner. Then there were those that celebrated Nepomuk as a defender of widows and orphans. Still others focused on the miracles attributed to the saint's intercessory powers.[31] These songs were often incorporated into a larger devotional text. Extolling the virtues of Nepomuk for ordinary believers, confraternities were particularly eager patrons of this type of literature.[32] Typical in this regard is Johann Fiebiger's *Holy Life*. Fiebiger, a former Lutheran, who had been so moved by the canonization proceedings in Prague that he converted, wrote a biographical meditation of Nepomuk in rhyming verse that saluted the saint as a powerful intercessor for sinners today. From Ljubljana to Poznań, from Cologne to Vienna, Catholic presses quickly flooded the market with this type of devotional literature.[33]

Of all the saints of eighteenth-century central Europe, Nepomuk was undoubtedly the most physically present, and it was the medium of sculpture that was most responsible for his seeming ubiquity. The monument on Charles Bridge served as a prototype for countless statues on bridges, squares and churches across the continent. Nearly forty were erected in Vienna while even a small town such as Bruck an der Leitha could boast of six Nepomuk monuments. These statues often became the focus of devotional rituals. On the saint's feast day trumpeters led processions of the faithful to these monuments where prayers were offered, hymns sung and litanies recited. In the Westphalian village of

---

[29] *Knihopis*, 7872–8339 (Nepomuk); 12594–12618 (Wenceslas).
[30] Schmidt, "Die volkstümliche Verehrung," pp. 103–4.
[31] Jan Josef Božan, *Slavíček rájský* (Hradec Králové: V. J. Tybely, 1719), pp. 644–5.
[32] See for example *Alles für alle* (Prague: Beringerin, 1706); *Swatý Jan z Nepomuku w Mladosti swé ku Křizi se vtikagjcý* (Prague, 1743).
[33] Johann Gottlob Fiebiger, *Heiliges Leben, Glorwürdiger Martyrer-Tod, und Herrliche Canonization des Böhmischen Thaumaturgi St. Johannis von Nepomuck* (Prague: J. N. Fitzky, 1736?); Pinsker, "Die Gesellschaft Jesu," pp. 62–3.

Reitberg a "Nepomuk way" was constructed with statuary marking seven stations of Nepomuk's life, death and glorification. Thesis sheets were also important as students frequently commissioned artists to produce a scene from the saint's life such as the one produced in 1699 (Figure 20). In 1720 a Capuchin friar singled out this medium as one of the most effective means of spreading the cult.[34] English visitors to Prague in 1734 commented that these early modern posters were nearly everywhere. From the rooms of local taverns to the city's many churches, thesis sheets were used both as decoration and devotional objects. It seems likely that this art form may not have been as ephemeral as many have assumed, for the specific illustration of Nepomuk identified by the travelers was in all likelihood one produced for a defense that had occurred nearly thirty years earlier.[35]

Painters also contributed to this campaign. Though the first illustration of the priest only dated from the beginning of the seventeenth century, once the iconography had been set in place, Nepomuk began appearing in cathedrals, churches and chapels with ever increasing regularity. In Vienna Franz Anton Maulbertsch created a series of Nepomuk drawings that were widely distributed as New Year's cards by a local confraternity. In Bohemia proper well over a 100 churches and chapels were dedicated to Nepomuk and filled with art highlighting his life and martyrdom. Ordinary believers were also likely to encounter images of Nepomuk through new forms of liturgical art. Chasubles and crosiers, monstrances and chalices, banners and antependiums, reliquaries and bells were frequently adorned with Nepomuk motifs. Outside the church there were many other contexts where one encountered the priest. Hundreds of medals were cast to commemorate various celebratory occasions connected to the saint: the discovery of his miraculously preserved tongue, his beatification, his canonization, and the erection of his new tomb. Cheaper versions of these medals were hawked by peddlers to visiting tourists as trinkets and charms while natives frequently wore Nepomuk pendants.[36] The saint also invaded domestic

---

[34] APH-AMKSV, Codex LXI, 90r–v. Of the 526 thesis sheets that survive today in Prague's National Library, there are more than twenty illustrations of Nepomuk. Anna Fechtnerová, *Katalog grafických listů univerzitních tezí uložených ve Státní knihovně ČSR v Praze*, 4 vols. (Prague: Státní knihovna ČSR, 1984), vol. IV, p. 741.

[35] "The travels of three English gentlemen, in the year 1734," in *The Harleian Miscellany* (London: White, 1810), vol. V, p. 359. The travel account speaks of a sheet of "one Paulus Woloczka," in all likelihood a reference to the 1707 sheet of Paulus Wodiczka (NK, inventory number 359).

[36] For a description of medals at Nepomuk's canonization see NA, ČDK IV B 1, Kart. 341; *Johannes von Nepomuk, 1393–1993* (Munich: Bayerisches Nationalmuseum, 1993), pp. 142–9; "The travels of three English gentlemen," p. 349.

20. Jan Nepomuk in glory, 1699 thesis sheet

space. Small devotional engravings, glass paintings and folding pictures filled the homes of eighteenth-century Bohemians. Even furniture and kitchen items such as ceramic jugs were decorated with Nepomuk iconography.

It is not without reason then that Nepomuk has been described by one scholar as "the quintessential saint of the baroque."[37] But though his image may have been virtually imprinted on the central European landscape, it is less clear what the new cult actually meant to its many devotees. This issue in fact was a significant point of contention for Czech scholars during the nineteenth and twentieth centuries. Many asserted that Nepomuk was a Habsburg invention foisted on the nation to suppress allegiance to the kingdom's true saint, Jan Hus, or as more modern scholars have put it, a tool of princely absolutism directed against the interests of the Bohemian estates.[38] While others countered this argument with equal vehemence, the debate reflected the extent to which the study of post-White Mountain Bohemia remained locked within tight nationalist parameters. Nepomuk was either an expression or denial of the true Czech nation. Viewed from a broader perspective, however, it is clear that from the very beginning there were multiple meanings to the Nepomuk phenomenon. It cannot be denied that Nepomuk was at least in part a Catholic foil to the heretical Hus. A 1710 play produced by the Piarists of Litomyšl celebrated the future saint as the direct antithesis of Hus. Not coincidentally, a polemic from the late sixteenth century intended to demonstrate that Hus was no true saint was reprinted in the years immediately preceding Nepomuk's canonization.[39] The struggle between the two was also depicted allegorically during the celebration of Nepomuk's 1721 beatification. The motif of a swan (Nepomuk) defeating a goose (Hus) was a notable feature of that festival's iconography.[40] During the canonization proceedings Nepomuk's supporters continued to portray him as a counter-Hus or at the very least a defender of orthodoxy against Protestant error. Such language can even be found in the papal bull officially proclaiming Nepomuk's sanctity, and later miracles would credit the martyr priest with striking Lutherans dumb.[41]

---

[37] Ludwig Andreas Veit, *Kirche und Volksfrömmigkeit im Zeitalter des Barock* (Freiburg i.B.: Herder, 1956), p. 69.

[38] Pinsker, "Die Gesellschaft Jesu," p. 59; Mezler-Andelberg, "Bemerkungen zur Verehrung," p. 31. The debate culminated in the early twentieth century with Josef Pekař. See his "Tři kapitoly z boje o sv. Jana Nepomuckého," reprinted in his *O smyslu českých dějin* (Prague: Rozmluvy, 1990), pp. 275–313.

[39] *Antitheton boemicum Joannis Huss* (Litomyšl: Kamenický, 1710); Petr Linteo z Pilzenburgku, *Gistá a Patrná Cýrkwe Swaté Znamenj* (Prague: Wickhart, 1725).

[40] Vlnas, *Jan Nepomucký*, p. 190.

[41] *Acta utriusque processus*, pp. 225, 241–2; Václav Oliva, ed., *Kanonizační bulla sv. Jana Nepomuckého* (Prague: Nákl. Tiskové Ligy, 1910), p. 26; Friedrich Nicolai, *Beschreibung einer Reise durch Deutschland und die Schweiz, im Jahre 1781* (Berlin, 1783), vol. II, p. 621.

Nepomuk must also be considered in the context of the Catholic Reformation. Following the prototype of Charles Borromeo, the sixteenth-century archbishop of Milan, he was held up as a symbol of ecclesiastical authority. The significance of Nepomuk as an opponent of secular power was surely not lost on Benedict XIII who had caused such a furor by so aggressively promoting the Feast of Gregory VII and the tactless breviary that praised the eleventh-century pope for courageously excommunicating his rival, Emperor Henry IV. Nepomuk was also the great defender of penance. During the sixteenth and seventeenth centuries the church assiduously promoted this sacrament, and Nepomuk was quickly enlisted in the campaign. Preachers as well as artists highlighted this theme using the silent priest as a model. The earliest known depiction of Nepomuk is as confessor, and next to his martyrdom, this motif was the most popular feature of his iconography. Throughout the eighteenth century confessional booths were decorated with images of the priest. In Munich the Asam brothers constructed an entire church as a shrine to Nepomuk and the sacrament of confession.

There were other major themes of the Catholic Reformation that were highlighted through Nepomuk's life. Along with Elizabeth of Hungary and Charles Borromeo, Nepomuk became one of the most important patrons of central Europe's poor and sick. In 1727 Vienna's Cardinal Sigismund von Kollonitsch built a "Nepomuk-Spital" to care for the city's destitute.[42] Nepomuk's devotion to Mary was another favorite motif of artists and a broader ideal that the church sought to propagate through his life. But beyond these standard themes of Catholic Reform, it was Nepomuk's role as divine intercessor that most captivated the popular imagination. In 1701 an Ursuline nun reported that Nepomuk had miraculously healed her paralyzed arm. Several years later a young girl from southern Bohemia attributed her rescue from the icy waters of a mill race to his supernatural intervention. Thousands came to his tomb at St. Vitus praying for his aid in some desperate cause and very quickly a long list of miracles was attributed to the new saint.[43] For many Nepomuk possessed almost talismanic powers in a fashion similar to the beloved St. Christopher, the patron of travelers. Some have argued that Nepomuk's popularity was based on a fusion of pre-Christian beliefs and rituals approved by the church. He was frequently

[42] Franz Matsche, "Die Darstellungen des Johannes von Nepomuk in der barocken Kunst – Form, Inhalt und Bedeutung," in *Johannes von Nepomuk* (1971), p. 53.

[43] See for example NA, APA I, B 60/1, 44r–56v; on Vienna see Matthias Fuhrmann, *Historische Beschreibung und kurz gefasste Nachricht von der Römisch. Kaiserl. und Königlichen Residenz-Stadt Wien* (Vienna: Krauss, 1767), vol. II, pt. 2, pp. 790–802.

referred to as the miracle worker. There was a particular link between the saint and magical practices with rain and water. In one Styrian hamlet Nepomuk's feast day was celebrated with a procession that reached a climax when the villagers threw his statue into a stream with the intent of purifying the water.[44]

There were also a variety of social groups that adopted Nepomuk as patron. Most obvious was the saint's connection with water. From raft makers to sailors, from millers to fishermen, those whose livelihood was in some way connected to rivers, lakes or seas often considered the saint their special protector. Even apothecaries and brewers whose potent potables were dependent on water quality regularly appealed to Nepomuk for aid.[45] Then there were educators and students who saw Nepomuk as their patron. Nepomuk, who had been a teacher of theology and canon law, was not infrequently depicted as a scholar with book in hand, a favorite theme of the Asam brothers in particular, and of course there were the many thesis sheets produced in his honor. The universities in Prague, Vienna and Breslau were especially active in the campaign for his canonization.[46] Outside central Europe Nepomuk was named patron of the Royal University in Mexico City in 1743. There was also the issue of speech. One of the most popular features of Nepomuk iconography was the saint's uncorrupted tongue (Figure 21). Over time the tongue proved to be a remarkably flexible metaphor alternatively signifying the priest's principled taciturnity or his remarkable eloquence. The canons of Mainz cathedral elevated him as a symbol of confidentiality while back in Prague the priest Krištof Hubatius saluted him as the great preacher of his day.[47] Nepomuk also emerged as an advocate of those slandered by their enemies. As early as 1720, Count Schönborn, bishop of Speyer, noted that many whose honor had been falsely impugned turned to the martyr for assistance. One of the more common illustrations of Nepomuk is the priest as victor over calumny. Holding his tongue aloft in triumph, Nepomuk stands astride the fallen body of Slander who is represented as a hag holding a knife in one hand and a trumpet in the other. In 1732 the Jesuits, in fact, officially designated Nepomuk as one of their patrons in the wake of what they perceived as a

---

[44] Nicolai, *Beschreibung einer Reise*, vol. II, p. 620; Mezler-Andelberg, "Bemerkungen zur Verehrung," pp. 34–5; Hans Koren, *Bauernhimmel* (Graz: Styria Verlag, 1974), pp. 53–8.

[45] Leopold Schmidt, "Johannesandachten und Nepomuklieder in Niederösterreich und Burgenland," *Jahrbuch des österreichischen Volksliedwerkes* 9 (1960), 20; Koren, *Bauernhimmel*, p. 54; Heinrich Schauerte, *Die volkstümliche Heiligenverehrung* (Münster: Aschendorff, 1948), p. 118; Jaroslav Polc, *Svatý Jan Nepomucký* (Rome: Křesťanská akademie, 1972), vol. II, p. 197.

[46] APH-AMKSV, Codex LXI, 112r–113r, 119r–120r, 123r–124v.

[47] Krištof Hubatius, *Kazatel Prorocký* (Prague: Laboun, 1730); Veit, *Kirche und Volksfrömmigkeit*, p. 70.

Forma Sacræ Linguæ B. Ioannis Nepomuceni

21. Uncorrupted tongue of Jan Nepomuk

series of libelous attacks stemming from the Chinese Rites controversy and their feud with the Jansenists.[48]

A final group to consider is the nobility. As a defender of honor, Nepomuk was in many ways a natural patron of this social group. Well before his canonization, many of the nobility regularly came and prayed

---

[48] Herzogenberg, "Zum Kult des heiligen Johannes Nepomuk," p. 28; Pinsker, "Die Gesellschaft Jesu," pp. 66–7.

before his tomb in the cathedral, and it was not long before his public image was shaped according to their standards. Through the end of the seventeenth century, Nepomuk was generally portrayed as an older full-bearded figure quite similar to standard depictions of the apostles and prophets. By the beginning of the eighteenth century, however, there was a noticeable shift in iconography. Nepomuk now appeared younger and more stylish, sporting a well-groomed and more fashionable mustache and beard, in short, the ideal cavalier. In his cenotaph memorial for Nepomuk on the exterior of Prague's cathedral, Ignaz Platzer based his design on Fischer's famous tomb of Count Vratislav of Mitrovice across the river in St. James Church.[49] Apart from the Wunschwitz and Althan families, there were a number of noble houses that sought to identify even more directly with Nepomuk. The Sternbergs, for example, had long been supporters of the cult. In the 1640s Freiherr Franz Matthias Karl had transformed the village house in which Nepomuk had been born into a church. At the time of his beatification some eighty years later, the Sternbergs supported the publication of a brief text describing the proceedings. They included an illustration that linked the family's coat-of-arms with its eight-pointed star with the five stars associated with Nepomuk. In Moravia Abbot Václav Vejmluva went one step further. He noted that the five v's found in his name corresponded to Nepomuk's five stars and actually incorporated three of those stars into his family's crest.[50]

If the Nepomuk cult could reflect the concerns of a variety of social groups, the same is true when we consider geography. As patron of Bavaria, protector of the university in Mexico, or a favorite saint of a circle of Roman cardinals, the Bohemian martyr was made native in a broad range of geographic settings. The spread of his devotion was in part fueled by a rivalry between the Spanish Bourbons and Austrian Habsburgs who sought to outdo each other in terms of loyalty to the new saint. But perhaps more important was the remarkable linguistic adaptability of the cult. This was a multilingual phenomenon from the very beginning. The canonization documents were composed in four major languages as were the many sermons delivered in Prague in fall 1729. Confraternities dedicated to Nepomuk in the Bohemian kingdom were nearly evenly split between German and Czech speakers.[51] In the German-speaking world the diversity

---

[49] Matsche, "Die Darstellungen des Johannes von Nepomuk," p. 48; *Johannes von Nepomuk, 1393–1993*, p. 204.
[50] *Formula et Ritus … St. Joannis Nepomuceni* (Prague: Hraba, 1721); Neumann, "Das ikonographische Programm," pp. 247–8.
[51] Vlnas, *Jan Nepomucký*, p. 175.

was even greater. In the 1780s the peripatetic writer and bookseller, Friedrich Nicolai, noted that songs in honor of Nepomuk tended to be written in dialect as high German was frequently seen as a Lutheran language. In the Westphalian context, Nepomuk was commonly known by the colloquial *Janbomsseens.* Swabians and others honored Nepomuk with religious verse composed in their local dialects.[52]

The most intriguing contrast that we find with Nepomuk geographically is his appropriation as a symbol of Bohemian identity and simultaneous adoption by the Habsburgs as an emblem of their wider imperial aspirations. Emperor Charles VI very consciously enlisted Nepomuk in the task of defining his imperium. Nepomuk was frequently deployed in the border areas to help create a sense of Habsburg identity in regions newly acquired by the family or under threat from confessional rivals. In the military zone of the Banat, the newly acquired territories of the Low Countries, or areas of Hungary recently recovered from the Turks, the Nepomuk cult was actively promoted by church and state authorities.[53] One of the best representations of this theme visually is a 1724 thesis sheet where Nepomuk passes on to the emperor the orb of world dominion while the figure of *Chronos* exclaims that the new Habsburg empire will have no geographic or temporal boundaries.[54] Such uses of Nepomuk contrasted sharply with those of the Czech antiquarians who tended to portray the saint as a local hero who defiantly confronted an over-grasping ruler or with civic institutions such as Prague's three town councils which celebrated him with great patriotic zeal.[55]

Nepomuk's tomb in St. Vitus is a striking example of the possible polyvalent readings of the saint. On the one hand, the tomb, which was remodeled three times between 1694 and 1736, was very much a specific dynastic statement. The emperor took an active role in its design, and like the *Karlskirche* in Vienna or the Reconciliation monument in Győr it was both a public representation of Habsburg piety and an important statement of imperial prestige.[56] At the same time this monument was an articulation of a culturally specific Bohemian piety. There were numerous references to patriotic themes including the Wenceslas crown that linked Nepomuk to the kingdom's greatest patron. Even more powerful were the memories

---

[52] G. Kapner, *Barocker Heiligenkult in Wien und seine Träger* (Munich: Oldenbourg, 1978), p. 61; Schauerte, *Die volkstümliche Heiligenverehrung*, p. 61.

[53] Koloman Juhász, "Der hl. Johannes Nepomuk als Schutzpatron des Banates," *Österreichische Zeitschrift für Volkskunde* 18 (1967), 89–90; Lasfargues, "Le culte mondial," pp. 239–43.

[54] "Ettaler Thesenblatt aus Philosophie aus der Ritterakademie auf Kaiser Karl VI. Vom Jahre 1724," reproduced in G. M. Lechner, ed., *Das Barocke Thesenblatt* (Göttweig: Stift Göttweig, 1985), pp. 113–20.

[55] APH-AMKSV, Codex LXI, 110r–111v.

[56] Matsche, *Die Kunst im Dienst der Staatsidee*, vol. I, pp. 208–12.

connected with the tomb. For a significant portion of the seventeenth century the cathedral's oldest relic, the Jerusalem Candelabrum, had been placed above Nepomuk's grave while the spot itself had been the site of numerous miracles and now rivaled the high altar as the devotional center of St. Vitus. Put simply, this was holy ground for Bohemian Catholics.[57]

As Moshe Sluhovsky has argued concerning St. Genevieve in early modern Paris, the base of a popular cult was frequently constructed on a series of multiple and at times conflicting readings of the same individual.[58] For central Europe Nepomuk is the perfect example. In Vienna he reflected the dynastic interests of the imperial family. In Prague he became popular with Czech patriots who saw the martyred priest as an appropriate role model silently but resolutely resisting Habsburg hegemony. In Rome he mirrored the concerns of the church and its claims of spiritual power. Most remarkably, all of this occurred without any apparent sense of contradiction. Whereas the promotion of the cult of Gregory VII had caused such an uproar, Nepomuk's sudden rise to prominence was accompanied with no similar outcry or controversy. He was a saint who seemed to cross cultural and linguistic boundaries effortlessly as reflected in one of the more interesting miracles connected to his canonization. During the 1729 proceedings in Rome there were reports of a simple Italian woman who miraculously began conversing in German, all this of course at a ceremony honoring a Czech-speaking priest.[59]

The appropriation of Nepomuk, then, was no simple and straightforward phenomenon. In chameleon-like fashion, the new saint was in many respects "all things to all people." What is clearer and easier to distinguish, however, is the extent to which this complicated cult reflected the culmination of a century-long process of reintroducing sanctity in the Bohemian kingdom. This was a process that had at least three stages. Immediately after White Mountain, ecclesiastical and secular leaders turned to the broader Catholic world for assistance. Perhaps best represented by the arrival of Norbert in 1627, it was through translation in particular that the church sought to reclaim lost territory. After the military resolution of 1648 and in an atmosphere of greater confidence, a now triumphant church worked especially through pilgrimage to bring the people to the holy by recovering the sacred at the local level. Though the import of relics continued, a thick

---

[57] Matsche, "Das Grabmal," pp. 102–3; *Acta utriusque processus*, pp. 235, 237, 240–1.
[58] Moshe Sluhovsky, *Patroness of Paris: Rituals of Devotion in Early Modern France* (Brill: Leiden, 1998), pp. 211–12.
[59] Kapner, *Barocker Heiligenkult*, p. 59.

network of shrines reminded the kingdom's inhabitants that they lived in a holy landscape where, long before the arrival of the heretics, saints had worked miracles, and the true faith had flourished. Now with Nepomuk a third stage had been reached. No longer was the holy merely connected to a specific relic or a local site with historical significance. Nepomuk was a saint intended for mass production. The statue on Charles Bridge was of course replicated countless times. Wax likenesses of Nepomuk also appeared in churches and were a special means of physically bringing the saint before the people.[60] Then there were the amulets, medals, and rosaries intended for private devotion. More significant was the fact that Nepomuk invaded the most ordinary of spaces. From the furniture of burgher homes to the jugs and gingerbread molds of peasant kitchens, the saint penetrated life at its most basic level. So great was his penetration at this level that the lottery in Vienna eventually made use of him.[61] Even two centuries later the poet and Prague native, Rainer Maria Rilke, gently poked fun at the saint's omnipresence with his clever rhyme:

> Aber diese Nepomucken!
> Von des Torgangs Lucken gucken
> Und auf allen Brucken spucken
> Lauter, lauter Nepomucken.[62]

Nepomuk's near ubiquity, then, reflects the extent to which the holy could mark virtually every aspect of life in the Czech lands. The Catholic triumph was so complete in fact that even the most profane elements of Bohemian society were not immune from the seemingly irresistible power of the sacred. Important in this regard is the case of the Jews. Nepomuk was purportedly responsible for the conversion of several in this community.[63] But what may be actually more illustrative of the transformative reach of the holy is the emergence of an unlikely cult that developed in the Prague ghetto parallel to the Nepomuk phenomenon.

MAKING A JEWISH SAINT

By the beginning of the eighteenth century the Prague ghetto was easily the most densely populated area of the Bohemian metropolis. Though always

---

[60] Franz Matsche, "Sekundärleiber des heiligen Johannes von Nepomuk," *Jahrbuch für Volkskunde* n.f. 6 (1983), 107–48.
[61] Kapner, *Barocker Heiligenkult*, p. 57.
[62] Rainer Maria Rilke, *Sämtliche Werke* (Frankfurt: Insel Verlag, 1955), vol. I, pp. 21–2.
[63] Kapner, *Barocker Heiligenkult*, p. 60.

crowded, now, according to a 1702 census, more than 11,500 people were shoehorned into this small district on the western side of Old Town. The Jews, in fact, constituted half the population of Old Town and more than a quarter of the entire city populace. Such numbers made the Prague ghetto one of the largest Jewish communities in all of Europe.[64] Though these statistics may have been worrisome to the city's Christian inhabitants, what may have been more ominous was the dramatic rate at which the ghetto had expanded. Only a century earlier the Jewish community had numbered slightly more than 2,000 inhabitants. Although the Rudolfine period is often remembered as a golden age of the city's Jewish settlement, the Prague of the great Maharal, David Gans and Mordechai Maisel, it was in the following decades of the seventeenth century that the Jews won some of their most important privileges. Thanks in large part to the negotiations of the financier Jacob Bassevi, Emperor Ferdinand II granted permission to enlarge the ghetto. His son Ferdinand III further expanded the rights of this community. The changes had dramatic results. In the span of thirty years the population of the ghetto increased more than five-fold. Not surprisingly, this soaring population concerned the Christian authorities. During the reign of Leopold I (1658–1705) there was a systematic attempt to stem this growth and roll back some of the earlier gains of the community.

The first significant steps were taken in 1679 when a Jewish Reduction Commission was established. Though a plan was drawn up to expel approximately one third of the community, it was never executed. But what the government did not accomplish, nature did. The plague of 1680 killed more than 2,000 of the ghetto's inhabitants. Though the population quickly recovered, an even more devastating event occurred nine years later when a fire destroyed nearly the entire settlement. The authorities saw the conflagration as an opportunity to reduce sharply or even eliminate completely the Jewish presence in the city. Proposals were floated that called for a new Jewish town outside the city walls, but in the end the ghetto remained though reconstruction was slow, and the size of the new neighborhood was scaled back significantly.[65] Numbers, however, would again climb in the now smaller settlement, and both city officials and the Habsburgs themselves continued to look for ways to pare back the Jewish presence. In 1726

---

[64] Jaroslav Prokeš, "Úřední antisemitismus a pražské ghetto v době pobělohorské. Redukční a extirpační pokusy z let 1679 až 1729," *Ročenka společnosti pro dějiny židů v Československé Republice* 1 (1929), 42; Alexandr Putík, "The Prague Jewish community in the late 17th and early 18th centuries," *Judaica Bohemiae* 35 (1999), 8.

[65] NA, ČDK, IV T 1, Kart. 793–4; Prokeš, "Úřední antisemitismus," 98–128; Václav Vojtíšek, "Po ohni židovského města pražského roku 1689," *Kalendář česko-židovský* 34 (1914–15), 61–71.

Charles VI passed the Familiants Laws restricting the marriage rights of Bohemian Jews, while in 1744 Maria Theresa took the final step and expelled them from Prague altogether. These official policies directed against the city's Jews were matched with popular expressions of anti-Semitism that became ever more frequent after the conclusion of the Thirty Years War. From his pulpit Bohumír Bílovský railed against the Jews claiming that they were marked with the sign of the beast. The wandering missionary Albrecht Chanovský told stories of blasphemous Jews whose evil acts were only miraculously thwarted by divine intervention. Antiquarians such as Jan Beckovský published tales of Host desecration and ritual murder, and in the streets songs circulated that decried the inhumanity and greed of this community.[66] In such a charged atmosphere it was inevitable that there would be episodic outbreaks of violence. University students in Prague were frequently involved as they viewed the tormenting of Jews a type of extracurricular activity. Between 1699 and 1702 there were eleven major riots alone.[67]

Against this backdrop of rising ethnic and religious tension the church pursued a dual strategy of indoctrination and isolation with the city's Jews. In the 1630s church leaders initiated a mission to the ghetto where every Saturday a congregation of Jews was compelled to assemble and listen to a Jesuit priest who labored through a homily in poor Hebrew. A special fund was also established to finance a hostel for young Jewish converts. Though none of these projects was terribly successful, throughout the century other schemes of mass catechization were occasionally discussed but rarely implemented. The church also used censorship in an attempt to weaken the intellectual vigor of the Jewish community. The Jesuits collaborated with the archiepiscopal consistory in an effort to clamp down on the production of Hebrew texts. This wave of repression culminated in the 1690s with an aggressive confiscation campaign. Copies of the Talmud, cabalist literature and prayer books were to be collected and presumably destroyed. A decree was even proposed that would forbid rabbis from preaching in the synagogues.[68] These unusually strong measures were at least partially a byproduct of the 1689 fire. Though numerous, Prague's Jews were in many respects

---

[66] Bohumír Bílovský, *Cantator Cygnus* (Olomouc: Jan Adam Avinger, 1720), pp. 411–12; A. Chanovský, *Správa křesťanská* (Prague, 1676), p. 5; Jan Beckovský, *Poselkyně starých příběhů českých*, ed. A. Rezek (Prague: Dědictví sv. Prokopa, 1879–80), vol. I, pp. 240, 245–6, 249, 252–3, 256–7, 259. My thanks to Zdeněk David for the Beckovský reference.

[67] Putík, "The Prague Jewish community," 24–6; I. Raková, "Bouře studentů pražské univerzity ve druhé polovině 17. století," *AUC, HUCP* 21, no. 2 (1981), 7–21.

[68] Milada Vilímková, *The Prague Ghetto* (Prague: Aventinum, 1993), pp. 60–4; Putík, "The Prague Jewish community," 28–39.

successfully quarantined in their ghetto. There were laws that restricted their movement on Sundays and other feast days. No Jew could cross Old Town Square when litanies were being sung at Bendl's Marian column. The 1689 fire changed much of this. While the ghetto was being slowly rebuilt, Jews were forced to take temporary residence in Christian homes. Archbishop Waldstein strongly opposed this mixed cohabitation. Priests were forbidden to visit such dwellings, and even last rites were refused to Catholics living in buildings with transient Jewish occupants. It was precisely in this tense and hostile atmosphere of the post-1689 period that an event occurred which further strained the already problematic relationship between Christian and Jew and gave rise to an informal cult around a new Hebrew "saint."

During the night of 26 February 1694, a certain Lazar Abeles was arrested and transported to the dank cells of Old Town Hall. Abeles, a glove maker by profession, was a member of a prominent Jewish family. His father, the respected Moses, was a *primator* of the community. Lazar, who was on his fourth marriage, had a reputation for violence and according to a Jewish informer in a fit of rage had murdered his young son, Simon. The body, which had been hastily buried, was exhumed. Medical experts from the university were called in, and an autopsy was performed. Though Lazar contended that his son had died from natural causes, the doctors concluded that the boy had been killed by a series of blows to his head and neck. After a lengthy interrogation of household members, another Jew and family acquaintance, the teenager Löbl Kurtzhandl, was also implicated in this conspiracy and brought into custody. In an effort to extract confessions both Abeles and Kurtzhandl were tortured. Abeles, in the end, was found dangling from a rope in his cell, presumably a victim of suicide. A less pleasant fate awaited Kurtzhandl. Resolutely maintaining his innocence, Kurtzhandl was pronounced guilty and sentenced to die beneath the wheel. At the place of execution, he admitted his guilt and begged for mercy. Though none was granted, the Jesuit attending him eagerly sought his conversion. After the executioner had delivered forty blows to the massive wheel which slowly crushed the young Jew, Kurtzhandl, according to Christian sources, relented and agreed to a baptism in exchange for one final stroke to end his protracted suffering.

This event would certainly not have been followed so closely or publicized so widely had it not been for one small but critical aspect of the story, a feature that in time colored all future accounts of the Abeles affair. Simon had evidently expressed some interest in Catholicism. In summer 1693 he left home, took up lodgings with Franz Kawka, a recent Jewish convert, and

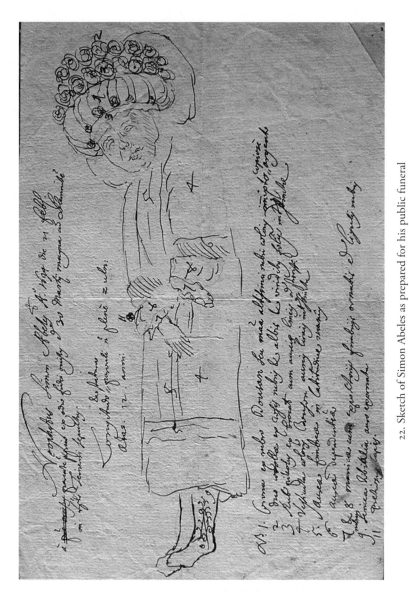

22. Sketch of Simon Abeles as prepared for his public funeral

began instruction with the Jesuits. For whatever reason, Simon's catechetical lessons were interrupted, and the boy returned home before he was baptized. Relations between father and son remained tense, and on 21 February 1694 the fatal incident occurred. Though the exact nature of the encounter between Lazar and Simon may never be known, ecclesiastical and civic authorities quickly claimed that overcome by rage Lazar and his accomplice had murdered the boy *ex odio fidei*. Never baptized, Simon now in death was cast as a martyred saint. Huge crowds came to view the murdered child who had been regally laid in state in the town hall chapel. At the end of March the archbishop himself officiated at his funeral as the body was ceremoniously transported across the square and buried in the Týn Church. The Abeles case also generated a significant paper trail. The archives closely document the trial, even including a rough sketch of the boy in his open casket (Figure 22).[69] In 1696 a compilation of many of these texts, *Processus Inquisitorius*, was published for a popular audience while in the same year Johann Eder, a Jesuit who had been involved in the affair, wrote his own account of the incident.[70] Publicists quickly realized that this story was suited for a variety of genres. Illustrated broadsheets, paintings, plays, songs and even an oratorio were produced memorializing the Abeles drama. News quickly spread beyond Prague. From Amsterdam to Königsberg, from Mainz to Florence, printers across the continent eagerly produced accounts of the tragic incident.[71]

In more modern times the Abeles case has continued to attract both scholars and amateur historians. At the beginning of the century the colorful journalist, Egon Erwin Kisch, worked through the archival sources to expose what he considered an anti-Semitic fraud. Most recently, Elisheva Carlebach has argued that this event was the beginning of a new form of anti-Jewish libel.[72] The Abeles story, however, has never been completely

---

[69] NA, SM, 1505, J 4/24, Kart. 945.

[70] *Processus Inquisitorius* (Prague: Endter, 1696); Johann Eder, *Virilis constantia pueri duodennis Simonis Abeles* (Prague: Typis Academicis, 1696); translated two years later as Johann Eder, *Mannhaffte Beständigkeit des zwölffjährigen Knabens* (Prague: Endter, 1698).

[71] Hayyim Druker, "Eyn neye klog lid benign fun rebbe Shimen" (Amsterdam, 1695); Johann Christof Wagenseil, *Belehrung der Jüdisch-Teutschen Red-und Schreibart* (Königsberg: Rhode, 1699), B4r–D3v; Lotharius Franz Fried, *Neupolierter und wohlgeschliffener Juden-Spiegel* (Mainz: Verlag des Authors, 1715); Italian translation of Eder, *Patimenti, e morte di Simone Abeles* (Florence: P. Matini, 1705).

[72] Egon Erwin Kisch, "Ex odio fidei...," in *Geschichte aus sieben Ghettos*, in Bodo Uhse and Gisela Kisch, eds., *Gesammelte Werke in Einzelausgaben* (Berlin: Aufbau Verlag, 1985), vol. VI, pp. 39–49; Elisheva Carlebach, *The Death of Simon Abeles: Jewish-Christian Tension in Seventeenth-Century Prague*. Third Annual Herbert Berman Memorial Lecture (New York: Center for Jewish Studies, Queens College, CUNY, 2003); Rachel L. Greenblatt, "A community's memory: Jewish views of past and present in early modern Prague," unpublished Ph.D. thesis, Hebrew University of Jerusalem (2006), pp. 109–19; Tommaso Caliò, *La legenda dell'ebreo assassino* (Rome: Viella, 2007), p. 84.

taken out of the ghetto and examined in its broader cultural context. The parallels with the Nepomuk phenomenon are undeniable, for at its most basic level the creation of an Abeles myth reflected the mood of Catholic triumphalism that was reaching its Bohemian climax in the late seventeenth and early eighteenth centuries. Here an examination of the *Processus Inquisitorius* is particularly illuminating. This text was a compilation of more than two dozen legal documents including forensic testimony, transcripts of interrogations and even letters from Emperor Leopold himself. These texts were carefully selected and compiled as a type of seventeenth-century legal thriller. By carefully sifting through the evidence as presented in the *Processus*, the reader would slowly uncover the lies and deceptions of the Jews and ultimately discover the truth. The truth, though, was more than the simple discovery that Abeles and Kurtzhandl were responsible for Simon's death, for the *Processus* also operated on a metaphysical level as well. As the preface states, it was God's miraculous providence and power that lay at the heart of this courtroom drama. The great mystery was not who killed Simon, but why one of the perpetrators converted while the other did not. Citing Romans 11, the author of the preface linked the confession and conversion of Kurtzhandl to the ultimate salvation of the Jews the apostle Paul had predicted.[73] Such a message was reinforced by an illustration of the *Processus*. The slain body of the boy lies in glory in the heavens while flanking him below on earth are the figures of Kurtzhandl and Lazar Abeles. Following the prototype of Christ and the two thieves, Lazar overcome by hate is seen dangling from his jail cell while Kurtzhandl to the surprise of amazed onlookers accepts God's love and promise of salvation through baptism (Figure 23).[74]

The use of the Abeles drama as a cosmic morality play is also a prominent theme of Johann Eder's *Virilis constantia*. Eder's published account, later translated into both German and Italian, reached an even broader audience. He contended that the obstinacy of Abeles and Kurtzhandl reflected a more general stubbornness of the Jewish community to recognize the truth of Catholicism.[75] A frontispiece illustration develops this theme further. The engraving is divided into two sections (Figure 24). To the right are symbols of the Jewish faith: a synagogue, an Old Testament priest and the Ten Commandments. On the left are figures demonstrating how the old has

---

[73] *Processus Inquisitorius*, A2v, A3r.
[74] Unpaginated illustration. The comparison to Christ and the two thieves is mentioned directly in the preface. *Processus Inquisitorius*, A2v.
[75] Eder, *Mannhaffte Beständigkeit*, A2v–r, 44–50.

23. Simon Abeles lying in glory

been superseded by the new. A magnificent cathedral has been exchanged for the synagogue. The pope now stands in for the priest while the keys of the kingdom and the Book of Life have replaced the stern mandate of the Mosaic law. At the center and as a bridge between the two worlds stands Simon atop the tree of life. This motif of Catholic triumphalism is also reflected in an oratorio that was composed to commemorate Simon's death. Cristoforo Angelo Rotondo's *Il neo-martire di Boemia* is a somewhat

24. Allegory of Simon Abeles from Johann Eder, *Mannhaffte Beständigkeit des zwölffjährigen Knabens*

surprising composition. One might have expected a musical drama that highlighted the treachery of Lazar, the saintly innocence of Simon and a last-minute revelation of the father's guilt. Instead we are presented with a more doctrinal, almost catechetical, composition. In the first part of the oratorio Simon, who is lost in a labyrinth of theological confusion, approaches the Jesuits for aid. They patiently explain to him the mystery of the trinity and incarnation. Including footnotes both to Scripture and the church fathers, Rotondo has young Simon master his lessons quickly and then decry the perfidy of the rabbis for hiding the clear truth of the gospels.[76] In the second half of the oratorio Simon confronts his father and Kurtzhandl. In a debate over the trinity and the divinity of Christ, Simon masterfully exegetes passages from the Old Testament to demonstrate how the old covenant is surpassed by the new. A stupefied Lazar and Kurtzhandl cannot refute the inspired boy who will also cite rabbinic texts to bolster his arguments.[77] Even the music reflected this spirit of triumphant Catholicism. Though the actual score has been lost, Rotondo in his letter to the reader noted that he deliberately matched a simpler setting of two voices with a richer polyphonic scheme in an effort to contrast the Jews' narrow and flawed understanding of the Old Testament with the church's fuller seven-fold sense of Scripture.[78]

As this literature attests, there was a striking series of parallels between Abeles and Nepomuk. The silent priest and the stoic Simon were both martyrs. They both underwent a type of canonization process. Nepomuk, of course, was subjected to a structured and formal review with the collection of written and oral testimony and the exhumation of his grave. With Abeles legal evidence and medical testimony were also carefully gathered and sifted. He, too, was exhumed and examined by qualified physicians. While the events connected to the opening of his grave may not have been as dramatic as the discovery of Nepomuk's miraculously preserved tongue, as we will see, the doctors were surprised by what they found. Then there were the celebrations, the meticulously planned festival for Nepomuk at St. Vitus and the magnificently staged funeral for Abeles in Old Town. Nepomuk was interred in the exuberant baroque monument in the cathedral. Abeles's final resting place, marked by a more modest memorial of pink marble, was in the Týn Church, Old Town's spiritual center. A matter of timing also links the two figures. Though the Abeles affair occurred in 1694, and the initial publications appeared shortly thereafter, renewed attention was given to the case during the years immediately preceding 1729 corresponding to a more general interest in sanctity connected to the historic canonization. In 1724 a popular summary of the incident appeared under the title, *A Short Account of the Life and Death of the twelve year old boy, Simon Abeles*, and in 1728 the *Processus Inquisitorius* was republished

---

[76] Cristoforo Angelo Rotondo, *Il neo-martire di Boemia* (Prague: G. Labaun, 1695), pp. 14, 15, 24.
[77] Ibid., pp. 45, 60.   [78] Ibid., pp. 6–7.

with a new portrait of the young martyr.[79] Substantial interest continued through the 1730s. During this decade the Jesuits staged plays commemorating Abeles's martyrdom in both Prague and Olomouc.[80]

Though these parallels between Nepomuk and Abeles are certainly suggestive, more evidence is needed before we can claim that the Jewish boy functioned as a type of saint in late seventeenth-century Prague. Critical here is the reaction of the church. Simon had died on 21 February. He had been buried the following day but was exhumed five days later after a Jewish informant had passed on his suspicions to municipal officials. The authorities took Simon's body to the cellars of Old Town Hall where the doctors began their examination of the corpse. Once the court proceedings had begun, the church was faced with a difficult decision. What were they to do with this child? The story had reached the public, and pressure was growing to treat him as a Christian martyr. The truth, however, was more complicated. Though Simon had demonstrated an interest in Christianity, his catechization was incomplete, and he had never been baptized. There were some doubts regarding his sincerity. Turning to his theologians for counsel, Archbishop Waldstein deliberated on this matter for some time. In the end his decision was firm and definitive. Though a baptism of water had never taken place, Simon had been baptized in his own blood, and as such he should be considered a martyr of the faith. He would be honored with a public funeral procession from Old Town Hall to the Týn Church where he would be laid to rest with the dignity and solemnity that his heroic death had merited.[81]

Once a decision had been reached, the authorities moved quickly on the matter. The corpse had remained in the basement after the medical examination, and a few days before the funeral, Johann Eder and two other Jesuits began preparing the body for a public viewing in the St. Lawrence chapel of Old Town Hall. As the priests began washing the boy, they were amazed to find that the skin was still soft and the joints remarkably pliant.[82] Eder was not the first to make this observation. The physicians who had initially examined Abeles had noted with some surprise that the corpse had appeared "gantz frisch." In his account of the Abeles affair, Johann Eder used even

[79] *Kurtzer Leben-und Todes Verfass des standhafften 12. jährigen Knabens Simonis Abeles* (Prague: Typis Academicis, 1724).
[80] *Agnus inter haedos* (Prague, 1738), summary in NA, JS III-415, Kart. 144, Fasc. 3.; *Amabili Christianae Fidei Constantia ab Hebraeo Adolescente Simone Abeles* (Olomouc, 1736), summary in NK, 52 A 40, #III.
[81] Letter of Archbishop Waldstein, 21 March 1594, in *Processus Inquisitorius*, pp. 65–6.
[82] *Processus Inquisitorius*, pp. 68–9.

stronger language to describe this startling discovery. Amazed that the body had defied the progressive stiffening of rigor mortis, he spoke of Simon's *incorruptum cadaver*.[83] Eder was clearly using the vocabulary of the hagiographer. With Abeles the natural process of decay and putrefaction had been halted and reversed. Many in fact remarked that his body emitted a sweet odor, an observation that was duly noted on his marble tombstone.

Eder and his colleagues quickly finished their preparations, and all was soon ready for a public viewing which began on 29 March and lasted two days. Details of the incident had circulated through the city, and there were very few who were ignorant of the proceedings. But it was the actual body that drew the crowds. News of its miraculous preservation had also spread, and as such, Simon was more than a mere curiosity, an exotic convert to the faith. He was physical proof of God's power and a sign of the church's definitive victory over Jewish lies and Protestant heresy. This drama had particularly intrigued the nobility who in short order became great champions of the new cause. Countess Sylvia Katharina Schlick submitted a petition to Archbishop Waldstein requesting permission to provide a special outfit for the murdered boy, a practice calling to mind the devotional activity of those noblewomen who had furnished the extensive wardrobe of the Prague Jesus.[84] Lying in a casket lined with a rich brocade of red samite, the elegantly dressed Simon attracted huge crowds who slowly filed by the boy in the Old Town Hall chapel. Though the municipal authorities sought to preserve the solemnity of the moment by stationing an honor guard outside the town hall, there was a mood of excitement and anticipation that could not be suppressed. Many wanted to touch the body. As Eder later related, they eagerly leaned over the coffin and kissed the hand. There was one individual who pulled off his valuable gold ring and attempted to place it on the boy's right hand in hopes of securing divine favor through Simon's intercession.[85] It was the blood, however, that caused the greatest stir. Those who passed by the body were supposedly amazed by the freshness of the injuries. Uncongealed blood was still present, and there was a great rush to dip handkerchiefs in the wounds. Catholic observers were quick to point out that even Protestants marveled at this miracle. One of the most avid of these relic seekers was a Lutheran dentist who left with a small supply of Simon's blood.[86] For those who could not obtain bodily fluids,

---

[83] NA, SM, 1505, J 4/24, Kart. 945, 27 February 1694. This fact was also noted in Hayyim Druker's "Eyn neye klog lid," stanza 12. My thanks to Rachel Greenblatt for this observation; Eder, *Virilis constantia*, pp. 63–4.

[84] *Processus Inquisitorius*, p. 69.   [85] Eder, *Virilis constantia*, p. 68.   [86] *Processus Inquisitorius*, p. 69.

the casket became the next target. Bits and pieces were sliced off and taken home as talismans. The situation became so chaotic that the authorities were forced to intervene. They placed a mesh net over the body and coffin to prevent further losses.[87]

The actual funeral ceremonies had been planned for 31 March. Nearly thirty years later, Jan Florián Hammerschmid remembered these obsequies as one of the great moments in the history of the Týn Church.[88] It certainly was one of the major civic events of the decade. Priests from every parish of Prague's three cities took part. The major confraternities assembled as well as members of the nobility, imperial officers, municipal representatives and church officials. The general public came in great numbers to the eventual chagrin of the event's organizers, for it proved difficult to control the crowds that day. The rites began at 8 a.m. in the St. Lawrence chapel where select representatives watched as Simon's body was sprinkled with holy water, and the coffin was ceremoniously sealed. Though the distance between Old Town Hall and the Týn Church was but a few hundred meters, the procession between the two buildings was an elaborately orchestrated event that must have taken several hours. There was a long stop at the Marian column to celebrate Simon's conversion as well as the singing of hymns and the recitation of litanies. The most prominent feature of the ceremonies was the emphasis on children. The liturgy in the St. Lawrence chapel had begun with an antiphonal reading of Psalm 112 [113], "Praise the Lord you children."[89] The Psalm was repeated in various forms throughout the day. Additionally, large groups of children dressed in matching costumes were the most conspicuous members of the cortege. This careful planning evidently produced the desired effect, for observers noted that the crowds were brought to tears at several points during the proceedings.

This emphasis on children was a strategic element of a larger plan. As they attempted to shape and direct the growing cult that was quickly developing around Simon, Archbishop Waldstein and other church leaders had a specific prototype in mind, Simon of Trent. This Simon was a fifteenth-century Christian boy who had been supposedly abducted by the Jews of Trent and ritually murdered. Though the case was controversial in its own day, Simon was venerated by many, and the story became well known across Europe. A famous woodcut of the incident was even included in the *Nuremberg Chronicle*. Popular pressure eventually forced the pope to

---

[87] *Kurtzer Leben-und Todes Verfass*, B8v–B9r.

[88] J. F. Hammerschmid, *Prodromus gloriae Pragenae* (Prague: Wolfgang Wickhart, 1723), p. 30.

[89] *Processus Inquisitorius*, p. 70.

confirm the local cult in 1588. Back in Prague, ecclesiastical officials had hoped from the very beginning to pattern the newly emerging cult after the Italian model. The precise timing of Abeles's funeral was actually determined by the feast day of the first Simon, 24 March. It was on this day that an announcement was made that the Abeles ceremony would be held on the octave of the feast, 31 March.[90] In later accounts of the Abeles story the parallels between the two Simons remained an explicit theme. The Jesuit plays of the 1730s have the young Abeles discovering a devotional image of Simon of Trent. In *Lamb among the Goats* the Jesuits devoted an entire scene to Abeles's meditation on the cruel death of his fifteenth-century predecessor. At the funeral itself there were scattered references or allusions to Simon of Trent.[91] Once the body had been sealed away, the tomb in the Týn Church did become a center of popular devotion in a fashion similar to the shrine in Trent. Five years after the event, the German Christian Hebraist, Johann Christoph Wagenseil, noted that devotion to Abeles continued to grow, and reports of miracles at his tomb had steadily increased.[92]

The theme of martyrdom was also carefully choreographed in the funeral. The red and white colors of Simon's outfit had been strategically chosen, white as the innocence of youth and red as the sign of martyrdom.[93] This color scheme appeared throughout the ceremony, most notably replicated in the red and white suits of the sixteen boys who carried Simon's coffin in the procession. The parallel here with Nepomuk is important as well. Though martyrs had been a prominent feature of the sixteenth-century Catholic world, only two were canonized between 1523 and 1767.[94] It is somewhat puzzling, then, to encounter two of them in the Czech lands during this relatively peaceful era. The historian of late antiquity, Robert Markus, has observed that it was principally through the use of martyrs that the fourth-century church made a critical adjustment from the cult of the persecuted to the faith of the privileged. By developing the cult of the martyrs, Eusebius and his successors sought to convince themselves that they in the now triumphant church were the true descendants of those believers who had suffered so cruelly under Nero and Diocletian.[95] A similar

[90] Eder, *Virilis constantia*, p. 67.

[91] *Agnus inter haedos*, Inductio VII; *Amabili Christianae Fidei*, Inductio I; Eder, *Virilis constantia*, pp. 75–81.

[92] Wagenseil, *Belehrung*, B4r. [93] Ibid., C2v.

[94] Peter Burke, "How to be a Counter-Reformation saint," in Kaspar von Greyerz, ed., *Religion and Society in Early Modern Europe 1500–1800* (London: Allen & Unwin, 1984), p. 51.

[95] R. A. Markus, "How on earth could places become holy? Origins of the Christian idea of holy places," *Journal of Early Christian Studies* 2 (1994), 268–9.

adjustment was occurring in early eighteenth-century Bohemia. After more than two centuries of religious turmoil, the Catholic church found itself in a radically different situation, no longer a persecuted and embattled minority. The focus on martyrs was a means to bridge this generational gap and maintain continuity by keeping the past alive. The contrast between Nepomuk and Abeles is quite instructive in this regard. These two figures divided by three centuries but united by martyrdom helped link the late medieval church with the contemporary world. Though the details had changed (a paranoid Christian king had been replaced by a sinister Jewish father) the great drama remained the same.[96]

Though one would have expected martyrdom to figure prominently in the retelling of the Abeles story, somewhat more surprising is the emphasis that the Catholic chroniclers placed on the theme of conversion. By conversion I do not mean Simon's individual decision to embrace Catholicism. Instead, the various compilers of the Abeles accounts construed conversion as a broader phenomenon. They saw Simon marking the beginning of a large-scale movement in the Jewish community. In nearly all of the texts produced in the wake of this affair, the narrative climax was not Simon's death nor the apprehension and conviction of his two murderers. It was, in contrast, the conversion of Löbl Kurtzhandl. In a short manuscript account of the Abeles incident in the Strahov library, five of the seven pages are devoted to Kurtzhandl's conversion. More than a quarter of the popular 1724 text is given over to this matter while the *Processus Inquisitorius* concludes with a lengthy description of Kurtzhandl's last days culminating with his baptism and "happy death."[97] Conversion was the central theme of Johann Eder's account. The first chapter opened with the Jesuit explicitly describing Abeles as a divine tool to bring the Jewish community to repentance.[98] Eder, in fact, began his narrative by recounting a number of Jewish conversions that had occurred in the years immediately prior to Abeles's death, including the story of the Christian midwife who in 1692 helped deliver a Jewish baby and then immediately christened him to the consternation of the assembled relatives.[99] The Jesuit devoted an entire chapter of his text to the conversions of those influenced by Simon's example. There was a Lithuanian boy who had known Abeles through

---

[96] See Eder's supporting observation. Eder, *Virilis constantia*, p. 81.
[97] "Pragensis Casus Anni 1694" (SK, Miscell. D H V 6, #17); *Kurtzer Leben-und Todes Verfass*, C4r–D4r; *Processus Inquisitorius*, pp. 85–93. These printed accounts are largely based on the manuscript of the Jesuit Johannes Brandstätter who oversaw Kurtzhandl's "conversion." "Mirabilis conversio Levi Kurtzhandl a Judaismo ad Catholicam fidem…," NA, APA I, C 98/ 1694 I/ Kart. 940.
[98] Eder, *Mannhaffte Beständigkeit*, p. 1.   [99] Ibid., pp. 2–5.

school and later converted when his family moved to Moravia. There was the girl, Sybilla, who had been so moved by his death and funeral that she was baptized in September 1694. Eder claimed that at least seventy Jews, primarily children, had sought Catholic baptism after Simon's martyrdom.[100]

The most miraculous of all these conversions according to Eder was the final confession and baptism of Löbl Kurtzhandl. Significant here is the role he assigned to the now dead Abeles. The Jesuit claimed that it was through the intercession of the *venerable martyr* that the stubborn Jew had in the last moment obtained God's mercy.[101] Eder in this text was merely reinforcing a message that the church had sought to communicate through Abeles's funeral. The young Simon was more than a brave martyr. He was a powerful patron and protector of converted Jews. One of these converts, Johannes Fanta, had composed a prayer that was prominently posted at the public viewing. Petitioning the martyr for divine assistance, Fanta appealed for the safety of all Jews who had rejected the lies of the rabbis for the truth of the Catholic church.[102] This theme was also scripted directly into the funeral procession of the following day. Of the eight major groups that participated in the procession, the most conspicuous was the one that came immediately behind the casket. Dressed with red belts that matched their new patron's color, a party of recently baptized Jewish children led the cortege.[103] Though Eder and other ecclesiastical leaders involved in this matter certainly saw the murdered boy as a new martyr saint, on a metaphysical level they viewed Abeles as a divine sign, for there was clearly an apocalyptic dimension to this entire drama as well. Eder considered the conversion and death of Simon a decisive turning point in the history of Prague's Jews. He was the first fruit of what would be an abundant harvest, with God's grace the beginning of the final and complete conversion of the city's ghetto. This point was also echoed in the *Processus Inquisitorius*. The preface raised an intriguing series of questions. Might Simon be an indication that human history was rapidly drawing to a close? Did his death belong to those series of portents that Christ foretold in Matthew 24? Was the fulfillment of St. Paul's prophecy in Romans 11 at hand? Was the long-awaited redemption of Israel near? Such were the musings of a triumphant church whose victory over heresy seemed complete and whose expectations were now set on eternal glory.

---

[100] Eder, *Virilis constantia*, pp. 81–9.   [101] Ibid., p. 89.   [102] Ibid., pp. 65–6.   [103] Ibid., p. 72.

Marc Fumaroli has reminded us that the seventeenth century was the age of eloquence, an observation that is particularly appropriate for the Czech lands. The rhetorical strategies of painters and preachers, of musicians and missionaries, were critical in a culture that in large part defined religious identity through signs and markers. This process of erecting signs and constructing markers reached a high point with Nepomuk and Abeles. Both are significant as they reflect slightly different facets of this complex process. Nepomuk illustrates the reach of the sacred. His seeming ubiquity either in statuary or other forms of representational art demonstrates how effectively Catholicism was able to penetrate nearly every aspect of Bohemian culture by 1740. The emphasis is different with Abeles. Here we see the remarkable transformative power of Catholicism, its potential to manipulate elements of even non-Christian cultures and reshape them into orthodox forms. In the hands of the church a rebellious Jewish adolescent is changed into a martyr and a saint. Not coincidentally, two years after Abeles's death a municipal court in Prague handed down its verdict on a contentious blasphemy case. When the court ordered the Jewish community to attach the inscription, "Holy, holy, holy, the Lord of Hosts," on to the great cross of the Charles Bridge, the Hebrew language itself became a literal marker of Catholic sanctity.[104]

---

[104] Alexandr Putík, "The Hebrew inscription on the crucifix at Charles Bridge in Prague," *Judaica Bohemiae* 35 (1999), 26–71.

Conclusion
Between force and persuasion

Sometime around 1614, the Italian artist Giovanni Pietro de Pomis completed one of the most dramatic representations of future Emperor Ferdinand II, an allegorical portrayal of his patron as a champion of Catholic Reform (Figure 25). Dressed in full armor, the archduke stands in the heavens leading a cosmic struggle against heresy. To his left three figures grapple with each other in the clouds. Truth with a star shining from her forehead has succeeded in dislodging the mask that has hidden Heresy's true features, the face of an ugly hag. The winged form of Chronos, however, intervenes and restrains her from completely vanquishing the enemy. The task of completing the mission is entrusted to Ferdinand. With a sword in one hand and the scales of justice in the other, a resolute Ferdinand has firmly planted his heel on the prone body of Heresy. The figure of Wisdom stands behind him ready to assist the young prince in this divine mission to rid the Habsburg lands, if not all of Europe, from the scourge of heresy.

De Pomis's canvas is in many respects an appropriate image with which to conclude, for it raises two fundamental issues central to this study. Most pointedly, it directs our attention to the relationship of force and persuasion. Thematically, we have primarily focused on the gentler arts of persuasion as we have explored the creative resources of early modern Catholicism. Bohemia's painters and preachers, missionaries and musicians, antiquarians and architects were remarkably imaginative and resourceful in their quest to restore the old faith. But as I have attempted to point out, force or at the very least the threat of coercion was never absent. Two recent monographs, in fact, prominently feature de Pomis's Ferdinand on their covers in their respective studies of how constraint and compulsion were used to quell dissent in Habsburg lands during this period.[1] The Bohemian situation certainly needs to be located in the broader setting of European Catholic reform. Ronnie Hsia conjures the

---

[1] Arno Strohmeyer, *Konfessionskonflikt und Herrschaftsordnung* (Mainz: Philipp von Zabern, 2006); Arno Herzig, *Der Zwang zum wahren Glauben* (Göttingen: Vandenhoeck & Ruprecht, 2000).

25. Ferdinand II as champion of the Counter-Reformation, Giovanni Pietro de Pomis

image of a battlefield to characterize a "militant" Catholic resurgence occurring in a region tightly wedged between a solidly Protestant north and a decidedly Catholic south. Indeed, he sees Bohemia as the site of some of the fiercest fighting in this confessional struggle over the contested middle ground that ranged from France to Poland. The assessment of Arno Herzig is even more extreme. Herzig observes that approximately one quarter of central Europe (the German lands, Austria and Bohemia) was forcibly returned to Catholicism. To understand this phenomenon he describes what he explicitly labels an early modern form of *Gleichschaltung*, a term of course normally associated with Nazi totalitarianism.[2]

[2] R. Po-Chia Hsia, *The World of Catholic Renewal, 1540–1770* (Cambridge: Cambridge University Press, 2nd edn 2005), pp. 61–81; Herzig, *Der Zwang zum wahren Glauben*, p. 12.

Despite the somewhat distorted picture that Herzig presents, it cannot be denied that coercion assumed ever greater importance during the reign of Charles VI at the close of our study. We have already noted the general spirit of Catholic triumphalism that accompanied the young Habsburg to the throne and was reflected in his various artistic commissions. We have considered the new legislation that he helped push through in Bohemia to counter the perceived threat of crypto-Protestantism and a series of even harsher and more restrictive mandates directed against the kingdom's large Jewish community. Charles VI was instrumental in establishing the general framework of Habsburg religious policy that remained in effect until the reforms of Joseph II at the end of the century. He sought to isolate the scattered Protestant enclaves of his domains, cut off their international connections and even deny the *ius emigrandi* which had been guaranteed at Westphalia. A system of permanent missions was established to convert these stubborn communities, and if all this failed, there was still the option of breaking up these Protestant outposts by forced labor, military service or transport to eastern regions such as Siebenbürgen. Charles was particularly active in Hungary. With the retreat of the Turkish menace and the settling of the Rákóczi uprising (1703–11) the Habsburgs had a freer hand to suppress Protestantism and reinvigorate Catholicism. The 1731 *Resolutio Carolina* confirmed older legislation against religious dissidents, placing all Protestant parishes under the supervision of Catholic bishops, outlawing conversion to either Calvinism or Lutheranism and excluding non-Catholics from public office.[3]

Where then does this leave us? This narrative of force seems to be leading us back to older historiographical traditions where stories of Habsburg repression fed so nicely into nationalist models, where the past was frequently presented in simplistic terms, where virtue was pitted against vice, coercion against freedom. A newer history of violence is emerging, though, where social conflict is presented in a more nuanced and methodologically sophisticated fashion. Such an approach could be useful in the Bohemian setting.[4] On the other side of the spectrum, scholarship on early modern religion often starts from an entirely different vantage point. Significant attention has been recently devoted to the complex set of issues surrounding

---

[3] Marc Venard, ed., *Histoire du Christianisme*, vol. IX, *L'âge de raison (1620/30–1750)* (Paris: Desclée, 1997), pp. 32–4; W. R. Ward, *Christianity under the Ancien Régime 1648–1789* (Cambridge: Cambridge University Press, 1999), pp. 62–7.

[4] See for example David Nirenberg, *Communities of Violence* (Princeton: Princeton University Press, 1996).

what Andrew Pettegree describes as the "culture of persuasion."[5] These two traditions meet for this study in Bohemia. The historian, however, must be careful not to embrace one without forgetting the other. The recatholicization of the Czech lands was a complicated interplay between force and persuasion. A squadron of soldiers often quite literally stood behind those resourceful missionaries who ranged across the countryside. The past is messy, and the historian must at times settle with ambiguity. The stories we tell may not be as emotionally satisfying as older narratives where hero and villain were more easily identifiable, but such accounts gloss over the rich complexity of the human condition. Jesuit activity in Bohemia is a case in point. Though I have attempted to make a few general observations concerning their work and challenge one or two older stereotypes, it is frankly problematic to draw too many conclusions for an organization whose members were involved in so many different pursuits and whose views represented a significant range of opinion. Were they advocates of the common folk or exploiters of the poor? Such questions are not generally helpful, for they are frequently based on naïve assumptions of human nature. Depending on context, Bohemia's Jesuits were both criticized and praised.[6]

If de Pomis's depiction of Ferdinand raises this thorny issue of force and persuasion, it also points us to a second question central to the study. Did this program of recatholicization work? The confident Ferdinand of the painting stands poised to finish off his foe and reestablish the true faith in his lands. Does the strident visual rhetoric of the artist, however, match reality? Here again we may be dealing with a *question mal posée*. More broadly, this is a problematic issue for the entire history of Christianity. How effective were the efforts of missionaries and other clerical elites in communicating the fundamental tenets of the faith to ordinary men and women? Historians of Christianity from late antiquity to modernity have long wrestled with variations of this basic question, and their responses more often than not have been negative. Such is certainly the case for the early modern period with scholars routinely citing examples of widespread doctrinal illiteracy across the continent. Protestant and Catholic reformers alike chronically bemoaned both religious indifference and confessional ignorance. But is this dogmatic yardstick the one we should use when

---

[5] Andrew Pettegree, *Reformation and the Culture of Persuasion* (Cambridge: Cambridge University Press, 2005).

[6] For anti-Jesuit polemic see Zdeňka Tichá, ed., *Verše bolesti, posměchu i vzdoru* (Prague: ČSAV, 1958), pp. 62–3.

measuring success and failure in the Czech lands? In Bohemia as in most of Europe, there was frequently a disjuncture between the idealistic goals of clerical elites and how confessional formation and church building actually occurred on the ground. Missionaries to this region were often disappointed by the tepid response to their exertions. There are annual letters of the Jesuits and reports from other missionaries in the field which noted that those with whom they worked were only Catholic in name. Old habits of mind were slow to pass. At the same time there were more optimistic appraisals of the situation. In 1651 a church commission reported to Ferdinand that the last heretic had disappeared from Bohemia. Teams of seventeenth-century statisticians deputized to count the kingdom's Catholics and non-Catholics also confirmed that the task of recatholicization was with a few exceptions nominally complete.[7] For whatever their value, these numbers hold steady all the way through the early twentieth century. Only 1–3 percent of the population officially converted to Protestantism with the 1781 Edict of Toleration, and 96 percent still registered as Catholic according to an 1890 survey. Not until the 1920s is there a significant drop in these figures.[8]

Statistics of course can be misleading, but at the very least they indicate that by the eighteenth century the vast majority of Bohemians officially identified themselves as Catholic, but even this conclusion is slightly ambiguous, for it does not explain how they construed issues of religious identity. To help clarify these questions and better assess the overall success and failure of Catholic Reform in the Czech lands, let me close with a few concluding observations. When the Counter-Reformation worked its way through central Europe, a number of Protestant enclaves successfully resisted the growing pressure to convert or emigrate. In this respect, Bohemia does stand out from many of its neighbors. Despite the determined efforts of the Habsburgs and the growing numbers of Polish immigrants, Silesia's Protestant community, though weakened, did not succumb. The Pietists of Teschen (Cieszyn) spearheaded a revival in the early eighteenth century while the Protestant schools of Breslau (Wrocław) continued to educate a Lutheran elite. Calvinism, of course, was not eradicated in Hungary, and in the more remote valleys of Upper Hungary, Slovak Lutherans were a persistent irritant to their immediate Catholic overlords. In the archbishopric of Salzburg Protestantism had been

---

[7] M. E. Ducruex, "La mission et le rôle des missionnaires dans les pays tchèques au XVIIe siècle," in *Transmettre la foi, XVIe–XXe siècle* (Paris: Ministère de l'éducation nationale, 1984), vol. I, pp. 32–4.

[8] M. E. Ducreux, "Entre catholicisme et protestantisme: l'identité tchèque," *Le débat* 59 (1990), 123–4.

essentially suppressed by the end of the sixteenth century only to reappear dramatically with revivals of the 1680s. The situation culminated fifty years later when in 1731–2 20,000 Lutherans were forced to pack their belongings and sent into exile across Europe and North America. In comparison, the Habsburgs and their allies settled matters in Bohemia in an effective and efficient fashion. Though there were occasional reports of secret Protestants, there was no organized infrastructure of a dissident church. So weak was their presence that in 1781 Bohemian Protestantism had to be jumpstarted by importing clergy from Hungary.[9]

Secondly, as I noted in the introduction, this study has focused not on interior patterns of belief but on public modes of representation. Interiority is difficult for the historian to measure and evaluate in the best of circumstances. Talkative Friulian millers who through their philosophical musings reveal the rough lineaments of that shadowy province of folk belief and popular piety are rare. More importantly, Bohemian sources of the seventeenth century are not as rich as the archival resources of a Spain or Italy that allow the researcher easier access to this fascinating world. With the destruction of war and the mass movement of peoples across the Czech lands this was an era of tremendous social dislocation. Even when peace returned, it must not be forgotten that the kingdom's gutted ecclesiastical infrastructure was only superficially restored. So many parishes remained vacant, and as late as the early eighteenth century, only one archbishop and six bishops oversaw the care of 4 million souls in Bohemia and Silesia. With the church so massively understaffed it is not surprising that we know precious little about lay religiosity. The records that we do have from this period tend to be more prescriptive than descriptive. A 1651 census is relatively thin on description. Only rarely does one find a line or two identifying the stubborn few who refused to convert.[10]

Given these conditions the historian must creatively use the sources available. One issue, however, does become clear over time. Bohemian Catholicism was a capacious religion. We have already seen to what degree Utraquism could be absorbed back into the Roman faith. Even before White Mountain it could be difficult to distinguish Catholic from Hussite. When Zbyněk Berka of Dubá (1551–1606) was nominated archbishop by Rudolf II, the papal nuncio Cesare Speciano protested, arguing that the candidate was actually raised in the Utraquist faith. Berka counter-attacked

---

[9] Ward, *Christianity under the Ancien Régime*, p. 111.
[10] See for example a short report of four Lutheran women of Dalovice village in Eliška Čáňová, ed., *Soupis poddaných podle víry z roku 1651, Loketsko* (Prague: Státní ústřední archiv v Praze, 1993), pp. 23–4.

by pointing to his credentials as a canon of Salzburg and an administrator in the Regensburg bishopric. Though he admitted his mother had lived and died as an Utraquist, he refused to condemn her, for her faith had been approved at the Council of Basel – this coming from a figure typically portrayed as a champion of the Counter-Reformation! At the same time key Habsburg allies such as Karl von Liechtenstein and Zdeněk Vojtěch Lobkovic could in their efforts to restore Catholicism defend the central feature of Utraquism, the lay use of the chalice.[11] As we saw in chapter 4, after White Mountain Bohemia's antiquarians slowly began to rehabilitate and assimilate elements of the Hussite legacy into their broader assessment of the kingdom's culture. Musicians and hymn writers did the same in their fields as well. The process of reclaiming the past continued into the late eighteenth and nineteenth centuries. In the 1780s Kaspar Royko, a professor of theology at the university in Prague, went as far as publishing a study on the Council of Constance which portrayed Hus as both a good Catholic and precursor of the Enlightenment. In the area of popular piety Marie-Elizabeth Ducreux has argued for the eighteenth century, a period when missionary reports and inquisitorial records become a more regular feature of the archives, that many men and women held on to older heterodox beliefs while publicly acknowledging their Catholic identity.[12] In the early twentieth century the Czech clergy were among the church's most voluble critics and progressive reformers. After national independence the more radical members of the Union of Czech Clergy would advocate clerical marriage, the adoption of Czech and Slovak in the liturgy, and the establishment of a Czechoslovak patriarchate.[13] Bohemian Catholicism was thus an expansive phenomenon slowly encompassing an increasingly larger scope of practice and belief as it adjusted to changing cultural and political conditions.

A final question remains unanswered. If the Catholic Reformation did not create a tight-knit community of men and women who had a clear understanding of core doctrines of faith and resolutely rejected all forms of heterodoxy, what did it accomplish in the Czech lands? Here we do have an answer that is less ambiguous. Bohemia's Catholic revival was most

---

[11] Cited in Petr Maťa, "Constructing and crossing confessional boundaries: the high nobility and the Reformation of Bohemia," in H. Louthan, G. Cohen and F. Szabo, eds., *Authority and Religion in Central Europe* (New York: Berghahn, forthcoming); Karl Bosl, ed., *Handbuch der Geschichte der böhmischen Länder* (Stuttgart: Hiersemann, 1974), vol. II, p. 291.

[12] Jaroslav Střítecký, "*The Czech Question* a century later," *Czechoslovak Sociological Review* 3 (1992), 61; M. E. Ducreux, "Entre catholicisme et protestantisme," 118–19.

[13] Ludvík Němec, *The Czechoslovak Heresy and Schism: The Emergence of a National Czechoslovak Church* (Philadelphia: American Philosophical Society, 1975), pp. 9–12.

successful in creating a corporate sense of identity. It may not have been on a sophisticated theological level, but certainly on a more basic plane there was a growing awareness of confessional belonging. What we saw occurring on the Charles Bridge with the layout of the statuary reminding passersby of their religious allegiances was a microcosm of this more general phenomenon. Bohemia's culture was chock-a-block with basic signs of confessional identity. New forms of religious art and music, an ever-increasing number of pilgrimage shrines, and the reappearance of the saints were all simple markers for ordinary believers. In this light the presence of outsiders was also significant. As we observed with the Abeles affair, one of the more disturbing features of Czech Catholicism was a distinct strain of anti-Semitism. Though it may be too much to argue that anti-Semitism was intrinsic to Bohemia's Counter-Reformation, it did serve an obvious and useful sociological purpose. The slurs and barbs of preachers, the scandalous stories of the antiquarians and the riots of students all helped reinforce a social order where the terms of inclusion and exclusion were clearly defined.

Abbreviations
Primary Source Collections: Archives and Libraries

National Archive, Prague
NA (Národní archiv)

Archival fonds of the National Archive
APA: Archiv pražského arcibiskupství (Archive of the Prague Archbishopric)
AZK: Archivy českých klášterů zrušených za Josefa II. (Archives of Bohemian cloisters dissolved by Joseph II)
ČDK: Česká dvorská kancelář (Bohemian Court Chancery)
JS: Jesuitika 1555–1774 (Society of Jesus)
NB: Náboženská bratrstva (Religious brotherhoods)
ŘK: Řád kapucínů (Capuchin Order)
ŘPi: Řád piaristů (Piarist Order)
ŘR: Řád redemptoristů (Redemptorist Order)
SM: Stará manipulace

Archive of the Prague Castle/Metropolitan Chapter of St. Vitus, Prague
APH-AMKSV (Archiv Pražského hradu-Archiv metropolitní kapituly u Sv. Víta)

Archive of the Charles University, Prague
AUK (Archiv Univerzity Karlovy)

Archive of the City of Prague
AHMP (Archiv hlavního města Prahy)

Strahov Monastic Library, Prague
SK (Strahovská knihovna)

National Library of the Czech Republic, Prague
NK (Národní knihovna České republiky)

University Library, Prague (now part of the National Library)
UK (Univerzitní knihovna)

Library of the National Museum, Prague
KNM (Knihovna Národního muzea)

Austrian National Library, Manuscript Division, Vienna
ÖNB, HSS (Österreichische Nationalbibliothek, Handschriftensammlung)

Select bibliography

PRIMARY SOURCES

Acta utriusque processus in causa canonisationis beati Joannis Nepomuceni martyris (Vienna: Schilgen, 1721)

Balbín, Bohuslav, *Bohemia docta*, 2 vols. (Prague: J. C. Hraba, 1777)

 Diva Montis Sancti, seu origines et miracula magnae Dei hominumque matris Mariae (Prague: Typis Universitatis Carolo-Ferdinandeae, 1665)

 Diva Turzanensis, seu Historia originis et miraculorum magnae Dei hominumque matris Mariae (Olomouc: Typis V. H. Etteli, 1658)

 Diva Wartensis, seu Historia originis et miracula magnae Dei hominumque matris Mariae (Prague: Formis Caesareo-Academicis, 1655)

 Epitome historica rerum Bohemicarum (Prague: Typis Universitatis Carolo-Ferdinandeae, 1677)

 Miscellanea historica regni Bohemiae, decas I, 1–8; decas II, 1–2 (Prague, 1679–88)

 Syntagma historicum quo illustrissimae et pervetustae stirpis, comitum de Guttenstein, origines et memoriae continentur (Prague: Typis Universitatis Carolo-Ferdinandeae, 1665)

 Vita B. Joannis Nepomuceni martyris (Augsburg: Typis J. J. Lotteri, 1725)

 Vita Venerabilis Arnesti (Prague: Kastner, 1664)

Beckovský, Jan, *Poselkyně starých příběhů českých*, ed. A. Rezek, 3 vols. (Prague: Dědictví sv. Prokopa, 1879–80)

Benrath, G. A., ed., *Die Selbstbiographie des Heidelberger Theologen und Hofpredigers Abraham Scultetus (1566–1624)* (Karlsruhe: Evangelischer Presseverband, 1966)

Bílovský, Bohumír, *Doctrina christiana animabus inservitura* (Olomouc: Jan Adam Avinger, 1721)

 Pia quadragesima (Opava: Jan Kašpar Braüer, 1721)

 Víno ze svadby v Káni a potřebnost roucha svadebního, ed. J. Vašica (Ve Staré Říši, 1932)

Bissel, J., *Leo Galeatus* (Amberg: Burger, 1677)

Božan, Jan Josef, *Slavíček rájský* (Hradec Králové: V. J. Tybely, 1719)

Bridel, Fridrich, *Básnické dílo* (Prague: Torst, 1994)

Chanovský, A., *Správa křesťanská* (Prague, 1676)

Comenius, J. A., *Historia persecutionum ecclesiae Bohemicae* (Amsterdam, 1648)

Eder, Johann, *Virilis constantia pueri duodennis Simonis Abeles* (Prague: Typis Academicis, 1696)

d'Elvert, Christian, ed., *Die Bestrafung der böhmischen Rebellion insbesondere die Correspondenz Ferdinand II. mit dem Fürsten Liechtenstein* (Brünn: A. Nitsch, 1868)

Emericus a Sancto Stephano, *Pragerisches Gross und Klein* (Prague: Höger, 1737)

Fama posthuma Ioannis Nepomuceni (Prague: Typis Academicis, 1641)

Habervešl of Habernfeld, Ondřej, *Bellum Bohemicum* (Leiden, 1645)

Hammerschmid, J. F., *Prodromus gloriae Pragenae* (Prague: Wolfgang Wickhart, 1723)

Hanegravio, Cornelio, *Compendio della vita, miracoli, et instituto del glorioso Patriarcha S. Norberto* (Rome: Giacomo Mascardi, 1632)

Hirnhaim, Hieronymus, *De typho generis humani* (Prague: Typis Georgii Czernoch, 1676)

S. Norberti Archiepiscopi Magdeburgensis (Prague: Typis Georgii Czernoch, 1676)

Holan Rovenský, Václav Karel, *Capella regia musicalis* (Prague: Georg Labaun, 1693)

Holyk, Georg, *Blutige Thränen des höchst bedrängten und geängsten Böhmer Landes* (Wittenberg: Meyer, 1673)

Jestřábský, Valentin Bernard, *Katechysmus Domácý* (Olomouc: Jan Adam Avinger, 1723)

Vidění rozličné sedláčka sprostného (Opava: Schindler, 1719)

Jireček, Josef, ed., *Paměti nejvyššího kancléře království českého Viléma hraběte Slavaty*, 2 vols. (Prague: I. L. Kober, 1866–8)

Kalista, Zdeněk, ed., *Korespondence Zuzany Černínové z Harasova s jejím synem Humprechtem Janem Černínem z Chudenic* (Prague: Melantrich, 1941)

Kamenitzky, Joachim, *Eigentlicher Entwurff und Vorbildung der vortrefflichen kostbahren und Welt-berühmten Prager Brucken* (Prague, 1716)

Khevenhiller, Franz Christoph, *Annales Ferdinandei* (Leipzig: Weidmann, 1721–6)

Koniáš, A., *Clavis haeresim claudens et aperiens* (Hradec Králové: V. J. Tybely, 1729)

Kořínek, Jan, *Staré paměti kutnohorské* (Prague: Typis Georgii Czernoch, 1675)

Kruger, Jiří, *Maiales Triumphi* (Litomyšl: J. Arnolt, 1669)

Küchelbecker, J. B., *Allerneueste Nachricht vom Römisch-Käyserl. Hofe* (Hanover: Förster, 1730)

Kurtzer Leben-und Todes Verfass des standhafften 12. jährigen Knabens Simonis Abeles (Prague: Typis Academicis, 1724)

Lamormaini, W., *Ferdinandi II. Romanorum imperatoris virtutes* (Antwerp: Apud Ioannem Meursium, 1638)

Lauritsch, Josef, *První věk rodičky Boží Rušánské* (Hradec Králové: V. J. Tybely, 1743)

Lerchenfels, Jan Sixt of, *Přenešení sv. Norberta* (Litoměřice, 1628)

Magni, Valerian, *De acatholicorum credendi regula iudicium* (Prague: Paulus Sessius, 1628)

Principia et specimen philosophiae (Cologne: Apud Jodocum Kalcovium, 1652)

Manni, Giovanni Battista, *Věčný pekelný žalář* (Prague: Jezuitská tiskárna, 1676)

Marek, Damascen, *Trojí chléb nebeský* (Prague: Hraba, 1728)

Miller, Johannes, *Historia Beatissimae Virginis Glacensis* (Glatz: Pega, 1690)

    Historia Mariascheinensis (Prague: In der Academischen Buchdruckerey des Collegii S. J., 1710)

Narratio translati e Saxonia in Boemiam sacri corporis beatissimi viri, Norberti (Prague: Paulus Sessius, 1627)

Octiduum S. Norberti triumphantis (Prague: Paulus Sessius, 1627)

Pešina, Tomáš, *Phosphorus septicornis, stella aliàs matutina* (Prague: Joannis Arnolti de Dobroslavina, 1673)

    Prodromus Moravographiae (Litomyšl: J. Arnolt, 1663)

    Thesaurus in lucem protractus, sive S. Mercurius, Maximus Orientis Martyr (Prague: Typis Joannis Arnolti de Dobroslavina, 1675)

Pick, Friedel, ed., *Denkschrift des Rektors Johannes Jessenius von Gross-Jessen an den Generallandtag von 1619 über Erneuerung der Prager Universität, Pragensia* 2 (1920)

    ed., *Die Prager Execution i. J. 1621. Flugblätter und Abbildungen, Pragensia* 5 (1922)

Písně nové, krátké naučení Křestanského náboženství v sobě obsahující (Prague: Burián Valda, 1588)

Podlaha, A., ed., *Dopisy reformační komisse v Čechách z let 1627–1629* (Prague, 1908)

Pontanus, G. B., *Bohemia pia* (Frankfurt: Apud Claud. Marnium & heredes Io. Aubrii, 1608)

Prägerische Execution (Prague: Albin, 1621)

Processus Inquisitorius (Prague: Endter, 1696)

Rosacius, Jan, *Koruna neuvadlá mučedlníkův božích českých* (n.p., 1621)

Rothe, Hans and Scholz, Friedrich, eds., *Svatováclavská bible*, 2 vols. (Paderborn: Schöningh, 2001)

Rotondo, Cristoforo Angelo, *Il neo-martire di Boemia* (Prague: G. Labaun, 1695)

Rozenplut ze Švarcenbachu, Jan, *Kancionál aneb Sebrání zpěvův pobožných* (Olomouc: Jiří Handl, 1601)

Schaller, J., *Beschreibung der königlichen Haupt- und Residenzstadt Prag* (Prague: Gerzabeck, 1795)

Scultetus, Abraham, *Krátká, avšak na mocném gruntu a základu Svatých Písem založená zpráva o modlářských obrazích* (Prague: Daniel Karolides z Karlsberka, 1620)

Skála ze Zhoře, Pavel, *Historie česká*, ed. Karel Tieftrunk, 5 vols. (Prague: I. L. Kober, 1865–70)

Stránský, Pavel, *Republica Bohemiae* (Leiden: Elzevir, 1634)

Středovský, Jan Jiří, *Sacra Moraviae historia sive vita ss. Cyrilli et Methudii* (Sulzbach: Lehmann, 1710)

Šteyer, Matěj, *Kancyonal Cžeský* (Prague: Jan Karel Jeřábek, 1687)

    Postylla Katolická (Prague: Archiepiscopal Press, 1737)

Táborský, Chrysostom Xaver Ignác, *Erschallende Lob-Stimm* (Olomouc: F. A. Hirnle, 1737)

Tanner, Jan, *Geschichte derer Helden von Sternen, oder deß uhralten und Ruhmwürdigsten Geschlechtes von Sternberg* (Prague: Hraba, 1732)

Muž apoštolský aneb život a ctnosti ctihodného pátera Albrechta Chanovského (Prague: Typis Universitatis Carolo-Ferdinandeae, 1680)

Swatá Cesta z Prahy do Staré Boleslawě (Prague: Typis Universitatis Carolo-Ferdinandeae, 1679)

Tanner, Matthias, *Societas Iesu apostolorum imitatrix* (Prague: Typis Universitatis Carolo-Ferdinandeae, 1694)

Societas Jesu usque ad sanguinis et vitæ profusionem militans (Prague: Typis Universitatis Carolo-Ferdinandeae, 1675)

"The travels of three English gentlemen, in the year 1734," in *The Harleian Miscellany* (London: White, 1810), vol. V, pp. 338–65

Tichá, Zdeňka, ed., *Verše bolesti, posměchu, i vzdoru* (Prague: ČSAV, 1958)

Veselý, Fabián, *Lehr-Geist- und Eyfer-volle Sonntags Predigen auf das gantze Jahr* (Augsburg: Veith, 1739)

Wagenseil, Johann Christof, *Belehrung der Jüdisch-Teutschen Red-und Schreibart* (Königsberg: Rhode, 1699)

Waldt, Ondřej František de, *Chwálo-Řeč, neb kázánj na některé Swátky* (Prague: Archiepiscopal Press, 1736)

SECONDARY MATERIAL

Adamson, John, ed., *The Princely Courts of Europe* (London: Weidenfeld & Nicolson, 1999)

Appuhn-Radtke, S., *Das Thesenblatt im Hochbarock* (Weißenhorn: A. H. Konrad Verlag, 1988)

Baďurová, A., *Bibliografie cizojazyčných bohemikálních tisků z let 1501–1800* (Prague: Knihovna Akademie věd České republiky, 2003), CD database

Baťková, R., ed., *Umělecké památky Prahy, Nové město/Vyšehrad/Vinohrady* (Prague: Academia, 1998)

Beissel, Stephan, *Wallfahrten zu unserer lieben Frau in Legende und Geschichte* (Freiburg i.B.: Herder, 1913)

Bílek, T. V., *Reformace katolická* (Prague: F. Backovský, 1892)

Bireley, Robert, "Ferdinand II: founder of the Habsburg monarchy," in T. V. Thomas and R. J. W. Evans, eds., *Crown, Church and Estates* (London: Macmillan, 1991), pp. 226–44

The Refashioning of Catholicism (Washington, D.C.: Catholic University Press, 1999)

Religion and Politics in the Age of the Counterreformation: Emperor Ferdinand II, William Lamormaini, S.J., and the Formation of Imperial Policy (Chapel Hill: University of North Carolina Press, 1981)

Blackbourn, David, *Marpingen: Apparitions of the Virgin Mary in Bismarckian Germany* (Oxford: Clarendon Press, 1993)

Blažíček, O. J., "Jan Jiří Bendl," *Umění* 30 (1982), 97–116

"Jan Jiří Bendl, Pražský sochař časného baroku," *Památky archaeologické* 4–5 (1934–5), 55–91

Blekastad, Milada, *Comenius* (Oslo: Universitetsforlaget, 1969)

Bobková-Valentová, Kateřina, *Každodenní život učitele a žáka jezuitského gymnázia* (Prague: Karolinum, 2006)

Bohatcová, Mirjam, *Česká kniha v proměnách staletí* (Prague: Panorama, 1990)

"Vzácná sbírka publicistických a portrétních dokumentů k počátku třicetileté války," *SbNMP* 27 (1982)

Bosl, Karl, ed., *Handbuch der Geschichte der böhmischen Länder*, vol. II (Stuttgart: Hiersemann, 1974)

Bukovský, Jan, *Loretánské kaple v Čechách a na Moravě* (Prague: Libri, 2000)

Bužga, Jaroslav, "Musiker und musikalische Institutionen im Zeitalter des Barocks," in Elmar Arro, ed., *Beiträge zur Musikgeschichte Osteuropas* (Wiesbaden: Steiner, 1977), pp. 351–9

Carlebach, Elisheva, *The Death of Simon Abeles: Jewish-Christian Tension in Seventeenth-Century Prague*. Third Annual Herbert Berman Memorial Lecture (New York: Center for Jewish Studies, Queens College, CUNY, 2003)

Catalano, Alessandro, *La Boemia e la riconquista delle coscienze: Ernst Adalbert von Harrach e la Controriforma in Europa centrale (1620–1667)* (Rome: Edizioni di storia e letteratura, 2005)

"Juan Caramuel Lobkowicz (1606–1682) e la riconquista delle coscienze in Boemia," *Römische Historische Mitteilungen* 44 (2002), 339–92

Châtellier, Louis, *La religion des pauvres: Les missions rurales en Europe et la formation du catholicisme moderne, XVIe–XIXe siècle* (Paris: Aubier, 1993)

Chaline, Olivier, *La Bataille de la Montagne Blanche* (Paris: Éditions Noesis, 1999)

Christian, William, *Local Religion in Sixteenth-Century Spain* (Princeton: Princeton University Press, 1981)

Conti, Vittorio, "*Consociatio civitatum*. L'idea di repubblica nelle *Respublicae Elzeviriane*," in Chiara Continisio and Cesare Mozzarelli, eds., *Repubblica e virtù* (Rome: Bulzoni, 1995), pp. 207–26

Coreth, Anna, *Pietas Austriaca*, trans. William Bowman and Anna Maria Leitgeb (West Lafayette: Purdue University Press, 2004)

Cygan, Jerzy, "Der Anteil Valerian Magnis an der Verteidigung des Piaristenordens," *Collectanea Franciscana* 38 (1968), 364–72

Valerianus Magni (1586–1661): "Vita prima," operum recensio et bibliographia (Rome: Institutum Historicum Capuccinum, 1989)

Čáňová, Eliška, "Vývoj správy pražské arcidiecéze v době násilné rekatolizace Čech," *SbAP* 35 (1983), 486–560

Čermák, Dominik, *Premonstráti v Čechách a na Moravě* (Prague: Nákl. Kanonie Strahovské, 1877)

Černý, František, ed., *Dějiny českého divadla*, vol. I (Prague: Academia, 1968)

Čornejová, I., "Das 'Temno' im mitteleuropäischen Kontext: Zur Kirchen- und Bildungspolitik im Böhmen der Barockzeit," *Bohemia* 34 (1993), 342–58

Tovaryšstvo Ježíšovo: Jezuité v Čechách (Prague: Mladá fronta, 1995)

David, Zdeněk, *Finding the Middle Way* (Baltimore: Johns Hopkins University Press, 2003)

Dewald, Jonathan, *The European Nobility 1400–1800* (Cambridge: Cambridge University Press, 1996)

Ditchfield, Simon, *Liturgy, Sanctity and History in Tridentine Italy* (Cambridge: Cambridge University Press, 1995)

"Martyrs on the move: relics as vindicators of local diversity in the Tridentine church," in Diana Wood, ed., *Martyrs and Martyrologies, Studies in Church History*, vol. XXX (Oxford: Blackwell, 1993), pp. 283–94

Ducreux, M. E., "L'hymnologie catholique tchèque de la Contre-Réforme," *Jahrbuch für Liturgik und Hymnologie* 30 (1985), 169–79

"La mission et le rôle des missionnaires dans les pays tchèques au XVIIe siècle," in *Transmettre la foi, XVIe–XXe siècle* (Paris: Ministère de l'éducation nationale, 1984), vol. I, pp. 31–46

"'Novost' hymnologického umění Adama Michny z Otradovic stručně naznačena," *Hudební věda* 38 (2001), 48–57

"Reading unto death: books and readers in eighteenth-century Bohemia," in Roger Chartier, ed., *The Culture of Print* (Oxford: Polity Press, 1989), pp. 191–229

"La reconquête catholique de l'espace bohémien," *Revue des Études Slaves* 60 (1988), 685–702

"Symbolický rozměr poutě do Staré Boleslavi," *ČČH* 95 (1997), 585–620

"Zum Thema Wallfahrt: das Beispiel Böhmens im 17. Jahrhundert," in R. Leeb, S. Pils and T. Winkelbauer, eds., *Staatsmacht und Seelenheil* (Vienna: Oldenbourg, 2007), pp. 98–108

Eade, John and Sallnow, Michael, eds., *Contesting the Sacred: The Anthropology of Christian Pilgrimage* (London: Routledge, 1991)

Eberhard, Winfried, *Konfessionsbildung und Stände in Böhmen (1478–1530)* (Munich: Oldenbourg, 1981)

Ekert, František, *Posvátná místa král. hl. města Prahy*, 2 vols. (Prague: Nákl. Dědictví sv. Jana Nepomuckého, 1883–4)

Elm, Kaspar, ed., *Norbert von Xanten* (Cologne: Wienand, 1984)

Evans, R. J. W., *The Making of the Habsburg Monarchy 1550–1700* (Oxford: Clarendon Press, 1979)

Rudolf II and His World (Oxford: Oxford University Press, 1973)

"The significance of the White Mountain for the culture of the Czech lands," *Bulletin of the Institute of Historical Research* 44 (1971), 34–54

Eybl, Franz, *Gebrauchsfunktionen barocker Predigtliteratur* (Vienna: W. Braumüller, 1982)

Fechtnerová, Anna, *Katalog grafických listů univerzitních tezí uložených ve Státní knihovně ČSR v Praze*, 4 vols. (Prague: Státní knihovna ČSR, 1984)

Forster, Marc, *Catholic Revival in the Age of the Baroque* (Cambridge: Cambridge University Press, 2001)

The Counter-Reformation in the Villages (Cornell: Cornell University Press, 1992)

Gebauer, J., *Die Publicistik über den Böhmischen Aufstand von 1618* (Halle: Niemeyer, 1880)

Gentilcore, David, *From Bishop to Witch: The System of the Sacred in Early Modern Terra d'Otranto* (Manchester: Manchester University Press, 1992)

Gindely, A., *Geschichte der Gegenreformation in Böhmen* (Leipzig: Duncker & Humblot, 1894)

Die Processierung der Häretiker in Böhmen unter Kaiser Karl VI (Prague: Verlag der königl. böhm. Gesellschaft der Wissenschaften, 1887)

Graham, B. F. H., *Bohemian and Moravian Graduals 1420–1600* (Turnhout: Brepols, 2006)

"The evolution of the Utraquist mass 1420–1620," *Catholic Historical Review* 92 (2006), 553–73

Greenblatt, Rachel L., "A community's memory: Jewish views of past and present in early modern Prague," unpublished Ph.D. thesis, Hebrew University of Jerusalem (2006)

Habermas, Rebekka, *Wallfahrt und Aufruhr: Zur Geschichte des Wunderglaubens in der frühen Neuzeit* (Frankfurt: Campus, 1991)

Hanzal, Josef, "Rekatolizace v Čechách – její historický smysl a význam," *SbH* 37 (1990), 37–92

Hassenpflug-Elzholz, Eila, *Böhmen und die böhmischen Stände in der Zeit des beginnenden Zentralismus* (Munich: Oldenbourg, 1982)

Heiss, Gernot, "'Ihro keiserlichen Mayestät zu Diensten…unserer ganzen fürstlichen Familie aber zur Glori': Erziehung und Unterricht der Fürsten von Liechtenstein im Zeitalter des Absolutismus," in E. Oberhammer, ed., *Der ganzen Welt ein Lob und Spiegel* (Munich: Oldenbourg, 1990), pp. 155–81

Hersche, Peter, *Der Spätjansenismus in Österreich* (Vienna: Verlag der Österreichischen Akademie der Wissenschaften, 1977)

Herzig, Arno, *Der Zwang zum wahren Glauben* (Göttingen: Vandenhoeck & Ruprecht, 2000)

Herzogenberg, Johanna von, "Marianische Geographie an böhmischen Wallfahrtsorten. Der Weisse Berg-Rimau in Südböhmen-der Heilige Berg," *Alte und moderne Kunst* 114 (1971), 9–21

"Zum Kult des heiligen Johannes Nepomuk," in *Johannes von Nepomuk* (Munich: Schöningh, 1973), pp. 25–35

Hojda, Z., *Kultura baroka v Čechách a na Moravě* (Prague: Historický ústav, 1992)

Holeton, David, "On the evolution of the Utraquist liturgy," *Studia liturgica* 25 (1995), 51–67

Holubová, Markéta, "Svatá Hora u Příbrami v obraze barokní doby," unpublished Ph.D. thesis, Charles University (2002)

Homerová, Klára, "Tisková cenzura v Čechách, 1621–1660," *SbNMP* 42–3 (1997–8)

Horák, F. and Tobolka, Z. V., *Knihopis československých tisků od doby nejstarší až do konce XVIII. století*, 2 vols., pts. 1–9 (Prague: V komisi knihkupectví F. Topiče, 1925–)

Horyna, Mojmír, *Jan Blažej Santini-Aichel* (Prague: Univerzita Karlova, 1998)

Hrejsa, Ferdinand, *Dějiny křesťanství v Československu*, 6 vols. (Prague: Spisy Husovy československé evangelické fakulty bohoslovecké, 1947–50)

Hrubý, F., *Lev Vilém z Kounic, barokní kavalír* (Brno: Státní oblastní archiv, 1987)

Hsia, R. Po-Chia, *The World of Catholic Renewal, 1540–1770* (Cambridge: Cambridge University Press, 2nd edn 2005)

Ingrao, Charles, *The Habsburg Monarchy 1618–1815* (Cambridge: Cambridge University Press, 2000)

Jireček, Josef, *Hymnologia Bohemica* (Prague: NKČSN, 1878)

Rukověť k dějinám literatury české do konce XVIII věku, 2 vols. (Prague: Tempský, 1875–6)

Johnson, Trevor, "Blood, tears and Xavier-water: Jesuit missionaries and popular religion in the eighteenth-century Upper Palatinate," in R. Scribner and T. Johnson, eds., *Popular Religion in Germany and Central Europe, 1400–1800* (New York: St. Martin's Press, 1996), pp. 183–202

"The recatholicisation of the Upper Palatinate (1621–circa 1700)," unpublished Ph.D. thesis, Cambridge University (1991)

Julia, Dominique, "Die Gegenreformation und das Lesen," in Roger Chartier and Guglielmo Cavallo, eds., *Die Welt des Lesens* (Frankfurt: Campus Verlag, 1997), pp. 359–70

Jungmann, Josef, *Historie literatury české* (Prague: Řiwnáč, 1849)

Kadlec, Jaroslav, *Bohemia Sancta* (Prague: Česká katolická charita, 1989)

Přehled českých církevních dějin, 2 vols. (Rome: Zvon, 1987)

Kalista, Zdeněk, *Čechové, kteří tvořili dějiny světa* (Prague: Garamond, 1999)

Česká barokní pouť (Žďár nad Sázavou: Cisterciana Sarensis, 2001)

Kaminsky, Howard, *A History of the Hussite Revolution* (Berkeley: University of California Press, 1967)

Kapner, G., *Barocker Heiligenkult in Wien und seine Träger* (Munich: Oldenbourg, 1978)

Karasek, A. and Lanz, J., *Krippenkunst in Böhmen und Mähren vom Frühbarock bis zur Gegenwart* (Marburg: N. G. Elwert Verlag, 1974)

Kaufmann, Thomas DaCosta, *Court, Cloister and City: The Art and Culture of Central Europe, 1450–1800* (Chicago: University of Chicago Press, 1995)

Kavka, F. and Petráň, J., eds., *Dějiny Univerzity Karlovy 1348–1990*, 4 vols. (Prague: Karolinum, 1995–8)

Kertzer, David, *Ritual, Politics and Power* (New Haven: Yale University Press, 1988)

Klitzner, Julius, *Hieronymus Hirnhaim* (Prague, 1943)

Konrád, Karel, *Dějiny posvátného zpěvu staročeského od XV věku do zrušení literátských bratrstev* (Prague: V. Kotrba, 1893)

Kopecký, Milan, *Staří slezští kazatelé* (Ostrava: Profil, 1970), 92–135

Kořán, Ivo, "Legenda a kult sv. Ivana," *Umění* 35 (1987), 219–39

Kramář, Vincenc, *Zpustošení Chrámu svatého Víta* (Prague: Artefactum, 1998)

Kriss-Rettenbeck, Lenz, ed., *Wallfahrt kennt keine Grenzen* (Munich: Schnell & Steiner, 1984)

Kroess, Alois, *Geschichte der böhmischen Provinz der Gesellschaft Jesu*, 3 vols. (Vienna: Opitz, 1910–38)

Kučera, J. and Rak, J., *Bohuslav Balbín a jeho místo v české kultuře* (Prague: Vyšehrad, 1983)

Kučera, Karel, "Raně osvícenský pokus o reformu pražské university," *AUC, HUCP* 4 (1963), 61–86

Kuchařová, Hedvika and Pařez, Jan, "Strahovští premonstráti a rekatolizace. Přístupy a problémy," in Ivana Čornejová, ed., *Úloha církevních řádů při pobělohorské rekatolizaci* (Prague: Univerzita Karlova, 2003), pp. 36–75

Kuchařová, Hedvika and Pokorný, Pavel, "Die St. Wenzels-Bibel im kulturhistorischen Zusammenhang," in Hans Rothe and Friedrich Scholz, eds., *Svatováclavská bible* (Paderborn: Schöningh, 2001), vol. II, pp. 551–85

Kutnar, F. and Marek, J., *Přehledné dějiny českého a slovenského dějepisectví* (Prague: Nakladatelství Lidové noviny, 1997)

Kyas, Vladimír, *Česká bible v dějinách národního písemnictví* (Prague: Vyšehrad, 1997)

Lasfargues, Yves, "Le culte mondial de Saint-Jean Népomucène aux XVIIe et XVIIIe siècles," unpublished Ph.D. thesis, Université de Paris (1965)

Louthan, Howard, "Mediating confessions in central Europe: the ecumenical activity of Valerian Magni," *Journal of Ecclesiastical History* 55 (2004), 681–99

Luebke, David, "The seditious uses of 'naïve monarchism' and Marian veneration in early modern Germany," *Past and Present* 154 (1997), 71–106

MacHardy, Karin, *War, Religion and Court Patronage in Habsburg Austria* (New York: Palgrave, 2003)

Maťa, Petr, *Svět české aristokracie (1500–1700)* (Prague: Nakladatelství Lidové noviny, 2004)

"Zrození tradice," *Opera Historica* 6 (1998), 513–50

Maťa, Petr and Winkelbauer, Thomas, eds., *Die Habsburgermonarchie 1620 bis 1740: Leistungen und Grenzen des Absolutismusparadigmas* (Stuttgart: Steiner, 2006)

Matsche, Franz, "Das Grabmal des hl. Johannes von Nepomuk im Prager Veitsdom," *Wallraf-Richartz-Jahrbuch* 38 (1976), 92–122

Die Kunst im Dienst der Staatsidee Kaiser Karls VI, 2 vols. (Berlin: de Gruyter, 1981)

Maur, Eduard, "Problémy farní organizace pobělohorských Čech," in Zdeňka Hledíková, ed., *Traditio et Cultus* (Prague: Karolinum, 1993), pp. 163–76

Melton, J. V. H., "The nobility in the Bohemian and Austrian lands, 1620–1780," in H. M. Scott, ed., *The European Nobilities* (New York: Longman, 1995), vol. II, pp. 110–43

Menčík, Ferdinand, "Censura v Čechách a na Moravě," *VKČSN* (1888), 85–136

Michna z Otradovic, Adam, *Das dichterische Werk: Česká mariánská muzika, Loutna česká, Svatoroční muzika*, ed. A. Škarka (Munich: Fink, 1968)

Mikulec, Jiří, *Barokní náboženská bratrstva v Čechách* (Prague: Nakladatelství Lidové noviny, 2000)

Pobělohorská rekatolizace v českých zemích (Prague: SPN, 1992)

Miller, Jaroslav, "Tištěné prameny o českém stavovském povstání z let 1618–1621 v anglických knihovnách," *FHB* 20 (2002), 133–213

Molnar, E., "The Catholicity of the Utraquist church of Bohemia," *Anglican Theological Review* 41 (1959), 260–70

Momigliano, Arnaldo, "Ancient history and the antiquarian," in A. D. Momigliano, *Studies in Historiography* (London: Weidenfeld & Nicolson, 1969), pp. 1–39

Neubauer, E., "Die Fortführung der Gebeine des Erzbischofs Norbert aus Magdeburg im Jahre 1626," *Geschichts-Blätter für Stadt und Land Magdeburg* 25 (1890), 15–46

Neumann, Jaromír, "Das ikonographische Programm der Wallfahrtskirche St. Johannes Nepomuk auf dem Grünen Berg," in *Festschrift Kurt Rossacher* (Salzburg: Verlag des Salzburger Barockmuseums, 1983), pp. 241–63

"Ikonologie Santiniho chrámu v Kladrubech," *Umění* 33 (1985), 97–136

Škrétové: Karel Škréta a jeho syn (Prague: Akropolis, 2000)

Nolan, Mary Lee and Nolan, Sidney, *Christian Pilgrimage in Modern Western Europe* (Chapel Hill: University of North Carolina Press, 1989)

Novotný, K. and Poche, E., *Karlův most* (Prague: Poláčka, 1947)

Oettinger, Rebecca Wagner, *Music as Propaganda in the German Reformation* (Aldershot: Ashgate, 2001)

O'Malley, John, *The First Jesuits* (Cambridge, MA: Harvard University Press, 1993)

Trent and All That: Renaming Catholicism in the Early Modern Era (Cambridge, MA: Harvard University Press, 2000)

Pagel, Walter, "Religious motives in the medical biology of the seventeenth century," *Bulletin of the Institute of the History of Medicine* 3 (1935), 97–312

Palmitessa, James, "The Prague uprising of 1611: property, politics and Catholic renewal in the early years of Habsburg rule," *Central European History* 31 (1998), 299–328

Panochová, Ivana, "Biblicismy v české architektuře 17. století," *Umění* 52 (2004), 198–217

Pelcl, F., *Abbildungen böhmischer und mährischer Gelehrten und Künstler*, 4 vols. (Prague: Gerle, 1773–82)

Petráň, Josef, *Staroměstská exekuce* (Prague: Rodiče, 2004)

Pettegree, Andrew, *Reformation and the Culture of Persuasion* (Cambridge: Cambridge University Press, 2005)

Podlaha, A., "Z dějin katolických misií v Čechách," *SbHKr* 4 (1895), 104–31

Posvátná místa Království českého, 7 vols. (Prague: Nákl. Dědictví sv. Jana Nepomuckého, 1907–13)

Polc, Jaroslav, *Svatý Jan Nepomucký*, 2 vols. (Rome: Křesťanská akademie, 1972)

Polišenský, Josef, "Komenský a české dějepisectví bělohorského období," *Acta Comeniana* 22 (1963), 61–83

ed., *Kniha o bolesti a smutku: výbor z moravských kronik XVII. století* (Prague: Nakladatelství Elk, 1948)

Pörtner, Regina, *The Counter-Reformation in Central Europe: Styria 1580–1630* (Oxford: Oxford University Press, 2001)

Preiss, Pavel, *František Antonín Špork a barokní kultura v Čechách* (Prague: Paseka, 2003)

Press, Volker, "*Denn der Adel bildet die Grundlage und die Säulen des Staates*. Adel im Reich 1650–1750," in E. Oberhammer, ed., *Der ganzen Welt ein Lob und Spiegel* (Munich: Oldenbourg, 1990), pp. 11–32

Purš, Jaroslav and Kropilák, Miroslav, *Přehled dějin Československa I/2 (1526–1848)* (Prague: Academia, 1982)

Putík, Alexandr, "The Hebrew inscription on the crucifix at Charles Bridge in Prague," *Judaica Bohemiae* 32 (1997), 26–71

"The Prague Jewish community in the late 17th and early 18th centuries," *Judaica Bohemiae* 35 (1999), 4–140

Raková, I., "Cesta k vzniku Karlo-Ferdinandovy Univerzity (Spory o pražské vysoké učení v l. 1622–54)," *AUC, HUCP* 24 (1984), 7–40

Rejzek, A., *Bohuslav Balbín T.J., jeho život a práce* (Prague: Nakladem dědictví Sv. Prokopa, 1908)

Renton, Barbara Ann, "The musical culture of 18th-century Bohemia with special emphasis on the music inventories of Osek and the Knights of the Cross," unpublished Ph.D. thesis, CUNY (1990)

Rezek, A., "Tak-zvaná 'Idea gubernationis ecclesiasticae' z času kardinála Harracha," *VKČSN* (1893), 1–7

Ridder-Symoens, Hilde de, ed., *Universities in Early Modern Europe, 1500–1800*, 2 vols. (Cambridge: Cambridge University Press, 1996)

Royt, Jan, "Křesťanská pouť po barokních Čechách," *ČL* 79 (1992), 323–39
  Obraz a kult v Čechách 17. a 18. století (Prague: Karolinum, 1999)
  ed., *Svatý Václav v umění 17. a 18. století* (Prague: Národní galerie, 1994)

Sehnal, Jiří, "Die Entwicklungstendenzen und Stilschichten im tschechischen barocken Kirchenlied," *Musica antiqua* 3 (1972), 127–60

Seibt, Ferdinand, ed., *Bohemia sacra* (Düsseldorf: Pädagogischer Verlag Schwann, 1974)

Seitz, W., "Die graphischen Thesenblätter des 17. und 18. Jahrhunderts: Ein Forschungsvorhaben über ein Spezialgebiet barocker Graphik," *Wolfenbütteler Barock-Nachrichten* 11 (1984), 105–13

Soergel, Philip, *Wondrous in His Saints* (Berkeley: University of California Press, 1993)

Sousedík, Stanislav, *Filosofie v českých zemích mezi středověkem a osvícenstvím* (Prague: Vyšehrad, 1997)
  "Jan Jesenský as the ideologist of the Bohemian estates' revolt," *Acta Comeniana* 11 (1995), 13–24
  "Der Scotismus in den böhmischen Ländern," *Collectanea Franciscana* 60 (1990), 477–503

Spiegel, Käthe, "Die Prager Universitätsunion (1618–54)," *MVGDB* 62 (1924), 5–94

Straka, C., *Přenešení ostatků Sv. Norberta z Magdeburku na Strahov (1626–1628)* (Prague: Kuncíř, 1927)

Sullivan, Henry, "Fray Juan Caramuel y Lobkowitz O. Cist.: the Prague years, 1647–59," in Michael McGrath, ed., *Studies in Honor of John Jay Allen* (Newark: Juan de la Cuesta, 2005), pp. 339–74

Sutthof, Ludger, *Gotik im Barock* (Münster: Lit, 1990)

Svátek, Josef, "Organizace řeholních institucí v českých zemích a péče o jejich archivy," *SbAPr* 20 (1970), 503–624
  Pražské pověsti a legendy (Prague: Paseka, 1997)

Svatoš, Martin, "Zur Mehrsprachigkeit der Literatur in den böhmischen Ländern des 17. und 18. Jahrhunderts," *WSJ* 46 (2000), 33–42

Svobodný, Petr, ed., *Joannes Marcus Marci: A Seventeenth-Century Bohemian Polymath* (Prague: Charles University, 1998)

Škarka, Antonín, "Kapitoly z české hymnologie," in *Půl tisíciletí českého písemnictví* (Prague: Odeon, 1986), pp. 190–302

Šorm, A. and Krajča, A., eds., *Mariánské sloupy v Čechách a na Moravě* (Prague: Antonín Daněk, 1939)

Teich, M., ed., *Bohemia in History* (Cambridge: Cambridge University Press, 1998)

Teplý, F., "Proč se stal Vilém Slavata z Chlumu a Košumberka z českého bratra katolíkem," *SbHKr* 13 (1912), 205–21; 14 (1913), 25–41, 171–81

Tipton, Susan, "'Super aspidem et basiliscum ambulabis...': Zur Entstehung der Mariensäulen im 17. Jahrhundert," in Dieter Breuer, ed., *Religion und Religiosität im Zeitalter des Barock* (Wiesbaden: Harrassowitz, 1995), vol. I, pp. 375–98

Tomek, V. V., *Geschichte der Prager Universität* (Prague: Haase, 1849)

Urbánek, Vladimír, "The idea of state and nation in the writings of Bohemian exiles after 1620," in Linas Eriksonas and Leos Müller, eds., *Statehood Before and Beyond Ethnicity* (Brussels: Peter Lang, 2005), pp. 67–83

Vašica, Josef, *České literární baroko* (Prague: Vyšehrad, 1938)

Veit, Ludwig Andreas, *Kirche und Volksfrömmigkeit im Zeitalter des Barock* (Freiburg i.B.: Herder, 1956)

Venard, Marc, ed., *Histoire du Christianisme*, vol. IX, *L'âge de raison (1620/30–1750)* (Paris: Desclée, 1997)

Vintr, Josef, "Jazyk české barokní bible Svatováclavské," *WSJ* 38 (1992), 197–212
"Komentář v české barokní bibli Svatováclavské," *LF* 117 (1994), 87–95

Vlček, Jaroslav, *Dějiny české literatury*, 2 vols. (Prague: Československý Spisovatel, 1951)

Vlček, Pavel, ed., *Umělecké památky Prahy, Malá Strana* (Prague: Academia, 1999)
ed., *Umělecké památky Prahy, Staré město/Josefov* (Prague: Academia, 1996)

Vlnas, Vít, *Jan Nepomucký, česká legenda* (Prague: Mladá fronta, 1993)
ed., *The Glory of the Baroque in Bohemia* (Prague: Paseka, 2001)

Volf, Josef, *Dějiny českého knihtisku do roku 1848* (Prague: Novák, 1926)

Ward, W. R., *Christianity under the Ancien Régime 1648–1789* (Cambridge: Cambridge University Press, 1999)

Wellek, R., "Bohemia in English literature," in *Essays on Czech Literature* (The Hague: Mouton, 1963), pp. 81–147

Winkelbauer, Thomas, *Fürst und Fürstendiener: Gundaker von Liechtenstein, ein österreichischer Aristokrat des konfessionellen Zeitalters* (Vienna: Oldenbourg, 1999)
Ständefreiheit und Fürstenmacht: Länder und Untertanen des Hauses Habsburg im konfessionellen Zeitalter, 2 vols. (Vienna: Ueberreuter, 2003)

Woolf, Daniel, *The Social Circulation of the Past* (Oxford: Oxford University Press, 2003)

Zíbrt, Čeněk, *Bibliografie české historie*, 5 vols. (Prague: Nákl. České akademie císaře Františka Josefa pro vědy, slovesnost a umění, 1900–12)
Z dějin českého knihtiskařství (Prague: Typografia, 1913)

Index

NEW STUDIES IN EUROPEAN HISTORY

Books in the series